Socioecology and Psychology of Primates

World Anthropology

General Editor

SOL TAX

Patrons

CLAUDE LÉVI-STRAUSS
MARGARET MEAD
LAILA SHUKRY EL HAMAMSY
M. N. SRINIVAS

MOUTON PUBLISHERS · THE HAGUE · PARIS
DISTRIBUTED IN THE USA AND CANADA BY ALDINE, CHICAGO

Socioecology and Psychology of Primates

Editor

RUSSELL H. TUTTLE

MOUTON PUBLISHERS · THE HAGUE · PARIS
DISTRIBUTED IN THE USA AND CANADA BY ALDINE, CHICAGO

to

Sherwood L. Washburn

General Editor's Preface

This collection of original research contributions, essays, and discussions on the socioecology and psychology of primates provides a wealth of new information about the ways in which natural habitats and social contexts may influence behavior; meat-eating and hunting in baboons, chimpanzees, and large carnivores; psychological capacities and tool behavior in primates; and the language skills of chimpanzees. Many chapters and discussions highlight modern techniques, approaches, and inferential strategies for obtaining results pertinent to functional and phylogenetic questions about man and other anthropoid primates. Studies of primates have so rapidly developed in this generation that only specialized journals can keep up with them. Each journal necessarily confines itself to a particular subject matter and sets limits to what it can publish. The present book and its two companion volumes therefore offer a unique variety of new information and ideas, often from younger people of different continents writing articles for discussion with a greater latitude that gives the published results vigor. This book required the creative energy of the brilliant young paleoanthropologist who organized the meetings and edited the results as much as it did the inspiration of an unusual international Congress.

Like most contemporary sciences, anthropology is a product of the European tradition. Some argue that it is a product of colonialism, with one small and self-interested part of the species dominating the study of the whole. If we are to understand the species, our science needs substantial input from scholars who represent a variety of the world's cultures. It was a deliberate purpose of the IXth International Congress of Anthropological and Ethnological Sciences to provide impetus in this direction. The *World Anthropology* volumes, therefore, offer a first glimpse of a human science in which members from all societies have played an active role. Each of the books is designed to be self-contained; each is an attempt to update its particular sector of scientific knowledge and is written by specialists from all parts of the world. Each volume should be read and reviewed individually as a separate volume on its own given subject. The set as a whole will indicate what changes are in store for anthropology as scholars from the developing countries join in studying the species of which we are all a part.

The IXth Congress was planned from the beginning not only to include as many of the scholars from every part of the world as possible, but also with a view toward the eventual publication of the papers in high-quality volumes. At previous Congresses scholars were invited to bring papers which were then read out loud. They were necessarily limited in length; many were only summarized; there was little time for discussion; and the sparse discussion could only be in one language. The IXth Congress was an experiment aimed at changing this. Papers were written with the intention of exchanging them before the Congress, particularly in extensive pre-Congress sessions; they were not intended to be read at the Congress, that time being devoted to discussions — discussions which were simultaneously and professionally translated into five languages. The method for eliciting the papers was structured to make as representative a sample as was allowable when scholarly creativity — hence self-selection — was critically important. Scholars were asked both to propose papers of their own and to suggest topics for sessions of the Congress which they might edit into volumes. All were then informed of the suggestions and encouraged to re-think their own papers and the topics. The process, therefore, was a continuous one of feedback and exchange and it has continued to be so even after the Congress. The some two thousand papers comprising *World Anthropology* certainly then offer a substantial sample of world anthropology. It has been said that anthropology is at a turning point; if this is so, these volumes will be the historical direction-markers.

As might have been foreseen in the first post-colonial generation, the large majority of the Congress papers (82 percent) are the work of scholars identified with the industrialized world which fathered our traditional discipline and the institution of the Congress itself: Eastern Europe (15 percent); Western Europe (16 percent); North America (47 percent); Japan, South Africa, Australia, and New Zealand (4 percent). Only 18 percent of the papers are from developing areas: Africa (4 percent); Asia-Oceania (9 percent); Latin America (5 percent). Aside from the substantial representation from the U.S.S.R. and the nations of Eastern Europe, a significant difference between this corpus of written material and that of other Congresses is the addition of the large proportion of contributions from Africa, Asia, and Latin America. "Only 18 percent" is two to four times as great a proportion as that of other Congresses; moreover, 18 percent of 2,000 papers is 360 papers, 10 times the number of "Third World" papers presented at previous Congresses. In fact, these 360 papers are more than the total of ALL papers published after the last International Congress of Anthropological and Ethnological Sciences which was held in the United States (Philadelphia, 1956).

The significance of the increase is not simply quantitative. The input of scholars from areas which have until recently been no more than subject matter for anthropology represents both feedback and also long-awaited theoretical contributions from the perspectives of very different cultural, social, and historical traditions. Many who attended the IXth Congress were convinced that anthropology would not be the same in the future. The fact that the next Congress (India, 1978) will be our first in the "Third World" may be symbolic of the change. Meanwhile, sober consideration of the present set of books will show how much, and just where and how, our discipline is being revolutionized.

In addition to the two companion volumes of this book, *Primate functional morphology and evolution* and *Paleoanthropology: morphology and paleoecology*, readers will be particularly interested in other volumes of the *World Anthropology* series which deal with archaeology; with biological, psychological, and linguistic anthropology; and with particular geographic areas of the Old World.

Chicago, Illinois   SOL TAX
August 25, 1975

Preface

This volume contains papers that were prepared for discussion in Session 411 at the IXth International Congress of Anthropological and Ethnological Sciences. The session was convened on September 4, 1973, at the Conrad Hilton Hotel in Chicago, Illinois.

Although a few papers were volunteered in response to the initial call for papers from the conference office, I solicited most of them with the intention of focusing discussion on a limited number of problem areas in behavioral primatology that are characterized by novel field and laboratory research and theoretic ferment. Small subsets of papers and two or four topics were discussed by two successive panels which included authors of papers in the session, other experts on one or more subjects treated in the papers, and reputable raconteurs.

Adriaan Kortlandt and Christian Vogel served with me as co-chairpersons and discussants during the entire session.

The first panel included Benjamin Beck, Gilbert Boese, Wolfgang Dittus, Kenneth Glander, Roger Peters, Duane Rumbaugh, Thomas Struhsaker, and V. P. Yakimov. They were principal discussants of papers in Sections I and II of this volume.

The second panel included Benjamin Beck, Roger Fouts, Philip Lieberman, Roger Peters, Duane Rumbaugh, and Thomas Struhsaker. They were principal discussants of papers in Sections III, IV, and V herein.

The format of discussion varied considerably during the session. But generally panelists were asked to summarize their own papers and to comment on related papers of other symposiasts. The topics and papers were then opened for discussion by the panel and the audience. In some instances the briefs were illustrated with slides.

The arrangement of this volume does not faithfully reflect the chronology of events in Session 411.

I prepared and edited typescripts of all discussions in the session and mailed them to the commentators for further editing, brief augmentation, and permission to publish. Summaries of papers were deleted from the typescript. So we have here a greatly condensed (but I hope no less mentally nutritious) rendering of the conference discussions.

Many persons contributed to the success of this adventure. Preeminent among them is Sol Tax, who was encouraging, challenging, and insightful about every aspect of the session and volume. His staff, especially Roberta MacGowan and Gay Neuberger, and my secretaries, June Ford and Susan Kurth, greatly expedited the preparation of manuscripts and correspondence with the contributors. It was also delightful to work with Jean Block and other staff members of the Midway Editorial Service and Karen Tkach and Peter Zoutendijk of Mouton Publishers.

Marlene Tuttle contributed in many ways to the development and completion of the project, especially assisting with typescripts of the discussions and the index. We are grateful to Nicole and Matthew Tuttle for their cooperation which permitted us to work together on the project.

The good cheer, cooperation, and communicativeness of the participants were overwhelming. We are very grateful for their colleagueship.

University of Chicago   RUSSELL H. TUTTLE
Chicago, Illinois
May 25, 1974

Table of Contents

General Editor's Preface   VII

Preface   XI

SECTION ONE: ECOLOGY, DIET, AND SOCIAL PATTERNING IN
MONKEYS AND APES

Ecology, Diet, and Social Patterning in Old and New World
   Primates   3
   by *C. M. Hladik*

Habitat Description and Resource Utilization: A Preliminary
   Report on Mantled Howling Monkey Ecology   37
   by *Kenneth E. Glander*

Social and Ecological Contrasts Between Four Taxa of
   Neotropical Primates   59
   by *Lewis L. Klein* and *Dorothy J. Klein*

Some Ecological, Distributional, and Group Behavioral Features
   of Atelinae in Southern Peru: With Comments on Interspecific
   Relations   87
   by *Norris M. Durham*

Comparison of the Behavior and Ecology of Red Colobus and
   Black-and-White Colobus Monkeys in Uganda: A Summary   103
   by *Thomas T. Struhsaker* and *John F. Oates*

Population Dynamics of the Toque Monkey, *Macaca sinica*   125
   by *Wolfgang P. J. Dittus*

The Descent of Dominance in *Macaca:* Insights into the
   Structure of Human Societies   153
   by *James Loy*

The Influence of Hormonal and Ecological Factors upon Sexual
   Behavior and Social Organization in Old World Primates   181
   by *Graham S. Saayman*
Social Behavior and Ecological Considerations of West African
   Baboons (*Papio papio*)   205
   by *Gilbert K. Boese*
Discussion   231

SECTION TWO: MEAT-EATING AND BEHAVIORAL ADAPTATIONS
TO HUNTING

Meat-Eating and Hunting in Baboons   245
   by *Robert S. O. Harding*
The Origin of Hominid Hunting: A Primatological Perspective   259
   by *Akira Suzuki*
Behavioral and Intellectual Adaptations of Selected Mammalian
   Predators to the Problem of Hunting Large Animals   279
   by *Roger Peters* and *L. David Mech*
Discussion   301

SECTION THREE: SELF-AWARENESS AND CAPACITIES FOR PERCEP-
TUAL INTEGRATION ACROSS SENSORY MODALITIES, LEARNING, SYM-
BOLIZING, AND INTELLIGENCE

Towards an Operational Definition of Self-Awareness   309
   by *Gordon G. Gallup, Jr.*
Capacities of Nonhuman Primates for Perceptual Integration
   Across Sensory Modalities   343
   by *Charles M. Rogers* and *Richard K. Davenport*
The Learning and Symbolizing Capacities of Apes and Monkeys   353
   by *Duane M. Rumbaugh*
Discussion   367

SECTION FOUR: LANGUAGE SKILLS OF APES AND THE EVOLUTION
OF HUMAN LANGUAGE

Capacities for Language in Great Apes   371
   by *Roger S. Fouts*

The Language Skills of a Young Chimpanzee in a Computer-
Controlled Training Situation 391
by *Duane M. Rumbaugh, E. C. von Glasersfeld, Timothy V.
Gill, Harold Warner, Pier Pisani, Josephine V. Brown,* and
C. L. Bell
Discussion 403

SECTION FIVE: CAPACITIES FOR TOOL BEHAVIOR AND HOMINID
EVOLUTION

Primate Tool Behavior 413
by *Benjamin B. Beck*

Discussion 449

Biographical Notes 453

Index of Names 461

Index of Subjects 467

Plates i–viii between 368–369

Ecology, Diet, and Social Patterning in Monkeys and Apes

Ecology, Diet, and Social Patterning in Old and New World Primates

C. M. HLADIK

Specialization in primate species appears in various ecological niches. Eaters of repugnant insects (*Perodicticus, Arctocebus, Loris*) and tough leaf eaters (*Lepilemur, Indri, Presbytis, Colobus*) are the most clear-cut examples. Among the many primate species that have differentiated in seventy-five million years, man is one of the less differentiated species from the ecological point of view. Consequently man is relatively more adaptable.

Some aspects of social structure are related to adaptation to ecological conditions. To demonstrate this, I will use the Ceylon primate population as an example that was studied in detail[1] and about which we obtained the most accurate quantitative ecological data. Comparisons with similar ecological studies undertaken in Madagascar[2] and in America (Barro Colorado)[3] as well as in Africa (Gaboon)[4] and consideration of numerous data collected by other investigators will allow us to see how far we can generalize a theory concerning the way the social patterning of the whole primate order is interdependent with environmental conditions.

I am indebted to Dr. Russell Tuttle for revising the English translation of this manuscript.

[1] Smithsonian Biological Program in Ceylon, under the direction of Dr. J. F. Eisenberg.
[2] Special concerns of Foreign Affairs (Paris), on the occasion of the International Conference of Tananarive, organized by Dr. J. J. Petter.
[3] Smithsonian Tropical Research Institute, under the direction of Dr. M. H. Moynihan.
[4] C. N. R. S. (France) Laboratory of Primatology and Equatorial Ecology, under the direction of Dr. A. Brosset.

For Plates, see pp. ii–vi, between pp. 368–369

ECOLOGICAL NICHES, FOOD AVAILABILITY AND ADAPTATIONS OF PRIMATE GROUPS AT THE POLONNARUWA FIELD STATION, SRI LANKA (CEYLON)

The Polonnaruwa field station is described in Hladik and Hladik (1972). We will mention here only some of its most important features. It is a semi-deciduous forest in the "dry zone" of Ceylon, where the annual rainfall is 1,700 millimeters. The very marked dry season is an important climatic factor considering that at the same latitude some moist evergreen forests do not have more rainfall.

The undergrowth of this forest has been cleared over a large area by archaeologists to bring to light ruins of a city of the twelfth century. In this area, which is very similar to the nearby forest (the canopy is intact except for vines), it was possible to observe in great detail the different species of primates, and to obtain good quantitative estimates of their natural diet (with control in the nearby forest). The whole area was surveyed and mapped, and we calculated the annual production of the different available foodstuffs. Using collecting baskets along a transection, a comparative estimate of the production in the primitive forest was made as a control.

Our field of detailed study covered 54.5 hectares, with a total length of two kilometers. Using an aerial photograph, all trees were mapped after ground identification. The canopy of each one of them was measured. Production was estimated from average measurements.

There are forty-seven species of trees. Though their spatial distribution is not uniform, it is interesting to consider it in relation to the use of the land and the foodstuffs by the different primate species.

Four primate species share the resources: two leaf monkeys of the same genus, *Presbytis senex* and *P. entellus*, one macaque, *Macaca sinica*, which chiefly uses the fruit resources, and a small nocturnal prosimian, *Loris tardigradus,* that can eat many sorts of repugnant insects.

Except for primates, mammalian fauna is fairly scarce at Polonnaruwa. There are no longer big predators (*Panthera*). Only the small nocturnal carnivores characteristic of the Ceylon dry zone (Eisenberg and McKay 1970), some rodents (two species of squirrels are often seen among the monkey groups), ruminants (*Axis axis*) and Tragulidae (*Tragulus meminna*) inhabit the area. Some cattle from a neighboring farm entered the undergrowth to feed on grass or shrubs but they did not interfere with the activity and feeding of the primates.

Presbytis senex

P. senex is a very unobtrusive species forming small groups of five to six individuals that always stay in the canopy (Plate 1). *P. senex* are not easy to observe. They hide their faces, move around a tree trunk or branch, and quickly flee. Our field station at Polonnaruwa is unique in that we were able to quantify diets by direct counting because of the clearance of undergrowth.

The yearly average of the diet of *P. senex* includes 60 percent leaves and shoots, 12 percent flowers and buds, and 28 percent fruits. One-half of this food is produced by only two tree species: *Adina cordifolia* and *Schleichera oleosa* from which fruits and flowers are eaten as well as shoots and mature leaves. The bulk of the food is obtained from no more than a dozen tree species; nevertheless *Presbytis senex* may eat small parts of many other trees.

The groups stayed in small territories that were three to four hectares wide (Rudran 1970, 1973; Manley f.c.). Shapes of the territories are shown in Figure 1. After mapping all trees at the field station, we were able to calculate the quantity of food available through the year for each of the groups (for details and methods of calculation, see Hladik and Hladik 1972).

Table 1 indicates the total food available per year for one monkey in each of the groups shown in Figure 1.

If we consider the spatial distribution of the food trees on the same scale as the home ranges, it seems fairly homogenous. The annual crop is about four tons of foliage (including an average of two tons of *Adina*) and about a hundred kilograms of *Adina* flower for a monkey

Table 1.   Total food in kilograms (fresh weight) available per year for one monkey in each group in Figure 1

	Adina cordifolia		*Schleichera oleosa*		Other trees
	leaves	flowers	shoots	fruits	leaves
A	1,300	60	240	65	1,100
B	3,500	160	380	105	2,200
C	2,100	100	420	115	2,200
D	4,700	215	350	100	2,000
E	3,500	160	510	160	2,000
F	1,000	50	200	55	2,800
G	6,500	300	300	85	5,800
H	600	30	130	35	1,000

whose annual needs are about 400 kilograms. Of course, the annual crop exceeds the annual need; but considering that the trees cannot stay very long if they are totally defoliated at regular intervals, the ratio of food requirement to food available which is actually 1 : 10 can be considered as a maximum permissible for leaf eaters using a large amount of young shoots. In fact, for one of the groups (Plate 1 and H on Figure 1) the total annual crop was less than two tons. We noted that some trees in their territory were dying because the leaves and shoots were eaten too frequently. These animals lived in that restricted area because the male of the neighboring group (G in Figure 1) was very aggressive. Conversely, group G had more food available in its home range than others.

Thus behavior and social structure strongly affect spatial distribution of the species and consequently the habitat use and ecology.

Social structure (see Rudran 1970, 1973) allows division into small groups that use small portions of the field area (Figure 1). The dispersion of the tree species used by *P. senex* is homogenous enough in those small portions to allow a regular division. On the other hand, many other vegetal species are not so evenly spread, and they are important in food production for other primate species (see below).

Social units of *P. senex* are "one-male groups" that include a few females and their offspring. Some males are necessarily excluded from these basic groups and may stay solitary or form "all-male groups." In these units, individuals are less powerful; they are chased away by the leaders of the "one-male groups" and they live in places neglected by others and which are obviously not the best food-producing areas.

Direct fighting between two groups was not often observed. Contact at the borders of the territories was infrequent. The animals do not have to move very much to find abundant food. Powerful calls emitted by the males early at dawn can be considered as territorial calls. These calls come from the different groups responding to each other. In this manner all of them learn about the location of neighboring groups as soon as the period of activity begins.

Similar types of morning calls are known in other species of leaf-eating primates.

Other species of leaf monkey possess many additional features described for *P. senex*, viz. small groups (with a fairly similar social structure) that move only short distances in a small territory, the source of food always being a few common vegetal species distributed homogenously.

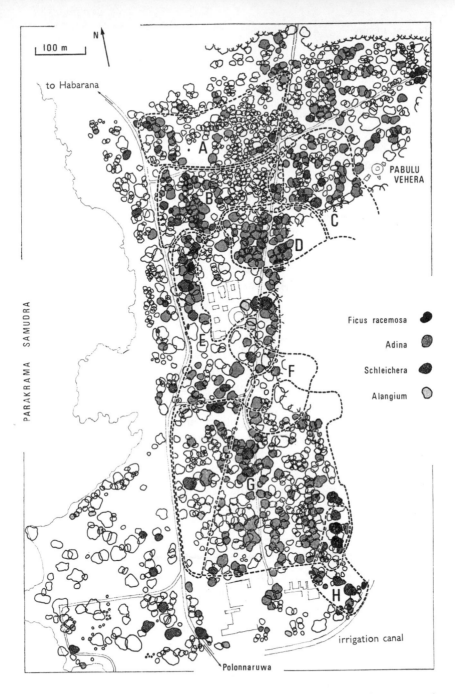

Figure 1. Aerial view of the field station at Polonnaruwa showing the canopy of all trees. This open forest is located on the shore of an artificial lake (Parakrama Samudra). The limits of the home ranges of *P. senex* are shown by dotted lines, after the data of Manley and Rudran. We note on this map the homogenous distribution of the main food species of *P. senex: Adina cordifolia* and *Schleichera oleosa*

Presbytis entellus

It is noteworthy to compare the gray langur, *P. entellus* (Plate 2), of the Polonnaruwa field station because of noticeable interspecific differences in ecology and social structures.

These monkeys form rather large groups (twenty to thirty individuals), and they are very conspicuous because they come down to the ground and stay there for long periods of time without fear of man.

The home ranges of the different groups of *P. entellus* (Figure 2) were mapped mainly after Ripley's data. They are wider than those of the *P. senex* groups; nevertheless the biomass of *P. entellus* is remarkably similar (ten to fifteen kilograms per hectare) due to the large size of the groups. The total biomass of folivorous mammals is very high (twenty-five kilograms per hectare), probably reaching the maximum allowed by the available vegetation, and the maintenance of two rather similar primate species in ecological niches can be explained only by subtle differences in diet and habitat use.

The diet of the gray langur (considered as an average for a one-year cycle) includes 48 percent foliage, 7 percent flowers, and 45 percent fruits. Thus, this last item is eaten in larger quantities by *P. entellus* than *P. senex*. *P. entellus* uses foliage mainly in the form of tender shoots and flushings while *P. senex* includes more mature leaves.

P. entellus also eats some different food plants from those chosen by *P. senex*. But the main difference is in the larger number of food plants included in the diet of the gray langur. The main crops are: *Walsura piscidia*, *Drypetes sepiaria*, and the various *Ficus* forming the bulk (as *Adina* and *Schleichera* do in *P. senex*).

The food plants used by *P. entellus* are also more widely scattered in the field as is shown in Figure 2. Nevertheless, if we consider their spatial distribution in the home range, we see that it is fairly even. That is to say, in the territories of each group there is approximately the same number of each one of these food-producing tree species. If the territories were not so large (and the groups were smaller, yielding an identical population density) these tree species would not be so

Table 2.   Annual mean production of trees for each individual living in the different territories shown in Figure 2

	Walsura shoots	*Drypetes sepiaria* shoots	*Drypetes sepiaria* fruits	*Ficus* spp. fruits	*Schleichera* fruits
North group	40	180	23.5	62.5	30
Central group	20	135	20	262	115
South group	(few)	>50	>10	197	40

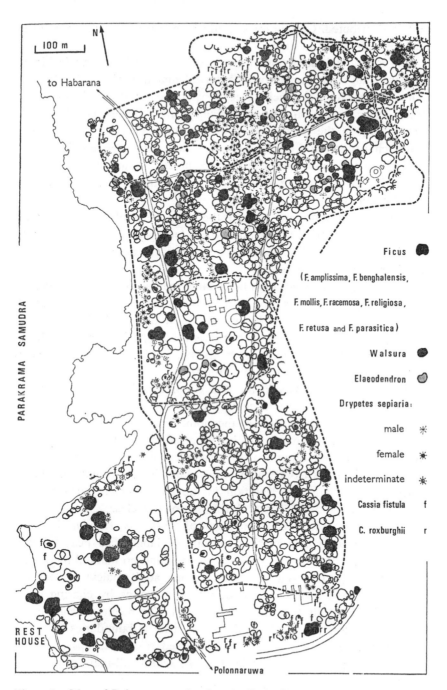

Figure 2. Map of Polonnaruwa showing the limits (in dotted lines) of the territories of three groups of *Presbytis entellus*, as for *P. senex* on Figure 1. Land use differs depending upon the scattering of food species in the field

evenly distributed. Certain ones would be missing in certain territories and over-abundant in others.

For each individual living in the different territories shown in Figure 2, there is an annual mean production calculated as shown in Table 2. An important food-producing tree, *Drypetes sepiaria*, which is concentrated in local spots on the general map is, nevertheless, equally distributed between the north and central groups. There are one female (producing fruits) and one and one-half male trees per individual (the data about the south group are not complete because the trees were counted after the fruiting season, but their distribution must be generally the same).

There are not too many *Ficus* in the home range of the north group. This group often tried to extend into the territory of the central group causing frequent battles between groups when the animals were feeding in *Ficus* near the boundaries.

Presbytis entellus feeds on a fairly large number of species. In Polonnaruwa, 90 percent of its food comes from twenty-three woody species. This total includes the twelve species used differently by the other *Presbytis* species. The gray langur uses other species for staple food, uses more fruits, and among leaves takes more shoots and tender leaves (27 percent of the total amount of food).

This greater selectivity in the diet is correlated with a slightly different general behavior and activity pattern. The group has to move more frequently and farther in the home range to find the different resources which are more widely dispersed. Some tree species have very short productive periods (for example the different *Ficus* species as well as the trees from which only young shoots are eaten). This is correlated with a social tradition in the group which permits using these different sources of food during seasonal cycles.

Nevertheless, the social structure of *Presbytis entellus* is quite loose. Jay (1965) characterized groups of langurs as peaceful and relaxed with very little intragroup aggression and no marked hierarchy. Adult males (mostly one dominant among adult males) protect the territory of their group against neighboring groups by chasing other males without really fighting (Ripley 1967). The results of such intertroop encounters in part determine the territorial boundaries.

In India, Sugiyama et al. (1965) observed smaller troops of *P. entellus* with only one adult male. Like *P. senex* "all-male groups" of *P. entellus* also occur.

This similarity in social structure of both species of *Presbytis* was observed at a lower level in our Polonnaruwa field station. In fact,

P. entellus were organized into large homogenous groups only during the dry season, and the larger groups lived in the most arid places: Jay (1965) found groups of 120 members in South India, and Ripley (1970) observed groups of sixty in Yala (southeast of Ceylon). The structure of the large groups is most effective as an anti-predator adaptation when the animals are on the ground. Many animals can watch and give alarm calls when a predator approaches, and females and young when fleeing can be protected by the more aggressive males who stay behind the group. Because, in the most arid zones, the gray langurs utilize water from water holes, the groups travel long distances on the ground (Beck and Tuttle 1972). In Polonnaruwa, they also seek water during the dry season and spend long periods on the ground to feed on the dried fruits of *Drypetes* and on the leaves of *Mimosa pudica*.

Conversely, during the monsoon season, the langur way of life is obviously more arboreal. The diet includes more foliage and more shoots (fruits are not so abundant) and the animals have to spend more time feeding in the canopy. At this time the groups often split into smaller units, and their social behavior tends to become more similar to that of *P. senex*. During the rainy season, *P. entellus* seems to be more disturbed by human observers, probably because it does not feel the reassuring presence of a large group. Like *P. senex* it uses a "spacing call" (morning whoop) that is not commonly heard during the dry season.

Thus the differences in social structure characterizing the two Ceylonese species of *Presbytis* are related to differences in ecology and habitat use and vary with these factors.

Macaca sinica

The toque macaque (*Macaca sinica*) is ecologically very different from the two species of *Presbytis*. The social structure of its population differs markedly as well. I will now refer to certain observations that Dittus made at the Polonnaruwa field station (see Dittus, this volume). He followed several groups of macaques in large sections of the Polonnaruwa forest and observed variations in population structures over several years. Thus his primatological information is of exceptional value.

I will only cite some aspects of the ecology of the toque macaque in

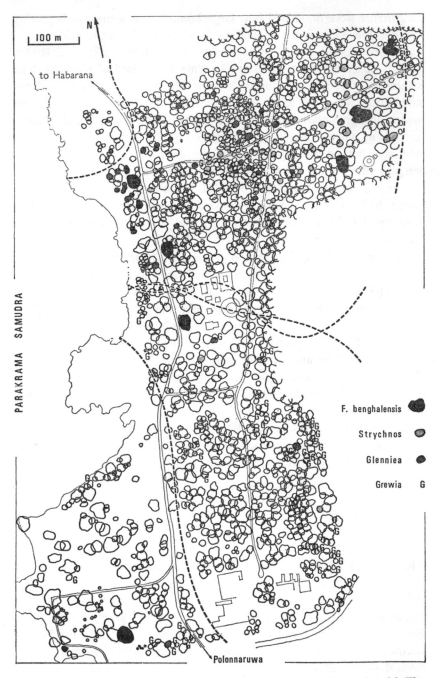

Figure 3.   A view of the canopy of Polonnaruwa, as shown in Figures 1 and 2. The dotted lines are the limits of the home ranges of two groups of macaques. The vegetal food species shown as examples are very scattered

order to clarify the most important ways in which it differs from other primates.

The diet of *Macaca sinica* is comprised chiefly of fruits (77 percent), with some green vegetal growth and flowers (14 percent) and a maximum of 5 percent fungae and 4 percent insects and small prey. The search for animal prey is the principal activity of the macaque. Because it is not abundant, the animals can get only very small quantities (according to Dittus the proportion can be even lower than our estimates). The fruit-eating primates must complement their diet with protein from animal prey and young vegetal shoots. They use many different species to compensate for the deficiencies in essential animo acids of the individual vegetal species (Hladik et al. 1971; 1973). Hence the toque macaque uses certain leaves and shoots like *Strychnos potatorum* and *Randium dumetorum*.

The fruits eaten come from many species widely dispersed in the field. The banyan, *Ficus benghalensis*, gives a fruit (which is eaten in large amounts) very rich in lipids, as do *Schleichera oleosa, Grewia polygama, Glenniea unijuga,* and *Drypetes separia.*

We can only make a general comparison of the distribution of these food-producing species (Figure 3) with what was accurately calculated for the leaf monkeys. *Ficus benghalensis* is more scattered in the field than any of the species used by the leaf monkeys and so are the other food trees utilized by the macaque. But their territories are very large. According to Dittus' observations, the two groups shown on our map (covering two kilometers) moved in a home range covering about twice the area described.

Despite the scattering of the main food trees, each group has very similar resources available because of the large size of its home range. In this perspective the dispersal of the important tree species seems to be "homogenous." But vegetal production is not an important factor, because it is very much greater than is the need — two tons of pulp of the fruit of *Schleichera oleosa* are available to the group located in the north on Figure 3 and the other species produce annually about one hundred times more than what is eaten (this also means that there is no competition with *Presbytis entellus* for fruits). In contrast, looking for prey means that the macaque must move in a very large home range, over irregular pathways to avoid destroying all of the game. The need for this is indicated by the fact that they actually obtain only a very small proportion of their food in animal proteins (compared with other primates of similar weight such as *Cebus,* which feeds on fruits, insects, and a few leaves).

The two groups of macaques which we studied included only twelve and thirteen individuals. Their territories were thirty and forty-five hectares, respectively. (Actually, we must consider their "area of land use" as equivalent to twenty-five and thirty hectares because there were partial territorial superpositions.) The biomass is two and one-half kilograms per hectare. This is the highest figure for primates at this trophic level.

The intragroup social organization is a linear hierarchy evident among males but not so marked for females. This organization allows a close integration of individuals, each with a precise role to play, and greater general efficiency when foraging or detecting predators because most of the time is spent on the ground.

This social model is common to many primate species with similar ecological background. The diet including small prey has the same effect on habitat use. It necessitates long journeys, sometimes on the ground, over a very wide territory.

Loris tardigradus

The slender loris, *Loris tardigradus*, also uses a portion of the animal resources of the Polonnaruwa forest.

We cannot compare social structures among such nocturnal Prosimiae to what we saw in the group of higher primates described above. Nevertheless, it is useful to examine a few examples to try to under stand how these primates with complex social structures may have evolved.

The slender loris comes from a branch that might be very close to the most primitive primate ancestor. Its exclusively insectivorous diet is composed of small prey found along branches and vines on which the loris moves very slowly in order to detect by smelling (Petter and Hladik 1970). It is likely that the persistence of this primitive form is due to its nocturnal cycle of activity, slow movements which make it unobtrusive and very specialized diet, which consists of repugnant insects, myriapods, and ants — which are neglected by other mammals.

We generally observed single lorises. The species is designated "solitary"; but this does not mean that there are no social contacts between the individuals of a population.

We located the individual home ranges in a population at Polonnaruwa (Figure 4) during a brief field study with Petter, on the edge of a secondary growth forest. The area used by one adult male or

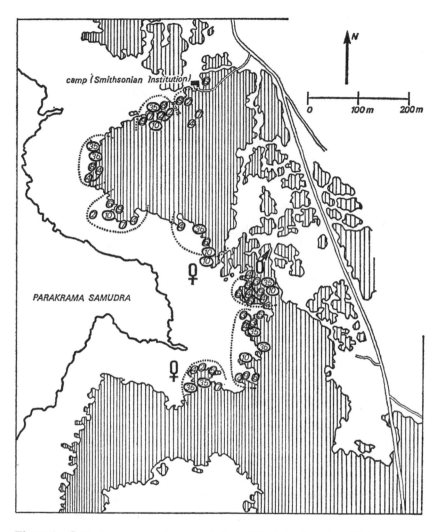

Figure 4.   Some home ranges in a population of *Loris tardigradus* at Polonnaruwa. The area depicted here is to the south of that shown in Figs. 1, 2, and 3. Each circled number indicates an observation in December, 1969. Home ranges are shown by dotted lines

female was about one hectare. Calculation of the corresponding bio-mass gives a fairly high weight for a secondary or tertiary consumer, 0.25 kilograms per hectare.

Social bonds among scattered individuals of this population probably correspond to what was described by Charles-Dominique (1971, 1972) for African Lorisidae: that is, one male individual territory is partially superimposed on one or several individual female territories. This type of primitive social structure is illustrated by the example of *Lepilemur* described below.

ECOLOGICAL NICHES AND SOCIAL STRUCTURES OF MALAGASY LEMURS

Along the banks of the Mandrare River, in the south of Madagascar, is a gallery forest very similar to the Polonnaruwa forest. Five species of lemurs occur in this gallery forest. *Lepilemur leucopus, Cheirogaleus medius* and *Microcebus murinus* are small nocturnal species. *Propithecus verreauxi* and *Lemur catta* are larger diurnal species.

There are similarities between the social organizations of these lemur populations and what was observed, in similar conditions, among the more evolved monkeys of Ceylon. From these similarities we can get an idea about the evolution of social groups of primates.

Lepilemur *and Other Nocturnal Forms*

The most primitive social organization was observed in the sportive lemur (Plate 3) (Charles-Dominique and Hladik 1971).

Individual territories observed in the field are shown in Figure 5. This type of social patterning corresponds to what was described for many other "solitary" primitive mammals. Each female protects its territory against other females but will share it for one or two years with one or several daughters. The male has a wider territory extended over one or several female territories and protects it against other males. As a result of this organization some extra males live outside of the population nucleus (peripheral males).

The most important part of the nocturnal activity of these animals is a motionless watching at the border of the territory. At the beginning of the night, *Lepilemur* makes some specific calls. By these sounds it clearly shows the neighboring animals what its location is at the moment. It is likely that the few animals living nearby are able to identify the sportive lemurs individually by their calls (differing slightly from one animal to another).

The food of *Lepilemur* is very abundant in all parts of the territory,

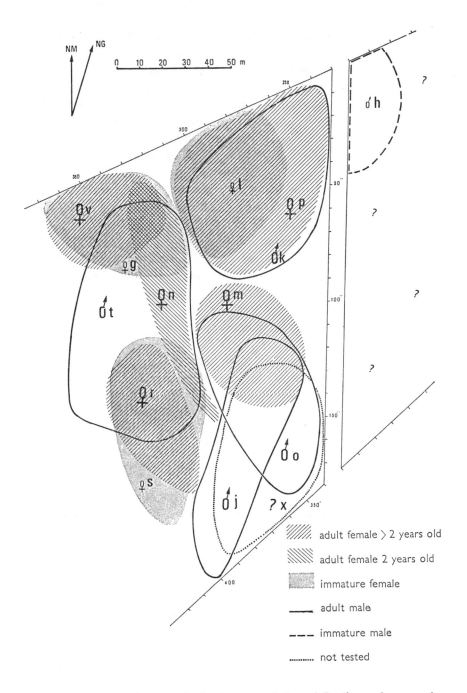

Figure 5.   The individual territories in a population of *Lepilemur leucopus*, in southern Madagascar. Territories of adult males cover territories of one or several females. The adult females are tolerant toward their daughters (territory in grey).

consisting chiefly of common foliage and flowers. This explains why the animals do not move much and why they spend most of their time watching competitors at the territorial boundaries.

This activity of territorial defense is complementary to the feeding activity. We demonstrated that during a short period the individual territory contains only 1.6 times the minimum amount of necessary food. Thus the surface area of the territories has been selected by this periodic limiting factor. As in the examples previously shown, the population density is precisely adjusted, through social and behavioral patterns, to the maximum available resources.

In the gallery forest, the biomass of *Lepilemur* reaches five kilo-grams per hectare (810 animals per square kilometer). We must con-sider, in the ecological system, a necessary balance between folivorous nocturnal lemurs and the larger diurnal forms that are also partly folivorous. Thus, the total size of folivorous biomass in this forest of Madagascar is almost similar to what we observed in the same type of forest at Polonnaruwa.

The *Loris* in Ceylon has a biomass twenty times lower than the bio-mass of *Lepilemur*. This difference is due to the differences in trophic level of the two species. The *Loris* only uses animal food. It is a secondary or third consumer in the trophic chain. This type of food is ten to one hundred times less abundant than vegetal food.

Yet social structures are very similar[5] in *Loris* and *Lepilemur* despite the very important differences in their ecologies. For both species, it seems most probable that this organization does not differ very much from that of the primates at the beginning of their evolution. Each of them, at the beginning of the process of differentiation, has become adapted to a highly specialized ecological niche. And so, from the beginning of the Tertiary era they maintained their morphological form as well as their social traditions. Like *Tamiasciurus* (Smith 1968) their population densities are adjusted to food availability only by the system of individual territories. But their social structures are already more sophisticated. The males have permanent contacts with one or several females for whom they "control" territories.

Other nocturnal lemurs, for example the mouse lemur *Microcebus* (Martin 1972), have similar social structures but with a higher level of gregariousness: several animals might gather in a common nest or hol-low tree trunk for the daily rest. From an ecological point of view, they are less specialized than the animals described above, eating insects,

[5]   The exact social structure of the *Loris* population is still to be studied.

fruits, gums, and foliage. We do not have precise information about all the different species of *Microcebus* but it is certain that they are transitional forms between *Loris* and *Lepilemur* which possess a primitive type of social structure.

Diurnal Lemurs Forming Structured Groups

The ecology and type of habitat use of the sifaka (*Propithecus verreauxi*) and the ring-tailed lemur (*Lemur catta*) is so reminiscent of the two species of *Presbytis* in Ceylon that we may consider them as an experimental model. Two groups of primates evolved separately in Ceylon and in Madagascar. Similar environmental conditions gave rise to partly similar social structures. Thus the social forms found in Madagascar must not differ much from the organization in the first groups of true monkeys.

Groups of sifakas are small, barely mobile units in a small territory. For instance, one group of three sifakas lived in one hectare (Petter 1962). Sifakas feed on leaves and fruits but their diet is less folivorous than the diet of *Presbytis senex* in Ceylon. The social units (Petter et al. i.p.) are "family groups" (in the usual Western meaning of the "family"), including only one couple and their offspring. The sifakas are concentrated a little higher in the gallery forest along the Mandrare River (Jolly 1966). In larger groups (four to six) there is more tolerance among males and among females (Sussman and Richard 1974). Indris (*Indri indri*) are more similar to the *Presbytis senex*, with a highly folivorous diet, but they live only in the moist forest of the eastern coast of Madagascar. They also form social units with only one couple (Petter i.p.). This can be considered as the most primitive type of group.

Groups of ring-tailed lemurs are larger, including twenty to thirty individuals (Jolly 1966). This recalls the groups of *Presbytis entellus* of Ceylon. Like these monkeys, ring-tailed lemurs eat leaves and fruits from many species. They often move on the ground over a fairly large territory. There is a hierarchy, with ranks of dominance among males and females. This linear hierarchy is an important factor in group adaptation to environmental conditions. It allows the presence of several males without loss of their aggressiveness, and thus better protection against predators for the whole group when it is moving on the ground, which is an essential aspect of searching out certain types of food distributed over the territory.

Sussman (1974) compared the *Lemur catta* with *Lemur fulvus* in Malagasy forests where both species occur. *Lemur fulvus* has a less sophisticated diet (three vegetal species yielded 80 percent of the food) and eats more leaves than *L. catta*. Comparing the diet and social organization of *Lemur fulvus* to those of *Presbytis senex* in Polonnaruwa, it is remarkable how similar they are. *Lemur fulvus* live in small groups without much hierarchy and remain in very narrow territories (Sussman 1974). The biomass may reach twenty-five kilograms per hectare like *P. senex*.

In these few examples of Malagasy lemurs, we note the great possibilities for variation of social structures but mostly for the diurnal species. The "solitary" mode of the nocturnal species is really a prototype of matriarchal society because the young are associated with their mother and share her territory during at least a short period. In the family groups, for instance among Indriidae, the male remains in permanent contact with one female. According to the environmental conditions, there may be some tolerance among adult males or females in wider groups. In more gregarious species of lemurs we observe instances where there is more tolerance among males or among females.

An intermediate social form between the "family group" and the multi-males group might be found in *Hapalemur griseus* (Petter et al. i.p.). These are small diurnal lemurs that live on the bamboos in swamp areas. They are tolerant enough to form small groups adapted to permanent guarding against dangerous predators like *Galidia*. The evolution of contact calls and alarm calls should also be considered as a criterion of adaptation to a hostile environment.

Identical variations in social patterning are found in lemurs and monkeys. In most cases closely similar ecological adaptations require the same type of social structure. Thus we can assume that the actual structures ("family groups") in the less specialized species of lemurs are the best representation of what was the intermediate social condition in the diverse phylogenetic radiations of the Old and New World monkeys.

ECOLOGY AND EVOLUTION OF THE SOCIAL ORGANIZATION IN THE NEW WORLD MONKEYS

The common ancestors of the primates were geographically separated at an early stage and, in the New World, they evolved towards many forms of the Platyrrhini. To exemplify these forms, I will refer to our observations between 1966 and 1968 on Barro Colorado Island (Panama). Determination of types and quantity of food available for each species will give an idea of its way of adaptation to the environment (Hladik and Hladik 1969).

Barro Colorado is a tropical rain forest. Most of the primate species live in this type of forest. Unlike areas discussed earlier it is not possible to get as precise quantitative data in rain forests. Ecological niches in a rain forest are generally more specialized because there are more animal and vegetal species.

On Barro Colorado Island there are still areas with young vegetation but most of it is mature forest. The dry season is marked by intensive sun radiation (no mist or clouds as in equatorial zones), and many trees defoliate at this time. It is semi-deciduous moist forest differing from the evergreen forest of the equatorial zone.

Five species of primates share the resources of this forest with specializations as in the examples of Ceylon and Madagascar. If we consider the ecological similarities and differences, the social patterning is found to be modeled in a series of similar types.

Alouatta palliata

The howler monkey, *Alouatta palliata* (Plate 4) is well known through the ethoecological studies of Carpenter. The groups include ten to twenty individuals. The howlers always stay in the upper canopy. They are the most folivorous among New World monkeys. But their diet is not markedly similar to the diet of *Presbytis* in Ceylon. The diet of *Alouatta* consists of 60 percent fruits and only 40 percent leaves. The ecological niche of the true folivores, in Barro Colorado, is filled by two species of sloth (*Bradypus* and *Choloepus*) which constitute the most important part of the biomass (Eisenberg et al. 1972).

With a group of ten howlers using fifteen to twenty hectares of forest, the biomass comes to a maximum of four kilograms per hectare. The howler consumes a fairly small number of vegetal species, especially several kinds of *Ficus* from which it can eat immature fruits as well as leaves. The groups do not move much because the food is easy to find in most parts of the territory. The well known call is equivalent to the morning call of other leaf-eating primates. It evidences presence in their territory without moving.

The distribution of the vegetal species used as food (Figure 6) is not as homogenous as it is in Polonnaruwa. This explains the need for a larger territory (as for the frugivores) to include enough of each kind of food tree. Consequently for the same density of the population groups will be larger than the "one-male group."

The concept of the "age-graded male troop," introduced by Eisenberg, Muckenhirn, and Rudran (1972) fits this case. According to these authors, howlers have the "one-male group" structure when the population density is low. When the density increases, several mature males may coexist in the same group. This situation corresponds to what was shown for the frugivorous-folivorous lemurs of Madagascar with the difference that, among lemurs, females are generally the less tolerant and the system is closer to a matriarchy.

In howler groups, cohesion is due to the tolerance between males. Nevertheless they might be chased away by the dominant male when they reach sexual maturity. According to population density they may become peripheral males or solitary.

Ateles geoffroyi

The red spider monkey, *Ateles geoffroyi*, was reintroduced on Barro Colorado by Moynihan. The nucleus of the population (six individuals in 1967) had a home range of forty hectares that is supposed to be adjusted to available food. Their biomass was about one kilogram per hectare.

Ateles is typically a frugivorous monkey. Its diet includes 80 percent fruits, is complemented by shoots and young leaves (20 percent) and a very small quantity of animal prey (less than 1 percent). Many species of fruits are used. So, ecologically, *Ateles* differs from *Aloutta* as much as *P. senex* differs from *P. entellus*. But the two Panamanian primate species, both frugivorous, are in a higher trophic level (with a lower biomass).

A great tolerance between individuals allows the formation of large troops of spider monkeys that can split into small units. These subgroups are organized around the females and their offspring (Eisenberg and Kuehn 1966) but the general shape of the social organization is the "age-graded male group."

Cebus capucinus

The white-throated capuchins (*Cebus capucinus*) are organized in more

Figure 6. Distribution of some food species used by the primates of Barro Colorado, mapped on two transections, twenty meters wide, crossing the home range of the different groups (see comments in the text)

structured groups over wide territories. One group whose feeding behavior we observed was made up of fourteen *Cebus* moving over a territory of ninety hectares (Oppenheimer 1968). As with the macaque, the chief activity of the capuchin is foraging for small prey (insects, spiders, and other invertebrates) found in hollow trunks or dead leaves (mostly on the ground, in the litter). This predatory behavior also involves long irregularly patterned walks over a large home range. Furthermore, the animals have to spread out when moving and keep contact by specific calls.

The diet of the capuchin includes 65 percent fruits, 20 percent animal prey, and 15 percent shoots, leaves, and stems. The maximum number of prey they can get in the forest litter is only a small fraction of the total amount they need. Therefore they are forced to be frugivores. We note that they get many more insects than the macaque in Ceylon do, and correlatively, their biomass is much smaller (0.5 kilograms per hectare). Thus they do not need a higher quantity of animal food per hectare.

If fruits are the main food of the capuchin, they are, nevertheless, selected in a particular way in relation to their chemical composition (Hladik et al. 1971). *Cebus* will select many fruits rich in lipids. For instance, among different palm trees it will take the fruits of *Scheelea zonensis*. (Conversely, the spider monkey will choose *Astrocaryum standleyanum* which gives more glucids.) In Figure 6, we note the abundance and rather even distribution of the *Astrocaryum* palm tree compared to the more scattered *Scheelea* palm tree. Again there is a correlation with the size of the territory, which is larger for the primate using the more scattered food-producing species. As among Ceylon primates this demonstrates the way the social structure adapts to an homogenous distribution of available food.

There is a linear hierarchy among female and male capuchins. But males of the age-class of four to five years are generally chased away (Oppenheimer 1968) showing a tendency towards the social type of "age-graded male group" (Eisenberg et al. 1972). Integration of individuals in a group of capuchins is accomplished through social exchanges like allogrooming. Grooming is more frequent in this species because it is necessary for animals that spend much time foraging in litter and dead wood to clean their fur. Some types of ritualized behavior such as the aggressive display and various ritualized responses permit the avoidance of true fights, and yet preserve a high level of aggressiveness in a group which is exposed to predators.

Saguinus geoffroyi

The feeding behavior of the rufus-naped tamarin, *Saguinus geoffroyi,*
does not differ very much from that of the capuchin, although the diet
is much more insectivorous. The tamarin is smaller than the capuchin
and thus it needs less food. In the same environment it captures about
the same number of small prey, so the relative proportion is higher.
Its average diet is 60 percent fruits, 30 percent insects, and 10 percent
green parts of vegetation.

The tamarin is becoming rare on Barro Colorado Island, probably
because it is specifically adapted to the edge of the forest and to the
secondary growth. It lives in thick vegetation and rarely comes down
to the ground. Social units are groups of six to nine individuals (Moynihan 1968) including one or several pairs of adults and their offspring.

So, among the Callithricidae (marmosets and tamarins) which are
the most primitive radiations of the New World primates, we already
find a sophisticated social pattern. But in most of the genera, the groups
are of the "parental type" (Eisenberg et al. 1972), which corresponds
to Petter's "family type." In such groups, an adult pair lives with permanent bonds, reinforced by social exchanges like grooming and bodily
contacts.

Aotus trivirgatus

The night monkey, *Aotus trivirgatus,* is a unique example of a true
monkey adapted to a nocturnal cycle of activity. On Barro Colorado
Island it lives either alone or in a small primitive group including at
most one adult pair and one or two infants (Moynihan 1964). *Aotus*
is among the least gregarious species of primates: there is no ritualized
display as in the social species, which serves to divert direct fighting
between individuals.

We have no precise ecological data about the night monkey, thus it
is difficult to make comparisons with other species. It does not seem
very specialized in its diet. It may be like some transitional forms of
lemurs.

ECOLOGICAL COMPARISON: PANAMA VS. CEYLON

I will now draw a parallel between the precise ecological data on
the Ceylon primates and those just described for the species of Barro
Colorado. In Figure 7b I show a division into more specialized ecological

niches in the rain forest. In the dry forest of Ceylon, the primate species are less specialized in their diet. Hence all of them cover the whole available food supply (from the insectivores to the more specialized folivores). In the rain forest of Barro Colorado they have to share the resources with other mammalian species. So, in Figure 7b, they are gathered in a narrower space according to their biomass which depends directly on the trophic level, i.e. the type of diet. Similar comparisons could be made with the primate species in Madagascar or in continental Africa but the ecological data are not yet accurate enough.

For a given species, the groups are more or less important not only in relation to their biomass and available food but also according to particular conditions of the environment (for example scattering of vegetal food species). The cohesion of large groups is due to the emergence of ritualized displays that make possible tolerance between the adults, male or female.

It is not possible to say whether ethological evolution of the social structures came from particular pressures of ecological conditions or if the adaptation to the environment followed these socioecological changes. What is certain is that correlation between those two conditions allows the survival of the different species.

SOCIAL LIFE AND ECOLOGY IN ANTHROPOID APES

A parallel evolution took place in the forests of the Old World, and there are many examples of convergences in socioecological adaptations rather similar to those shown in our examples (Struhsaker 1969). But there is no place where ecological data have been collected in much detail.

We studied *Pan troglodytes troglodytes* in the forest of Gaboon for one year (Hladik 1973).

The chimpanzee is a true frugivore which complements its diet with green plants and a few insects or other invertebrates (68 percent fruits, 28 percent leaves and bark, 4 percent insects; see Figure 7a). Occasionally it eats small game animals. This particular predatory behavior is very interesting to consider in itself (Goodall 1965; Teleki 1973) but it has no true consequences for nutritional needs because the average quantity of meat eaten is very low. Furthermore this type of food is used only by adult males and a few females; the juveniles, whose protein needs are the highest, have no access to the meat.

This hunting and meat-eating behavior could be compared with what is known about primitive human tribes of hunter-gatherers. For them, meat-eating is a pleasure as well as an opportunity to organize festivities with social exchanges. But precise ecological data show that their diet is almost entirely vegetarian (80 percent fruits and roots collected by women; Woodburn 1968). In human populations, the meat of the game is a significant source of proteins, but it is not a compulsory need considering that some kinds of insects are included in the food gathered by women (e.g. caterpillars are richer in proteins and lipids than meat).

In the diet of the chimpanzee the proportion of animal food as well as the fruits and other vegetal parts may vary from one place to another. This is not surprising if we consider that the geographical range

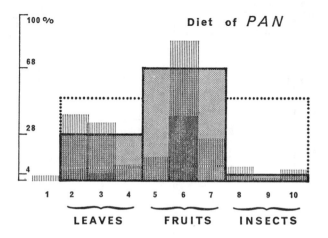

Figure 7a.   Example of the diet of the chimpanzee (*Pan troglodytes troglodytes*). This diagram is made with the same symbols as those used for the diets of other primates in Figure 7b.

Each of the grey parts of the three squares is proportional to the corresponding type of food ingested in a year:
Leaves (28 percent), in the left square;
Fruits (68 percent), in the central square;
Insects (4 percent) in the right square.

A more detailed account of the types of food ingested and their daily variations is expressed by the hachured columns as follows:
1. Minerals (earth) occasionally ingested.
2. Barks and twigs ⎫ Leaves
3. Leaves, buds and pith ⎬ and
4. Flower buds and gums ⎭ twigs
5. Immature fruits ⎫
6. Sweet fruits ⎬ Fruits
7. Seeds and arils ⎭
8. Ants, termites, and small arthropods (*Orthoptera*) ⎫ Insects
9. Large arthropods (*Orthoptera*) ⎬ and
10. Eggs, fledgings, and other large prey ⎭ other prey

of *Pan troglodytes* crosses more than half of the African continent, with three subspecies living in many different environments. Goodall described termite "fishing" behavior by East African chimpanzees. They use a long twig as a "tool" to catch the insects. In several hours of such activity a chimpanzee may obtain a large amount of animal

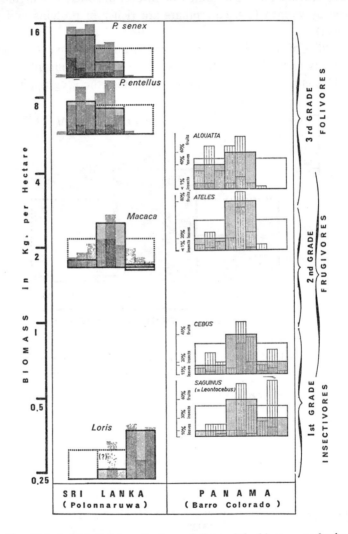

Figure 7b.   Relationship between the type of diet and the biomasses of primates in two different field stations.

Each primate species is characterized by its "dietogram" symbolized as in Figure 7a. Its level on the present diagram corresponds to its biomass.

It is clear that the different types of diet are directly correlated with the biomass, thus affecting social patterning.

protein and fat. Chimpanzees in the rain forest of Gaboon find most of their animal protein in several species of ants' nests. They spend a large part of their time looking for these prey in the manner of gatherers more than hunters. Thus they get a regular supply through gathering. Hunting per contra is an activity of high risk and low return (Lee 1968). In one day we saw 120 grams of insects eaten by chimpanzees (up to 6 percent of the total food amount) gathering the small nests of *Macromiscoides aculeatus,* one of which contains only 0.2 grams of ants and larvae. Other ants eaten in large quantities are *Œcophylla longinoda, Polyrhachis militaris* (Plate 5), and *Paltothyreus tarsatus.* The last species is "fished" with a stick as was described for termites.

To have a regular supply of large quantities of insects, chimpanzees need very wide territories. We have no good data for Gaboon about the size of this area. In the rain forest of East Africa, the densities observed by Reynolds (1965) correspond to a biomass of 1.5 kilograms per hectare, which is somewhat lower than the biomass of the macaque in Polonnaruwa which also feeds on fruits and a small proportion of insects.

Social traditions in local populations of chimpanzees make the use of special techniques possible. An example is the way *Panda oleosa* or *Coula edulis* nuts are opened (Rahm 1971). The hard shells are cracked with a branch of hard wood or a heavy stone used as a hammer. This technique is ignored by the chimpanzees living in the rain forest of Gaboon in spite of the local abundance of *Coula* and *Panda.* But the variety in the types of food eaten and recognized by the chimpanzees is impressive; we collected 210 specimens of food in the primary forest of Ipassa (Gaboon).

The social unit does not appear to have great cohesion. Sometimes small temporary groups of chimpanzees split or rearrange themselves sometimes in a few hours. It seems that subtle, permanent bonds exist on the larger scale of a "regional population" (Sugiyama 1968). Some fifty individuals are acquainted with each other, maintaining "friendly" interrelations. This type of big "group" lives in a home range much larger than any other territory of frugivorous primates.

The gorilla (*Gorilla gorilla*), studied by Schaller (1963) in a montane forest, forms smaller social units (six to seventeen individuals) that can fit in the category of "age-graded male groups." One male is dominant and the others become more or less peripheral. The gorilla is a leaves-and-fruit eater and there is some similarity with the social patterning of folivorous primates. But territories are among the largest ever seen for primates (twenty-five square kilometers for one group of ten adults).

This could be explained by the large number of species included in the diet. More than 100 vegetal food species were collected by Schaller. Only the chimpanzee, being more frugivorous, has a wider range (see Suzuki, this volume).

More classical correlations are found in two species of Hylobatidae, in Malaya. The gibbon, *Hylobates lar*, is predominantly a frugivore while the siamang, *Symphalangus syndactylus*, eats more leaves and shoots of many vines, including many species of *Ficus* (Chivers 1972). Both species live in small familial groups maintaining distances by specific calls. But the more folivorous siamang has a territorial area which is only half the size of the territory of the gibbon.

CONCLUSION

We started this comparative study with a few examples in which the knowledge of precise ecological data allowed comparison of several sympatric primate species. But we were only demonstrating the correlations between the types of social patterning and the resources and habitat use in an supposedly stabilized environment.

Long term mechanisms for regulating population densities were not examined. The most rapid fluctuations may depend on the groups' social structure. In the case of increasing population density, certain species have slight differences in group structure. The males are more aggressive and may kill most of the new-born infants. Eisenberg et al. (1972) showed that this way of limiting the population is not "social pathology" at all because in this case, the "one-male group" is the structure best adapted to the environment. Wynne-Edwards (1962) showed other general mechanisms regulating the population according to available resources but many of them have yet to be verified by ecological observations of primates.

Social patterning is modeled by environmental conditions but it also comes after a long evolution of each systematic group: so we find now different expressions of it. This conclusion is shared by Struhsaker (1969) and Eisenberg et al. (1972). More general laws (Crook and Gartlan 1966) only concern a few precise predators by having a large, ground-living primates adapt against predators by having a large, structured group with a linear hierarchy. The most sophisticated unit with many males is the baboon troop (DeVore and Hall 1965). Among forest-living species, the more terrestrial primates are also the larger groups with ranks of dominance among males. But the occurrence of large, polyspecific groups among arboreal primates of the rain forest (Gautier and Gautier 1969) cannot be explained by the same ecological factor.

Group structure is more directly affected by the way the whole population uses food resources. Similar examples are clear for all leaf-eating primates: the biomass is high; they are organized in small units ("family" type or "one-male group"); they have narrow territories; and all of them use territorial calls.

In other cases, similarities are not so clear. But some authors speak about folivorous or frugivorous forms or just about arboreal primates without any precise ecological definition. Many field studies concerning the ethology, structure, and composition of primate groups have been carefully carried out, but very few ecological and quantitative data are available, especially on the diet. That is why we quote only a few examples in this text. The last example mentioned (the comparison between the gibbon and the siamang) only refers to the actual time these two species spend feeding on fruits or leaves and not really to the weight eaten. Among Chivers' projects is the collection of complementary quantitative data. In a few years the ecology will be clearly known. The same could be said of the gorilla and of many other primate species. The exact proportions of the different components of the diet must be known at least to elucidate what the impact of the species is on the environment and how it is integrated with it.

With such precise quantitative data we can hope to separate into finer classes the ecological types of primates as follows:

1. The first grade: from typical types of insectivores (*Loris, Arctocebus*) with a gradation towards diets including fruits and insects (*Saguinus, Saimiri*) in large proportion (see Figure 7b).

2. The second grade: diets combining insects or other invertebrates and green parts of vegetals, in fairly small proportions, with a main complement of fruits and/or seeds (*Cebus, Cercopithecus, Macaca, Papio, Pan*, etc.).

3. The third grade: from the frugivores-folivores obtaining their proteins mostly from the leaves (*Ateles, Gorilla, Alouatta*) toward the more specialized folivores-frugivores with a complex stomach (*Presbytis, Colobus*) or special caecum (*Indri, Lepilemur*).

Among the forms of insect-eating primates are the prosimians of continental Africa. For these last species, the ethoecological studies of Charles-Dominique (1971, 1972) showed the very exact specializations in the diet of five species living in the rain forest. Charles-Dominique also remarked on the importance of the vegetal gums in the diet of certain species (*Euoticus elegantulus, Perodicticus potto*). This last type of feeding which we are actually investigating might be very different from the frugivore type and more similar to the leaf-eating specialization shown in our third grade.

The classical term *omnivore* has generally applied to the first or second grade of primate ecological types, including all transitional types. Now it should be avoided, because it is used with different definitions by different authors.

In all these ecological categories, there may be variations in the social patterns of the internal structures of the social units but they are most closely correlated with the mode of sharing local resources.

REFERENCES

BECK, B. B., R. TUTTLE
   1972   "The behavior of gray langurs at a Ceylonese waterhole," in *The functional and evolutionary biology of primates*. Edited by R. Tuttle, 351–377. Chicago: Aldine-Atherton.

CHARLES-DOMINIQUE, P.
   1971   Eco-éthologie des Prosimiens du Gabon. *Biologia Gabonica* 7(2): 121–228.
   1972   Comportement et écologie des Prosimiens nocturnes. Ecologie et vie sociale de *Galago demidovii. Zeitschrift für Tierpsychologie,* supplement 9:7–41.

CHARLES-DOMINIQUE, P., C. M. HLADIK
   1971   Le *Lepilemur* du sud de Madagascar: écologie, alimentation et vie sociale. *La Terre et la Vie* 25:3–66.

CHIVERS, D. J.
   1972   "The siamang and the gibbon in the Malay peninsula," in *Gibbon and siamang*. Edited by D. M. Rumbaugh, 103–135. Basel: S. Karger.

CROOK, J. H., J. S. GARTLAN
   1966   Évolution of primate societies. *Nature* 210:1200–1203.

DE VORE, I., K. R. L. HALL
   1965   "Baboon ecology," in *Primate behavior*. Edited by I. DeVore, 20–52. New York: Holt, Rinehart and Winston.

EISENBERG, J. F., R. E. KUEHN
   1966   *The behavior of* Ateles geoffroyi *and related species*. Smithsonian Miscellaneous Collections 151(8):1–163.

EISENBERG, J. F., G. M. MC KAY
   1970   An annotated checklist of the recent mammals of Ceylon with keys to the species. *The Ceylon Journal of Science, Biological Sciences* 8(2):69–99.

EISENBERG, J. F., N. A. MUCKENHIRN, R. RUDRAN
1972   The relation between ecology and social structures in primates. *Science* 176:863–874.

GAUTIER, J. P., A. GAUTIER-HION
1969   Les associations polyspécifiques chez les *Cercopithecidae* du Gabon. *La Terre et la Vie* 23:164–201.

GOODALL, J.
1965   "Chimpanzees of the Gombe Stream Reserve," in *Primate behavior*. Edited by I. DeVore, 425–473. New York: Holt, Rinehart and Winston.

HLADIK, A., C. M. HLADIK
1969   Rapports trophiques entre végétation et primates dans la forêt de Barro-Colorado (Panama). *La Terre et la Vie* 23:25–117.

HLADIK, C. M.
1973   Alimentation et activité d'un groupe de chimpanzés réintroduits en forêt gabonaise. *La Terre et la Vie* 27:343–413.

HLADIK, C. M., A. HLADIK
1972   Disponibilités alimentaires et domaines vitaux des primates à Ceylan. *La Terre et la Vie* 26:149–215.

HLADIK, C. M., A. HLADIK, J. BOUSSET, P. VALDEBOUZE, G. VIROBEN, J. DELORT-LAVAL
1971   Le régime alimentaire des Primates de l'île de Barro-Colorado (Panama): résultats des analyses quantitatives. *Folia Primatologica* 16:85–122.

JAY, P.
1965   "The common langur of North India," in *Primate behavior*. Edited by I. DeVore, 197–249. New York: Holt, Rinehart and Winston.

JOLLY, A.
1966   *Lemur behavior. Madagascar field studies*. Chicago: The University of Chicago Press.

LEE, R. B.
1968   "What hunters do for a living, or, how to make out on scarce resources," in *Man the hunter*. Edited by R. B. Lee and I. DeVore, 30–48. Chicago: Aldine.

MANLEY, G.
f.c.   "Aspects of the ecology of *Presbytis senex*."

MARTIN, R. D.
1972   "A preliminary field-study of the Lesser Mouse Lemur," in *Behavior and ecology of nocturnal Prosimians. Zeitschrift für Tierpsychologie* (supplement) 9:43–89.

MOYNIHAN, M. H.
1964   *Some behavior patterns of Platyrrhine monkeys. I. The Night Monkey* (Aotus trivirgatus). Smithsonian Miscellaneous Collections 146(5):1–84.
1968   *Some behavior patterns of Platyrrhine monkeys. II.* Saguinus geoffroyi *and some other Tamarins*. Smithsonian Miscellaneous Collections.

34   C. M. HLADIK

OPPENHEIMER, J. R.
  1968   "Behavior and ecology of the white-faced monkey *Cebus capucinus,* on Barro Colorado Island, Canal Zone." Unpublished doctoral dissertation, University of Illinois, Urbana, Illinois.
PETTER, J. J.
  1962   Recherches sur l'écologie et l'éthologie des Lémuriens malgaches. *Mémoires du Muséum National d'Histoire Naturelle,* série A, 27(1):1–146.
  i.p.   "A study of population density and home range of *Indri indri* in Madagascar," in *Prosimian biology.* Edited by R. Martin, G. A. Doyle, and A. C. Walker, 75–108. London: Duckworth.
PETTER, J. J., C. M. HLADIK
  1970   Observations sur le domaine vital et la densité de population de *Loris tardigradus* dans les forêts de Ceylan. *Mammalia* 34(3): 394–409.
PETTER, J. J., Y. RUMPLER, R. ALBIGNAC
  i.p.   "Les lémuriens de Madagascar," in *Faune de Madagascar.* Paris: O.R.S.T.O.M. and C.N.R.S.
POIRIER, F. E.
  1970   "The Nilgiri Langur (*Presbytis johnii*) of South India," in *Primate behavior; developments in field and laboratory research.* Edited by L. A. Rosenblum, 251–383. New York and London: Academic Press.
RAHM, U.
  1971   L'emploi d'outils par les Chimpanzés de l'Ouest de la Côte d'Ivoire. *La Terre et la Vie* 25:506–509.
REYNOLDS, V., F. REYNOLDS
  1965   "Chimpanzees of the Budongo Forest," in *Primate behavior.* Edited by I. DeVore, 368–424. New York: Holt, Rinehart and Winston.
RIPLEY, S.
  1967   "Intertroop encounters among Ceylon gray langurs (*Presbytis entellus*)," in *Social communication among primates.* Edited by S. A. Altmann, 237–253. Chicago: University of Chicago Press.
  1970   "Leaves and leaf monkeys: the social organization of foraging in gray langurs (*Presbytis entellus thersistes*)," in *Old World monkeys.* Edited by J. R. Napier and P. H. Napier, 481–509. New York and London: Academic Press.
RUDRAN, R.
  1970   "Aspects of ecology of two subspecies of purple-faced langurs (*Presbytis senex*)." Unpublished thesis, University of Ceylon, Colombo.
  1973   Adult males replacement in one-male troops of purple-faced langurs (*Presbytis senex senex*) and its effect on population structure. *Folia Primatologica* 19:166–192.
SCHALLER, G. B.
  1963   *The mountain gorilla: ecology and behavior.* Chicago and London: University of Chicago Press.

SMITH, C. C.
1968 *The adaptive nature of social organization in the genus of tree squirrel* Tamiasciurus. Ecological Monographs 38:31–63.
SUGIYAMA, Y.
1968 Social organization of chimpanzees in the Budongo Forest, Uganda. *Primates* 9:225–258.
SUGIYAMA, Y., K. YOSHIBA, M. D. PATHASARATHY
1965 Home range, mating season, male group and inter-troop relations in Hanuman langurs (*Presbytis entellus*). *Primates* 6:73–106.
SUSSMAN, R. W.
1974 "Ecological distinctions in sympatric species of lemur," in *Prosimian biology*. Edited by R. Martin, G. A. Doyle, and A. C. Walker, 75–108. London: Duckworth.
SUSSMAN, R. W., A. RICHARD
1974 "The role of aggession among diurnal prosimians," in *Aggression, territoriality and xenophobia in the primates*. Edited by R. L. Holloway, 49–76. New York: Academic Press.
STRUHSAKER, T. T.
1969 Correlates of ecology and social organization among African cercopithecines. *Folia Primatologica* 11:80–118.
TELEKI, G.
1973 The omnivorous chimpanzee. *Scientific American* 228(1):32–42.
WOODBURN, J.
1968 "An introduction to Hadza ecology," in *Man the hunter*. Edited by R. B. Lee and I. DeVore, 49–55. Chicago: Aldine.
WYNNE-EDWARDS, V. C.
1962 *Animal dispersion in relation to social behaviour*. Edinburgh and London: Oliver and Boyd.

Habitat Description and Resource Utilization: A Preliminary Report on Mantled Howling Monkey Ecology

KENNETH E. GLANDER

INTRODUCTION

In the past decade there has been an increasing awareness of the relationship between primate social organizations and their environments (Crook and Gartlan 1966; Denham 1971; Eisenberg et al. 1972). The literature to date contains many studies of primate social behavior, but the concomitant investigations of ecological parameters are absent. Eisenberg et al. (1972) have suggested that this "lack of sound ecological studies" prevents insight into the adaptiveness of primate social systems. True, almost every paper on primate behavior does contain a few paragraphs giving geographical location, rainfall, temperature extremes, etc., and a generalized description of habitat cover ("thorn scrub," "open savanna," "tropical wet forest," "evergreen seasonal forest") to describe the study site. But, unfortunately, even this cursory ecological information often is gathered incidental to the behavioral study.

Conspicuous by its absence is detailed information about the natural diets of free-ranging primates in general and herbivorous primates in

I wish to thank Dr. Russell Tuttle for suggesting howlers as a research project and for his guidance and advice throughout the study. I am grateful to the Werner Hagnauers for allowing me to work on Hacienda La Pacifica. I also wish to express my appreciation to Dr. Paul Opler for identifying the trees and to Dr. Norman Scott for developing and implementing the capture and marking technique and for his help in the capture of my study group. In addition, thanks go to C. Opler, T. Opler, and B. Scott for their help in mapping the trees. J. Bradbury, R. Carroll, D. Janzen, P. Opler, and S. Vehrencamp critically commented on the manuscript. The field work was supported in part by National Science Foundation Grant GS 31733.

particular. Often leaf-eating primates, such as howling monkeys (*Alouatta* spp.) are assumed to have an unlimited food supply and, therefore, not to be food limited (Carpenter 1934; Altmann 1959; Hladik et al. 1971). Observations of howlers dropping what appeared to be food (Carpenter 1934; Altmann 1959; Hladik et al. 1971) and leaving a tree before all of the apparent food was eaten (Carpenter 1934; Richard 1970) are given as evidence for an overabundance of available food.

The gathering of such fundamental information as (1) the natural diet of free-ranging primates, (2) the distribution of resources, and (3) the seasonality of resources can help provide the needed prerequisites for the correlations between environment and social structure. Indeed, is it better to specialize on a single resource or to feed on a wide variety of plant foods? What are the habitat similarities or differences which may be shaping various primate social systems? And, how might these ecological variables influence a primate's behavior?

This paper presents the results of the first six months of a twelve-month study aimed at providing a detailed description of the habitat as well as quantifying information on resource utilization by one group of mantled howling monkeys (*Alouatta palliata*) inhabiting a riparian forest in Costa Rica. Included in this report are 1365 hours of animal observation during 117 days from September 1, 1972, through March 2, 1973.

The Study Area

The study was conducted at Hacienda La Pacífica, Guanacaste Province, Costa Rica (10°28′N, 85°07′W). The ranch is 45 meters above sea level and is located in the Lowland Tropical Dry Forest life zone (Holdridge 1967). Most (92 percent) of the yearly average of rainfall (1,561 millimeters) falls between May and November, based on ten-year records (1960–1969) of the Servicio Meteorólogico de Costa Rica. During the dry season, which extends from December through April, strong trade winds blow from the northeast. It is during this time that most of the trees in the dryland areas and some in the riparian forest drop their leaves and remain leafless for most of the dry season (Janzen 1967).

Approximately one-fourth of the ranch is in forest which has been disturbed in various degrees while the remainder has been cleared for farming. In clearing, total deforestation is not practiced; rather, windbreak strips and riparian forests are often left to protect against wind and water erosion.

The study site consisted of narrow bands of riparian forest on the banks of the Río Corobici with wider strips of dry deciduous forest extending laterally into the fields on either side. The river strips were the width of a single tree in some places, about 60 meters wide at the widest point, and 640 meters in length. One of the dry forest strips was 30 meters wide by 170 meters long, and the other was 80 meters wide by 140 meters long. The study area could be divided into riparian and dry regions (these distinctions were based on the kinds, proportions, and phenologies of tree species present) with the river dividing the riparian forest, resulting in four distinct regions (Figure 1). There were cleared fields surrounding all of the range except to the northeast where the riparian forest continued upstream.

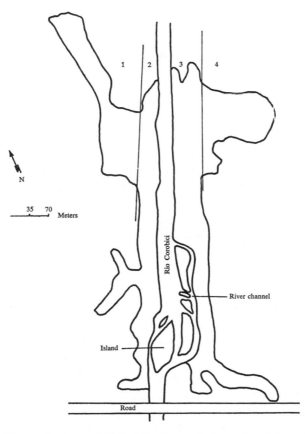

Figure 1. The study site as delimited by Group 1. Areas 1 and 4 are dry regions while Areas 2 and 3 are riparian

Group Composition

During the period of this report my study group (Group 1) consisted of two adult males, six adult females, and five juveniles. A juvenile is defined as an animal not carried by an adult but less than two years old (see Table 5 for names and weights).

Another group (Group 2) occasionally moved into the study area from upriver. It consisted of six adult males, sixteen adult females, twelve juveniles, and two infants. An infant is any animal that is carried continuously by an adult.

Methods

Because the primary concern of this study was to analyze the relation-ship between the habitat and the monkeys, the initial two months were devoted to obtaining detailed parameters on the environment. Each tree (a self-supporting woody plant more than four meters in height) within the study group's range was numbered consecutively, and tree heights, diameters, and canopy depths were measured. The trees were also identified as to species where possible.

One of the difficulties of observing arboreal animals is the prob-lem of being able to see all, or even a few of the subjects. Other in-vestigators have employed various observational methods in an effort to overcome the problems of visibility and the bias of individual animal observability intrinsic to the study of a free-ranging primate inhabiting forested areas (McClure 1964; Chalmers 1968; van Lawick-Goodall 1968; Beck and Tuttle 1972). Prior to this study I developed a method that I call Randomized Individual Observation (RIO) which was used successfully throughout this field work. RIO is based upon the strategy of continuously monitoring the behavior of one animal per day. A dif-ferent subject animal may be observed each day or the same animal may be observed for several successive days. The order of individual observation is determined by a random digit table.

RIO is designed to eliminate any possible bias that the investigator may unintentionally introduce into the order of individual observations because of personal preference or the ease with which certain ages and/or sex classes may be observed. By concentrating on a single animal the observer is not distracted by the movements of other animals and can follow the subject animal for longer periods of time. There is then much less unproductive observation time which must be filled with educated guesses. Using RIO, data can be collected on the duration of activities and time-energy budgets can be calculated.

Unambiguous recognition of each individual within the study group is an absolute necessity for the successful employment of RIO. To facilitate positive identification of the thirteen members of my study group, leather collars with metal tags of different colors were put around the necks of the six adult females. The adult males could be distinguished by physical characteristics. The juveniles were too small for collars and could be differentiated by their size and close association with a tagged female. To capture the animals, a controlled dose of Anectine (*Succinylcholine chloride*) was delivered by a CO_2 gun. A large piece of canvas, rigged with handles, was used to catch the animals as they fell from the trees.

Observations were usually begun about 0500 (on several days observations were begun at 0400) and terminated at 1800 or at sunset. Prior to 0500 I would place myself in position under the subject animal for the day, using a headlamp to verify the individual's identity. Howlers seldom move at night and are fairly easy to locate the next morning if their position for the previous night is known. During two all-night observations the animals being observed did not move at all other than to shift positions. On many mornings the subject animal was found in the same location in which it had been the preceding night. Occasionally animals changed branches but usually moved less than twenty-five feet and seldom changed trees. Although they did not move very much at night, Group 1 was observed traveling through the trees on several nights around midnight, and often began feeding well before dawn (as early as 0400) and continued feeding past sunset (as late as 1830). During this study sunrise occurred at about 0510 and sunset about 1755. Once located, the subject's position in relation to the positions of other animals in the tree was noted and the continuous monitoring of the subject's behavior was initiated.

The time of onset of any new activity and the activity were noted. If the activity was feeding, the tree number (for later species identification), location in the tree, feeding posture, and part of the tree eaten were recorded. An attempt at quantifying the amount eaten was made by counting mouthfuls, or in some instances, the number of fruits eaten, in order to determine relative importance of the various tree species. In quantifying the feeding data two stop-watches were used simultaneously. A record was also kept of the numbers of the trees through which the animals moved. This information will be used to view area utilization.

In order to compare the howlers' movements with food seasonality a weekly record was kept of the flowering, fruiting, and leaf production of the numbered trees.

RESULTS

During the first six months of the study the four areas of the study site, as delimited by the study group, contained a total of 1,348 trees representing ninety-two species from thirty-eight families (Table 1).

Table 1.   A complete list of the tree species present in the study site. The species are arranged alphabetically by family with the common name in quotation marks and the number of individuals in parentheses. If the species is a food source, the part(s) of the tree used as food is listed. An asterisk indicates the species was utilized as a primary source of food. A # indicates a dioecious tree species

---

ANACARDIACEAE
  Anacardium excelsum "Espavel" (68)
      new leaf petiole, pedicel, flowers, new leaves
  # *Astronium graveolens* "Ronron" (7)
      flower buds, leaves
  Mangifera indica "Mango" (8)
      green & ripe fruit
  #*Spondias mombin* "Jobo" (14)
      fruit, leaf pulvinus, new leaves, leaves
  #*Spondias nigrescens* (7)
      leaf pulvinus, flower buds, fruit
  Spondias purpurea "Jocote" (31)
      leaves
ANNONACEAE
  Annona holosericea "Anona" (7)
  Annona purpurea "Soncoya" (3)
  Sapranthus palanga "Palanca" (5)
APOCYNACEAE
  Rauwolfia sp. (1)
ARALIACEAE
  # *Sciadodendron excelsum* "Jobo de lagarto" (1)
BIGNONIACEAE
  Crescentia cujete "Calabacero jicaro" (7)
  Godmania aesculifolia "Corteza de chivo" (23)
  Tabebuia neochrysantha "Corteza

de chivo" (30)
      flowers, flower buds
  Tabebuia rosea "Roble de sabana" (32)
      flowers, flower buds
BIXACEAE
  Bixa orellana "Achiote" (6)
BOMBACACEAE
  Bombacopsis quinata "Pochote" (4)
      leaves
  Ceiba pentandra "Ceiba" (6)
  Ochroma lagopus "Balsa" (1)
BORAGINACEAE
  Bourreria quirosii (2)
      flower buds, flowers
  Cordia alliodora "Laurel" (39)
      leaves
  # *Cordia collococca* (17)
      leaves, flower buds
  Cordia dentata (194)
      fruit
  # *Cordia panamensis* (5)
BURSERACEAE
  #*Bursera simaruba* "Indio des-nudo" (18)
      new leaves, leaves
CAESALPINACEAE
  Hymenaea courbaril "Guapinol" (61)
      new leaves
  Schizolobium parahybum "Galli-

Table 1 (continued)

nazo" (6)
  flowers, fruit
Cassia grandis "Carao" (1)
CAPPARIDACEAE
  Capparis indica (2)
  Crataeva tapia (1)
CARICACEAE
Carica papaya "Papaya" (1)
  leaves
  Stemmadenia obovata (2)
COCHLOSPERMACEAE
  Cochlospermum vitifolium "Poro-
  poro" (30)
  flower buds
ELAEOCARPACEAE
  * *Muntingia calabura* "Capulin" (7)
  fruit, flowers, leaves
FABACEAE
  * *Andira inermis* "Carne asada" (30)
  new leaves
  Dalbergia retusa "Cocobola" (11)
  * *Gliricidia sepium* "Madera negra"
  (103)
  leaves, new leaves, flowers, fruit
  Lonchocarpus costaricensis (6)
  Lonchocarpus hondurensis (2)
  flowers, fruit
  * *Lonchocarpus minimiflorus*
  "Chaperno" (66)
  flower buds, flowers
  * *Pterocarpus hayesii* "Sangre de
  drago" (4)
  new leaves, leaves
FLACOURTIACEAE
  Casearia aculeata (7)
  Casearia arborea (6)
  Laetia thamnia (2)
Xylosma flexuosum (2)
HIPPOCRATACEAE
  Hemiangium excelsum (9)
LAURACEAE
  Ocotea veraguensis (1)
MALPIGHIACEAE
  Byrsonima crassifolia "Nance" (2)
MELIACEAE
  Cedrela mexicana "Cedro amargo"
  (5)
Guarea luxii (13)
  new leaves
  Swietenia humilus "Caobo" (11)
* *Trichilia cuneata* (5)

new leaves, leaves, flowers
Trichilia sp. (12)
MIMOSACEAE
  Albizzia adinocephala "Gavilana"
  (1)
  new leaves
  Albizzia sp. (2)
  Enterolobium cyclocarpum
  "Guanacaste" (13)
  leaves, flower buds, flowers
  * *Inga vera* var. *spuria* (3)
  new leaves, flowers
  Lysiloma seemannii "Quebracho"
  (22)
  * *Pithecellobium longifolium* "Soto-
  caballo" (16)
  new leaves, flowers
  * *Pithecellobium saman* "Cenicero"
  (10)
  new leaves, leaves, flowers, fruit
MORACEAE
  Brosimum costaricanum "Ojoche"
  (1)
* *Cecropia peltata* "Guarumo" (4)
  leaf petiole, fruit, new leaves
Chlorophora tinctoria "Mora" (7)
  leaves
  * *Ficus sp.* "Higuerón" (3)
  new leaves
MYRTACEAE
  * *Eugenia salamensis* (76)
  fruit
  Psidium guajava "Guayaba" (1)
NYCTAGINACEAE
Pisonia macranthocarpa "Petrono"
  (6)
OLACACEAE
  Schoepfia schreberi (4)
PAPILIONOIDEAE
  * *Myrospermum frutescens* (13)
  leaves, new leaves, flowers
PIPERACEAE
  Piper tuberculatum (1)
  leaves
POLYGONACEAE
Coccoloba caracasana "Papaturro
  blanco" (9)
  new leaves
ROSACEAE
  * *Licania arborea* "Alcornoque" (29)
  new leaves, flower buds

Table 1 (continued)

RUBIACEAE
  Calycophyllum candidissimum
  "Madrona" (17)
    leaves
  Chomelia spinosa (3)
    leaves
Genipa caruto "Guazitel" (2)
  Guettarda macrosperma (2)
    leaves
RUTACEAE
  Citrus limetta "Lima dulce" (1)
Zanthoxylum procerum (4)
    leaves, new leaves
SAPINDACEAE
  Thouinidium decandrum (16)
SAPOTACEAE
  * *Manilkara achras* (6)
    fruit
  * *Mastichodendron tempisque* (6)

    flower buds, flowers, fruit
SIMAROUBACEAE
Picramnia latifolia (1)
Simarouba glauca "Olimo" (7)
    leaves, fruit
STERCULIACEAE
  Guazuma tomentosa "Guacimo"
  (185)
    new leaves
  Sterculia apetala "Panama" (3)
TILIACEAE
  Apeiba tibourbou "Peine de mico"
  (4)
  Luehea candida "Guacimo
  macho" (54)
    new leaves
  Luehea speciosa "Guacimo
  molenillo" (4)
    flower buds, flowers

There are fifteen species (16 percent) represented by only one individual while the most numerous tree species, *Cordia dentata*, numbered 194. In this particular life zone a riparian habitat can be defined by the presence of *Anacardium excelsum* and *Pithecellobium longifolium*. There are twenty (22 percent) dioecious tree species in the study site. These twenty species include 10 percent of the total number of individuals (134 of 1,348). Dioeciousness of a species affects the monkeys by reducing the number of individuals which provide fruit because only the female trees produce fruit. Of such species Group 1 fed on the fruit of *Cecropia peltata* (one female of four individuals), *Spondias mombin* (six females of fourteen individuals), *Spondias nigrescens* (four females of seven individuals), and *Chlorophora tinctoria* (four females of seven individuals).

Two of the species found in my study site are not indigenous to this area, i.e. *Mangifera indica* and *Citrus limeta*. *M. indica* is used as an occasional food source.

Group 1 spent two days feeding in Area 1, seven days feeding in Area 4, and the remaining 108 days feeding along the river, with sixty-four days in Area 2 and forty-four days in Area 3. The visits to Area 1 were to feed on *Manilkara achras* and *Mastichodendron tempisque* flower buds and flowers. The seven days spent in Area 4 were all during the *Cordia dentata* fruiting season. During the dry season the trees of these two areas (except *Hymenaea courbaril*) dropped their leaves and remained bare while the riparian area species were flowering, fruiting, and producing new leaves.

The howler's movements throughout the range appeared to be co-ordinated with the trees' phenology. For example, in several instances the group moved from one side of the river to the other when indi-viduals of *Pithecellobium longifolium* on the opposite river bank began to produce new leaves. Often new leaves, fruit, flowers, and buds are a bright color and visible for long distances against the backdrop of green leaves or brown branches. Possibly the odor of the fruit also caused howlers to determine that a move would be rewarded. Because the group moved through its range quite frequently, it also might have been obtaining direct cues of events which would occur in the near future, such as flowering or new leaf production.

At first glance Group 1 appeared to be generalists because they utilized 54 percent (fifty of ninety-two) of the species available to them. But when only the species primarily used as resources by Group 1 were considered, they were shown to be much more selective in their food choice. Only 23 percent (twenty-one of ninety-two) of the total species available to Group 1 were used as primary resources. A primary resource is defined as one which has been utilized as a food source more than seven times.

Many of the fifty species were utilized by Group 1 only once or twice. For example, one of the adult males was observed to feed on leaves of *Carica papaya* for less than three minutes on a single occa-sion; an adult female took only two bites of new leaves from a single *Guazuma tomentosa*; and once a juvenile and adult female were seen to feed briefly on leaves of a *Bombacopsis quinata*. Other species not noted with an asterisk in Table 1 were utilized more frequently than those mentioned above, but not as regularly as the primary resources. The howlers may have had limited access to the food item because of the seasonality of the food, or possibly they may have been using that particular resource at the time to balance their diet or because some-thing else which might have been preferred was not available. It is probable that some of these species which are not primary food sources at this time may become primary sources of food as the trees change seasonally.

Also, it may be that these trees contained substances which in higher concentrations were toxic to the monkeys but could be tolerated when eaten in smaller amounts. Certain ruminant artiodactyls can eat small amounts of toxic plant substances (Pearson 1965) and squirrels ingest small amounts of seeds containing canavanine which in large amounts is probably toxic (Janzen 1971a). Many tropical plants have high concentrations of "secondary compounds" in their seeds or foliage which may be toxic to the plants' predators (Janzen 1970, 1971b). For example, *Gliridicia sepium* is called mata-ratón (mouse killer) in Puerto Rico: the toxic seeds, bark, leaves, and roots are used to kill rats and mice (Little and Wadsworth 1964). There were 103 *G. sepium* individual trees present in the study site. Group 1 fed on the flowers of eighteen of the 103 individuals and only on the mature leaves, new leaves, and fruit of four of the 103 individual trees, two of which were located in Area 2 and two of which were located in Area 3. The foliage of these four trees may have had a lower toxin content.

Most of the food sources of the study group were contained in five families (Anacardiaceae, Fabaceae, Mimosaceae, Moraceae, Sapotaceae). New leaves of *Anacardium excelsum* and *Andira inermis* were eaten but not the mature leaves. The family Anacardiaceae contains a resinous exudate which can be very caustic. Some people cannot eat mango fruit because of this resin. *A. excelsum* produced a very large fruit crop per tree but the monkeys only ate the small fleshy stalk (pedicel), probably due to toxins in the fruit itself which were not present in the pedicel. The shell of the related *Anacardium occidentale* fruit contains a poisonous oil: cardol oil (Little and Wadsworth 1964).

The family Moraceae probably also contains toxic secondary compounds because the howlers fed only on new leaves of *Ficus* sp. as well as the new leaves and the leaf petioles of new and mature leaves of *Cecropia peltata* plus the fruit of each of these species. *C. peltata* has an ant species which inhabits the hollow areas of the trunk and patrols the leaves and fruit. The ant may serve as an effective deterrent against some invertebrate and vertebrate predators.

The two families, Mimosaceae and Sapotaceae, are somewhat less sharply defined as to presence or absence of toxic compounds. Only the fruit and flowers of *Manilkara achras* and *Mastichodendron tempisque* were eaten. The fruit, flowers, new leaves, and mature leaves of *Pithecellobium saman* were eaten while mature leaves and fruit of *Pithecellobium longifolium* were not eaten but the new leaves were actively sought by Group 1.

Cordia dentata fruit were available for only two weeks, but during that time the fruit represented a major part of the daily food intake as judged by the amount of time spent feeding. *Muntingia calabura* produced flowers, fruit, and leaves throughout the year and, although it comprised a very low percentage of the feeding time for any day, it was available every day. Probably the limiting factor in *M. calabura* use as a food source was its location in the range and the availability of other resources. If the group passed through any *M. calabura* trees they almost always fed in them during the dry season, but they did not make special detours just to feed in *M. calabura* and utilized only two trees (both in the southern part of Area 3) of the seven trees in the range, probably because the other five were not located in areas frequently visited by the group members (all five were located in the northwestern part of Area 3). Utilization of *M. calabura* decreased to almost zero during the wet season.

During the time *Andira inermis* produced new leaves it served as a major daily food source. The twenty-one *A. inermis* on the east side of the river produced new leaves first and for ten days served as Group 1's major food source. As the leaves of the individuals on the east side of the river began to mature the group moved to the west side where the other *A. inermis* were then beginning to produce new leaves.

Some species provided the study group with more than one type of food, e.g. *Anacardium excelsum*. The howlers ate the very new leaves (less than two inches long), new leaf petioles, flower buds, flowers, and the fleshy fruit pedicels. Because *A. excelsum* began to flower, produce new leaves, and fruit at the end of the wet season and continued this production into the dry season, it was one of the major sources of food during the dry season. Another species which provided more than one type of food and was an important food source during the dry season as well as throughout the year was *Pithecellobium saman*. The howlers fed on mature leaves during both the wet and dry season and also fed on the new leaves which were produced in October and March. The fruits of *P. saman* were also eaten during the dry season just before they began to mature. The fruit, in earlier stages of development, also was eaten during the rest of the year because it takes one year from the time of pollination for the fruit to mature. Flowers usually occur in March and April and were also sought by Group 1. Because of an extremely dry wet season this past year, some of the *P. saman* individuals in the drier areas produced a crop of flowers during October and November, 1972.

The fruits of *Spondias mombin* and *Eugenia salamensis* were important food sources for Group 1. Both of these fruits were taken from the trees by mouth and swallowed after being briefly chewed. The adults were seen to tilt their heads back when chewing *S. mombin* fruits, which are very juicy, thus swallowing as much of the juice as possible. Apparently the monkeys select the fruit of *S. mombin* by color from a distance, for upon entering a fruiting tree they would look around before moving to a certain area. They then appeared to accept or reject a particular fruit by odor, sniffing each one before eating it.

From the monkey's viewpoint, the year just past was not a good one in regard to the quantity of *E. salamensis* fruit. Of the seventy-six trees in the range, only four produced fruit. Possibly a lack of rain at a critical time resulted in the small fruit crop, or *E. salamensis* may produce a fruit crop every other year.

Feeding Postures

Although howlers have a prehensile tail and may use it in feeding, my study group often fed in the sitting or standing posture. Juveniles seemed to spend more of their feeding time hanging. Adults appeared to adapt their feeding posture to the conditions required to feed (Table 2). Three important determinants of whether sitting or hanging was used were the shape of the tree, the kind of food eaten, and the location of the food in the tree. If the food ingested was in a tree with a narrow, confined canopy, the food was likely to be in an upright position and could be reached by sitting in adjacent branches. If the tree had a wide spreading canopy the lower one-half of the canopy was usually either horizontal or arched toward the ground and the food could only be reached by hanging from the same branch or a branch above the food. Any food located in the upper half of this type of tree was likely to be positioned above the branch and could be reached by sitting on the branch. Normally most fruit hung below the level of a branch and could only be reached by hanging. This was especially true of large fruit of *Mangifera indica*, *Spondias mombin*, and *Eugenia salamensis*. *Cordia dentata* fruit are borne in a cluster which projects upward and were usually eaten while sitting on adjacent branches.

Size difference was probably the main reason for juveniles hanging more than adults while feeding. Because they weighed less (three to five pounds as compared to ten to eleven pounds) they could get out to the ends of very small branches which bent under their weight, making it almost impossible to reach any food other than that lower down. However, if these terminal branches were upright, i.e. in the upper center of the tree, the juvenile like the adult was more likely to feed sitting. In trees such as *Pithecellobium saman* and *Ficus* sp. adults often spent their entire feeding time of fifteen to thirty-five minutes sitting. As yet there does not appear to be any individual preference by any member of Group 1 for either sitting or hanging.

Often while feeding in the sitting posture the tail was wrapped around an adjacent branch. Though it did not support any weight, it probably acted as a safety device against any sudden movement by other monkeys in the immediate vicinity or a strong gust of wind which can occur suddenly in the dry season. In certain situations the tail was used as a counterweight to offset the weight of the animal balanced on top of a branch while reaching out toward some nearby food. In these instances the tail was not anchored but was held free.

Feeding Rates

Part of the time spent in a resource tree by the monkeys was spent foraging for food. Foraging is defined as the time spent in a food tree either visually searching for food or moving from place to place within the tree. Foraging and feeding times appeared to depend upon the species used as a food tree. There was very little foraging time in *Licania arborea* when feeding on leaves, while 50 percent of the time was spent foraging in *Anacardium excelsum* when feeding on "pedicels" (Table 2). The number of pedicels eaten per unit time was a result of the number of fruit available in a tree (Table 3).

Mouthfuls of leaves per minute were counted in an effort to get an idea of the feeding rate and the amount ingested. Hladik et al. (1971) counted the number of leaves and then weighed a sample of the same species to determine the weight of food ingested. They estimated that an adult weighing 17.6 pounds ingested forty-two ounces of food. I took twenty-two ounces of mash from the caecum of a dead howler weighing eight pounds. This monkey's stomach was completely empty.

Drinking

Several members of Group 1 were seen to drink water from cisterns formed at the base of several branches or from holes in large branches. In all cases rain water had gathered in these areas, and the howlers hung by their tails with their heads down and inserted their heads into the opening. None of the members of Group 1 were seen to drink from the river, even though many of the trees had branches which touched the water. During the dry season the howlers apparently got all of the moisture they required from their food as the waterholes in the trees dried up from lack of rain.

Table 2.   Feeding and foraging times for several species of trees with postures used and tim spent in each posture. All information is from Group 1

Animal	Food type	Tree species	Time in tree	Actual feeding time		Feeding time hanging		Feeding time sitting	
			seconds	seconds	percent	seconds	percent	seconds	percent
Baker	NLFL	*Pithecellobium saman*	720	373	52	280	75	93	25
Scar	FRST	*Anacardium excelsum*	420	267	64	180	68	87	32
Yellow	FR	*Pithecellobium saman*	240	215	89	36	19	179	81
Scar	FRST	*Anacardium excelsum*	480	244	50	0	0	244	100
Scar	NL	*Ficus* sp.	540	248	45	56	23	192	77
Scar	FRST	*Anacardium excelsum*	1560	794	51	218	27	576	73
Scar	NLFB	*Licania arborea*	1200	997	83	273	27	724	73
Green/red	FL	*Lonchocarpus hondurensis*	480	470	98	390	83	80	27
Baker	FLFR	*Lonchocarpus hondurensis*	540	535	99	535	100	0	0
Green/red	FBPE	*Schizolobium parahybum*	960	692	72	159	24	533	76
Green/red	LE	*Pithecellobium saman*	480	260	54	0	0	260	100
Green/red	NL	*Inga vera* var. *spuria*	660	525	79	240	45	285	55
Green/red	LE	*Pithecellobium saman*	720	660	91	0	0	660	100
Green/red	LE	*Calycophyllum candidissimum*	600	600	100	0	0	600	100
White/red	FL	*Gliricidia sepium*	600	252	42	35	14	227	86
Green	FL	*Gliricidia sepium*	600	215	35	15	7	200	86
Green	NL	*Andira inermis*	1620	1440	89	610	42	830	68
Dogcollar	NL	*Licania arborea*	780	780	100	84	11	686	89
Blue	NL	*Andira inermis*	720	685	95	0	0	685	100
Green/red	FB	*Mastichodendron tempisque*	900	675	75	343	51	332	49

52   = percent of time in the tree spent feeding
NLFL   = new leaves and flowers
FRST   = fruit stalks (pedicels)
FR   = fruit
NL   = new leaves
NLFB   = new leaves and flower buds
FL   = flowers
FLFR   = flowers and fruit
FBPE   = flower bud petiole
LE   = leaves
FB   = flower buds

Effects of Monkeys upon the Habitat

Group 1 acted as seed dispersal agents for many of the tree species present in their range. In most instances the seeds were not damaged by chewing and passed through the gut unharmed to be dropped in the fecal matter. I have retrieved viable seeds of *Spondias mombin*, *Eugenia salamensis*, *Manilkara achras*, and *Cordia dentata* from howler

Table 3.   Number of *Anacardium excelsum* fruit picked and dropped after eating the pedicel

Tree number	Animal	Number of fruit	Time seconds
72	White/red	6	240
99	Green	5	60
109	Green	5	60
72	Green	26	480
126	Scar	26	360
126	Baker	45	267
72	Scar	32	244
72	Scar	106	794

feces. These seeds have been found in all parts of Group 1's range, although individuals of each species are not located in all areas of the range. An even wider dispersal of *S. mombin* seeds resulted from the fact that Group 1 inhabited a riparian forest and the fact that *S. mombin* seeds without the flesh float (*S. mombin* seeds with flesh sink). The howlers ingested the fruit, digested the fleshy pulp from the seeds, and expelled the seeds in their feces. When the howlers were either feeding or moving over the river at the time of defecation, the feces would drop into the water, and the seeds would float downstream. One seed dispersal agent (howlers) provided access to another (water).

Some possible negative effects of intensive feeding by the howlers can be demonstrated with *Cecropia peltata* and *Bursera simaruba*. Constant feeding pressure has apparently contributed to the death of two of the four *C. peltata*. Because *C. peltata* is dioecious, an indirect result of the loss of these two trees, if they were males, may be the lack of fruit production by the remaining females. Because *B. simaruba* is also dioecious a similar reduction of fruit may result from the method of feeding employed by the howlers in these trees. To reach the desired leaves the howlers broke off the terminal twigs. However, only three of the eighteen individual *B. simaruba* served as resources for the howlers. The canopy of these three trees was noticeably less dense than those receiving no feeding pressure from the howlers.

Also, feeding pressure on the flowers may affect the eventual size of the fruit crop. If the flower production is small the feeding could reduce the size of the fruit crop. Many species produce a vast number of flowers, many times the number of the eventual fruit crop, to attract pollinators, i.e. *Anacardium excelsum* produced an estimated 500,000 flowers with about 35,000 fruit set. Even the loss of about one percent of the flowers of these trees to the howlers could affect the eventual seed production by reducing nectar flow and pollination visits.

The howlers did remove a large number of green fruit while feeding upon the pedicels of *A. excelsum* fruit, perhaps up to 10 percent of the trees' fruit crops, thereby lowering the number of fruit which reached maturity. The green fruit was picked from the trees with the mouth, grasped with either hand, the pedicel bitten off, and the fruit dropped.

DISCUSSION

Although my study group fed on 54 percent of the available tree species, only 23 percent of the total available tree species can be considered to be important or primary food sources. The twenty-one tree

Table 4.   Utilization of the primary food species by Group 1

Tree species	Individual trees			Months during which tree species served as food and food type selected					
	# pres.	# used	% used	Sep.	Oct.	Nov.	Dec.	Jan.	Feb.
Anacardium excelsum	68	45	66		NL	NLPE	NLPE	NLPE	FRST
Andira inermis	30	19	63				NL	NL	NL
Bursera simaruba	18	5	27	NL	NL	LENL			
Cecropia peltata	4	3	75	FR	PE	PE	PE	NL	
Eugenia salamensis	76	3	3	FR	FR				
Ficus sp.	3	3	100	NL	NL	NL	NL	NL	NL
Gliricidia sepium	103	18	17	LE	LE	LE	LE	FL	FL
Inga vera var. *spuria*	3	2	67		NL		FL		NL
Licania arborea	29	15	50	NL	NL	NL	NL	NL	NL
Lonchocarpus minimiflorus	66	15	23	FL	FL	FL			
Manilkara achras	6	5	83		FR	FR	FR		
Mastichodendron tempisque	6	5	83	FBFL				FBFL	FBFL
Muntingia calabura	7	2	28			LE	LE	FR	FR
Myrospermum frutescens	13	1	7	LE	LE		LE	FBFL	LENL
Pithecellobium longifolium	16	12	75	NL		NL	NL	NL	NL
Pithecellobium saman	10	8	80	LENL	NLFL	LEFL	LEFR	LE	LE
Pterocarpus hayesii	4	2	50	NL	NL	NL			NL
Schizolobium parahybum	6	5	83					FL	FL
Spondis mombin	14	5	36	FR	FR	FR	FR		
Spondias nigrescens	7	7	100	FR	FR	FR	FRPU	PU	
Trichilia cuneata	5	5	100	LE	LE	LE	LE	LE	LE

NL	= new leaves	FBFL = flowers and flower buds
NLPE	= new leaf petiole	NLFL = new leaves and flowers
FRST	= fruit stalk (peticel)	LEFL = leaves and flowers
LENL	= leaves and new leaves	LEFR = leaves and fruit
FR	= fruit	FRPU = fruit pulvinus
PE	= leaf petiole	PU = pulvinus
LE	= leaves	FL = flowers

Table 5. Composition of my study group for the six months of this report

Animal	Sex	Date	Weight	Mother	Comments
Scar	male	6/22/73	13 lb. 12 oz.	—	
Baker	male	6/19/73	15 lb. 6 oz.	—	
White/red	female	6/22/73	9 lb. 1 oz.	—	
Blue	female	6/19/73	11 lb. 6 oz.	—	
Yellow	female	6/19/73	10 lb. 3 oz.	—	
Green	female	6/19/73	10 lb. 11 oz.	—	
Green/red	female	6/19/73	11 lb. 8 oz.	—	
Dogcollar	female	8/16/72	11 lb. 3 oz.	—	
Charlie	male	6/22/73	8 lb. 2 oz.	Yellow	
Able	male	3/25/73	5 lb. 4 oz.	White/red	
Bonnie	female	1/12/73	4 lb. 5 oz.	Dogcollar	
Shadow	male	—	—	Green/red	
Infant	male	—	—	Blue	Disappeared 1/20/73

species classed as primary food sources contained 53 percent (709 of 1,348) of all the trees in Group 1's range (Table 4). However, this is not an accurate picture of the overall selectivity of Group 1. They utilized only 257 individual trees of the 1,348 trees available to them in their range. In addition, Group 1 did not feed on all individuals of a tree species in its range, but in most cases on only a select few. An extreme example of this selectivity was demonstrated by Group 1 feeding on the mature leaves of only four of the 103 individuals of *Gliricidia sepium* present in the range. Possibly these figures represent the number of individuals required to provide all of the nutrients the howlers needed. If we can assume that all individuals of a tree species contain similar nutrients, then the monkeys should feed equally on all of the individual trees within a food species. In the same manner, if it can be assumed that all species of trees can be utilized as food sources, howlers should be expected to demonstrate little selectivity between tree species in their choice of food, or at most only demonstrate individual peculiarities. Such is not the case for my study group. Rather, the monkeys returned to the same individual trees and fed selectively on certain species, certain individual trees, and selected parts of those trees at certain seasonal stages.

This selectivity within a food species (e.g. *Gliricidia sepium* with four of 103) as well as between species (twenty-one of ninety-two) may be the result of secondary substances produced by the trees as a deterrent to herbivores thereby narrowing the feeding niche of the howler. In opposition to this constriction is the howler's need to meet nutritional demands. The sampling of more tree species (fifty of ninety-two) may indicate that it is highly advantageous for howlers to maintain a sufficiently diverse gut flora and fauna in order to survive even a slight perturbation of the available resources (Janzen, personal communication).

The secondary substances which the plants have evolved as defenses against herbivores may be of critical importance both to the individual animal and to group social behavior. The action of these plant toxins may be direct as demonstrated by the rat poison made from the bark and leaves of *Gliricidia sepium*. Or, it may be indirect in the manner of tannins, as found in mature oak leaves, which bind proteins into indigestible complexes (Feeny 1970). An even more indirect effect of the plant toxins might be the subtle interference with the animals' reproductive cycles, such as occurs in insects (Ellis et al. 1965).

Plant secondary substances may have played an important role in primate evolution. The presence of intestinal flora may permit herbivores to ingest a diet high in secondary substances which would be toxic to them without the gut flora to detoxify the toxins, e.g. rodents living on a high oxalate diet (Shirley and Schmidt-Nielsen 1967). Possibly the protection offered by the intestinal flora allowed herbivorous primates to invade an ecological niche not available to animals without such an adaptive mechanism. Because caffeine and nicotine are alkaloids (Whittaker and Feeny 1971) man's ability to tolerate many toxins in his food and his use of plant-derived stimulants and hallucinogenics may be a legacy of his herbivorous ancestors.

The suggestion of an unlimited food supply for a herbivore, such as the howler, implies an animal which can use a wide variety of available plant food and which has evolved the ability to detoxify a broad range of toxic materials found in these foods. The detoxification of a wide range of plant foods containing many different toxic compounds requires the herbivore to expend a majority of its energy and nutrients to maintain the detoxification mechanisms necessary to handle this variety of toxins (Whittaker and Feeny 1971). Prior to the present fieldwork previous investigators concluded that the range of a howler group contained more food than the group would ever be able to utilize, and that food availability played no part in limiting the population density (Carpenter 1934; Altmann 1959; Chivers 1969; Hladik et al 1971). They would probably agree with Hairston, Smith, and Slobodkin (1960) that herbivores are not limited by the available food, but by other factors, such as disease and predators, which keep their number from increasing until all the food is eaten. In viewing the relationship between the howlers and the potential food available in their habitat, I would propose that the idea first suggested by Stahl in

1888 (Fraenkel 1959), "that not all that is green is palatable," be considered before *a priori* conclusions as to the quantity or quality of available food are made.

My study group utilized only a fraction of the tree species available in their range, only certain individuals of some food species, and less than 20 percent of the total number of trees present in their range. Their lack of activity may be the price howlers pay, in terms of maintaining their detoxification system, for feeding on the particular tree species which meet their nutritional requirements. It seems highly unlikely that the howler can maintain a detoxification system necessary to meet the added demands that ingestion of all available resources would place upon their digestive systems.

An apparent independence of free water during the dry season can be related to a finding of Feeny (1970) that the water content of immature leaves is higher than mature leaves. Many of the riparian trees, which are primary food species, produce new leaves during the dry season. Therefore, it is very likely that the howlers acquire sufficient water from their food and do not need to drink from the river.

Hladik et al. (1971) suggest that an exclusive fruit diet would be deficient in proteins. Indeed, even on those days when fruit made up most of the daily intake of food, Group 1 always ingested some leaves, possibly, as Hladik et al. (1971) have suggested, to balance the diet. It is this need for a balanced diet which may explain why howlers leave a tree before the available food is depleted. Also, departure may indicate that the howlers have ingested as much of that food as they can detoxify.

To the degree that contemporary studies can elucidate the ecology and behavior of early hominids, detailed information on the diet of extant primates may be important. Fossil evidence of plants or of pollen are sometimes available from the area which a fossil primate probably inhabited. Knowing the relationship between an extant primate and its habitat can provide an insight into some of the selection pressures which may have acted on the extinct primates, such as a gradual change in climate which resulted in an alteration in the composition of tree species and thus in the primates' resources.

REFERENCES

ALTMANN, S. A.
    1959   Field observations on a howling monkey society. *Journal of Mammalogy* 40:317–330.

BECK, B. B., R. TUTTLE
  1972   "The behavior of gray langurs at a Ceylonese waterhole," in
         The functional and evolutionary biology of primates. Edited by
         R. Tuttle, 351–377. Chicago: Aldine.

BERNSTEIN, I. S.
  1964   A field study of the activities of howler monkeys. *Animal Be-*
         havior 12:92–97.

CARPENTER, C. R.
  1934   A field study of the behavior and social relations of howling
         monkeys (*Alouatta palliata*). *Comparative Psychology Monographs*
         10:1–68.

CHALMERS, N. R.
  1968   Group composition, ecology, and daily activities of free-living
         mangabeys in Uganda. *Folio Primatologica* 8:247–262.

CHIVERS, D. J.
  1969   On the daily behavior and spacing of howling monkey groups.
         Folio Primatologica 10:48–102.

COLLIAS, N. E., C. SOUTHWICK
  1952   A field study of population density and social organization in
         howling monkeys. *Proceedings of the American Philosophical*
         Society 96:143–156.

CROOK, J. H., J. S. GARTLAN
  1966   Evolution of primate societies. *Nature* 210:1200–1203.

DENHAM, W. W.
  1971   Energy relations and some basic properties of primate social or-
         ganization. *American Anthropology* 73:77–95.

EISENBERG, J. F., N. A. MUCHENHIRN, R. RUDRAN
  1972   The relation between ecology and social structure in primates.
         Science 176:863–874.

ELLIS, P. E., D. B. CARLISLE, D. J. OSBORNE
  1965   Desert locusts: sexual maturation delayed by feeding on senescent
         vegetation. *Science* 149:546–547.

FEENY, P. P.
  1970   Seasonal changes in oak leaf tannins and nutrients as a cause of
         spring feeding by winter moth caterpillars. *Ecology* 51:565–580.

FRAENKEL, G. S.
  1959   The raison d'être of secondary plant sustances. *Science* 129:
         1466–1470.

HAIRSTON, N. G., F. E. SMITH, L. B. SLOBODKIN
  1960   Community structure, population control, and competition.
         American Naturalist 94:421–425.

HLADIK, C. M., A. HLADIK, J. BOUSSET, P. VALDEBOUZE, G. VIROBEN,
  J. DELORT-LAVAL
  1971   Le régime alimentaire des primates de l'île de Barro-Colorado
         (Panama). *Folia Primatologica* 16:85–122.

HOLDRIDGE, L. R.
  1967   *Life zone ecology.* San Jose, Costa Rica: Tropical Science Center.

JANZEN, D. H.
  1967   Synchronization of sexual reproduction of trees within the dry
         season in Central America. *Evolution* 21:620–637.
  1970   Herbivores and the number of tree species in tropical forests.
         American Naturalist 104:501–528.
  1971a Escape of juvenile *Dioclea megacarpa* (Leguminosae) vines from
         predators in a deciduous tropical forest. *American Naturalist*
         105:97–112.
  1971b Seed predation by animals. *Annual Review of Ecology and System-
         atics* 2:465–492.
JOLLY, A.
  1972   *The evolution of primate behavior.* New York: Macmillan.
KENOYER, L. A.
  1929   General and successional ecology of the lower tropical rain-
         forest at Barro Colorado Island, Panama. *Ecology* 10:201–222.
LITTLE, E. L., JR., F. H. WADSWORTH
  1964   *Common trees of Puerto Rico and the Virgin Islands.* Washington,
         D.C.: U.S. Department of Agriculture.
MC CLURE, H. E.
  1964   Some observations of primates in climax diptocarp forest near
         Kuala Lumpur, Malaya. *Primates* 5:39–58.
NEVILLE, M. K.
  1972   The population structure of red howler monkeys (*Alouatta seni-
         culus*) in Trinidad and Venezuela. *Folia Primatologica* 17:56–86.
PEARSON, H. A.
  1965   Rumen organisms in white-tailed deer from south Texas. *Journal
         of Wildlife Management* 29:493–496.
POPE, B. L.
  1966   The population characteristics of howler monkeys (*Alouatta ca-
         raya*) in Northern Argentina. *American Journal of Physical An-
         thropology* 24:361–370.
RACENIS, J.
  1952   Some observations on the red howling monkey (*Alouatta seni-
         culus*) in Venezuela. *Journal of Mammalogy* 33:114–115.
RICHARD, A.
  1970   A comparative study of the activity patterns and behavior of
         Alouatta villosa and *Ateles geoffroyi*. *Folia Primatologica* 12:
         241–263.
SHIRLEY, E. K., K. SCHMIDT-NIELSEN
  1967   Oxalate metabolism in the pack rat, sand rat, hamster, and white
         rat. *Journal of Nutrition* 91:496–502.
VAN LAWICK-GOODALL, J.
  1968   The behaviour of free-living chimpanzees in the Gombe Stream
         Reserve. *Animal Behaviour Monographs* 1(3):161–311.
WHITTAKER, R. H., P. P. FEENY
  1971   Allelochemics: chemical interactions between species. *Science*
         171:757–770.

Social and Ecological Contrasts Between Four Taxa of Neotropical Primates

LEWIS L. KLEIN and DOROTHY J. KLEIN

From October, 1967, through November, 1968, observations were made of four neotropical primates (*Ateles belzebuth, Alouatta seniculus, Cebus apella,* and *Saimiri sciureus*) sympatric in the floodplain forest of the Colombian national park, La Macarena. The park is situated approximately 3° North latitude between 73 and 74° West longitude, and comprises about 11,000 square kilometers (4,250 square miles). It consists of three very general types of terrain: a small mountain range approximately parallel to the eastern cordillera of the Andes, foothills, and floodplains. Two-thirds of the park's area consists of floodplains, primarily of three rivers, the Guejar, Ariari, and Guayabero, and several of their smaller tributaries. These rivers ultimately drain into the Orinoco. The study site on the north bank of the Guayabero and most of the areas surveyed were located on or near floodplains, terrain which was inundated either yearly or at least once every several years. Forests found at the study site were not, however, floristically uniform, despite their extensive continuity, taxonomic heterogeneity, freedom from slash-and-burn agricultural practices, and annual inundation. At the approximately three-square-mile study site, a sector of a much larger continuous forest, eight different types of vegetational community were identified, using gross criteria of presence and abundance of several easily identifiable trees or readily apparent differences in forest structure.

CENSUS METHODS

Ateles belzebuth was the primary subject of these observations. Experience during the survey period consistently revealed that the number of

animals encountered at any one location, even on the same day, was extremely variable. In making a census of the populations, therefore, we
adopted the following methodological criteria and standards for determining the number and composition of animals moving and in contact
with one another at any given time.

1.   Census counts were tallied only when animals were kept under observation for a minimum period of fifteen minutes.

2.   Tallies were considered complete only if no additional spider monkeys were seen or heard moving nearby for the same minimum period of
fifteen minutes and if no spider monkey vocalizations were heard from
areas within 200 yards not traceable to one of the animals under observation or already counted.

It was assumed that these counts included all those individuals poten-
tially in constant or at least frequent intermittent and audible contact
with one another. Spider monkeys so considered were also usually
simultaneously engaged in similar or complementary activities, e.g.
feeding, resting, grooming, and travelling.

We made 498 counts meeting the above criteria in an eleven-month
period between December 4, 1967, and November 22, 1968. Visual
contact with these units, hereafter referred to as subgroups, was maintained by one or both of the observers for sixty-six minutes on the average. Contact with any single subgroup was considered terminated if all
members of the subgroup were lost to sight or if a new subgroup formed
either by merger or division and persisted for a minimum of fifteen
minutes.

SUBGROUP SIZES

The median subgroup encountered over the eleven-month period was
composed of 3.5 independently locomoting spider monkeys. Infants
under one year were not considered independent. Subgroups of two
comprised 21 percent of the total number of subgroups; this was the
modal size subgroup. Subgroups of four individuals represented 16 percent of the total, and isolated animals, 15 percent of the total. Subgroups
of eight or more comprised 15 percent of the subgroups. (See Table 1.)

SUBGROUP SPACING

Distances as great as one-half mile between different subgroups did not
appear to be unusual. Estimates of this kind were made possible by the

Table 1. Percentage of subgroups consisting of one to eight or more independently locomoting *A. belzebuth*

Subgroup size	Frequencies	Percent of total subgroups
1	75	15
2	105	21
3	72	14
4	78	16
5	36	7
6	36	7
7	20	4
8–22	76	15
Total:	498	99

observers' ability to recognize individual animals and the ability of one observer to follow an animal or animals as it left a subgroup it had been with while the other observer stayed and moved with the remaining animal or animals. Spacing between members of what were considered the same subgroup varied with the ongoing activity but was rarely more than 200 yards. In general, interanimal spacing was greater between feeding than resting spider monkeys; spacing also tended to be uniform within large and medium-sized fruiting trees. (For further detail see Klein 1972.)

Subgroups of the most commonly observed sizes as well as isolates were observed when the animals were engaged in all types of major activities. There was no indication that subgroups assembled into larger units or reassembled at specific "lodge" trees before nightfall for sleeping (cf. Carpenter 1935). On twenty-six separate occasions subgroups were followed for several hours until after dusk when all activites had terminated. The median size subgroup on these occasions was three, the mode two, and the range one to eleven, which was not too different from the subgroup statistics of all observations. On several of these occasions we were able to recontact and follow the same animals the next morning until they made renewed contact with other conspecifics. It was quite clear, then, that at least occasionally, and probably more often, they had been sleeping at distances at least as great as one-quarter to one-half mile from members of the same social group.

ISOLATES

Seventy-five instances of isolated animals were recorded, constituting 15 percent of the total number of subgroups observed. Observer contact was maintained on the average for fifty-five minutes before the animal either encountered others (22 percent of cases) or was lost to sight (78 percent of cases). Adult females without infants constituted 66.7 percent of the total number of isolates; females with infants, 10.7 percent of cases; adult males, 22.7 percent of cases. No juvenile or infant was ever observed isolated for longer than a few minutes. The maximum periods that animals were actually observed continuously and known to remain isolated were as follows: adult female, eight and a half daylight hours and then overnight; adult female with infant, six hours; adult male, one and a half hours. It was concluded that temporary isolation of most adult spider monkeys for periods as long as one to three days was a regular occurrence at the study site. (See Table 2.)

Table 2.   Frequency and biological status of isolated *A. belzebuth* at study site

	Number of observed isolated *A. belzebuth* of O group	Number of observed isolated *A. belzebuth* of O, S, and H groups combined	Percent composition of O group isolates*	Percent composition of isolates* of O, S, and H groups combined
Isolated male	13	17	20	23
Isolated independent female	45	50	69	67
Isolated female with infant	7	8	11	11
Isolated juvenile	0	0	0	0
Total frequency:	65	75		

*   Isolated animals comprised 15 percent of all scored subgroups.

SUBGROUP COMPOSITION

The composition of all subgroups was variable. Subgroups composed entirely of females, entirely of males, and bisexual subgroups containing one to five adult males were observed on occasion.

Subgroups of females without males comprised approximately 45 percent of observed subgroups. These maleless subgroups ranged in size from two to eleven females. They were observed for periods ranging from fifteen minutes to almost twelve hours. In the latter case, the same group was recontacted and followed most of the next day, during which time they still had not made contact with a male. There was no indication that subgroups without males were any more or less stable than subgroups with males.

Subgroups composed entirely of adult males comprised approximately 4 percent of all observed subgroups. They ranged in size from two to four animals. These all-male subgroups were observed to remain isolated from other conspecifics for periods ranging from fifteen minutes to three and a half hours. Because males were more difficult to follow than females, subgroup stability was assumed to be approximately similar to that of exclusively female subgroups.

The remaining subgroups censused were composed of adults of both sexes. The number of males present ranged from one to five, and some subgroups were observed in which males outnumbered females. (See Tables 3, 4, 5.)

Table 3. Composition of subgroups of four or more independently locomoting *A. belzebuth*

	Frequency		Range of subgroup sizes
Bisexual subgroups	152 (66 percent)		4–22
Bisexual with two or more adult males		76 (33 percent)	4–22
Bisexual with one adult male		76 (33 percent)	4–10
Subtotal:		152 (66 percent)	
Single-sexed groups	77 (34 percent)		4–11
Entirely male		2 (1 percent)	4
Entirely female with no dependent young		13 (6 percent)	4–5
Entirely female with dependent infants or juveniles		13 (6 percent)	4–8
Entirely female with and without dependent young		49 (21 percent)	4–11
Subtotal:		77 (34 percent)	
Total:	229 (100 percent)		

SUBGROUP ASSOCIATIONS — AN EXAMPLE

As a consequence of our ability to identify individually most spider monkeys at the study site, it became clear that the same animals were at times both isolated and members of subgroups of all sizes and compositions. Subgroup membership over a period of days was usually unstable. However, their composition was drawn from a larger, mutually exclusive

Table 4. Composition of subgroups of three independently locomoting
A. belzebuth

	Frequency	Percent
♂ ♂ ♂	3	4
♂ ♂ ♀	2	3
♂ ♂ ♀inf	2	3
♂ ♀ ♀	10	14
♂ ♀ ♀inf	1	1
♂ ♀ Juv	11	16
♀inf ♀inf ♀inf	1	1
♀inf ♀inf ♀	0	0
♀inf ♀inf Juv	7	10
♀inf ♀ ♀	1	1
♀inf Juv Juv	0	0
♀inf ♀ Juv	9	13
♀ ♀ ♀	11	16
♀ ♀ Juv	12	17
♀ Juv Juv	1	1
Juv Juv Juv	0	0
Total:	71	100

Table 5. Composition of subgroups of two independently locomoting
A. belzebuth

	Frequency	Percent
♂ ♂	11	10
♂ ♀	26	25
♂ ♀inf	1	1
♂ Juv	1	1
♀ ♀	23	22
♀ Juv	23	22
♀ ♀inf	8	8
♀inf ♀inf	3	3
♀inf Juv	8	8
Juv Juv	1	1
Total:	105	101

network of animals that usually interacted peacefully with one another.

The subgroup membership protocols of one known animal should serve to illustrate the degree of stability and unstability occurring. Mo, an adult female who gave birth to a female infant on or around January 29, 1968, was encountered on 54 percent of those days at the study site on which spider monkeys were continuously observed for fifteen minutes or longer.

Mo was observed as an isolate on two occasions, September 17 and September 20, 1968. On September 17 she was initially encountered in a tree with an adult male at 9:00 A.M. He left her at 9:20 and from that time until 2:20 P.M., when she and her infant were lost to sight, she made no contact with other conspecifics. She was isolated for five hours. Mo was relocated again on September 20, still accompanied only by her infant. Contact was maintained with her at that time for two hours. The following day she was seen in a subgroup of ten to twelve animals.

Besides being observed as an isolate, Mo was also seen in subgroups of most sizes. She was a member of subgroups of two to four animals in 38 percent of all our encounters with her; of subgroups of five to seven animals on 26 percent of encounters; and of subgroups of eight or more animals at the remaining 35 percent of encounters. (See Tables 6 and 7.)

Table 6. Frequency with which the adult female Mo was observed in subgroups of one to eight or more independently locomoting spider monkeys and in association with one or more of the following: males — Crestless, E–D, Two–Dot, Scar–Face; females — H–F, B–F, W–C, H–M

	Number of occasions	Number of observed associations with:							
		Males				Females			
		Crestless	E–D	Two–Dot	Scar–Face	B–F	W–C	H–F	H–M
Isolated:	2	–	–	–	–	–	–	–	–
Subgroups of:									
2	14	1	1	0	0	0	0	3	0
3	16	0	0	1	0	2	1	7	1
4	26	4	2	1	0	3	5	7	1
5	12	2	2	2	0	2	3	3	1
Subgroups of:									
2–5	68	7	5	4	0	7	9	20	3
Subgroups of:									
6	18	5	6	4	0	8	7	6	3
7	8	1	2	2	0	3	4	4	1
8 or more	52	25	32	27	0	38	35	38	16
Total:	148	38	45	37	0	56	55	68	23

Her most frequent associates, aside from her infant, who was seen with her at all times, were a specific female juvenile between two and three years of age on 68 percent of all encounters; an adult female who gave birth around April 5, 1968, on 32 percent of all encounters; and a single adult female who gave birth to probably her first infant in the first week of November, 1968, on 57 percent of all encounters. Mo was, at various times, also seen in subgroups with three different and clearly distinct adult males. She was seen in the company of all three of these

Table 7.   Percentage of subgroups containing Mo and AT LEAST one male, and/or one additional female with infant, one female with juvenile, one unattached juvenile, and one independent female

	Percentage of subgroups containing at least:				
	One male	One additional female with infant	One female with juvenile	One unattached juvenile	One independent female
Subgroups of:					
2	14	21	0	42	21
3	6	44	19	69	44
4	23	31	35	62	62
5	42	33	50	92	58
2–5	21	32	18	68	57
6	56	33	67	72	72
7	75	62	50	100	88
8+	94	73	100	98	98

males, any combination of two, or any one of these males singly. These associations were observed to last for periods as long as five hours or more. Although Mo's association patterns were extensive, there were certain well-known spider monkeys at the study site with which she was never observed, e.g. a specific adult male with extensive scarring around his mouth (Scar-Face). Not only was she never observed in pacific proximity to this monkey, she was also never observed with any of that male's identifiable female and male associates.

GROUP AFFILIATION

On the basis of such patterns of individual animal association, it was discovered that at the study site there were three mutually exclusive social units of spider monkeys whose members did not interact peacefully with one another, although spatial proximity between them occasionally occurred (see below). The members of each social unit appeared to share a common home range. The size of the home range of the social network studied most intensively was approximately one to one and a half square miles; those of the other social groups were either the same or larger. Home ranges of these mutually exclusive networks of groups partially overlapped, approximately 20 to 30 percent. The frequency with which different parts of the home range were utilized appeared to be a function of the preference of specific animals and of such factors as tree density, canopy height, vegetative associations, amount of time elapsed since the last intergroup agonistic interaction, and seasonal changes in the availability of ripe fruit.

Relations between individuals of the different social networks were usually agonistic, conspicuously so in the case of adult males. For example, although E-D, one of the males we observed most often, frequently associated in both small and large subgroups with other males more often than with any particular females, he was never observed moving in a subgroup either with the male Scar-Face or with any of Scar-Face's identifiable male or female associates. On several occasions E-D and Scar-Face or E-D and some of Scar-Face's associates were observed within 100 yards of one another. Proximity of this degree was usually associated with aggressive displays and vocalizations, chasing, or active avoidance. On one such occasion E-D and Scar-Face were observed within 100 to 200 yards of one another, whooping and growling in each other's direction. Throughout this observed interaction E-D was either in physical contact with or within twenty feet of one of his two frequent adult male associates and a male juvenile who also growled, whooped, and charged in Scar-Face's direction. After about an hour of displays, these three males moved away, followed by several female associates who had remained inconspicuously nearby during the confrontation. On another occasion, E-D, who had been traveling in a subgroup with four adult females and one juvenile female, was observed marking branches with saliva and sternal gland secretions and charging toward two male associates of Scar-Face after having moved to within seventy-five feet of them. Although Scar-Face was not with them at that time, he was observed in the company of these two males about thirty minutes subsequent to the agonistic interaction with E-D.

ATELES FEEDING BEHAVIOR

Methods of Study

Data on *A. belzebuth* diet were obtained by observations of feeding and checks of fecal material. Relative percentage importance of specific food items was determined from data on the durations of all individual animal feeding bouts — animal feeding minutes. Each feeding bout was considered to have terminated when the individual spider monkey (1) had clearly ceased eating for a period of three minutes or more; (2) was observed engaging in an activity incompatible with feeding, e.g. resting;

(3) moved into another tree; or (4) began eating a different substance. Termination times could be most accurately recorded when animals moved out of the tree they had been feeding in; fortunately, this was the way most feeding actually ended. Adult *A. belzebuth* were observed only three times over the year eating more than one type of substance successively within the same tree, e.g. leaves and fruit. From our experience with captive *A. belzebuth*, we were able to ascertain that ingested solids, i.e. seeds and rinds, pass through the intestinal tract in solid feces from four to twelve hours after consumption. This allowed us roughly to gauge the representativeness of the dietary data obtained by observations of feeding animals. The correspondence was usually good. (For further detail see Klein 1972.)

Results

The feeding duration data revealed that over the year ripe fruit comprised the overwhelming part of *Ateles'* diet. About 83 percent of all feeding was on ripe fruit and included more than fifty different taxa. The remaining feeding time was spent on tree leaves and buds (5 percent), epiphytic leaves and stems (2 percent), and dead or decaying wood (10 percent). Flowers were positively observed to have been eaten on only two occasions, in both cases by a juvenile. Nonripe fruit constituted less than 1 percent of the diet. No clearcut instances of *Ateles* eating either invertebrates, mammals, birds, reptiles, or amphibians, or the eggs of insects, amphibians, or birds were observed, although some termites, fig insects, or other invertebrates may have been eaten inadvertently. All published reports of *Ateles* eating vertebrates or invertebrates (e.g. Richard 1970; Carpenter 1935; Wagner 1956) were carefully scrutinized, and none appear to be based upon actual observations, in contrast to inferences. (For detail see Klein 1972.) (See Table 8.)

Table 8. Relative amounts of time spent by *A. belzebuth* between February 1, 1968, and November 22, 1968, eating fruits, leaves and stems, flowers, and wood

Types of edible substance consumed	Percentage of total feeding time observed
Fruit	83
Tree leaves and buds	5
Epiphytic leaves and stems	2
Dead wood	10
Flowers	>.1
Insects, animals, and eggs	0

CHARACTERISTICS OF TREES FROM WHICH *A. belzebuth* ATE RIPE FRUIT

Trees from which *A. belzebuth* ate ripe fruit ranged in height from fifty to a hundred and fifty feet and in crown width from approximately twenty-five to more than two hundred feet in diameter. Fruit was borne in almost all cases at least forty feet from the ground. In many of the important fruit-bearing trees under ninety feet tall, with the exception of palms, fruit appeared to be most abundant either around the crown or on a side with relatively greater lateral exposure.

There was no single or general spatial pattern of fruit tree dispersion or of fruit concentrations within single trees and no temporal pattern of ripening to which all, or even most, of the commonest type of large trees at our study site conformed. It was convenient to distinguish, therefore, the following categories of fruiting trees at the study site.

Type I trees were widely dispersed throughout the forest and individually bore ripe fruit over a relatively brief period from a few days to a week. Type I trees were subdivided on the basis of crown diameter and/ or the degree to which the ripe fruit they bore was concentrated within them. Type Ia trees were those whose crowns were greater than sixty feet across. Most of the figs used by the primates at the study site were of this category. All their fruit ripened in a very short period and most were widely dispersed. Type Ib trees bore ripe fruit briefly, their crowns were moderately broad (between twenty-five and sixty feet across), and the distribution of fruit within the tree scattered. No important *Ateles* food tree was included in this category. Type Ic trees were those whose fruit ripened in a short period and whose crowns were narrow, under twenty-five feet across (e.g. a species of *Pseudolmedia*).

Type II trees generally grew in close proximity to others of the same kind but bore ripe fruit over slightly longer periods than did Type I, usually for one or two weeks. On the basis of crown diameter, they were subdivided into Type IIa, very broad crowned trees (e.g. *Brosimum)* and Type IIb, moderately broad crowned trees (e.g. a second species of *Pseudolmedia*). No Type IIc trees, those with narrow crowns, were an important food source for *Ateles*.

Type III trees were widely dispersed, as were Type I, but in contrast to Type I, they bore ripe fruit over a considerably longer period of time, two to four weeks. Type IIIa trees had crown diameters greater than sixty feet (e.g. *Simarouba*) and Type IIIb trees had crown diameters of about twenty-five to sixty feet (e.g. *Virola* sp., *Heisteria* sp., *Protium* sp., and *Rheedia* sp.).

Type IV trees occurred, as did Type II, in close proximity to others of the same taxon, but they bore ripe fruit for longer periods, from two to four weeks. Type IVa trees with crown diameter greater than sixty feet were *Chrysophyllum* sp. and *Callophylum* sp. Type IVb trees had crown diameters less than sixty feet but more than twenty-five feet (e.g. *Hyeronima* and *Pouteria*).

Type V trees were widely dispersed, as were Types I and III. However, Type V trees bore at least some ripe fruit over very long periods of time, from one to three or four months. They all had small crown diameters, under twenty-five feet, and their fruits were circumscribed within even narrower boundaries. Palms of the genera *Euterpe* and *Iriartea* fell into this category and constituted an important food source of *A. belzebuth.*

MATURE AND IMMATURE FRUIT   Almost all the fruits *A. belzebuth* were observed to eat appeared either from color and/or taste to be fully mature. The ratio of observed animal feeding time devoted to ripe versus unripe fruit was a hundred to one. Green fruit was eaten in significant amounts only during periods in which ripe fruit was scarce or nonexistent. Thus, utilization of specific taxa of trees for food was usually limited to those periods in which some specimens bore ripe fruit.

FRUIT SIZE AND FEEDING COMPETITORS   Ripe fruits observed to have been eaten frequently by *A. belzebuth* ranged in size from those less than an eighth of an inch in diameter to some more than two inches, including certain *Inga* sp. whose pods frequently exceeded twelve inches in length, although in this case only the seeds and some of the pod flesh were consumed. This wide range in fruit sizes meant that *A. belzebuth* shared and competed with other arboreal-feeding vertebrates of disparate sizes, including birds as small as *Forpus* parrots (five to six inches long) and mammals as large as coatimundis (two feet from head to base of tail). Those animals observed to have most frequently eaten fruits also eaten by *A. belzebuth* included *Alouatta seniculus,* observed to have utilized thirteen of the taxa used by *Ateles; Cebus apella,* twelve taxa; *Ramphastos tucanus* (white-throated toucan), *Pipile cumanensis* (white-headed piping guan), and *Saimiri sciureus,* six taxa.

FRUIT STRUCTURE   Almost all the ripe fruits observed to have been eaten frequently by *A. belzebuth,* with the exception of *Ficus* sp., contained a single seed or seeds clearly distinguishable from and harder than the surrounding flesh, pulp, juice, or aril. Additionally, about 50 percent of the fruits had a leathery or hard outer covering (pericarp). Adults swallowed most of the seeds whole, and intact and recognizable seeds comprised the major volume of their feces in most cases.

DAILY VARIETY   Individual *A. belzebuth* were usually observed to have eaten two or more varieties of ripe fruit within any one day. On only one of the sixty-seven days on which we were able to observe spider monkeys for four or more hours, were they observed to have eaten just one variety of mature fruit. On the remaining sixty-six days of four or more hours of observations, the number of different taxa of mature fruit eaten ranged from two to nine, with a median of 3.3 varieties per day. Over the entire year, an average daily rate of one taxon of ripe fruit per ninety-five minutes of daily observation time was recorded, but the variety of ripe fruits available and eaten varied from period to period. The diet of *A. belzebuth* at its most monotonous level consisted of one new variety of ripe fruit per 195 minutes of daily observation time; their diet at its most diverse level consisted of one new variety of ripe fruit approximately every hour. (See Table 9.)

Table 9.   Average number of different taxa of fruit eaten daily during successive periods of the year

Inclusive dates	Number of different fruits eaten daily	Minutes of observation	Rate at which different fruits are eaten daily in minutes of observation time
February 1–14	46	3,252	1 fruit per 71 minutes
February 15–29	45	4,252	1 94
March 1–12	35	3,679	1 105
April 1–13	45	3,822	1 85
April 18–30	27	2,410	1 89
May 1–14	34	2,480	1 73
May 16–27	24	1,267	1 53
June 18–24	5	245	1 50
September 5–13	13	1,818	1 140
September 16–29	24	2,329	1 97
October 2–14	12	2,314	1 193
October 15–22	14	2,175	1 155
November 11–22	22	2,360	1 107

CORRESPONDENCE BETWEEN DIETARY CHANGES, SUBGROUP SIZE, AND SUBGROUP STABILITY

Median and modal subgroup size, subgroup stability, and the frequency of isolates varied over the year. If just those months in which observation conditions were at least moderately good are considered (i.e. ignoring the period of extensive forest flooding), intermonth variations in median subgroup size ranged from 2.2 to 5.6 animals. Subgroups of eight or more spider monkeys accounted for over 20 percent of the subgroups counted during the months of May and October and represented less than 10 percent of all subgroups encountered during the months of December, 1967, and January, September, and November, 1968. Isolated but individually recognizable spider monkeys were encountered every month of the year, but they made up more than 10 percent of the total number of subgroups observed in December, 1967, and January, April, September, October, and November, 1968. The frequency with which isolated independent spider monkeys were encountered does not appear to be a simple negative reflection of the frequency with which large subgroups are formed, because in October, 1968, the relative frequencies of encounters both with isolated animals and with large subgroups of eight or more animals were considerably higher than usual. (See Table 10.)

Table 10.   Intermonth variations in subgroup size of all *A. belzebuth* observed at study site

Months	Median	Mode	Range	Number of encounters	Percent of encounters with isolated individuals	Percent of encounters with subgroups of eight or more
January	2.9	3	1–17	64	17	2
February	4.0	2	1–18	103	5	16
March	4.3	4	1–10	48	4	12
April	3.7	2	1–11	82	12	15
May	5.6	3	1–20	43	7	40
June–August	2.7	1	1–6	19	32	0
September	2.2	2	1–11	47	28	6
October	5.2	1	1–22	44	21	43
November	2.2	2	1–11	36	25	3
December	1.5	1	1–4	12	50	0
Total over year:	3.5	2	1–22	498	15	15

Some of these grouping tendencies appeared to correspond with the changing conditions of abundance, dispersion, and variety of ripe fruit available. The general picture of correspondence was the following. At those times of year (September, December, and January) when small, widely dispersed trees bearing ripe fruit for lengthy periods of time (Type V trees — palms) were the most important and almost sole source of ripe fruit for spider monkeys (in September palm fruits accounted for 53 percent of observed feeding time), *Ateles* social organization reflected maximal group fission and subgroup stability. Isolated animals were observed frequently during September (28 percent of all subgroup encounters) and appeared to remain isolated for periods ranging from several hours to several days, and almost all subgroups were composed of four or fewer animals (80 percent of those observed for more than fifteen minutes). The median subgroup size was 2.2, the mode 2. Subgroups appeared to be relatively stable; the mean duration of observation time per subgroup was ninety minutes during September, when *Ateles* were eating mainly palm fruit. The situation was probably the same for the month of December, 1969, but fewer data were collected.

In contrast, in October, when large trees bearing ripe fruit for short to moderately lengthy periods (Type IIa trees) constituted the most important source of food for spider monkeys (over 60 percent of their diet was composed of a single taxon of this type, *Brosimum*), large, relatively stable subgroups were more frequent. Median subgroup size was almost five animals; subgroups smaller than five accounted for less than 50 percent of all observations, and groups of eight or more animals comprised more than 40 percent of our encounters. Mean observation time per subgroup was ninety-five minutes.

Correspondence between fruiting patterns and subgroup sizes and dispersion was considerably more complicated when a greater variety of trees with differing patterns of dispersion and ripening characteristics were bearing mature fruit in quantity. For example, in February a wider than average variety of fruits was available and frequently used by spider monkeys. These included trees of Types Ia, Ic, IIb, IIIb, and IVb. The size and composition of subgroups during this period reflected the annual statistics, although subgroups appeared to be less stable than usual. Median subgroup size during February was 4.0, subgroups of eight or more individuals accounted for 16 percent of subgroups censused, while the number of isolates was infrequent, 5 percent. Mean duration of observation time per subgroup was 70.1 minutes, relatively unstable in contrast to September and October.

Some additional kinds of observations and arguments reinforce the view that size and stability of spider monkey subgroups were affected by the types and amounts of ripe fruit available at any one time. First, although dominance interactions and overt aggression were observed relatively infrequently between spider monkeys of the same social group (thirteen supplantations and sixty more intense episodes of intragroup agonistic interactions observed over 627 hours of observation), a large

percentage of those observed occurred when at least one of the participants was feeding (40 percent of the supplantations and 23 percent of the
agonistic interactions). All but two of these episodes occurred when
animals were feeding on trees with crowns smaller than sixty feet on
substances restricted to an area less than twenty-five feet in diameter
(Types Ic and V). Second, the number of spider monkeys that would
simultaneously feed in any single fruiting tree was relatively limited, e.g.
compared with *Saimiri* at the study site. The number of simultaneously
feeding spider monkeys observed within the same tree, in fact, was also
frequently smaller than the number of individuals included in the same
subgroup. Ten *Ateles* was the maximum number of animals ever observed feeding in the same tree at the same time, and numbers greater
than eight were observed in exceptionally large trees on only a few occasions, and then for only a few minutes. These maximum figures were
smaller than the maximum number observed resting in similarly sized
trees and even the very same trees when they were not bearing fruit. For
example, fifteen independently locomoting animals were observed resting
within a single *Brosimum* tree for thirty minutes. Trees preferred as day-
time resting sites were large trees not bearing ripe fruit, such as *Brosimum, Chrysophyllum,* and *Ficus* (Types IIa, IVa, and Ia).

The following were probably also related: (1) adult spider monkeys
that were feeding generally appeared to be evenly spread out within
fruiting trees, and frequently a change of location by one animal was
soon followed by location changes re-establishing a uniform spread; (2)
spider monkeys were frequently observed waiting for periods of at least
several minutes on the periphery of a fruiting tree, entering only after
some other individuals had exited; and (3) all spider monkeys appeared
reluctant to rest in the same tree they had just been feeding in, although
in some cases the same trees when not bearing ripe fruit were observed
to be preferred resting sites.

The features reviewed so far concerning the characteristics of important food sources (i.e. tree dispersion, seasonal fruiting, and fruit concentrations), seasonal correspondences between these characteristics and
subgroup sizes and stability, and feeding space and agonistic interactions
combine in a way that appears to make palm fruit a central factor in
understanding the social organization of spider monkeys. Palm fruits appeared to have been eaten by spider monkeys most frequently when
other fruits were scarce and during those periods when very small subgroups were most frequent. At the study site they represented a relatively
unique source of food for several reasons. (1) Many palm trees of certain
species bore ripe fruit over exceptionally long periods, perhaps as great

as three to four months, although (2) frequently, only a very small proportion of the fruit was ripe on any given day. Thus, from the standpoint of a spider monkey, palms may constitute a very reliable, if sparse, source of food. (3) The fruits of each palm tree all grow within a rather compact cluster, which makes it difficult for more than one animal to feed simultaneously without making actual physical contact with one another. (4) At the study site, the trees of the two most important species of palms in the diet of *A. belzebuth*, i.e. *Iriartea ventricosa* and *Euterpe* sp., were found over large sectors of appropriate terrain either uniformly or randomly dispersed, rather than clumped. As a consequence of these characteristics of dispersion, and in combination with the other characteristics of palms noted above, feeding from a large number of palms by any single individual spider monkey would have probably increased the possibility of becoming a participant in agonistic interactions and would have required a considerable amount of travel for minimal amounts of mature fruit at a time when nonpalm sources of food were usually in short supply. Maximal dispersion and minimal association with conspecifics would appear to be an adaptive response of animals with as specialized a feeding base as spider monkeys appear to have.

COMPARISONS WITH SYMPATRIC TAXA

It was quite clear that the degree of daily variability and seasonal change in *Ateles* subgrouping was not characteristic of the other primate taxa sympatric with *Ateles* at the study site, which shared many of the same fruit sources and inhabited the same trees. (See Table 11.)

Table 11. Estimated study site population densities, group size, and number of groups present

	Estimated population density per square mile	Range of group size[1]	Number of groups utilizing 3-square-mile study site
S. sciureus	50–80	25–35	3–6
C. apella	15–25	6–12	4–6
A. seniculus	30–75	3–6	6–15
A. belzebuth[2]	30–40	17–22	3

[1] Independently locomoting animals
[2] See text for methods of determining total group size from subgroup data

Alouatta seniculus

Alouatta seniculus were observed at the study site for approximately seventy hours. They were observed on fifty-two occasions for minimal periods of fifteen minutes, and on twenty-one of these occasions for an hour or more. Groups were considerably smaller than those reported for Barro Colorado Island (see, e.g. Carpenter 1965; Chivers 1969) and ranged in size from three to six animals. All groups encountered contained at least one adult male. Most groups consisted of one adult male and two to three females with associated immatures. The few groups observed with two mature males were uncommon, and the second male in all observed cases appeared to be either very old or subadult. In contrast to *Ateles, A. seniculus* females were not observed without males nearby, although instances of one or two isolated adult male howlers were seen.

Relative to *Ateles* subgroups, the composition and membership of these bisexual groups of howlers was both stable and cohesive. Distances between members of each bisexual group rarely exceeded fifty to a hundred feet, the crown diameter of one or two large trees. Occasionally several howler groups were contacted on successive days in the same general area, but at certain seasons groups of howlers concentrated at distances at least as far as one-quarter mile from where similar concentrations were observed at other times (see Klein and Klein 1973). Group size and composition did not appear to be affected by seasonal shifts of habitat use.

Our unsystematic observations of howler feeding habits were in general quite consistent with what has been described for *A. palliata* on Barro Colorado Island (Hladik and Hladik 1969). Major proportions of their diet consisted of mature and immature leaves and mature and immature fig fruit. Also included were quantities of ripe fruit, decaying wood, and leaf stems. They were never observed to eat palm fruit at our study site, nor are palms listed in the specific food catalogues for *A. palliata* of Carpenter (1934) or Hladik and Hladik (1969) (cf. Neville 1972).

In contrast to palm fruit, the fruit of fig trees (*Ficus* spp.) appears to play a more important role in the diet of *Alouatta* than of *Ateles*. Several unidentified species of *Ficus* were observed to have been eaten more frequently than by *Ateles*. In addition, a greater number of *Ficus* species were observed to have been eaten more frequently by *Alouatta* than by *Ateles*. These disparities in favor of *Alouatta* were noted despite the lesser amounts of time spent in visual contact with them than with *Ateles*.

Moreover, on three separate occasions spider monkeys were observed to have ignored the fruit of large fig trees through which they passed, although howlers were feeding in them just before or after. In contrast, ripe fruit of large trees other than *Ficus* were rarely ignored by spider monkeys, unless they had been feeding in the same type of tree immediately beforehand.

A similar feeding difference appears to be characteristic of the populations of the two genera on Barro Colorado Island. Altmann (1959), for example, notes: "During the first two weeks of the present study, about 95 per cent of the diet of the howlers of the laboratory group consisted of figs. After that, the diet shifted to about 50 per cent figs." Hladik and Hladik (1969: 63) note:

The different species of *Ficus*, particularly *F. insipida*, played a primary role in the diet of howlers (more than 50% of the biomass of all quantitative samples; immature fig fruit composed 100% of the contents of one specimen's stomach). The genus *Ficus* furnished mature fruit several times in a year at complementary periods. [Translated from the French.]

Of additional interest are the radical differences between the genus *Ficus* and the palms with respect to (1) tree size, (2) distribution of fruit, and (3) length of fruiting period. In general, those figs that by growth pattern are or become trees are usually among the largest trees in the evergreen forest, bear large quantities of fruit throughout their crowns or at least on many of their branches, and bear ripe fruit over an extremely brief period, generally on the order of three to four days, falling into our category Type Ia (Hladik and Hladik 1969; Condit 1969; L. Klein, personal observation).

Although no data are available on the subject, it is thought that differences between *Ateles* and *Alouatta* with respect to the differential utilization of figs and palms may have a physiological basis. Several types of figs are known to be very high in nitrogen (Hladik and Hladik 1969), latex, and a proteolytic enzyme, ficin (Condit 1969). On the other hand, the flesh of many palms contains exceptionally large amounts of vegetable oils (Corner 1966).

The comparative dietary difference between *Ateles* and *Alouatta* with respect to figs and palm fruits illustrates one of the dangers of grossly labeling primates in terms of dietary categories such as frugivorous, insectivorous, etc. Furthermore, it also illustrates one of the problems with using a more refined approach based on percentage differences as long as categories as gross as "fruits," "leaves," "insects," etc., continue to be used. Such categories may be overly simple and even misleading when more specific dietary substances are the actual differentiating factors. Although howler monkeys are definitely more herbivorous (folivorous) and less frugivorous than spider monkeys, they also eat more immature fruit and fig fruit than do spider monkeys.

It is suggested that the howlers' extensive use of such food as mature leaves, Type Ia figs, and green fruit mitigated the effects of seasonal change and seasonal scarcity on feeding competition and social cohesion.

Saimiri sciureus

Saimiri sciureus were observed at the study site on sixty-eight occasions for fifteen or more continuous minutes, for a total of approximately sixty hours. On eighteen of these occasions they were observed for an hour or more. The longest continuous observation of a group of *Saimiri* lasted about two hours. Those group counts which were made under the best conditions of visibility noted between twenty-five and thirty-five independently locomoting animals and included at least several adult males, with the exception of two clear-cut encounters with isolated adult male *Saimiri*.

These bisexual groups of *Saimiri* were considerably more cohesive than comparably sized *A. belzebuth* groups. Except for the temporarily isolated males, the distances between individual squirrel monkeys of the same group rarely, if ever, exceeded fifty to a hundred yards.

The formation of subgroups as defined in this paper was not observed to be characteristic of squirrel monkeys. The groups did not seem to be restricted to any particular part or sector of the study area at any particular time of the year.

The major portion of the diet of *Saimiri* as measured by feeding time appeared to consist of flushed, agile, and cryptically camouflaged insects. (For greater detail see Klein 1972; Thorington 1967.) Vegetable products such as leaves and ripe fruits did not appear to be exceptionally attractive to squirrel monkeys even if they were available in abundance, and *Saimiri* appeared to satiate themselves rapidly on these substances. Insects were frequently sought even when ripe fruit was immediately at hand.

The fruits observed to have been used most frequently by squirrel monkeys were those that occurred either abundantly scattered throughout the very large trees (Type Ia) or those that were borne on trees growing in close proximity to others of the same taxon and bearing fruit at about the same time (Type II and IV trees). Squirrel monkeys, like howler monkeys, were not observed eating palm fruits. They, too, may have been unable to digest these highly dependable but concentrated sources of food.

Major dietary differences between *Saimiri* and *Ateles* may be related to their respective patterns of social spacing. *Saimiri sciureus* collect much of their food by foraging, i.e. feeding as they move between and through fruiting or nonfruiting trees. Movement is usually continuous, and stationary feeding at a single location for more than ten-second intervals is rare. *Saimiri* were frequently observed investigating numerous places where insects were likely to be found and catching, killing, and ingesting insects such as katydids, grasshoppers, caterpillars, arachnids, and cicadas. Within limits, the number of mobile insects discovered and eaten by each individual squirrel monkey may be positively affected by the cumulative amount of branch and leaf disturbance, which in turn would be at least a partial function of the number of animals moving in relative proximity to one another when feeding. Cohesive social groups of small primates foraging extensively on cryptic but mobile insect prey may thus increase the foraging efficiency of most individual animals.

Spider monkeys do relatively little, if any, foraging, i.e. feeding while moving. It is difficult to imagine how foraging would be advantageous to spider monkeys, which are predominantly frugivorous, unless they were capable of supplementing their diet with insects and significant quantities of stems and leaves. This they were not seen to do, and they do not seem capable of effectively doing so even in captivity (Klein and Klein, personal observation).

Additionally, predation pressures were almost certainly higher on *S. sciureus* than on any of the other diurnal primates at the study site. The formation of cohesive groups of these rather active and, for their size, relatively far-ranging primates (home range estimated to be one-quarter to one-half square mile) may have had significant adaptive advantages in this respect as well.

Cebus appella

The data on *Cebus apella* grouping patterns were not nearly as adequate as the information on *A. belzebuth*. Nevertheless, certain features did become evident and were consistent with more complete reports of another species of the same genus (Oppenheimer 1968).

C. apella were observed at the study site for approximately fifty-five hours. They were encountered on approximately 200 occasions: sixty-three of these contacts were maintained for fifteen minutes or longer, and several periods of observation persisted for about two hours. The number of independently locomoting *C. apella* observed at any one time ranged from one to twelve; the median was approximately eight. Groups of this size always included adult animals of both sexes. Contacts with what appeared to be isolated *C. apella* occurred twice; both encounters persisted only a little longer than fifteen minutes. On one additional occasion, a group of one adult female and a juvenile were observed feeding in a tree for about one hour. Four to twelve animals comprised the remaining group counts, and six or more accounted for 75 percent of the total.

Distances between individual *C. apella* considered to be part of the same group ranged from a few feet to 150 to 200 yards. When foraging, the progression was usually considerably more spread out than *Saimiri*. More than half our encounters with *C. apella* occurred when they were in close proximity to — usually intermixed with — larger groups of foraging *Saimiri* (Klein and Klein 1973).

The diet of *C. apella* was considerably more diversified than that of *A. belzebuth*. Besides fruit, they were also observed eating flowers, insects, small vertebrates, leaf buds, and leaf stems. In comparing the diets of *Cebus capucinus, Alouatta villosa,* and *Ateles geoffroyi,* Hladik and Hladik (1969: 82) came to a similar conclusion concerning the capuchins' catholicity, calling them "the most 'opportunistic' of all the Barro Colorado Island primates." A considerable portion of capuchin feeding time appeared to be devoted to searching for insects. Hladik and Hladik (1969) estimated that by weight the overall diet of *C. capucinus* consisted of 20 percent prey animals. Time devoted to foraging for insects probably comprises a considerably greater percentage of feeding time. Prey occasionally included small vertebrates, e.g. frogs and squirrels (Klein 1972; Oppenheimer 1968). Although some overlap with *Saimiri* insect and arachnid prey occurred (see Klein and Klein 1973), an important portion appeared to be different (Thorington 1967). The brown capuchins were frequently observed investigating, prying open or apart dead pieces of bark, branches, vines, palm sheaths, and certain types of insect nests.

Many of the fruits eaten by *C. apella* were among those most important in the diet of *A. belzebuth*. Significantly, these also included two of the most important palms, *Iriartea exorrhiza* and *Euterpe* sp. Moreover, the flowers of at least one of these palms (*Euterpe*) and the leaf stems of the other (*Iriartea*) were also eaten by capuchins, to the probable detriment of the future production of fruit.

Several social aspects of feeding which were noted above in the course of explaining seasonal changes in spider monkey subgroup size and dispersion were also observed to be characteristic of capuchins. For example, rigid spacing between individual adult *C. apella* simultaneously feeding in the same tree was sometimes apparent if they remained for a long enough period. Competition over certain feeding locations at times appeared to be even more conspicuous between capuchins than between spider monkeys. For example, more than one adult capuchin feeding simultaneously from a single palm tree was never observed, whereas two adult *Ateles* were observed on several occasions feeding simultaneously in a single palm, and once two adult *Ateles* fed simultaneously alongside one another while a third occasionally reached in from an adjoining tree. Obvious supplantations and agonistic interactions in or around a palm tree were also observed to occur relatively more frequently between capuchins than between spider monkeys.

Why, then, were capuchin groups not affected in the same way or at least to the same degree as *Ateles* by periodic fluctuations in fruit availability and concentration?

We suggest that there are two major dietary factors, although one is judged to be probably more important than the other. First, many of the insects most frequently utilized by *C. apella,* appeared to encourage relatively constant movement and avoidance of repetitive daily travel paths. For example, among the locations in which *C. apella* were most frequently observed searching for and catching insects were arboreal snags of dead branches and palm sheaths caught on lianas or small trees. As a consequence of foraging through these structures, much of the detritus fell to the ground. Intermittent rather than daily foraging over the same areas probably increased the overall supply by allowing new accumulations of decaying vegetation to develop where important varieties of insects could subsequently be easily accessible to the manipulative capuchins. However, continual movement in pursuit of better and more accessible sources of insects meant that there was little feeding advantage to be gained by remaining near exclusive or restricted sources of fruit even if they represented a highly stable source of food. This appeared, it will be recalled, to be one of the major causes of wide dispersion between extremely small subgroups of *Ateles.*

Perhaps even more important in stabilizing group size and cohesion in *C. apella* relative to *A. belzebuth* was the considerably more diversified nature of the capuchins' diet. The degree of daily eclecticism precluded the possibility that any individual capuchin, in contrast to individual spider monkeys, could at any time entirely inhibit the feeding behavior of other group members, despite the fact that it could, while in possession or proximity, prevent some conspecifics from eating a specific item or from approaching a specific source. In fact, *C. apella* of the same group were frequently observed feeding simultaneously on different substances while they remained in visual contact. It was their most common practice and contrasted radically with spider monkeys, whose diet was considerably more restricted; the latter were at times wholly dependent upon just a few scattered but dependable sources of food and were rarely observed feeding on different substances in sight of one another. Spider monkeys usually either ate, waited, or departed. They rarely appeared to have some less desirable food substance close at hand.

Also related to this dietary difference may be the apparently considerably greater propensity of *C. apella* to organize significant aspects of their daily social behavior around status differences and conspicuous signaling of submission and appeasement. Their communicatory repertoire appears to include visual signals, which at least in form, duration, discreteness, complexity, and function are most similar to the Old World monkeys of the genera *Papio* and *Macaca*. The fact that many of the better-studied Old World taxa also appear to be characterized by relatively constant and frequent intragroup visual contact and feed upon a rather similarly broad spectrum of different substances, usually in sight of one another, may be of adaptive significance in this respect.

CONCLUDING IMPLICATIONS

1.   Variations in the social organization of four diurnal neotropical primates sympatric at a river-plain forest sector of approximately three square miles were described. The observations reaffirm what has become increasingly clear from work on Old World primates (e.g. Hall 1965; Struhsaker 1969; Aldrich-Blake 1968), i.e. that a wide range of different but taxonomicaly correlated social organizations can occur within any single type of forest habitat despite the fact that the sympatric primates are all essentially arboreal and share to varying extents specific dietary items.

2.   Traditional classification of primate diets into fruit, leaves, and insects obscures important differences clearly relatable to feeding competition and social behavior. There are a host of possible differences, both crosscutting and subdividing these traditional categories, some of which have been noted by others (e.g. Hladik and Hladik 1969). For our work, within the category of ripe fruit, specific differences between palm and fig fruit turned out to be an important discriminatory feature between

the feeding behavior of howler and spider monkeys. This difference, in turn, was argued to be relatable to differences in social cohesion via competitive feeding. In addition, ripening, dispersion, and crown-diameter characteristics of different fruiting trees were seen to be an important factor regulating *A. belzebuth* subgroup size, subgroup stability, feeding and resting patterns, and the frequency of agonistic interactions. Similarly, varying dietary emphases on either cryptic and mobile insects or concealed and sedentary ones may explain some of the described social differences between *Saimiri* and *Cebus*.

3.   It was found impossible, however, to relate characteristics of food supply to social organization in any abstract manner without taking into consideration differences in taxa-specific feeding choices and strategies — some of which appear to be both physiologically and anatomically based. For example, differences in the ability and propensity to obtain and ingest large quantities of mature leaves, insects hidden beneath bark and accumulation of leaf detritus, insects protected by spines or stingers, and rapidly leaping but camouflaged leaf-eating insects may depend upon characteristics of gastrointestinal anatomy and physiology, manual dexterity, rapidity of movement, and motor-visual coordination. A dietary factor that appeared to be of major importance, but one that is generally overlooked in discussion of primate socioecology, was the degree to which specific primates are able to utilize in an expeditious manner varied substances in any single day. To different extents this modified the competitive effects of fruit tree dispersion and the abundance and concentration of ripe fruit. It has been suggested that rigid spacing, appeasement gestures, and the frequency of supplantations are related to the relatively great diversity of the diet of capuchin monkeys. In contrast, the flexibility and individual "fission-fusion" social grouping patterns of spider monkeys appear to be based upon a considerably more restricted range of potential food substances available each day. The considerable importance of sparse, widely dispersed ripe palm fruit, along with extreme concentration of the ripe fruit on any one tree, was correlated with minimal group size and maximal occurrence of isolated adult spider monkeys of both sexes.

4.   Implied in some of the material reviewed, but not discussed, was that simple positive correlations between vegetation or fruit density and single primate taxon population densities cannot be supported without considerable additional information on intertaxon dietary differences and the nature and extent of feeding competition both between primate species and between primates and sympatric mammalian, avian, and perhaps invertebrate taxa.

5.   The outlined descriptive material on social grouping in *A. belzebuth* suggests that "fission-fusion" social grouping as the outcome of association preferences of individual adult animals of both sexes within definable social networks has evolved independently in at least two taxonomically distinct primate families: Cebidae and Pongidae (Nishida 1968). This suggests that the factors responsible are more likely to be ecological than phylogenetic (cf. Kummer 1971).

REFERENCES

ALDRICH-BLAKE, F. P. G.
   1968   A fertile hybrid between two *Cercopithecus* spp. in the Budongo Forest, Uganda. *Folia Primatologica* 9:15–21.

ALTMANN, S. A.
   1959   Field observations on a howling monkey society. *Journal of Mammalogy* 40:317–330.

CARPENTER, C. R.
   1934   A field study of the behavior and social relations of howling monkeys. *Comparative Psychology Monographs* 10(2).
   1935   Behavior of red spider monkeys in Panama. *Journal of Mammalogy* 16:171–180.
   1965   "The howlers of Barro Colorado Island," in *Primate behavior: field studies of monkeys and apes*. Edited by I. DeVore, 250–291. New York: Holt, Rinehart and Winston.

CHIVERS, D. J.
   1969   On the daily behaviour and spacing of howling monkey groups. *Folia Primatologica* 10:48–102.

CONDIT, I. J.
   1969   *Ficus: the exotic species*. University of California, Division of Agricultural Sciences.

CORNER, E. J. H.
   1966   *The natural history of palms*. Berkeley: University of California Press.

HALL, K. R. L.
   1965   "Ecology and behavior of baboons, patas, and vervet monkeys in Uganda," in *The baboon in medical research*. Edited by H. Vagtbord, 43–61. San Antonio: University of Texas Press.

HLADIK, A., C. M. HLADIK
   1969   Rapports tropiques entre végétation et primates dans la forêt de Barro Colorado (Panama). *La Terre et la Vie* 1:25–117.

KLEIN, L.
   1972   "The ecology and social organization of the spider monkey, *Ateles belzebuth*." Unpublished doctoral dissertation. University of California, Berkeley.

KLEIN, L., D. KLEIN
1973   Observations on two types of neotropical primate intertaxa associations. *American Journal of Physical Anthropology* 38:649–653.

KUMMER, H.
1971   *Primate societies: group techniques of ecological adaptation.* Chicago: Aldine-Atherton.

NEVILLE, M. K.
1972   The population structure of red howler monkeys (*Alouatta seniculus*) in Trinidad and Venezuela. *Folia Primatologica* 17:56–86.

NISHIDA, T.
1968   The social group of wild chimpanzees in the Mahali mountains. *Primates* 9:167–224.

OPPENHEIMER, J. R.
1968   "Behavior and ecology of the white-faced monkey, *Cebus capucinus*, on Barro Colorado Island." Unpublished doctoral dissertation, University of Illinois, Urbana.

RICHARD, A.
1970   A comparative study of the activity patterns and behavior of *Alouatta villosa* and *Ateles geoffroyi. Folia Primatologica* 12: 241–263.

STRUHSAKER, T. T.
1969   Correlates of ecology and social organization among African cercopithecines. *Folia Primatologica* 11:80–118.

THORINGTON, R. W., JR.
1967   "Feeding and activity of *Cebus* and *Saimiri* in a Colombian forest," in *Progress in primatology.* Edited by D. Starck, R. Schneider, and H. J. Kuhn, 180–184. Stuttgart: Fischer.

WAGNER, H. O.
1956   Freilandbeobachtungen an Klammeraffen. *Zeitschrift für Tierpsychologie* 13:302–313.

Some Ecological, Distributional, and Group Behavioral Features of Atelinae in Southern Peru: With Comments on Interspecific Relations

NORRIS M. DURHAM

The vast forests of eastern Peru stretch from just north of the equator to approximately 18° south latitude and encompass almost 60 percent of the country (Map 1). Within this region live many species of nonhuman primates including *Ateles*, *Lagothrix*, *Cebus*, *Aotus*, *Saimiri*, *Alouatta*, and a great variety of Callithricinae. They are distributed from lowland canopy forests to highland wet forests. In general, the lowland canopy forests extend from approximately sea level to between 600 and 800 meters up the eastern slopes of the Andes. Above this altitude, depending on latitude and other ecological determinants, rise the highland wet forests (montane forests) to as high as 2300 meters. The transition from highland to lowland forest is characterized by obvious though gradual changes in the general ecosytem composition: frequency and distribution of floral types, size and production of trees common to both areas, and frequency and number of animal species. This is due, in part, to the substantial difference in precipitation between the two regions: as high as 7250 millimeters in the highland compared to a maximum of 4950 millimeters in the lowland, and to variations in temperature. The division and fluctuating composition of forest zones, then, is for the most part based on the direct effects of rainfall and on altitude which creates the temperature gradient (Durham 1971).

The eastern slopes of the mountains form a pattern of intricately

The author wishes to express gratitude to researchers of the Institute of Andean Biology and the Field Station of the Pennsylvania State University at Nunoa, Peru. Special thanks are due Dr. C. R. Carpenter, Dr. Paul T. Baker, Dr. Charles J. Hoff, Sr. Celestino Colinonsky, Sr. Cezar Vargas, and Sr. Víctor Barreda M.

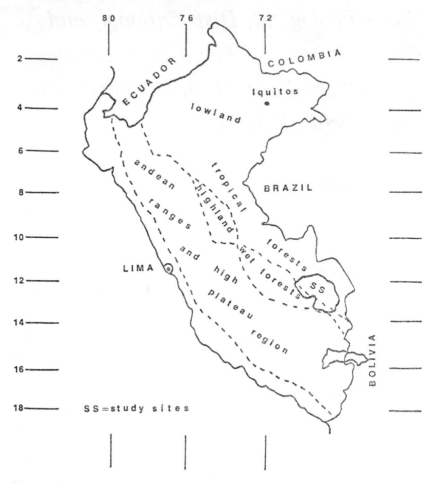

Map 1.   Peru

dissected landscape with steep gradients etched by rapid flowing streams. At higher altitudes the valleys are V-shaped and narrow, gradually widening to the lowland forests. With each sharp decrease of 300 to 400 meters the streams widen, eventually forming the characteristically large and majestic rivers of the tropical canopy forest.

The principal trees found in the Peruvian forests are members of the following families: Apocynaceae, Bombaceae, Caryocaraceae, Euphorbiaceae, Lauraceae, Leguminoseae, Mellaceae, Myristiceae, Rubiaceae, Sapotaceae, and Stercullaceae (Bazan 1969). The general composition of the tropical forests up to an altitude of approximately

1600 meters, depending upon latitude, may be broken down as follows:

1.   Hardwoods — this group is made up of mainly mahogany, cedar, arrowwood, *Inga* species, and two species of fig. There are a total of eleven species of hardwoods, but the remainder have not yet been formally classified.

2.   Softwoods — here the principal trees are a native cotton, cacao, Tinta, or native lime, two species of *Yarina*, and fourteen others known only by the common name.

3.   Palms — the twelve species of palm are the predominant form of growth, with the exception of vines, lianas, and bromeliads. They vary from the tall *Palmetto* to medium-sized spiny palms to the feather palm, a woody shrub rarely over six feet in height. Above the highland wet forests (approximately 1600 meters) the cloud forest begins and is composed of mainly the hardwoods and four species of palm including the palmetto.

Animal life is quite varied in all forest areas. Varieties of orioles, parrots, parakeets, cockatoos, cocks-of-the rock, doves, harpy eagles, black hawks, vultures, toucans, and many types of hummingbirds are ubiquitous in the canopy forest as high in altitude as 900 meters. Above this, parrots and cockatoos are conspicuously absent.

Second only to the insects and spiders in total numbers, the reptiles are represented by three species of lizards, dozens of species of turtles and tortoises, and an unknown number of snakes, some venomous. Great quantities of fish are found in the large lowland rivers including saltwater varieties of skates and rays. In the higher forests, the frequency of piscine species decreases until finally in the cloud forest only two or three are found.

The most frequent forms of mammalian life encountered are rodents, although tapirs (*Tapirus terrestris*) and collared peccaries (*Tayassu tapacu*) were often noted. Other species of mammals observed, including the nonhuman primates to be discussed separately, were jaguars (*Panthera onca*), ocelots (*Felis pardalis*), jaguarundi (*Felis yagouaroundi*), margays (*Felis wiedi*), tayras (*Eira barbara*), grisons (*Galictis* spp.), and otters (*Lutra* spp.).

It is the purpose of this paper to discuss the general ecology and behavior of five species of Cebidae (*Ateles paniscus, Lagothrix lagothrica, Aotus trivirgatus, Saimiri sciureus, Cebus albifrons*) found in the highland wet forests and/or the lowland canopy forests of southeastern Peru. In addition, comments will be made on observed group sizes, group composition, and interspecific interactions.

The data presented were gathered during a detailed survey and intensive, long-term study of nonhuman primate life with emphasis on the ecology and behavior of the black spider monkey, *Ateles paniscus*. The survey concentrated on four distinct areas differing in altitude by at least 300 meters: Río Piachaca (1424 meters) and San Gaban-Río San Juan (889 meters) in the department of Puno; Karos-Pilcopata area (576 meters) in the department of Cuzco; and Salvación-Río Madre de Dios (275 meters) in the department of the Madre de Dios. (See Table 1 for Code.) From January 21 to March 4, 1969, the investigator traveled by truck, boat, and foot through the areas recording two types of data: ecological and distributional. The ecological factors consisted of altitude, temperature, humidity, precipitation, and cloud cover; all were recorded on an hourly basis. In addition, preliminary estimates were taken of preferred food, resting, toilet, and sleeping trees at the different altitudes in order to evaluate the areas in terms of potential available support of groups. Factors such as ecological influences on diurnal and annual activity cycles, and group dynamics are reported elsewhere (Durham 1971, f.c.). Distributional data gathered included number of groups or subgroups per species, their sizes, and location (Table 1).

RÍO PIACHACA (STUDY AREA A)

This area represents the highest altitude at which nonhuman primates were observed during the entire study. It is situated just below the cloud forest at 13.7° south latitude and 70.4° west longitude. There are three main rivers in the area: Ríos Piachaca, San Gaban, and Churumayo. One of the five main roads into the canopy forest, the Mucusani-Tocoroni follows the Río San Gaban and bisects the region.

Diurnal temperature range is 14.5° to 25.1° centigrade with the cooler periods occurring during May, June, and July. Annual rainfall averages 7250 millimeters, but there is no actual dry season.

Although sparsely inhabited, the region does produce some lumber, limes, and sugar cane. The steep gradient of the Andean foothills and limited level land make it generally an inhospitable area for colonization or large-scale agriculture.

SAN GABAN-RÍO SAN JUAN (STUDY AREA B)

A few hours down the eastern slopes of the mountains lies the village

Table 1.   Group size and location of nonhuman primates in southeastern Peru

Codes Sites	A Piachaca 1424 meters	B San Gaban — Río San Juan 889 meters	C Karos — Pilcopata 576 meters	D Salvación — Madre de Dios (Manu) 275 meters
Species *Ateles* *paniscus*[1]	XV — 4 XVI — 4 XVII — 3	I — 5 II — 7 III — 6 IV — 5	V — 9 VI — 10 VII — 10 VIII — 11 IX — 11	X — 14 XI — 14 XII — 15 XIII — 17 XIV — 25 XVIII — 18 XIX — 13
Lagothrix *lagothrica*[2]	None	A — 6 B — 6 F — 7 G — 6	D — 14 H — 10 J — 11	E — 12 C — 11 K — 14 L — 14
Aotus *trivirgatus*[2]	AB — 2 AC — 1 AD — 2	AA — 18–26	AE — 20–25 AG — 21–30 AJ — 3	AF — 30–33 AH — 28–35
Saimiri *sciureus*[2]	None	None	None	SA — 8 SB — 10–19 SC — 12–23 SD — 9–11 SE — 16–17
Cebus *albifrons*[2]	CA — 6	CB — 8 CC — 10 CD — 12	CF — 10 CG — 11	CH — 9 CJ — 10

[1] Roman numerals = subgroup + group identification number for *Ateles* and run in order of first observation, thus group I at B was observed first. Following Arabic numeral indicates group size. At Study Sites A & B, units were apparently stable groups, XIII, XVIII, and XIX at D and VI and VIII at C seemed to be sub-groupings.

[2] Codes are similar to above with Arabic letter for group identification and numerals for group size or estimated size. Thus, group A of *Lagothrix* was the first observed; group AA (group A of *Aotus*) was first; group SA (group A of *Saimiri*) was first; group CA of *Cebus*; etc.

of San Gaban. The area is highland wet forest with approximately 5875 millimeters of rain per year and a limited dry season during the month of June and part of July. Five families live in the village and practice swidden agriculture on small garden plots along the river.

Here the river valley widens and the gradient of the mountains decreases. The temperature ranges from 18° to 35.5° centigrade daily with a slight decrease during the dry season. Observation areas were approximately six kilometers to the northeast towards the Río San

Juan at 13.5° south latitude and 70.3° west longitude.

This was the highest altitude at which brown woolly monkeys, *Lagothrix lagothrica,* and the night monkeys, *Aotus trivirgatus,* were observed. This also was the uppermost limit for the broad stretches of bamboo thickets and true gallery forest characteristic of the lowland canopy forest.

KAROS-PILCOPATA (STUDY AREA C)

Bordering on the lowland forest, this study area is representative of a transitional zone between the two forest types. Although annual rainfall is high, 5250 millimeters average, the foothills are low, rolling ridges with rather slight gradients.

The observation points are located approximately twelve kilometers southheast of the small village of Karos and fourteen kilometers northeast of the larger town of Pilcopata between the Río Pinni and the Río Pini Pini. This is approximately 13.1° south latitude and 71.4° west longitude. Diurnal temperature range is 20° to 37.5° centigrade. The dry season averages two and one-half months from mid-June until late August.

SALVACIÓN-MADRE DE DIOS (STUDY AREA D)

The final observation areas are located in the lowland canopy forest of the department of the Madre de Dios. The region has since become a protected national preserve in tribute to its untouched and natural condition. The entire area is bordered by rivers on three sides: the Carbón, Alto Madre de Dios, and Manu. At the far side of the park a broad swamp completes the natural boundary.

Average annual rainfall of 4950 millimeters is perceptibly lowei than in the other study areas and correspondingly, diurnal temperature ranges are higher at 21° to 42° centigrade. Consequently, there is a longer, more definite dry season lasting from the end of May to the beginning of September.

On a plateau averaging 250 to 275 meters in altitude, the rivers of the Madre de Dios tend to drain to the southeast and east, and therefore are actually separate from the Amazon drainage basin to the north.

The observation areas are located at 12.6° south latitude and 71.1° west longitude, three kilometers east of the military post at Salvación and twenty-one kilometers into the National Park at the end of the Río Carbón. The entire region is heavily canopied with many small streams which become wide rivers only during the wet season.

The forest areas of the three departments surveyed are the least populated of this tropical zone due to limited dependable communication routes, no major source of commercial outlet, and rivers navigable only by powered canoes or balsa rafts. However, due to this inaccessibility, southern forest areas offer vast untouched regions of high research and conservation potential.

THE BLACK SPIDER MONKEY (*ATELES PANISCUS*)

The *Ateles paniscus* groups represent one of three species of Ceboidea observed at all four survey areas. While no animals were noted above 1450 meters, it is probable that farther north towards the equator, animals will be found at higher altitudes. However, it is doubtful that *Ateles paniscus* lives higher than 2300 to 2500 meters at the equator since it has been suggested that this is the latitudinal limit for most preferred food trees of this species (Vargas, personal communication).

During the study nineteen groups were observed which varied in size from three to twenty-five members. This does not include two adult all-male subgroups of three and five respectively which were observed in the lowland canopy forest at 275 meters altitude, and three apparent isolated animals.

Mean group sizes decreased sharply from 18.5 at 275 meters to 11 at 576 meters, and then less sharply to 7 at 889 meters and 4.5 at 1424 meters. The figure of 4.5 per group is probably near the minimum number which may be found at higher altitudes closer to the equator (Durham 1971).

All highland forest groups had one male while lowland groups ranged from zero to three males. At the two highest study sites, no group had more than one male. A breakdown of the approximate mean number of animals per age category per group is as follows: at 275 meters, 3.75 males, 6.1 females, 5.6 subadults and juveniles, and 1.1 infants; at 576 meters, 2.2 males, 4.2 females, 3.2 subadults and juveniles, and 0.6 infants; at 889 meters, 1.0 males, 1.7 females, 2.5 subadults and juveniles, and 0.5 infants; and finally, at 1424 meters, there was a mean of 1.0 males, 1.3 females, 1.3 subadults and juveniles, and no infants were observed. Thus, not only does group size diminish with altitude, but the structure of groups tends to shift. Adult females are the most noticeable reduction dropping from an average of 6.1 per group at the lowest study site to 1.7 at 889 meters. A most interesting feature is that at 889 meters there is a tendency for groups to have more animals of the subadult/juvenile category than adult females.

As reported previously, five of the principal food trees tend to decrease in total number per square kilometer as the altitude increases. This has the effect of decreasing the amount of biomass supportable, altering composition, and probably causing the increase in size of territory at higher ranges.

From the steep highland wet forests of the Andean slopes overlooking V-shaped valleys to the lowland canopy forests of the Madre de Dios, *Ateles paniscus* is found in moderate abundance. Depending on seasonal and other factors, population density ranges from six per square kilometer in the higher altitudes to twenty-four per square kilometer in the lower areas. Total numbers and densities may be lower toward the Amazon River where the concentration of animal collecting and hunting for pelt or food is at its highest. This is due to the great potential of the larger rivers of the Amazon Basin as communication routes and the advantages of immediate sale and/or export in the port city of Iquitos (Durham f.c.).

Ateles paniscus prefer three combinations of food conditions: they live and feed in areas within pockets of (1) *Inga*, *Lupuna*, and Palmetto, or (2) *Ficus* and *Lupuna*, or (3) palmetto, *Tinta*, and *Ficus* trees. They are rarely found within three to four kilometers of any human settlement of two families or more and seem to occur in a clumped and uneven distribution.

Ateles paniscus groupings seem to be characterized by small, apparently permanent groups at the two higher study areas (A and B), larger subgroupings at the lower areas (C and D), and various combinations of these in the lower areas.[1] For example, group X at the Salvación-Madre de Dios study site D numbered fourteen animals: one adult male, seven adult females, six subadults and juveniles. This group had its own subgroupings of three adult females, two adult females and four subadults and juveniles, and varying combinations of the remaining five animals. This was, therefore, considered a definite or permanent group having little or no contact with other groups or subgroups. On the other hand, XIII, XVIII, and XIX were in reality subgroups which regularly broke up and exchanged members.

[1]   For this reason, reasonably permanent subgroups were regarded as groups for comparative analysis. In terms of biomass relationships the nomenclature is immaterial because the same correlations still hold true.

In addition, these three were observed only twice to defend territory. On the average, these three numbered seventeen, eighteen, and thirteen respectively. Each was comprised of periodic clusters of females, females and young, males, and males and females. Similar conditions have been reported by Carpenter (1935) and Klein (personal communication). The difference is two-fold:

1.   Subgroups XIII, XVIII, and XIX did not defend territories against each other, and only came together for an extended period during the extended dry season when certain preferred fruits and nuts were available although they exchanged members on twenty-six different occasions.

2.   Groupings at higher altitudes are considerably more permanent although smaller with formations gathering since food supply is apparently balanced throughout the year. Therefore, it appears that *Ateles* has such behavioral flexibility as to allow relatively efficient adaptation under many differing environmental and social conditions (Durham f.c.).

HUMBOLDT'S WOOLLY MONKEY (*LAGOTHRIX LAGOTHRICA*)

Humboldt's woolly monkey is a widely distributed primate species found in heavy canopy forest, highland wet forest, and occasionally seen along small streams on the eastern slopes of the Andes. Until recently, only limited behavioral and organizational data have been available, therefore it is important to present some preliminary observations gathered in the 1969 study.

The observations took place at three of the four study sites and included both highland wet forest and lowland canopy forest (Table 1).

Woolly monkeys are large, rather robust animals. There appears to be a greater difference in body size between males and females than found in other ceboid species. There was a decided preference for the mid-canopy of the forest but on two occasions they were observed to come to the ground in order to cross narrow mountain streams.

The most frequently eaten foods were the buds and fruit of several *Ficus* spp., *Lupuna*, *Cecropia*, and palmetto. Additional fruits, nuts, and young shoots were eaten in varying degrees but mainly during the wet season and at times when the apparent preferred foods were less readily available. Groups generally fed together in small clusters in one or two trees at a time and rarely spread out as is characteristic of *Ateles* or *Cebus*.

The concept of suspensory behavior as applied to many other nonhuman primates is entirely appropriate for woolly monkeys. Animals hung by the tail to feed, crossed from one tree to another using the arms and tail, or dropped as much as twenty feet. Only occasionally, in 8 percent of locomotor movements, did they display the characteristic hand over hand movements with assisting tail that is referred to as semibrachiation.

Groups varied in size from six or seven in the highland wet forest to from ten to twenty in the lowland canopy area, but due to the limited observation hours, no CLEAR relationship of group size or com-composition to altitude can be demonstrated. However, as reported above for *Ateles paniscus*, it may be expected that goups nearer the equater will range to higher altitudes as far as potential food sources allow. During the period of observations reported here no groups were seen at altitudes higher than 1000 meters. In nine of all groups observed, females normally outnumbered males. One highland group had two males and one adult female, and one lowland group had three males and three females. No unisexual subgroups or groups were observed.

Woolly monkeys are extremly mild-tempered animals. Although sometimes hunted for food, they display little fear of man. Frequently during the wet season, they raid banana plantations, and in one instance a lowland group lived only 75 meters from a small farm. This temperance is carried over into the maintenance of what seemed to be territories and social relationships with other species of nonhuman primates, notably *Ateles* and *Cebus*. Each male moved forward in the tree to a position in front of his group while the corresponding female went high into the trees on an almost vertical line with the male. Both would then gaze intently, emitting only a soft cooing sound for several minutes with the protector male and female of the opposing group doing the same. Then each male would move back to his group and continue some individual activity such as feeding or resting, but still quite obviously observing the other group. The adult female followed his example but remained at her high position. When one group moved away, the female moved down into the remaining group or over to another tree and the male seemed to relax. When two groups of woollys met on either side of what may be referred to as territorial corridors, that is, open areas that seemed to separate groups, a quiet reaction from the protector male of each group and the largest or oldest female was observed. In two cases the corridor was of low growing bamboo about ten meters wide, winding around for over a hundred meters. Each meeting was apparently fortuitous and took place at a different point along the corridor. Other corridors were not as conspicuous, but became apparent whenever two or more groups met. This is the extent to which woollys exhibited territorial behavior, if it may be called that. Responses to potential predators, e.g. margays or ocelots, were the same with the adult male moving out ahead of the group and the adult female high above him. Potential avian predators apparently did not distress woollys at all.

Natives of the region informed the observer that woollys were known to attack and were considered most dangerous, but neither of these statements was supportable by personal observations.

As stated above, groups varied in size according to area observed. While no clear relationship exists between group number or composition and altitude, certain other features indicate that food supply may be affecting such group dynamics. One of the principal foods eaten during the wet season is the lupuna. However, this tree is rarely found over 1000 meters, the altitudinal limit for woollys observed during this study. Therefore, it might be assumed that while not the most frequently eaten food, the fruit of the lupuna may in fact be one of the staples that must be utilized during the long wet seasons. In the higher region from 600 to 1000 meters where the tree bears small fruit in fewer numbers there is more than likely a substitute fruit or the young buds and shoots are eaten instead, or a combination of different foods. The primary cause for the demarcation of lupuna production and growth may be an ecological feature such as soil, rainfall pattern, or resistance to cold. Nonetheless this seems to be a rather different situation from that reported for *Ateles paniscus*, where preferred foods seem also to be staples and thus influence the range and distribution of these animals into the higher altitudes.

Larger groupings or colony formations have been reported for many species of nonhuman primates. Woolly monkeys seem to form colonies on a seasonal basis during the three and one-half months of the dry season in the lowland canopy forest. At this time most of the preferred foods mentioned above are at the peak of production. Groups begin moving into an area heavy in growth of *Ficus, Inga* sp., palmetto, and tinta, a medium-sized tree which bears a sweet, green lime of large size, which is preferred even by humans. The animals move into these areas by group and begin feeding. After arrival, females and young begin mixing. Females groom other females or young animals;

juveniles and older infants play. Births, however, were not observed during the dry season and, as has been suggested, there may be no reproductive seasonality in *Lagothrix*. Curiously, adult males holding any high dominance rank or control positions (probably a preferred term since dominance in woollys is extremely difficult to ascertain) in their respective groups rarely share in the interactions. Occasionally, they will groom an adult female or another adult male from their respective groups. But, in general, these control males feed alone with a quiet alertness similar to that described earlier when encountering other woollys. The only overt aggressive encounters were observed during this period of mass feeding or colony formation. Of seven fights observed, two involved adult females, three involved a male and female, and two involved adult males. Each was accompanied by shrill screaming, and occasional biting. Each was explosive in nature, but in only two cases did the fight stimulate the occurrence of another fight or a redirection of aggression toward two different animals.

At the end of the dry season, colony disintegration began to take place. As far as could be determined groups left in what appeared to be the company of ones they first appeared with. That is, group E came in with and left with group K; and group C came and left with group L. The cause of the disintegration is at this point unclear. During the last few days of August, rainfall slowly increased. At this time groups began to disperse, moving back to their respective territories or ranges.

OBSERVATIONS ON OTHER TAXA

Large feeding groups of twenty-five to thirty-five *Aotus trivirgatus* were encountered at the B, C, and D study site areas up to an altitude of 1000 meters while two isolated pairs were observed as high as 1500 meters in certain valleys leading from Cuzco to the Madre de Dios. The feeding groups were noted in the early evening (7:00 to 9:00 P.M.) when the animals moved into clusters of lime or orange trees near cultivated regions. They were normally observed in low clusters of trees, but occasionally were as high as 30-35 meters in the mid-canopy.

Saimiri sciureus were found in gallery forests of the lowland canopy forest (Study Site D) in groups of approximately eight to twenty-three animals. They were most easily seen, undisturbed, from a slow-moving canoe or raft, fifty to one hundred feet from shore. They ranged from ground level to mid-canopy depending on conditions.

Among those groups observed at each survey site, *Cebus albifrons* is the most abundant. Groups varied in size from eight to twelve in the highland forest to eighteen to thirty-four in the lowland canopy forest. They inhabited most valley systems, mountain slopes, and all lowland forests. In most cases *Cebus* was sympatric with *Ateles* and occasionally *Lagothrix*, but at the expense of the latter two species.

INTERSPECIFIC RELATIONS

Recently, attention has been drawn to the fact that extremely complex interactions may occur between different species of neotropical primates, such as *Saimiri-Cebus* associations and *Ateles-Alouatta* associations (Klein 1973: 649-654).

The differences presented from the data gathered in Peru are based on *Ateles-Lagothrix*, *Cebus-Lagothrix*, and *Cebus-Ateles* interactions.

Ateles, *Cebus*, and *Lagothrix* are direct competitors for at least three foods. One important type of food (tinta) is eaten by *Ateles* and *Cebus*, but not *Lagothrix*.

Ateles and *Cebus* range over wider areas not only when traveling but also when feeding or resting. *Ateles* moves higher into the canopy and has a wider vertical distribution while *Lagothrix* and *Cebus* tend to range in the mid- and lower-canopy areas (Figure 1).

When interactions occur between *Ateles* and *Cebus* they tend to be aggressive if food is involved (seventeen occasions), but passive if groups are resting or traveling within 20-30 meters of each other (twenty-three occasions). No play, body contact, or grooming occurred. Thus, interactions tend to be both passive and active but apparently based on spatial separateness and/or feeding competition.

In contrast, *Cebus* and *Lagothrix* interactions (sixteen occasions) tend to be hostile but passive. *Lagothrix* use the same "guardian" techniques described above with the control male and female becoming alert and moving forward to a better vantage point between their own group and the *Cebus*. The *Cebus* made a wide detour around the woollys and no fighting or chasing occurred. This reaction may be based on social incompatability.

When *Ateles* and *Lagothrix* do come into visual contact which is rare (two occasions), passive and mutual annoyance is observed, but there are no displays, "guardian" behavior, or whooping as defense.

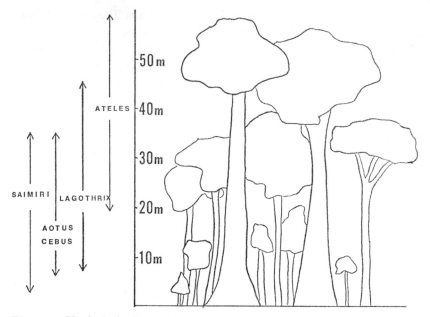

Figure 1.   Vertical distribution in Peru

Instead, both groups separate rather quickly. This seems to be a mutual avoidance condition.

In none of these interspecific relations could a mutual advantage be determined, but one-sided advantages were observed for *Ateles* if woollys and *Cebus* were nearby. The *Cebus* left almost immediately. On one occasion *Cebus* stripped a small *Ficus* tree of almost all fruit before being chased by an *Ateles* subgroup. However, it was too late to be of advantage since there was little left for *Ateles* to eat. Herein might be one reason for the reactions of both *Ateles*, during feeding, and *Lagothrix* at all times.

SUMMARY

This article has presented some general features of ecology, distribution, and group behavior of *Ateles paniscus* and *Lagothrix lagothrica*. The data were collected during a long-term field study of the behavior and ecology of *Ateles paniscus* in southern Peru in 1969. The following were the salient features:

1.   Distribution of the animals at the study sites was presented.
2.   Grouping behavior in *Ateles* and *Lagothrix* was discussed and

found extremely different in type and form.

3. Other nonhuman primates observed were noted.
4. Interspecific relations between *Ateles-Lagothrix, Ateles-Cebus*, and *Cebus-Lagothrix* were discussed.

REFERENCES

BAZAN, Q.
  1969 *Botanical features of the Peruvian forest*. Lima: Lima Geographical Society.
CARPENTER, C. R.
  1935 Behavior of red spider monkeys in Panama. *Journal of Mammalogy* 16(3). American Society of Mammalogy.
DURHAM, N. M.
  1971 Effects of altitude differences on group organization of wild black spider monkeys (*Ateles paniscus*). *Proceedings of Third Congress of the International Primatological Society*. Basel: Karger.
  f.c.   Distribution of nonhuman primates in southern Peru.
KLEIN, L. L.
  1973 Observations on two types of neotropical primate inter-taxa associations. *Proceedings of the Fourth Congress of the International Primatological Society. American Journal of Physical Anthropology* 38(2).

Comparison of the Behavior and Ecology of Red Colobus and Black-and-White Colobus Monkeys in Uganda: A Summary

THOMAS T. STRUHSAKER and JOHN F. OATES

INTRODUCTION

The leaf-eating monkeys of the Old World constitute the subfamily Colobinae of the family Cercopithecidae. The majority of colobines occur in India and Southeast Asia; only three occur in Africa: the olive, black-and-white, and red colobus. The alpha taxonomy of the African Colobinae is in a confused state. The various forms of red colobus are placed either in *Procolobus, Piliocolobus,* or *Colobus.* The olive colobus is usually placed in *Procolobus* and the black-and-white colobus in *Colobus* (Verheyen 1962; Dandelot 1968; Kuhn 1967, 1972; Rahm 1970; Groves 1970). The olive colobus is monotypic, whereas there are fourteen recognized forms of red colobus placed in one or six species, and as many as sixteen to twenty–two forms of black-and-white colobus included in two to four species (Napier and Napier 1967; Dandelot 1968; Rahm 1970).

We wish to thank the National Research Council and Mr. M. L. S. B. Rukuba, Chief Conservator of Forests, Forest Department of Uganda, for permission to study in Uganda and in the Kibale Forest. The staff of the Uganda Forest Department at Fort Portal and the Kanyawara Station were extremely helpful throughout our studies. Plant material was identified for us by Mr. A. B. Katende, assistant curator of the herbarium at Makerere University of Kampala, and Dr. Alan Hamilton, formerly of the Department of Botany, Makerere. We are grateful for many fruitful discussions on the subject of this article with Drs. Tim Clutton-Brock, Peter Marler, and Steven Green. Financial support was provided by the New York Zoological Society, Rockefeller University, United States National Science Foundation grant number GB 15147, and United States National Institutes of Mental Health grant number 1 R01 MH 23008–01, for which we are grateful.

This report is based primarily on two studies in the Kibale Forest of western Uganda, East Africa. Both studies were conducted in compartment 30 of the Kibale Forest, which is located adjacent to the Kanyawara Forest Station (0° 34′ North, 30° 21′ East, elevation 1,530 meters). The study area was comprised of mature rain forest, transitional in form between montane and lowland rain forest. The data considered here come from Struhsaker's study of the red colobus (*Colobs badius tephrosceles*) from May, 1970, through March, 1972, and Oates's study of the black-and-white colobus (*Colobus guereza occidentalis*) from October, 1970, through March, 1972. The emphasis of both studies was behavioral and ecological. Each study concentrated on one social group of the respective species.

This article concentrates on the differences and similarities in the social behavior and ecology of these two species and offers hypotheses to explain them. The reader is referred to our separate and detailed reports (Struhsaker i.p.; Oates 1974) for the basic data and information on methodology.

ECOLOGICAL COMPARISON OF THE TWO HOME RANGES

Although both studies were conducted in the same forest block, the home range of the main study group of red colobus (CW group) did not overlap the range of the main guereza group (group 4). The areas most heavily used by the two groups were separated by 900 to 950 meters. However, the northeast part of CW group's range was almost contiguous with the southwest corner of group 4's range.[1]

Botanically, the two home ranges were very similar. Strip enumerations of all trees that were at least ten meters tall were made in the home ranges of the two groups.[2] Based on these samples, the density of trees of this size class was estimated at 328 per hectare in the range of the badius group and 274 per hectare in the guereza home range. Much, if not all, of this difference in tree density is explained by the

---

[1] On the map grid system, which is explained in our detailed studies, the northeasternmost quadrat occupied by CW group was +4 +1 and the southwesternmost quadrat used by group 4 was +5 —1. This means that the extreme ends of the ranges of the two groups came within less than 100 meters of each other. The two quadrats most heavily used by the badius group were —2 —13 and —5 —13; the most heavily used quadrat of the guereza group was +11 +1.

[2] All trees within 2.5 meters of the enumeration trail were tallied. A total area of 1.43 hectares was enumerated by this method in the range of the badius group and 0.81 hectares in the home range of the guereza group.

fact that 41 percent of the area enumerated within the guereza range had been selectively timbered in 1969. The guereza group, however, used this area little compared with the undisturbed mature forest, where the tree density was higher. Based on the same samples, the estimated number of tree species per unit area in the badius home range was lower (36 per hectare) than in the guereza range (47 per hectare). This difference is probably attributable to the difference in the size of the area sampled in the two ranges. The number of new species tallied in enumeration increases very rapidly in the initial several hundred meters, but as more area is covered, the number of new species encountered increases at a much lower rate. Consequently, enumerations covering relatively small areas have proportionally more species than do enumerations covering larger areas.

The tree-species composition of the two ranges was very similar. Only the ten most common species were considered, because these ten species comprised the majority of trees enumerated; 79.4 percent in the badius home range and 80.3 percent in the guereza range. Comparing the densities of the ten most common tree species in the two ranges revealed no significant difference and confirmed our impression that the two areas were very similar botanically (Table 1).[3]

In contrast to the general similarity in vegetation in the two areas, there was at least one pronounced difference in the primate faunas. There were definitely more groups of guereza in the vicinity of the guereza study area than in the badius study area (Table 2). The reason(s) for this pronounced difference in guereza density is not known. However, one obvious implication of this difference is that in the guereza study area, with its higher density of guereza groups, the probability of intergroup encounters is much higher than for groups of guereza living in the vicinity of the main study group of badius. In addition, there may also have been slightly fewer badius groups in the guereza area than in the badius range, but the reality of this difference is less certain. The other differences in relative abundance of primate species in the two areas are probably not significant (Table 2).

---

[3] Wilcoxon's signed-ranks test for two groups arranged as paired observations (Sokal and Rohlf 1969) was used to compare the estimated densities in Table 1. Comparing the densities of the ten most common trees in the badius range with their densities in the guereza range revealed no significant difference ($p = 0.084$, two-tailed). Similarly, comparison of densities of the ten most common trees in the guereza range with their densities in the badius range revealed no difference ($p > 0.10$, two-tailed).

Table 1. Comparison of densities of ten most common tree species ($\geq$ 10 meters tall) in two study areas at Kanyawara, Kibale Forest, Uganda

Density (number/hectare) of ten most common trees in badius study area and density of same species in guereza study area

Species	Badius area	Guereza area
Diospyros abyssinica	65.7	27.2
Markhamia platycalyx	58.0	56.8
Celtis durandii	34.3	49.4
Uvariopsis congensis	25.2	19.7
Teclea nobilis	21.0	7.4
Funtumia latifolia	14.7	11.1
Strombosia scheffleri	14.7	11.1
Parinari excelsa	10.5	0
Chaetacme aristata	8.4	9.9
Millettia dura	7.6	0

Density (number/hectare) of ten most common trees in guereza area and density of same species in badius area

Species	Guereza area	Badius area
Markhamia platycalyx	56.8	58.0
Celtis durandii	49.4	34.3
Diospyros abyssinica	27.2	65.7
Uvariopsis congensis	19.7	25.2
Bosqueia phoberus	18.5	2.8
Strombosia scheffleri	11.1	14.7
Funtumia latifolia	11.1	14.7
Chaetacme aristata	9.9	8.4
Celtis africana	8.6	2.1
Teclea nobilis	7.4	21.0

Table 2. Relative abundance of primate species in two study areas at Kanyawara, Kibale Forest, Uganda
$\bar{x}$ number of groups per census*

Species	Guereza area	Badius area
Colobus badius	2.90	3.80
Colobus guereza	3.30	0.84
Cercopithecus ascanius	2.90	2.77
Cercopithecus mitis	1.70	1.80
Cercopithecus lhoesti	0.10	0.32
Cercocebus albigena	0.30	0.39
Pan troglodytes	0	0.14

* Fifteen censuses were made by Oates in the guereza area along a census route 4,000 meters long. Forty-four censuses were made by Struhsaker in the badius area along a census route 4,020 meters long.

COMPARISON OF SOCIAL STRUCTURE AND SOCIAL BEHAVIOR

Group Size and Composition

The badius of the Kibale Forest lived in considerably larger social groups than did the guereza. Badius groups numbered about 19 to 80, with a central tendency of approximately 50, whereas guereza groups ranged in size from 8 to 15, averaging 10.5. The main study group of badius averaged 20 in number and that of guereza 12. There was always more than one fully adult male in each badius social group, with the ratio of adult females to adult males varying from about 1.5 to 3.0. In marked contrast, there was usually only one fully adult male and three to four adult females in groups of guereza. The adult membership of social groups was relatively stable for both species. Solitary subadult and adult males of both species were quite common.

Inter-individual Spacing

In an attempt to describe the spacing patterns between members of a social group, a series of samples was taken in which the distance between a specific individual monkey and its neighbors was estimated. Results from 155 such samples on seven individual badius have been compared with the results from 170 samples on ten individual guereza. This comparison clearly shows how much more cohesive were guereza groups than badius groups. For example, the mean number of neighbors within 2.5 meters of all ten guereza sampled was 2.8. In contrast, there was an average of only 0.86 neighbors within 2.5 meters of the seven badius sampled. These differences are highly significant $(0.01 > p > 0.002$, Wilcoxon two-sample test for the unpaired case). This pattern persisted even when the comparison was broken into specific age–sex classes. For example, the adult male guereza had an average of 2.6 members of his group within 2.5 meters of him, and the three adult males of the badius group had averages of 0.32 to 0.68 members of the group within 2.5 meters. The differences between the females of the two species were not of the same order of magnitude, but still the guereza adult females averaged 1.6 to 3.7 more neighbors within 2.5 meters of them than did the badius adult females, whether they were in possession of a newborn infant or not. Thus, the members of the guereza group were more closely spaced than were the members of the badius group.

Grooming Relations

In both species the adult females performed the majority of grooming. Adult female guereza not only groomed more than would be expected on the basis of their proportional representation in the group membership, but also received more grooming than would be expected by chance. This differs from the badius females who, although they groomed more than would be expected, received about as much grooming as would be expected by chance. Adult male badius were groomed more than would be expected by chance. The single adult male guereza in the main study group received about as much grooming as would be expected by chance, but he groomed others very rarely. Juvenile badius appeared to perform more grooming than did juvenile guereza, although part of this difference may be attributable to possible differences in aging criteria in the two studies.

Social Relations of Newborn Infants

Newborn infant badius were neither handled, groomed, nor carried by other monkeys in the group. Juveniles and young juveniles often approached the mother and infant and tried to touch the neonate, but the mother always responded with threat gestures. Infant badius first made contact with monkeys other than their own mothers when they were about 1 to 3.5 months old. In sharp contrast to this, neonate guereza were often carried and handled by other females in the group. This attention was given primarily by adult females and to a lesser extent by immature monkeys. Newborn guereza were most attractive to other group members during the first month after birth.

Relations among Adult Males

The adult males in the main study group of badius formed a kind of subgroup. They characteristically maintained close spatial proximity and stable, long-term membership in the group, and they displayed cohesive and united effort in aggressive episodes with other badius groups. In addition, there was a stable and linear dominance hierarchy among them, which was defined as priority of access to space, food, and grooming position. Correlated with this dominance hierarchy were fixed roles in a stylized encounter called the present type II. Dominant males gave the present type II to their subordinate males. This display seemed to reinforce their dominance relations and may have also strengthened the ties of their subgroup and at times reduced agonistic tension. The manner in which membership in this subgroup was achieved is not clearly understood. However, it seemed to involve a slow familiarization between young males and adult males. Initially, the young males harassed the adult males, but as they grew older, the roles reversed, with adults harassing the old juvenile and subadult males. Eventually, it would seem, the maturing male either attains membership in the subgroup or leaves the group altogether.

No such subgroup was observed among the one-male social groups of guereza, and it appears that maturing males either leave or are forced out of the group before reaching full physical maturity. It also seems possible that a young and developing male may, on occasion, force the harem male out of the group.

Mating Systems

Neither badius nor guereza is panmictic. Assortative mating is, however, achieved in different manners and to different extents in the two species. The single adult male in the guereza study group performed all heterosexual mounts. In the main study group of badius, there was a good correlation between dominance and copulatory success. The dominant male performed at least 84 percent of all heterosexual mounts during the first part of the study. The other two adult males copulated very little. During the second half of the study, a young male attained sexual and physical maturity and eventually became the dominant male in the group. In this transitional period, the previously dominant male performed only 42.7 percent of the mounting, the remainder being divided unequally among the other three males (30.0, 19.1, and 5.5 percent; in 2.7 percent cases the male was not properly seen and therefore not identified). Clearly, badius males reproduce differentially, but apparently not to the extent of guereza males. However, one should not exclude the possibility that the degree of assortative mating in guereza is, in fact, very nearly the same as that in badius, because guereza live in smaller groups, so that each harem male may serve fewer females than do some badius males. In a hypothetical case, single guereza males in four different harems containing five, four, three, and two females respectively would be equivalent to one badius group containing fourteen females in which the mating was assorted among four males on a 35.7, 28.6, 21.4, and 14.3 percent basis.

Intergroup Relations

The intergroup relations of these two species are quite different. The main study group of badius had very extensive, if not complete, overlap in its home range with two other badius groups. The relations of these three groups were usually aggressive, involved only the subadult and adult males, and seemed to be based on an intergroup dominance hierarchy, which was independent of spatial parameters. No matter where any two of the three groups met in their home ranges, one usually supplanted the other. Direction of successful supplantation varied enough, however, to suggest that in some cases the outcome depended on which particular males of the two groups happened to meet. These three groups used an area of approximately 50 hectares[4] to the virtual exclusion of all other badius groups. The four or five other badius groups who entered this 50-hectare area did so very infrequently and were usually chased out immediately.

Guereza groups had preferred areas in their home ranges which they defended against, and from which they could readily chase, other guereza groups. However, these preferred areas were not used to the exclusion of other groups. The element of exclusive use is often considered to be the prime factor defining territoriality (Pitelka 1959) — on this basis, the guereza groups in the Kibale Forest do not have territories. One might think of their intergroup relations as being based on dominance relationships which are dependent on spatial parameters, i.e. the boundaries of the preferred areas of each group. However, Burt's (1943) definition of territoriality, which emphasizes the defense of a specific area, would apply to the guereza situation.

COMPARISON OF ECOLOGY

Home Range

The main study group of badius had a home range of about 35 hectares, approximately twice that of the guereza group (15 to 16 hectares). However, consideration of the differences in size and biomass between the two groups reveals that the biomass density was about the same, i.e. 118 kilograms/35.3 hectares for the badius group (3.34

---

[4] It is unlikely that all 50 hectares were used by these three groups, because some were unsuitable habitat for badius, but it is also unlikely that any other badius groups used these areas.

kilograms/hectare) and 61 kilograms/15.5 hectares for the guereza group (3.94 kilograms/hectare). Nonetheless, the overall biomass density of badius was considerably greater than that of the guereza because of the much more extensive overlap in home ranges of the badius groups and the much larger size of the typical badius group. In the vicinity of the main study group of badius, the biomass density of badius was estimated at about 1,760 kilograms/square kilometer and that of guereza at only 64.7 kilograms/square kilometer. Even in areas of greater density, the estimated guereza biomass density did not exceed 570 kilograms/square kilometer.

Daily Ranging Patterns

The distance traveled by both study groups was extremely variable, but in general the badius group traveled further each day than did the guereza group. During fifty-four days in which the badius group was followed continuously from sunrise to sunset, it traveled an average of 648.9 meters/day, but this daily distance varied from 222.5 to 1,185 meters. In sixty days the guereza group moved an average of 535.1 meters/day, varying from 288 to 1,004 meters. A t–test comparing the day ranges of the two species showed that on the average the badius group moved significantly further each day than did the guereza group (t = 3.12, df = 112, $0.01 > p > 0.001$).

Distance traveled per day is only one way of viewing ranging patterns and certainly tells little of how the animals utilize their home range or how they distribute their time in space. Our most detailed analysis of ranging patterns consisted of superimposing a grid system over the daily range maps and then plotting the amount of time the groups spent in specific 0.25-hectare quadrats of the grid system. This analysis gives us several measures of ranging patterns.

Our monthly samples were collected during five continuous days of observation. During these five-day periods the badius group used an average of 45.1 quadrats per five-day sample, varying from 27 to 65 (N = 7). The guereza group tended to use fewer quadrats during the five-day sample, averaging 29.8 quadrats per sample and varying from 14 to 44 (N = 12).

A more refined analysis of ranging patterns measured the dispersion of time in space. For this analysis, we used the Shannon–Wiener information measure (Wilson and Bossert 1971) to compute a diversity index that reflected the diversity in ranging patterns. In months when the group distributed its time evenly among quadrats, its index of ranging diversity was high. Months when the group spent the majority of its time in a few quadrats gave a low index of ranging diversity. Again, it is apparent that the badius group generally had a more diverse pattern of ranging than did the guereza group. The monthly index of ranging diversity averaged 3.240 over seventeen months (range 2.742 to 3.779) for the badius group and 2.719 over twelve months (range 2.098 to 3.174) for the guereza group.

On both a daily and five-day basis, the badius group had a more diversified pattern of ranging than did the guereza group, as indicated by daily travel distance, number of quadrats used per month, and monthly indices of quadrat utilization diversity. These differences are almost certainly related to the differences in the number of monkeys and biomass in the two groups. For example, although the guereza group used only 66.6 percent as many quadrats during the five-day sample as did the badius group, their group size was only 55 to 60 percent and their biomass 51 percent that of the badius group.

One final analysis concerns the annual ranging pattern. We have already shown that the badius group had a larger home range than the guereza group, but we have not yet considered distribution of time in these ranges. The Shannon–Wiener information measure was again used, but in this case the computation was made on all the ranging data for a twelve-month period. In contrast to the preceding analysis, the indices of quadrat utilization diversity for the two species were very similar: badius 5.025 and guereza 5.465. Thus, although the badius group had a larger home range and a more diverse monthly ranging pattern, their proportional distribution of time in space during a twelve-month period was much like that of the guereza group.

Time Budgets

There were very pronounced differences between the two species in the allotment of time to various activities. The badius spent considerably more of their time feeding (44.5 percent) and moving (9.2 percent) and less of their time resting (34.8 percent) than did the guereza (19.9, 5.4, and 57.3 percent respectively). These differences in time budgets could be related to dietary differences. For example, the more diversified diet of the badius may require that species to feed and move more than the guereza, with its more monotonous diet. The nature of these different foods may also involve different rates of digestion and may thereby necessitate different amounts of time devoted to resting, presumably when much of the digestion occurs. These data also suggest that the two species may have some very basic metabolic differences which are related to the energy content of their respective diets, but in the absence of physiological data, further speculation seems unwarranted.

Vertical Stratification

Although the heights preferred by the two species in the forest are not strikingly different, several thousand height estimates of the monkeys tabulated at half-hourly intervals suggest that the guereza prefer slightly lower heights than do the badius. In terms of ecological niche separation, feeding heights are probably most important. Of the feeding observations for badius, 25 percent occurred from 3 to 13.5 meters above the ground, 50 percent between 13.5 and 25.5 meters, and 25 percent from 25.5 to 37.5 meters or higher. In contrast, 50.4 percent of the feeding observations for guereza in the same forest compartment occurred below 13.5 meters, only 38.2 percent between 13.5 and 25.5 meters, and 11.4 percent above 25.5 meters. These differences may contribute to niche separation between the two species, but they are relatively insignificant when compared with dietary differences.

Diets

Although both species are herbivorous and justly qualify as leaf eaters, their diets differ in many ways.[5] The guereza diet was found to be much more monotonous than that of badius. Indices of food-species diversity were computed each month for the two species using the Shannon–Wiener information measure. In seventeen months this index for badius averaged 2.606 and varied from 1.973 to 3.051. In fourteen months the same index for guereza averaged only 1.720, ranging from 1.205 to 2.152. In only two months was the badius index as low as the highest guereza index. The monotony of the guereza diet was due primarily to its heavy concentration on one common tree species, *Celtis durandii*. This species provided the major source

[5] Data on monkey food items were collected by recording frequency, rather than duration, of feeding.

of food for guereza in all fourteen months, sometimes comprising as much as 68.5 percent of the monthly diet.

Both species fed heavily on young leaves, but the blades of mature leaves played a much more important role in the diet of guereza than in badius. In one month mature leaf blades were the most important dietary item for guereza, constituting 32 percent of the food eaten. The badius, in contrast, rarely ate the blades of mature leaves. During a twelve-month period only 2.3 percent of the badius diet contained mature leaf blades. The badius did, however, regularly eat the petioles of mature leaves and in the same twelve-month period this item constituted 18.5 percent of their diet. Guereza, by contrast, rarely ate leaf petioles. Fruits were more important in the guereza diet than in that of the badius, and they were among the five most important food items in thirteen of the fourteen months. In one month fruits comprised as much as 34.2 percent of the guereza diet. On the other hand, fruit accounted for only 4.8 percent of the badius annual diet.

A more precise way of comparing the diets of these two species is to measure the percentage overlap in the specific food items eaten each month. In this analysis we employed the same methods as those used by Holmes and Pitelka (1968). In any given month, the percentage overlap in diet is the sum of the shared percentages of specific food items common to the two species in that month. For example, if in January, 1972, the badius diet contained 50 percent leaf buds of species A, 25 percent mature leaf petioles of species B, 25 percent floral buds of species C, and none of species D, and the guereza diet contained 25 percent leaf buds of species A, none of species B, 25 percent mature leaves of species C, and 50 percent young leaves of species D, then the percentage overlap in the diets of guereza and badius for this month would be 25 percent (leaf buds of species A). Percentages of overlap in diets were computed for the last twelve months of the study (April, 1971, to March, 1972; Table 3). Dietary overlap between badius and guereza was generally very low. The mean monthly overlap was 7.1 percent with a range of 2.0 to 15.7 percent. This is much lower than the intermonthly overlap in diet of badius during seventeen months (136 monthly pair combinations): the mean overlap in diet between months was 24.3 percent with a range of 9.3 to 50.0 percent. In only 13 of these 136 monthly combinations was the overlap in the badius diet lower than the maximum overlap in the badius–guereza comparison, i.e. 15.7 percent. None of the intermonthly comparisons for badius had overlaps in diet that were as low as the mean overlap in the badius–guereza diet.

Table 3. Percentage overlap in diet (specific food items) of *Colobus badius* and *Colobus guereza*

Month	Percent overlap
April, 1971	7.29
May	3.64
June	4.70
July	3.77
August	4.54
September	15.68
October	12.71
November	2.00
December	13.25
January, 1972	3.36
February	9.81
March	4.30

We conclude from this that overlap in food habits was very slight between these two species. Furthermore, the little overlap that did occur involved very common species and common food items. In the four months when diet overlap was greatest, most of this overlap was accounted for by *Celtis durandii* (7.2 percent in September, 8.9 percent in October, 10.0 percent in December, and 3.0 percent in February). In all of these cases, the young leaves, leaf buds, and/or fruits of this species accounted for most of the overlap. All of these items were extremely abundant. It will be recalled from Table 1 that *Celtis durandii* was one of the most common trees in the forest and as such probably does not constitute a food source that limits the population of either colobus species. Consequently, we conclude that the slight overlap in diet between these two species did not constitute competition for food. Additional support for this conclusion was obtained by observing the food habits of badius living within the home range of the main study group of guereza. Their food habits did not differ substantially from those of the main study group of badius.

DISCUSSION

How can we account for these interspecific differences from an evolutionary standpoint? There are at least three obvious possibilities: (1) the social structures may be specialized adaptations to the Kibale habitat; (2) the social structures originally may have been adaptations to other habitats which nevertheless have permitted a certain amount of success in Kibale; and (3) the third possibility concerns the phylogenetic proximity of the two species: just how closely are they related? Obviously, these three possibilities are not mutually exclusive.

Adaptation to Kibale-like Habitat

In the first hypothesis we suggest that the small and cohesive social groups of guereza which defend fixed areas ("territories") against neighboring groups are adapted to the efficient exploitation of a monotonous diet whose chief component (*Celtis durandii*), has a high density, a high cover index (a function of crown size and tree density), and a uniform dispersion (Struhsaker i.p.). In addition, the phenology of this species provides an abundance of preferred guereza food at most times of the year. The concentration of guereza on a food species of this nature permits partitioning of the habitat into territories and, in combination with the small group size, also permits relatively restricted ranging patterns on a daily and monthly basis. An important feature of guereza social behavior which probably contributes to both stability in group membership and group defense of territories is the attention given to newborn infants by other members of the group. Such attention, we suggest, is important to the rapid and complete integration of neonates into the social group. The close spatial cohesion between members of guereza groups is probably related to their emphasis on a monotonous diet and a high-density food source (in terms of both tree density and item density on a given tree) and not to their territoriality, because territoriality in other primate species, e.g. vervets (*Cercopithecus aethiops* [see Struhsaker 1967]), is not necessarily accompanied by close inter-individual spacing within the group. Differential mating is achieved in guereza by the one-male social groups, from which other adult males are excluded. The ecological significance of this exclusion, if any, is not apparent, particularly because the extra-group males utilize the same food resources in the same areas as do the social groups. The significance of this exclusion of all but one adult male from social groups is more probably involved with outbreeding, gene flow, and assortative mating, rather than with feeding ecology *per se*.

The ecological adaptation of the badius social structure is less apparent. There is no obvious reason for having large, multi-male groups in order to exploit a large home range and a great diversity of foods. Although it is tempting to suggest that a greater diet diversity indicates a greater diversity in ranging pattern, the data for the main badius study group do not support this suggestion (Struhsaker 1974). Nor was any correlation found between the pattern of food dispersion and ranging diversity. In fact, the badius ranging-pattern diversity was more closely related to the frequency of intergroup conflicts and intergroup proximity (Struhsaker 1974). Greater inter-individual distance between members of a badius group might, however, be related to their more diversified diet. By feeding on a greater variety of foods, the badius encounter a greater variety of food dispersion patterns, many of which are not densely spaced. The absence of group territoriality in badius may be related to their great dietary diversity, which in turn may dictate a home range larger than can be efficiently defended in a rain forest habitat. The extensive overlap in the home ranges of three groups may permit each group to use a larger area than would be possible if, given the same group density, they defended territories. Their intergroup dominance relations effectively determine which group has priority of access to any food source, but the distribution of food sources is such that the supplanted group never appears to have difficulty in immediately locating another ample food source. The fact that these three groups appear to defend and exclude other groups from an area of about 50 hectares may be viewed as a kind of territoriality and is probably related to food allocation.

Several of our results and conclusions have been substantiated by Clutton-Brock (1972) during his two-month study of badius and guereza in the Kibale Forest and his nine-month study of badius in the Gombe Park of Tanzania. He found, for example, that the guereza had a less diverse diet, moved less each day, and had a smaller monthly range than did the badius. He also speculated that guereza might be able to subsist primarily on mature leaves at certain times of the year, a speculation substantiated by the studies of Oates (1974). In an attempt to explain the adaptive significance of the badius social structure, Clutton-Brock (1972) suggested that a single large group having relatively little overlap in home range with other groups was advantageous:

1) because food is heavily clumped, so that each food source (usually a group of trees in shoot or flower) can usually support the greater part of the troop at one time, 2) because it permits an integrated use of the animals' food supply. If the whole area was used by several troops, troops would be likely to visit areas where the supply of shoots had been cropped immediately previously by another troop.

Although this hypothesis may be applicable at Gombe, which seems to have a much lower density of badius groups than Kibale, it clearly does not apply to the Kibale Forest, where there is extensive and near-ly complete overlap in home ranges of badius groups. Our study found that groups supplanted one another, and on some occasions these sup-plantations were clearly over clumped food sources. In such cases it seemed that because of their dietary diversity and abundance of food, the supplanted group had no difficulty in readily locating another suit-able food source. Furthermore, badius groups usually left a clumped source of food before they had depleted it, even without being sup-planted by another group. Clutton-Brock (1972) goes on to suggest that the higher proportion of young growth in the diet of badius, com-bined with their larger group size, results in a day range larger than that of guereza. However, it is clear from our studies that not only does young growth usually constitute a high proportion of the guereza diet, but when one considers the differences in biomass between groups of the two species, the differences in day ranges are virtually eliminated (see above).

The lack of attention to newborn infants or the lack of opportunity to express this interest by other group members may result in a looser attachment of juvenile badius to their group. Although the data are sparse, there is some suggestion that the juvenile class is the most mo-bile element in the badius society and that juveniles frequently shift be-tween groups. This could be the way in which most outbreeding is achieved by badius.

Adaptation to Habitat Different from That of Kibale

Surveys in many other parts of East Africa indicate that guereza is most successful in relatively young secondary forest and that it often succeeds in narrow strips of riparian forest and very small patches of relict forest. Guereza can successfully occupy old and mature rain forests, but they are much less numerous there than in younger forests. The social structure of guereza is more clearly adaptive in an eco-logical sense for a species inhabiting secondary and riparian forests than for one inhabiting mature rain forest. Many of the habitats in which guereza seem most successful are characterized by few tree species and pronounced dry seasons, when young, succulent plant growth is usually absent. Such an environment would clearly select for an herbivore that could survive on a monotonous diet and, at cer-tain times of the year, on mature leaves alone. The small area of some of these habitats would also select for small group size and close inter-individual spacing because of the small and clumped nature of the food resources. Territoriality would be one means of allocating food resources among groups in such a situation. The suggestion that small group size is related to small- or low-density food resources is indirectly supported by evidence from studies of other species. For example, two subspecies of red colobus, *C. badius temminckii* and *C. badius rufomitratus*, live in relatively dry woodlands where food is considered to be more seasonal and generally less abundant than in the rain forest. Both of these subspecies live in considerably smaller social groups than do the subspecies living in rain forests. Another example is the vervet monkey (*Cercopithecus aethiops*) of Amboseli, Kenya, whose average group size declined in apparent response to a reduction in food supplies (Struhsaker 1973). Clutton-Brock (1972) has also suggested that guereza may, in fact, be better adapted to a drier habitat than to the rain forest, again because of their more monotonous diet and ability to subsist exclusively on mature leaves at certain times of the year.

Considering the overall distribution of badius, we conclude that the species is adapted primarily to the rain forest. Some populations and subspecies, however, are able to succeed in relatively dry and seasonal habitats, including savanna woodland and riparian and relict patches of forest. As noted above, these populations generally live in smaller social groups than do those living in rain forest. Presumably, this is a function of food availability. Clutton-Brock's (1972) suggestion that the dietary dependency of badius on young growth limits them to habitats that provide young growth throughout the year, thus restricting them to rain forest habitats, seems tenable, with the possible exceptions of *C. badius temminckii* and *C. badius rufomitratus*.

Phylogeny

As mentioned in the introduction, the taxonomy of the African Colobinae has not been worked out to the satisfaction of all. As far as this paper is concerned, the major question is whether or not badius and guereza are rightfully members of the same genus. Because species of different genera are phylogenetically more distant than species of the same genus, the former are assumed to have been separated over a relatively longer period of time and to have had evolutionary histories more different from each other than have species of the same genus. The extent of these differences in the duration and nature of their evolutionary histories may be of considerable importance in explaining the current differences in the behavior and ecology of badius and guereza. Our behavioral and ecological data demonstrate that these two species are very different. Marler's (1969, 1970) and our studies on guereza and badius vocalizations also show pronounced differences. Whether the magnitude of the differences described by these studies warrants placing guereza and badius in different genera cannot be stated with certainty at this time. However, the osteological evidence that has been used to place them in the same genus is no more compelling than our data suggesting that they should be placed in different genera. Clearly, more data of a different sort are needed before a satisfactory conclusion can be reached. Detailed and comparable data on karyology and serology could be extremely useful. Barnicot and Hewett-Emmett (1972) have examined red cell and serum proteins of badius, and Sarich (1970) presents information on the immunology of *Colobus polykomos*, but comparable data for badius and guereza are not available.

Comparison with Other Colobinae

There are few data on other Colobinae which permit the kind of comparison we have been able to make with guereza and badius. However, it appears that guereza is much more like the majority of Indian and Asiatic Colobinae than is badius. *Presbytis johnii* (Poirier 1970), *P. cristatus* (Furuya 1961–1962; Bernstein 1968), *P. senex* (Eisenberg, Muckenhirn, and Rudran 1972), and some populations of *P. entellus* (Yoshiba 1968; Vogel 1971) all live in small social groups having only one fully adult male. Furthermore, these species are all territorial and, as among guereza, other members of the group handle and carry newborn infants. These studies support the conclusion that attention to infants enhances closer cohesion among group members, which in turn facilitates their united effort in defending territories against neighboring groups. Exceptions to this are some populations of *P. entellus* (Jay 1965; Vogel 1971) in which the groups are large, have several adult males, and are not territorial but still practice "aunt" behavior toward neonates. In some ways these exceptional entellus groups resemble the badius more closely than they resemble the guereza.

Ecological comparisons with other Colobinae are equally difficult because of the paucity of data. Hladik and Hladik (1972) described the food habits of *P. senex* and *P. entellus* at Polonnaruwa, Ceylon, and their results suggest some parallels with the guereza–badius comparison. For example, like guereza, senex eats more mature leaves and fruit than does entellus, which is more like badius in its food items. Furthermore, senex has a less diverse diet than does entellus, also consistent with the parallel between guereza and badius.

We feel that one of the main lessons emerging from this comparison is that gross classifications of habitat and food habits are poor predictors of social behavior and social organization among primates. The forest-dwelling leaf eaters can have very different societies, as demonstrated by *Colobus badius* and *Colobus guereza*.

REFERENCES

BARNICOT, N. A., D. HEWETT-EMMETT
   1972   Red cell and serum proteins of *Cercocebus, Presbytis, Colobus* and certain other species. *Folia Primatologica* 17:442–457.
BERNSTEIN, I.
   1968   The lutong of Kuala Selangor. *Behaviour* 14:136–163.
BURT, W. H.
   1943   Territoriality and home range concepts as applied to mammals. *Journal of Mammalogy* 24:346–352.
CLUTTON-BROCK, T. H.
   1972   "Feeding and ranging behaviour of the red colobus monkey." Unpublished doctoral dissertation, Cambridge University, Cambridge, England.
DANDELOT, P.
   1968   *Primates: Anthropoidea*. Smithsonian Institution Preliminary Identification Manual for African Mammals 24:1–80. Washington: Smithsonian Press.
EISENBERG, J. F., N. A. MUCKENHIRN, R. RUDRAN
   1972   The relation between ecology and social structure in primates. *Science* 176:863–874.
FURUYA, Y.
   1961–1962   The social life of silvered leaf monkeys (*Trachypithecus cristatus*). *Primates* 3:41–60.
GROVES, C. P.
   1970   "The forgotten leaf-eaters and the phylogeny of the Colobinae," in *Old World monkeys*. Edited by J. R. Napier and P. H. Napier, 555–588. New York: Academic Press.
HLADIK, C. M., A. HLADIK
   1972   Disponibilités alimentaires et domaines vitaux des primates à Ceylan. *La Terre et la Vie* 26:149–215.

HOLMES, R. T., F. A. PITELKA
 1968   Food overlap among coexisting sandpipers on northern Alaskan tundra. *Systematic Zoology* 17:305–318.
JAY, P.
 1965   "The common langur of North India," in *Primate behavior.* Edited by I. DeVore, 197–250. New York: Holt, Rinehart and Winston.
KUHN, H.-J.
 1967   "Zur systematik der Cercopithecidae," in *Neue Ergebnisse der Primatologie.* Edited by D. Starck, R. Schneider, and H.-J. Kuhn, 25–46. Stuttgart: Gustav Fischer.
 1972   On the perineal organ of male *Procolobus badius. Journal of Human Evolution* 1:371–378.
MARLER, P.
 1969   *Colobus guereza:* territoriality and group composition. *Science* 163:93–95.
 1970   Vocalizations of East African monkeys I. Red colobus. *Folia Primatologica* 13:81–91.
NAPIER, J. R., P. H. NAPIER
 1967   *A handbook of living primates.* New York: Academic Press.
OATES, J. F.
 1974   "The ecology and behaviour of the black-and-white colobus monkey (*Colobus guereza* Rüppell) in East Africa." Unpublished doctoral dissertation, University of London.
PITELKA, F. A.
 1959   Numbers, breeding schedule, and territoriality in the pectoral sandpipers of northern Alaska. *Condor* 61:233–264.
POIRIER, F. E.
 1970   "The nilgiri langur (*Presbytis johnii*) of South India," in *Primate behavior: developments in field and laboratory research.* Edited by L. A. Rosenblum, 251–383. New York: Academic Press.
RAHM, U.
 1970   "Ecology, zoogeography, and systematics of some African forest monkeys," in *Old World monkeys.* Edited by J. R. Napier and P. H. Napier, 589–626. New York: Academic Press.
SARICH, V. M.
 1970   "Primate systematics with special reference to Old World monkeys: a protein perspective," in *Old World monkeys.* Edited by J. R. Napier and P. H. Napier, 175–226. New York: Academic Press.
SOKAL, R. R., F. J. ROHLF
 1969   *Biometry: the principles and practice of statistics in biological research.* San Francisco: W. H. Freeman.
STRUHSAKER, T. T.
 1967   Social structure among vervet monkeys (*Cercopithecus aethiops*). *Behaviour* 29:83–121.
 1973   A recensus of vervet monkeys in the Masai-Amboseli game reserve, Kenya. *Ecology* 54:930–932.
 1974   Correlates of ranging behavior in a group of red colobus mon-

keys (*Colobus badius tephrosceles*). *American Zoologist* 14:177–184.

i.p.   *Behavior and ecology of red colobus monkeys.* Chicago: University of Chicago Press.

VERHEYEN, W. N.
1962   *Contribution à la craniologie comparée des primates.* Annales de la Musée Royale de l'Afrique Centrale, série 8vo, Sciences Zoologiques 105. Tervuren, Belgium.

VOGEL, C.
1971   Behavioral differences of *Presbytis entellus* in two different habitats. *Proceedings of the Third International Congress of Primatology, Zurich* 3:41–47. Basel: Karger.

WILSON, E. O., W. H. BOSSERT
1971   *A primer of population biology.* Stamford, Connecticut: Sinauer Associates.

YOSHIBA, K.
1968   "Local and inter-troop variability in ecology and social behavior of common Indian langurs," in *Primates: studies in adaptation and variability.* Edited by P. C. Jay, 217–242. New York: Holt, Rinehart and Winston.

Population Dynamics of the Toque Monkey, *Macaca sinica*

WOLFGANG P. J. DITTUS

INTRODUCTION

Fundamental to any understanding of the adaptation of animals to their natural environment is the knowledge of their numbers and life and death characteristics. The data on population dynamics to be presented here is based on a three and one-half year field study of the toque macaque, *Macaca sinica* (Linnaeus 1771) of Sri Lanka (Ceylon). Publications dealing with aspects of ecology and behavior are in preparation.

The toque macaque, a member of the family Cercopithecidae, shares the subgenus *Zati* (Reichenbach 1862) with the bonnet macaque, *M. radiata* (Geoffroy 1812), of southern India and possibly *M. assamensis* (McClelland 1839) of northeastern India and Burma (Hill and Bernstein 1969). In its range *M. sinica* is confined to the forested regions of Ceylon, and three subspecies have been recognized; *M. s. sinica* (Linnaeus 1771), *M. s. aurifrons* (Pocock 1931), and *M. s. opisthomelas* (Hill 1942),

Research was supported, in part, by National Science Foundation grant GB-3545, awarded to Dr. John F. Eisenberg; National Institute of Mental Health grant Ro1MH15673-01; -02; research grant 686 from the National Geographic Society; and Smithsonian Institution Foreign Currency Program grant SFC-7004, awarded to Dr. J. F. Eisenberg and Dr. Suzanne Ripley. It is a pleasure to express my gratitude to Dr. John F. Eisenberg whose support, advice and kind encouragement made this research a reality. I thank especially Messrs. S. M. S. Farook, S. Waas, G. DeSilva for their devoted assistance in the field; Miss L. Andradi and Mrs. Wy Holden for secretarial help; and the staff of the Polonnaruwa camp for the maintenance of our camp. I also wish to thank Drs. D. Kleiman, H. K. Buechner, and N. A. Muckenhirn for valuable editing of the manuscript. This paper is from a Ph.D dissertation to be submitted to the department of Zoology, University of Maryland.

For Plate, see p. vii, between pp. 368–369.

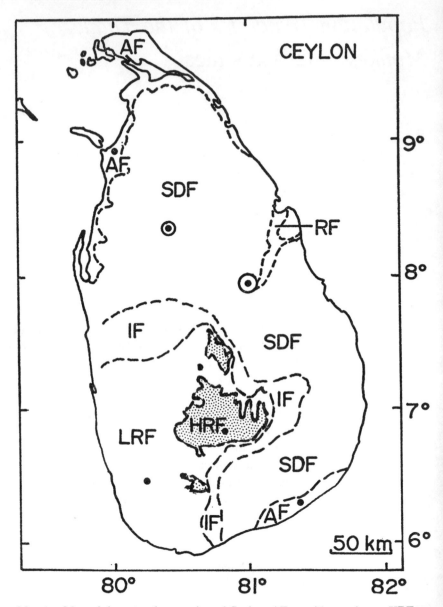

Map 1.   Map of the natural vegetation of Ceylon; AF = arid zone forest; HRF = highland rain forest; IF = intermediate forest; LRF = lowland rain forest; RF = riverine forest; SDF = semideciduous forest (after Fernando 1968). Study sites are marked with a dot; Polonnaruwa, the main site, is encircled; Anuradhapura, the secondary site, has a smaller circle

of the low country dry zone, low country wet zone and central hill country, and highlands respectively (Eisenberg and McKay 1970). Other primates in Ceylon are the langurs, *Presbytis entellus* and *P. senex* of the subgenera *Semnopithecus* and *Kasi* respectively, and the prosimian, *Loris tardigradus* (Phillips 1935).

The toque monkey is long tailed and is agile both on and above ground. Its popular name refers to a well formed cap-like whorl of hair (toque) radiating symmetrically outward from the center of its head (Plate 1). It is generally more colorful than its nearest relatives, the pelage varying geographically from dusky brown to golden yellow. The ears and lower lips are black and the face of adult females is usually varying degrees of red. Adult males frequently have black and/or red spots on the face. Facial coloration in both sexes generally becomes more intense with age, and is not strongly associated with the reproductive condition.

The main site for this study was in the semideciduous forests of Polonnaruwa in the north central dry zone. Anuradhapura, a secondary study site, is in the same zone, but is ecologically somewhat more disturbed than Polonnaruwa. Less detailed, comparative information was collected over a wide range from the Wilpattu and Ruhunu National Parks in the northwest and southeast arid zones respectively, the Sinharaje Forest Reserve in the lowland rain forest, Udawattekelle Sanctuary, Kandy, in the midland rain forest, and the Ohiya and Horton Plains region of the highland forests (Map 1).

In both the arid zones, the toque macaque was limited in its distribution to gallery forests and to areas surrounding other sources of permanent water. Troops living within towns, as reported for the rhesus, *M. mulatta* (e.g. Southwick et al. 1965: 111–159), were not found. In general macaques occurred wherever a semblance of natural forest with a permanent source of water was available.

Nearly all of the Polonnaruwa study site lies within a religious and archaeological sanctuary, therefore most of the animals were not seriously harassed and not as shy as they might have been in a "wilder" situation. Botanically, the study site can be considered a peninsula of forest bounded by water and cultivation, and continuous with extensive expanses of forest by only a narrow neck (Map 2). The forest within the study site generally resembled that natural to the area; however, areas surrounding important archaeological sites had been cleared of the shrub layer, and much of the periphery bordered on either abandoned or active cultivation. Cattle grazing occurred in parts of the study site. All species of Ceylon primates occurred there as did most of the native smaller mammals. Only elephants, *Elephas maximus;* sambar deer, *Cervus uni-*

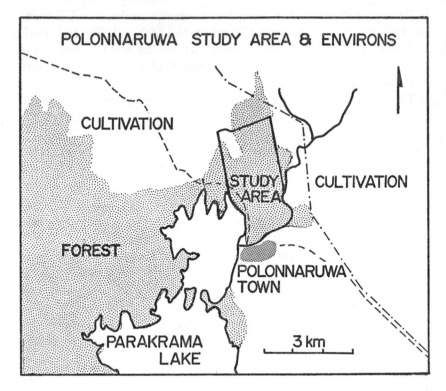

Map 2.   The Polonnaruwa Study Area. The irrigation channel (solid line) delimits the southern portion of the study area. The main road and the railway are marked by dashed and dashed and dotted lines respectively

color; wild boar, *Sus scrofa;* bear, *Melursus ursinus;* and leopard, *Panthera pardus;* were absent.

The study site encompassed approximately six square kilometers. Here eighteen troops representing 446 animals were censused. An additional 198 animals from Anuradhapura are considered in this report.

METHODS AND MATERIALS

Observations were made with the aid of Leitz Trinovid 7 x 42 binoculars. Data were initially recorded with a Philips Norelco portable cassette tape recorder, but, owing to its unreliable performance in the field, all data were eventually written by hand. Data were taken in as complete a form as possible in the field itself, thereby precluding supplementary notes after field hours.

Upon arrival in Polonnaruwa, I began to memorize the individual characteristics of animals from many different troops. This was a never-ending process, but by the end of the study, I could readily identify approximately 175 animals, which permitted the maintenance of many long-term individual records. Some individuals from the main study troops could be approached to within two meters or less; animals from less habituated troops usually maintained a ten- to thirty-meter distance from the observer.

In censusing, a troop was followed until all members of a troop had been noted. With a particularly shy or large troop this occasionally involved several days of contact. Individual characteristics of each animal were recorded to reduce the chance of recounts. The best method was to concentrate on each age and sex class separately, making sure that all individuals were accounted for. The final counts are the result of many double checks. Depending on the troop, censusing was conducted by either one observer or myself plus an assistant. For very shy troops, we occasionally used cooked rice to lure animals into the open for better observation.

Age Classification

For all infants of known date of birth, a record of morphological changes with age for the first year was maintained, including the color and distribution of fur, development of head hair, and degree of pigmentation of skin, especially the ears and dorsum of the hands and feet. Rather than ascribing "infant 1" or "infant 2" categories to infants, estimated ages were recorded. For purposes of these data, "infants 1" are those less than six months old, "infants 2" are six months to one year old.

The ages of juveniles were estimated less accurately, but, since toque monkeys have a narrow birth peak from December to February (Dittus, unpublished data), the one- and two-year-olds especially could be distinguished by size differences. As I followed the development of several juveniles for three years or more, it became evident that growth rates were much less than originally anticipated; therefore, the following juvenile classes were established: juveniles 1, aged one to two years; juveniles 2, aged two to three and one-half years; and juveniles 3, aged three and one-half to five years. The ages of juveniles were estimated by comparison with those of known ages.

Young females were considered adult with the first pregnancy at four and one-half to five years old. Males, on the other hand, were not fully

adult until seven, possibly eight, years of age, as judged by their morphological maturation. Subadult males from five to seven years of age had
the size of an adult female, but were smaller and morphologically less
developed than an adult male.

Adults were classified according to five broad categories: young, young
to middle aged, middle aged, old and senile. A host of subtle morphological changes, similar to those criteria one might use in subjectively
assessing the ages of humans, formed the basis of this classification.

With increasing age the following changes occured: erosion and tar-
tarization of the teeth, wrinkling of the facial skin, loosening of folds of
body skin especially near the eyelids, lips, and cheek pouches. The degree of facial pigmentation often intensified with age, and facial hair became more prominent. In addition, the pelage of old or senile individuals
was frequently dull, and some hair loss occurred especially on the tail.
Senile males were also very lethargic, and like senile females commonly
exhibited signs of illness. The numerical age ranges attributed to adult
age classes were arbitrarily determined by dividing the number of adult
years by the number of adult age classes.

RESULTS

Longevity

Captive records indicate that macaques may live up to thirty years or
more (Jones 1962; Dathe 1971). Some individuals in the field appeared
and behaved as though extremely old and I would challenge the assumption that free-ranging primates do not approach the longevity of captive
specimens. I have assumed that thirty years is the approximate maximum
longevity, but for isolated cases this may still be a slight underestimation.

Fertility

Fertility (m_x) refers to the number of offspring born to a female per unit
time. Although it is customary to express fertility or natality on the basis
of the entire female cohort, I have given estimates based on only the
adult or reproductively mature females. Tables 1 and 2 give estimates of
fertility over several seasons for Polonnaruwa and Anuradhapura respectively. The maximum estimates include females judged to be preg-

Table 1.   Estimates of fertility (m_x) for Polonnaruwa (N = 154 births)

| Year | Number of adult ♀♀ | Fertility | |
		Maximum	Minimum
68–69	27	.741	.704
69–70	43	.721	.698
70–71	76	.724	.697
71–72	78	.634	.590

Average = .688 infants/adult ♀/year.
Average = .411 infants/♀ of any age/year

Table 2.   Estimates of fertility (m_x) for Anuradhapura (N = 38 births)

| Year | Number of adult ♀♀ | Fertility | |
		Maximum	Minimum
69–70	31	.593	.323
70–71	36	.700	.417

Average = .508 infants/adult ♀/year.
Average = .269 infants/♀ of any age/year

nant at the time troops were sampled for newborn infants, whereas the minimum estimates preclude them.

A test for the significance of differences between two independent proportions utilizing a deviate of the unit normal curve (z) (Ferguson 1966) indicated that there was no significant difference (z = 1.36, p = 0.158) between the highest (m_x = 0.741) and lowest (m_x = 0.590) fertility estimates in Polonnaruwa for the four seasons sampled. Therefore, the mean value of 0.688 infants/adult female/year is taken as representative and was used in further calculations. The mean fertility value in Anuradhapura (m_x = 0.508) was significantly less than that of Polonnaruwa (z = 2.906, p = 0.006). However, this difference might be attributable to sampling error, since I censused for only one week at the end of the three to four month birth-season in Anuradhapura, and many infants born earlier might have died prior to the sampling period. Moreover, there was no significant difference (z = 0.841, p = 0.280) between the average maximum fertility estimates for Polonnaruwa (m_x = 0.705) and Anuradhapura (m_x = 0.647).

In the Polonnaruwa and Anuradhapura populations, there was no correlation between the fertility of females and the size of the troop (N = 26 troops). In the Polonnaruwa population, where more detailed records were maintained, there were differences in the fertility of females of different ages (Table 3), the senile females being significantly lower

Table 3.   Age specific fertility rates (m_x)*

Age class	Age in years	Number of adult ♀♀	Number of infants	Number of adult ♀ seasons	Average number of infants born/ adult ♀/year
Young	5–10	10	19	27	.704
Young- middle age	10–15	9	21	29	.724
Middle age	15–20	6	13	16	.813
Old	20–25	8	23	26	.885
Senile	25–30	5	4	14	.286

*   Adult females were sorted according to 5 age groups each being approximately 5 years in duration. The number of seasons of observation differed between females. An adult-female-season refers to one year of observation of one adult female. Fertility per age group is the sum of infants born to females of the given age group divided by the total of adult female seasons for that age group.

($m_x = 0.286$) than the average ($z = 1.36$; $p = 0.158$). This low fertility results from the incorporation of post-reproductives into the estimates, menopause being defined as two or more successive years without a birth. Approximately 10 percent of the adult female cohort (or 3 percent of the total population) consisted of senile females of which 60 percent were past menopause. Fertility seems to increase with age and remains high right up to menopause. Thereafter the probability of death for a female is extreme; the longest duration of life for a post-reproductive female was three years.

Sex Ratio at Birth

Over four seasons in Polonnaruwa and Anuradhapura, 165 newborn infants were recorded: seventy-six males, sixty-six females, plus twenty-

Table 4.   Sex ratio at birth

	Year	Number of infants Males	Females
Polonnaruwa:	1968–1969	2	0
	1969–1970	4	7
	1970–1971	21	14
	1971–1972	22	26
Anuradhapura:	1970–1971	8	7
	Total	57	54

Ratio ♀:♂ = 1.056.

three for which the sex could not be determined. More females than males are undoubtedly included in the undetermined category since the vulva of a female infant was much more difficult to positively identify than was the penis of a male under field conditions.

The data in Table 4 represents the total number of infants of each sex from several troops in four birth seasons. To cancel observational bias, only those counts where the sex of all the infants in the troop had been positively established are considered, thus data from troops where the sex of one or more infants was not determined are not included. The ratio of females to males was 1.056, which does not differ significantly from 1.000 ($z = 0.209, p = 0.390$).

Life Table

It is convenient to summarize life and death processes of a population by means of a life table (Deevey 1947: 283–314). This requires a knowledge of the number of animals of different ages that are alive at a given point in time. The life table information presented here is based upon a thorough survey of all troops in the Polonnaruwa study population conducted in October 1971.

It is common to express the number of individuals alive at any age as a fraction of the total number alive. Such fractions are usually put on a "per thousand" basis. That is, one assumes that the data are based on a

Table 5.   The number of immature *M. sinica* of different age and sex classes*

	Age class	Age (years)	Males Number observed	Males $l_x/1,000$	Females Number observed	Females $l_x/1,000$
Values per	Infant-1	0–½	38	1,000	38	1,000
half year	Infant-2	½–1	30	789	21	553
Average	Infant	0–1	68	1,000	59	1,000
values	Juvenile-1	1–2	23	605	18	474
per	Juvenile-2	2–3½	30 ⎫	526	18 ⎫	316
annum	Juvenile-3	3½–5	30 ⎭		18 ⎭	
	Subadult ♂	5–7	23	303	—	—
	Adult ♂	7–30	48 (see Table 6)		—	—
	Adult ♀	5–30	—	—	111 (see Table 6)	
Total			222		224	

*   The conversion to l_x per 1,000 of the observed number of infants and juveniles of different ages and sex, as determined from eighteen troops (N = 446) in Polonnaruwa.

cohort of 1,000 animals that theoretically began life together and ran the gamut of death risks together (Quick 1963: 190–228). "l_x" is defined as the number of individuals alive at time or age "x", and "d_x" as its converse, the number of individuals dead at age "x." The rate of mortality "q_x" refers to the proportion of animals dying that enter a particular age class. It assumes that each age class begins with a cohort of 1,000 individuals. The mean expectation of life is expressed by the symbol "e_x" and refers to the average length of life of a population or cohort, and the average length of life remaining for those individuals that have reached a given age class.

Tables 5 and 6 present the observed data separately for the sexes and its conversion to $l_x/1,000$. The age and sex classification of juveniles and infants was ascertained for all eighteen troops (Table 5). However, the breakdown of adults into different age classes was ascertained with confidence for males in fourteen of the eighteen troops, and for females in eleven of the eighteen troops (Table 6). Comparison of the proportions of adults of each sex to the total number of animals in the respective

Table 6.   The number of adult *M. sinica* of different age and sex classes*

Age class	Age (years)	Males Number observed	$l_x/1,000$ per annum	Females Number observed	$l_x/1,000$ per annum
Young ♂	7–10	10	104	—	—
Young ♀	5–10	—	—	21	152
Young to middle age	10–15	13	81	19	138
Middle age	15–20	11	69	17	123
Old	20–25	5	31	15	109
Senile	25–30	1	6	8	58
Total		40		80	

*   The conversion of l_x per 1,000 of the observed number of adults of different ages and sex, as determined from fourteen troops for the males and from eleven troops for the females in Polonnaruwa.

troop totals indicates less than a four percent difference for females and less than 1 percent for males; therefore, the proportions of adults of different ages from Table 6 were extrapolated to all eighteen troops for further derivation of vital statistics (Table 7).

The peak of the birth season is December to February, thus, by the time of the October census, all surviving infants had attained the infant 2 class. To maintain a logical integrity or unity of the population cohort, the few infants 1 born during or just prior to October were not included

Table 7.   Life table for a population of 446 *M. s. sinica* in Polonnaruwa

Age class		Age (years) l_x	Males			Females			
			d_x	q_x	e_x l_x	d_x	q_x	e_x	
Values per	Infant-1	0–½ 1,000	211	211	5.3 1,000	447	447	5.4	
half year	Infant-2	½–1 789	184	233	5.6 553	79	143	8.3	
	Infant	0–1 1,000	395	395	4.5 1,000	526	526	4.8	
	Juvenile-1	1–2 605	79	131	6.2 474	158	333	8.6	
	Juvenile-2	2–3½ ⎫							
		⎬ 526	74	141	5.0 316	55	174	10.7	
	Juvenile-3	3½–5 ⎭							
Average	Subadult ♂	5–7 303	99.5	328	5.1 —	—	—	—	
values	Young adult ♂	7–10 104	7.7	74	10.5 —	—	—	—	
per	Young adult ♀	5–10 —	—	—	— 152	2.8	18	16.6	
annum	Young to								
	middle age	10–15 81	2.4	30	9.0 138	3.0	22	13.0	
	Middle age	15–20 69	7.6	110	5.2 123	2.8	23	9.3	
	Old	20–25 31	5.0	161	3.5 109	10.2	94	5.2	
	Senile	25–30 6	1.2	200	2.5 58	11.6	200	2.5	

*   Age categories are variable in length according to recognizable classes. Statistics, however, were calculated according to the constant interval of one year, and then averaged per age class.

in the census. Numbers of "infant 1" (thirty-eight infants of each sex) were determined by multiplying the number of adult females in the census (111) by the average fertility rate (0.688) infants/adult female/year. This is equivalent to determining the number of newborn infants recruited into the censused troops during the birth season preceding October.

Because of the high death rates in infants, the first year data are divided into two six-month intervals. For consistency with the rest of the life table, the same data are given again on a yearly basis. In both sexes the observed frequencies for the juvenile 2 and 3 classes were the same; this is probably due to sampling error, that is, some of the smaller juveniles 3 should have been classed as juveniles 2. Thus, one value has been used to represent both classes in Table 7. To calculate l_x and d_x values as per age class, one need only multiply the given yearly averages by the number of years accorded the age class. Note that the average q_x and e_x values for senile animals is 200 and 2.5 respectively, when in fact for the twenty-ninth to thirtieth year these values are as expected: $q_x = 1,000$ and $e_x = 0.5$. The mean life expectancy of the entire cohort is based on the yearly average for the infant class, and for males is 4.5 years, and females 4.8 years.

Figure 1 graphically summarizes the life and death characteristics of males and females at different ages. In both sexes, notice the loss of young animals and the dramatic stabilization, or increase in the proba-

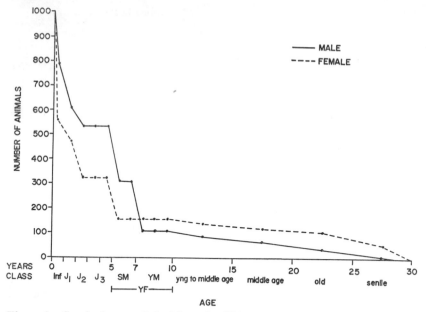

Figure 1.   Survival curve. Subadult males (SM) are 5 to 7 years old, young adult males (YM) are 7 to 10 years old, and young adult females (YF) are 5 to 10 years old. "Inf," "J," and "Yng" are infant, juvenile, and young, respectively

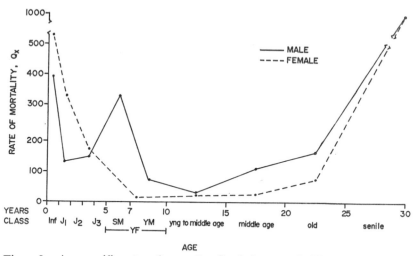

Figure 2.   Age-specific rates of mortality. Symbols are as in Figure 1

bility of survival with the attainment of adulthood, which for females is approximately two years earlier than for males. Mortality in infant and juvenile females is higher than in like-aged males, but drops below male mortality as females become adult. Male mortality rates peak during the

Table 8. Approximate life table of a population of 194 *M. s sinica* from Anuradhapura

Age class	Age (years)	Number observed	Males l_x	d_x	q_x	Number observed	Females l_x	d_x	q_x
Infant	0–1	17	1,000	471	471	22	1,000	364	364
Juvenile-1	1–2	9	529	98	185	14	636	395	621
Juvenile-2 and 3	2–5	22	431	55	128	16	241	43	180
Subadult ♂	5–7	9	265	102	384	—	—	—	—
Adult ♂	7–30	24	61	2.7	44	—	—	—	—
Adult ♀	5–30	—	—	—	—	61	111	4.4	40

subadult stage at approximately five to seven years of age and level off again with the attainment of adulthood, but remain higher than the female rates throughout adult life. Senile females are more numerous than senile males, therefore, females are slightly longer lived than are males, as already suggested by the estimates of e_x for the respective cohorts. Figure 2 clearly illustrates the difference in the rates of mortality (q_x) at different ages between the sexes.

A similar census was taken in Anuradhapura. Complete counts were obtained on two troops in March 1970, and five troops in March 1971. An incomplete count of a very large troop of at least fifty-one animals is also included. Two or three troops had the birth peak in the fall, whereas the rest peaked in the spring (Dittus, unpublished data); in one troop there were no infants of one year or less at the time of the census. Further, it was not possible to classify all adults into different age groups. As a result, the life table (Table 8) for Anuradhapura is incomplete and ought to be considered only as a rough approximation.

In general, the Anuradhapura data resemble those of Polonnaruwa, indicating a high rate of mortality during infancy which then decreases to a minimum toward adulthood. There is a slight peak of mortality in the subadult male stage, and a slightly higher rate of mortality in adult males than in adult females.

The rates of mortality between the sexes in the infant stage seemed to differ; in Anuradhapura, infant males suffered a greater mortality than did females during their first year. In the yearling stage, however, female mortality far surpassed that of males and, as in Polonnaruwa, remained somewhat higher in females until approximately five years.

Comparing rates of mortality for the first two years of life, q_x in Polonnaruwa is 474 for males and 684 for females, whereas in Anuradhapura

Table 9.   A comparison of proportions of age classes in adults between the populations of Anuradhapura and Polonnaruwa

		Percent			
	Total N	Young and young to middle age	Middle age	Old	Senile
Adult males:					
Anuradhapura	17	53–59	35–41	6	0
Polonnaruwa	40	57	38	12	3
Adult females:					
Anuradhapura	28	61	21–29	4–11	7
Polonnaruwa	80	50	21	19	10

q_x is somewhat higher for both sexes: 569 for males and 759 for females.

Although data on the frequencies of different age classes in adults were insufficient to incorporate into the life table, some indication of the age structure can be gained from the limited sample that was taken. Table 9 compares the percentages of adults of different age classes in Anuradhapura with those of Polonnaruwa. The age classes "young" and "young to middle age" are combined.

Again the age structure of adults in Anuradhapura closely approximates that of Polonnaruwa. However, there was a lower proportion of old and senile animals in Anuradhapura. Assuming a long-term constancy of fertility rates, this might reflect a greater rate of mortality in old age in this population.

Mortality

An important question concerns the causation of the observed mortalities. Death is rarely observed, but instead may or may not be inferred by assessing the circumstances surrounding an individual's disappearance. Although predation is a major factor in mortality, its effects are not random; social and ecological factors potentiate mortality differently among the age and sex classes. This is a complex situation and will be dealt with in detail in future publications.

All five observations of death through predation involved dogs. Dogs are the main predators not only of the macaques, but also of the grey langurs, *P. entellus*, as is evident from the numerous attempts by dogs to catch both species, and by these monkeys' intense alarm responses to dogs. The sight of a jackal, *Canis aureus*, also produced alarm and avoidance, even though jackals appeared to show no great interest in the macaques. Of the cats, only the fishing cat, *Felis viverrina,* and the jungle cat, *Felis chaus,* were of sufficient size to be dangerous to the macaques, but there is no information regarding their interaction with macaques. Leopards were absent from the study site.

The response to the python, *Python molurus pimbura,* and the poisonous snakes, cobra, *Naja n. naja,* and Russell's viper, *Vipera russelli pilchella,* was one of alarm, avoidance, and curiosity (nomenclature according to Deraniyagala 1955: 1–121). Nonpoisonous snakes did not elicit these responses.

Alarm and avoidance reactions were elicited by the low flight of most large eagles or hawks, particularly the sea eagle, *Haliaectus leucogaster;* serpent eagle, *Spilornis cheela spilogaster;* tank eagle, *Ichthyophaga ichthyaetus plumeiceps;* hawk eagle, *Spitzaetus cirrhatus ceylonensis;* Brahminy kite, *Haliastur indus indus;* the fish owl, *Ketupa zeylonensis zeylonensis;* and the forest eagle-owl, *Bubo nipalensis blighi* (nomenclature according to Henry 1971). These birds probably prey only on the younger animals and, indeed, these give the most intense responses to raptors. A forest eagle-owl was observed carrying away a captive infant purple-faced langur, *P. senex,* that had been sleeping by itself. Men occasionally harassed the monkeys, but, with one possible exception, did not kill them in the study area.

Migrations

With the exception of one equivocal observation, females were never observed to migrate. In males, migration was confirmed in adults, subadults, and older juveniles 3, but rarely in younger juveniles, and never in infants.

Migrations were of two kinds: (1) Temporary excursions from the troop lasting from a fraction of a day to several days while attempting to consort with estrous females of other troops. These males always returned to the home troop, and, during long absences, visited for short intervals. (2) Occasionally, some males did not return, but became permanent members of another troop. The data presented here refer only to permanent migrations.

Solitary males, in the sense that they were completely independent of a troop, were never found. Whenever single males were encountered and followed, they returned to a troop within a few hours at most. One all-male subgroup was peripheral to the largest troop in the study area (forty-three members including the subgroup). Its composition varied, especially in the membership of its younger juveniles, but, essentially it consisted of two adult males, one subadult, and six to seven juveniles. The youngest juveniles, three juveniles 2 and one juvenile 1, were born in the main troop and were non-permanent members of the peripheral subgroup. One juvenile 2 from a neighboring troop was also a temporary resident.

Records concerning migrations were maintained on twenty-six subadult and juvenile 3 males (Table 10), and twenty-seven adult males (Table 11).

Table 10.   Histories of twenty-six adolescent males, with reference to their migrations

7	Known to have migrated permanently. Later three of these disappeared.
1*	Emigrated temporarily and subsequently disappeared.
4*	Became permanent members of an all-male subgroup peripheral to their maternal troop. Later two of these disappeared.
4	Remained resident members of the same troop for the duration of the period of observation. All of these were relatively young.
10	Disappeared under unknown circumstances.

* See text.

Table 11.   Histories of twenty-seven adult males, with reference to their migrations

10	Remained resident members of the same troop throughout the period of observation.
8	Are known to have migrated.
9	Disappeared under equivocal circumstances.

For the subadult and juvenile 3 males, referred to as adolescent males, an exact estimate of the rates of migration from the data in Table 10 is not possible, but the range might be indicated. The number of days adolescent males were under observation varied between individuals, but totalled 8831 adolescent-male-days of observation. The acquisition of permanent membership in a new troop was ascertained for seven adolescent males (Table 10). With a minimum of seven migrations in 8831 adolescent-male-days, we obtained 0.00079 migrations per adolescent-male-day, or, each adolescent male migrated once on the average of every 3.47 years. In Table 10 I have marked with an asterisk five males whose migratory status is equivocal; if these might be considered as true migrants, then with a total of twelve migrations the rate of migration would be once every 2.01 years.

Ten adolescent males disappeared without trace, and an additional six disappeared subsequent to one migration, or from the all-male subgroup.

The eventual fate of death is probable for most of these sixteen males; a supposition based first on the high probability of death in this age group ($q_{4-7} = 722$), and second on the fact that the Polonnaruwa study site is almost a closed "island" bounded by water and cultivation (Map 2), making it unlikely that any but the exceptional male could succesfully emigrate from the study area.

Since death and migration are not mutually exclusive, migration, or an attempt at migration, possibly to the northernmost parts of the study area which were not intensively investigated, should not be ruled out for at least a few of the sixteen males with unknown final destinies. Clearly, the actual rate of migration is above the minimum indicated.

Of the eight adult male migrants in Table 11, six migrated once, two migrated twice, giving a total of ten migrations; five animals immigrated from unknown origins, and five migrated between known troops.

Of the nine that disappeared four were very old and probably died of senility and illness, three of these were obviously becoming progressively weaker through physical impairment. A fifth animal was captured and probably killed by a cultivator.

The disappearance of three males coincided with the establishment of new dominant males, which in two cases were immigrants. One of the disappearing males was multiply wounded during battles for dominance. The circumstances suggest that these three males were evicted from their troops; their fate may or may not have been death. The troop of the ninth male habitually "stole" from a rice mill; he may have been killed.

These data indicate a minimum of ten and a maximum of fourteen migrations if the possibility of emigration is admitted for the last four males with unknown fates.

For adult males the total number of adult-male-days of observation was 21,436. A minimum of ten migrations yields a rate of 0.00047 migrations per adult-male-day, or, each adult male migrated on the average of once every 5.83 years. The maximum of fourteen migrations gives a rate of 0.00065 migrations per adult-male-day, or, each adult male migrated once every 4.21 years. A male that lives to a ripe old age would be expected to change troop membership on the average of five to six times in his lifetime.

All ten emigrations were known to have been by subordinate males who had recently dropped in the dominance hierarchy. Eight of the immigrants were known to have been attracted to the troop by estrous females. The ensuing competition with resident males caused a hierarchical reorganization with subsequent emigration by the resident losers in two cases.

Net Reproductive Rate, R_0

It is of interest to know whether a population of animals is increasing its numbers ($R_0 > 1$), decreasing ($R_0 < 1$), or at equilibrium ($R_0 = 1$). The net reproductive rate, or recruitment rate, is commonly defined as the average number of female infants produced by a female in her lifetime. There are several ways of estimating R_0 from my data.

First, how many female infants born per breeding female live to breeding age? The mean life expectancy of a female having reached breeding age is 16.58 years (Table 7). With a sex ratio at birth of 1 : 1 (Table 4), the birth rate for infant females is $\frac{1}{2} \times 0.688$ per adult female per year. Therefore, the average number of female infants born per adult female in a lifetime is $16.58 \times \frac{1}{2} \times 0.688 = 5.70$. The probability of an infant female dying prior to reaching breeding age is the sum of the d_x values up to four and one-half years of age, or 822 per 1000 (Table 7). That is, of 5.70 female infants born, 82.2 percent die, or 4.69. R_0, the number of infant females born per adult female that live to breeding age is 5.70 minus 4.69 = 1.01.

Employing the usual formula for R_0, the sum of the products $l_x m_x$ for each age class "x," then $R_0 = 0.9976$.

A third estimate of the recruitment rate, also called replacement rate, comes from directly observing the number of juvenile females that begin breeding and subtracting the number of adult females that cease breeding. Records were maintained on fifty-three adult females (from eight troops) resulting in 48,104 female-days of observation over three and one-half years.

During this time, nine juvenile females had their first birth, giving 0.069 female recruits per female year. Four adult females died, three senile females reached menopause, and one pathological female with a malformed pelvis, crippled hind leg, injured jaw, and a generally weak condition was never noted to give birth. Another female missing her left arm gave birth three times but her infants died at an early age suggesting that she was not fully competent in maternal care. She had noticeable difficulty in lending arm support to her infant during arboreal travel.

This amounts to eight, possibly nine, females, or a rate of 0.062 to 0.069 females being lost to the breeding population per adult female year, which nearly or exactly cancels those entering the breeding state (0.069 per female year). Although this estimate might incorporate elements of chance or interpetation, it does reiterate that the net reproductive rate, R_0, for the Polonnaruwa study population is at or very near equilibrium.

The Number and Biomass of Macaques per Unit Area

The home ranges of fifteen troops were ascertained on the basis of a minimum of 100 hours, and a maximum of several thousand hours of observation per troop. The home ranges of these troops were continuous with one another, and those of immediately adjacent troops overlapped considerably. Together they formed what might be considered a small deme that was surrounded mostly by water and cultivation. The home ranges of three troops, however, overlapped only partially with troops considered in this estimate. To adjust for this, only that fraction of the number of animals in the three troops that was proportional to the amount of home range overlap with the rest of the deme was incorporated in the density estimate, which is: 295 individuals inhabiting 296 hectares, or one individual per hectare.

To obtain biomass estimates, animals were weighed in the field, using a spring weighing scale suspended from a tree support. Animals were enticed to sit in a pan which contained known amounts of food. Because of the persistent domination of the food pan by high ranking animals and the apprehension some animals had of the apparatus, it usually took a day or more to weigh ten animals. Table 12 summarizes the weights of animals of different age and sex.

Table 12.   Weights of macaques of different age and sex

Age class	Average weight (kilogram)	Number of animals weighed (N = 76)
Infant-1 (18 days old)	0.44*	1
Infant-2 (0.6 yrs. old)	0.91	1
Juvenile-1	1.35	5
Juvenile-2	2.00	9
Juvenile-3	3.00	11
Subadult ♂	4.10	9
Adult ♂	5.72	16
Adult ♀	3.59	24

*   This estimate is based on the weight of a male infant, *Macaca nemestrina*, at the age of 18 days, born in the National Zoological Park, Washington, D.C.

To calculate the biomass of the study population, weight differences with age and sex were taken into account (Table 13). Further adjustment was made in accordance with the proportion of the three bordering troops that shared only part of their home range with the other twelve troops. These calculations yield 869 kilograms of macaque inhabiting 296 hectares, or three kilograms per hectare. Considering that part of an ani-

Table 13. Total weights of animals wholly and partially inhabiting 296 hectares

	AF	AM	SM	J_3	J_2	J_1	I	Adjustment for partial residency	Total weight (kilogram)
Troops 1–12									
Number of animals	73	31	18	36	28	31	37		
Weight-kilogram	262	177	74	108	56	42	37	none	756
Troop Oval									
Number of animals	8	4	1	2	3	2	3		
Weight-kilogram	29	23	4	6	8	3	3	76 kg × 0.8	61
Troop Bout									
Number of animals	8	3	1	3	6	4	3		
Weight-kilogram	29	17	4	9	12	5	3	79 kg × 0.5	40
Troop G									
Number of animals	4	1	1	2	3	2	0		
Weight-kilogram	14	6	4	6	6	3	0	39 kg × 0.3	12
Total weight									869

AF = adult female, AM = adult male, SM = subadult male, J = juvenile, I = infant.

mal's weight represents dead contents of the alimentary tract, the estimate might be over by a very small fraction.

DISCUSSION

The population of toque macaques in Polonnaruwa is the first example of a primate population, to my knowledge, where the net reproductive rate, R_o, has been found to be near equilibrium. Information from two other populations for which extensive data are available, the Takasakiyama colony of Japanese macaques, *M. fuscata* (Itani et al. 1963: 1–42; Carpenter and Nishimura 1969: 16–30), and the Cayo Santiago colony of rhesus, *M. mulatta* (Koford 1965: 160–174), indicates that both of these colonies, which are artificially provisioned with food, have increased their numbers three and one-half times over ten years and seven fold over twelve years respectively.

For the sake of comparison with *M. sinica,* I have taken the data on *M. mulatta* from Koford (1965: 160–174) and that on *M. fuscata* from Itani et al. (1963: 1–42) and Carpenter and Nishimura (1969: 16–30) and have calculated the proportion dying at different ages, d_x per 1,000, separately for the male and female cohorts. Because of inter-observer differences, fine distinctions between ages were not possible, and the values given here are approximations within broad age categories. The main point of interest is that the rates of mortality for infants and juveniles in both of the provisioned colonies were less than those for the wild population of *M. sinica*. The value of $d_x/1,000$ for males between birth and seven years old was 825 for *M. mulatta*, 765 for *M. fuscata*, and 895 for *M. sinica*. Similarly for females between birth and the end of the fourth year of life, mortality was 737 in *M. mulatta*, 680 for *M. fuscata*, and 849 for *M. sinica*.

The discrepancy is greatest between females, that is, more females reach breeding age in the provisioned colonies than in the wild population of toque macaques. This is reflected directly in the proportions of immatures to adults in these populations. Immature females account for 57.4 percent of the female cohort in *M. fuscata*, but only 45.5 percent in *M. sinica*, whereas immature males account for 79.9 percent of the male cohort in *M. fuscata* and 75.2 percent in *M. sinica*. I was not able to extract equivalent information from Koford's data. In a population that is increasing its numbers a greater proportion of immatures to adults would be expected.

An examination of the rates of fertility shows that *M. sinica*, a population at equilibrium, has the lowest value, $m_x = 0.688$ infants per female per year, when compared with the growing populations of *M. fuscata*, $m_x = 0.723$ infants per female per year (calculated from the data of Itani et al. 1963), and $m_x = 0.850$ infants per female per year in the rhesus of Cayo Santiago (Koford 1965: 160–174).

These data suggest that the equilibrium in the population of *M. sinica* in Polonnaruwa is achieved through lowered fertility and increased mortality in the infant and juvenile classes, especially in females.

Figure 2 illustrates that in Polonnaruwa mortality in males reaches a peak (neglecting infants and senile males) at six years of age. This coincides with a peak of migration rates, between four and seven years old approximately. Migrations occur almost exclusively in the breeding season, when competition between males for estrous females is greatest and when wounding from intra-specific fighting is most common. As mentioned, emigrating adult males are those that have recently attained low status. Unless an immigrating adult establishes himself as a dominant in the host troop, he, with the adolescent immigrants, is relegated to a spatially peripheral position and low status access to resources (Dittus, unpublished data. Of the six instances where the physical condition of peripheral immigrants was known before and after migration, all were conspicuously thinner as well as being wounded (three had large or many wounds) following migration. Although death through wounding or starvation was never directly observed, the evidence strongly suggests a causal relationship between the rigors of migration and mortality.

The pattern of mortality in males of *M. sinica, M. mulatta,* and *M. fuscata* appears to be similar. Mortality begins to surpass that of females between the fourth and fifth year, and reaches a peak at six years in *M. sinica* and *M. mulatta* and then attenuates with the advent of adulthood. In *M. fuscata* a similar peak is attained but at a slightly older age, eight to nine years and drops to a low only at about fifteen years old. As in *M. sinica,* these peaks of mortality coincide approximately with a peak in migration rates in *M. mulatta* and *M. fuscata.* Koford's data (1965: 160–174; 1966: 1–7) indicate that for the rhesus of Cayo Santiago in the years 1960 to 1963 the peak age at migration was six to seven years old in males, yet the rate for three to five year olds was also quite high, and Boelkins' and Wilson's (1972) data, which were collected from the same colony between 1965 and 1967, indicate the peak to be in the three to five year range. Ages of "solitarization" in *M. fuscata* of the Koshima and Ohirayama troops occur between the sixth and the twelfth year of life (Kawai and Yoshiba 1968), which correlates closely with the peak of death in males of this species in Takasakiyama. Any significance to this coincidence assumes, of course, that the peaks of mortality and migration occur at the same age between these Japanese colonies. In the rhesus of Cayo Santiago, an increase in wounding and mortality from fighting during the breeding season has been established by Vandenbergh and Vessey (1968: 71–79) and Wilson and Boelkins (1970: 719–724) respectively, although no direct link between mortality and migration has been established.

In Polonnaruwa every older juvenile 3 or subadult male migrates once in two to three and one-half years or less. This means in effect, that all males leave their maternal troops during adolescence. Further, although the rate of migration for adult males is less than for the adolescent males, the data strongly indicate that adult males do not remain with the same troop throughout their lives. Unless one postulates the return of males to their maternal troops when adult, emigration by itself would seem to provide an effective barrier to sibling or mother-son matings, or at least render such matings extremely unlikely.

If the rates of migration in *M. sinica* hold for other congenerics, then the contradictions between the reports of Sade (1968: 18–38; 1972: 378–398) and Missakian (1973b: 621–624) regarding factors preventing or inducing inbreeding are understandable since migration for rhesus on the sixteen hectare islet of Cayo Santiago is extremely limited. Patterns atypical of the wild situation may emerge as a consequence. The value of long term studies of a species in its natural habitat is underscored.

The density of *M. sinica* in the Polonnaruwa habitat was one macaque per hectare. No estimate of density for *M. fuscata* at Takasakiyama is given, but, from a scale and map provided by Mizuhara (1963), the combined home ranges of the troops in 1952 is approximately 1.75 square kilometers, which with 220 animals at the onset of provisioning (Itani et al. 1963: 1–42) converts to 1.3 macaques per hectare. The density of rhesus in their natural habitats in India ranges from 0.2 to 0.5 macaques per hectare in forests, and up to 8.8 per hectare in towns (after Neville 1968: 111–123; Southwick 1961: 698–710). Clearly, the densities of these species in their natural habitats are of the same order of magnitude. The high density of 8.8 rhesus per hectare in a town, Neville (1968) attributes to the nature of the food sources. Artificial provisioning of food has "exploded" the Takasakiyama colony to 4.5 per hectare by 1962 and especially the rhesus of Cayo Santiago to twenty-five per hectare by 1962 (after Koford 1965: 160–174) and forty-four per hectare by 1968 (after Missakian's 1973b report of 700 rhesus by 1968). Taking the average weight of a rhesus macaque to be 7.9 kilograms (after Napier and Napier 1967), the carrying capacity of Cayo Santiago is over 110 times greater than that of Polonnaruwa. Hence, a tolerance for densities far above those found in the wild is indicated at least in the rhesus, in the presence of a superabundance of food. Interestingly, Boelkins and Wilson (1972: 125–140) noted a decline of fertility and an increase in adult male mortality at the extreme densities between 1964 and 1967. A high tolerance for the proximity of individuals seems almost self-evident in a group-living species. Within the range of densities found in forest habitats, it is unlikely, therefore, that density *per se* is a factor limiting population growth.

The Polonnaruwa area is subject to a dry and wet season annually. Hladik and Hladik (1972: 149–215) have profiled the corresponding seasonal availability of various woody plant foods for the three large primates in Polonnaruwa, and Rudran (1973: 41–60) with similar information has related this to the seasons of birth and mating in *P. senex.*

Refuges and sleeping trees are always abundant for *M. sinica,* but a season of food scarcity is prevalent (Dittus, unpublished data). At this time animals spend almost all their daylight hours in search for food, which is generally of low nutritional value (Dittus, unpublished data). The animals of several troops in sub-optimum habitat are of lesser weight and generally exhibit a poorer physical condition than normal (Dittus, unpublished data). These facts, together with a low density of less than 0.3 macaques per square kilometer in the arid zone forest of the Wilpattu National Park (Eisenberg et al. 1972: 863–874) suggest that the availability of food, at least in part, determines the carrying capacity of the forest and the level of equilibrium of the population. The two folivorous species of langur, *P. entellus* and *P. senex*, both maintain densities far greater than the frugivorous-omnivorous macaque with whom they share the Polonnaruwa habitat (Eisenberg et al. 1972: 863–874).

Compared to Polonnaruwa, the habitat in Anuradhapura was generally much less benign. The shrub layer has been cleared almost completely in most areas and the density of trees was less, thereby depriving animals of refuges and sources of food. This unfavorable situation also brought them into closer conflict with garden owners and dogs. Animals in the two largest troops (fifty-one and thirty-three members) were noticeably undernourished, and most troops had one or more individuals with signs of human harassment including cut tails, broken bones, missing hands (amputated as "punishment" for thievery) or wire collars. In light of this, it may be significant, that the most vulnerable age classes, the very young and the old, constituted a lesser proportion in the Anuradhapura population than in Polonnaruwa. That is, increased harshness of the environment and predation had the effect of accentuating the peaks of the age-specific rates of mortality very early and late in life and left unaffected the overall pattern of mortality. This conclusion asumes that rates of fertility in Anuradhapura had been more or less constant over several generations.

SUMMARY AND CONCLUSIONS

In the population of toque macaques in Polonnaruwa, mortality rates differed with respect to age and sex, and the highest probability of survival was found in animals as they attained effective breeding age. For young adult females the probable average number of years of life remaining (e_x) was 16.6, and for young adult males it was 10.5 years. Prior to these ages the risk of death for both sexes was extreme. In females nearly 85 percent ($d_{0-5} = 849$) of all deaths occurred prior to adulthood, and in males nearly 90 percent ($d_{0-7} = 895$) of all deaths occurred prior to seven years. The peak in female mortality was during the first few weeks of life, whereas in males risks of death were greatest for adolescents, approximately 72 percent ($q_{4-7} = 722$) of which died between the age of four and seven years. That is, 27 percent ($d_{4-7} = 273$) of total male mortality is concentrated in this short phase. This high mortality in adolescent males is associated with their expulsion from their maternal troops, or attraction to another troop, predominantly during the mating season. Progressive debilitation through food deprivation which was attributable to low status in the host troop, and exacerbated through injury from competitive fights with other males for estrous females, is thought to be a principal cause of death. The high rates of mortality early in life had the effect of greatly reducing the overall or mean life expectancy of the male and female cohorts to 4.5 and 4.8 years respectively.

A comparison with the Anuradhapura population, where there was more predation pressure and access to food sources was less favorable, indicates that the peaks of mortality early and late in life are accentuated, rather than the overall pattern of mortality.

The density of macaques in Polonnaruwa is one animal per hectare, or up to forty-four times less than the provisioned colony of rhesus on Cayo Santiago, yet the net reproductive rate of *M. sinica* at Polonnaruwa is near one. Ecological data (Dittus, unpublished data) suggest that the macaques in Polonnaruwa are saturating their habitat, but density *per se* is not regarded as a major factor maintaining the equilibrium. Rather, it is proposed that the age and sex composition of the population and its net reproductive rate is attuned to the availability of food, and is regulated through socioecological mechanisms. The nature of the latter will be explored in future publications.

REFERENCES

BOELKINS, C. R., A. P. WILSON
  1972 Intertroop social dynamics of the Cayo Santiago rhesus (*Macaca mulatta*) with special reference to change in group membership by males. *Primates* 13(2):125–140.

CARPENTER, C. R., A. NISHIMURA
  1969 The Takasakiyama colony of Japanese macaques (*Macaca fuscata*). *Proceedings of Second International Congress of Primatology Atlanta* 1:16–30.

DATHE, H.
  1971 Hohes Lebensalter eines Javaneraffens, *Macaca irus* (Cuv.). *Zool. Garten N.F.* 40(6):328–329.

DEEVEY, E. S.
  1947 Life tables for natural populations of animals. *Quarterly Review of Biology* 23(4):283–314.

DERANIYAGALA, P. E. P.
  1955 *A colored atlas of some vertebrates from Ceylon, Serpentoid Reptilia.* Ceylon National Museums Publication 3:1–121.

EISENBERG, J. F., G. M. MCKAY
  1970   An annotated checklist of recent mammals of Ceylon with keys to the species. *Ceylon Journal of Science* 8(2):69–99.

EISENBERG, J. F., N. A. MUCKENHIRN, R. RUDRAN
  1972   The relation between ecology and social structure in primates. *Science* 176:863–874.

FERGUSON, G. A.
  1966   *Statistical analysis in psychology and education* (second edition). New York: McGraw-Hill.

FERNANDO, S. N. U.
  1968   *The natural vegetation of Ceylon.* Colombo: Lake House Bookshop.

HENRY, G. M.
  1971   *A guide to the birds of Ceylon* (second edition). New York: Oxford University Press.

HILL, W. C. O., I. S. BERNSTEIN
  1969   On the morphology, behaviour and systematic status of the Assam macaque (*Macaca assamensis* McClelland 1839). *Primates* 10:1–17.

HLADIK, C. M., A. HLADIK
  1972   Disponibilités alimentaires et domaines vitaux des primates à Ceylan. *La Terre et la Vie* 1972(2):149–215.

ITANI, J., K. TOKUDA, Y. FURUYA, K. KANO, Y. SHIN
  1963   The social construction of natural troops of Japanese monkeys in Takasakiyama. *Primates* 4(3):1–42.

JONES, M. L.
  1962   Mammals in captivity — primate longevity. *Laboratory Primate Newsletter* 1(3):3–13.

KAWAI, M., K. YOSHIBA
  1968   Sociological study of solitary males in Japanese monkeys. *Proceedings of Eighth Congress of Anthropological and Ethnological Sciences* 1:259–260.

KOFORD, C. B.
  1965   "Population dynamics of rhesus monkeys on Cayo Santiago," in *Primate behavior.* Edited by I. DeVore, 160–174. New York: Holt, Rinehart and Winston.
  1966   Population changes in rhesus monkeys: Cayo Santiago, 1960–1965. *Tulane Studies in Zoology* 13(1):1–7.

MISSAKIAN, E. Z.
  1973a   The timing of fission among free-ranging rhesus monkeys. *American Journal of Physical Anthropology* 38:621–624.
  1973b   Genealogical mating activity in free-ranging groups of rhesus monkeys (*Macaca mulatta*) on Cayo Santiago. *Behaviour* 45(3–4): 224–240.

MIZUHARA, H.
  1963   "Japanese macaque (*Macaca fuscata fuscata*)." Unpublished manuscript.

NAPIER, J. R., P. H. NAPIER
   1967   *A handbook of living primates.* London and New York: Academic
          Press.
NEVILLE, M. K.
   1968   Ecology and activity of Himalayan foothill rhesus monkeys (*Ma-caca mulatta*). *Ecology* 49:111–123.
PHILLIPS, W. W. A.
   1935   Manual of the mammals of Ceylon. *Ceylon Journal of Science.*
          Colombo.
QUICK, H. F.
   1963   "Animal population analysis," in *Wildlife investigational tech-niques.* Edited by H. S. Mosby and O. H. Hewitt, 190–228. Wash-ington, D.C.: The Wildlife Society.
RUDRAN, R.
   1973   The reproductive cycles of two subspecies of purple-faced lan-gurs (*Presbytis senex*) with relation to environmental factors. *Folia Primatologica* 19:41–60.
SADE, D. S.
   1968   Inhibition of son-mother mating among free-ranging rhesus mon-keys. *Science and Psychoanalysis* 12:18–38.
   1972   "A longitudinal study of social behavior of rhesus monkeys," in *Functional and evolutionary biology of primates.* Edited by R. H. Tuttle, 378–398. Chicago: Aldine Press.
SOUTHWICK, C. H., M. A. BEG, M. R. SIDDIQI
   1961   A population survey of rhesus monkeys in northern India: II. Transportation routes and forest areas. *Ecology* 42(4):698–710.
   1965   "Rhesus monkeys in North India," in *Primate behavior.* Edited by I. DeVore, 111–159. New York: Holt, Rinehart and Winston.
VANDENBERGH, J. G., S. VESSEY
   1968   Seasonal breeding of free-ranging rhesus monkeys and related ecological factors. *Journal of Reproduction and Fertility* 15:71–79.
WILSON, A. P., R. C. BOELKINS
   1970   Evidence for seasonal variation in aggressive behavior by *Macaca mulatta. Animal Behavior* 18:719–724.

The Descent of Dominance in Macaca: Insights into the Structure of Human Societies

JAMES LOY

INTRODUCTION

Several recent works have attempted to explain human conduct in terms of behavioral universals using data from a wide variety of animal species (Lorenz 1963; Ardrey 1966). That these attempts faltered because of an uncritical use of comparable data (or the use of non-comparable data) in no way diminishes the soundness of the approach itself. Count (1958) pointed out that vertebrate (mammalian, primate) species exhibit variations on a common biogram or "way of living" based upon a common neurological morphology. Investigations into the nature of any single variant therefore also yield information about the total biogram and all other variants.

Man's behavior and social organization have long been viewed as unique in the animal world. A more correct approach, however, is to view the human condition as a primate biogram variant, and to discover man's unique features by first elucidating his primate substratum. Anthropologists Tiger and Fox (1971) utilize this approach in their book *The imperial animal.*

This study attempts to apply the biogram approach to an inves-

Much of the author's original research was done at the La Parguera, Puerto Rico, primate colony, a facility of the Caribbean Primate Research Center. This center is supported by Contract Number NIH-DRR-71-2003 from the Division of Research Resources of the National Institute of Health, Public Health Service, Department of Health, Education and Welfare. Thanks go to the staff of the La Parguera colony for their assistance. The manuscript profited from critical reviews by Doctors C. H. Conaway and D. S. Sade, and by Kent M. Loy, to all of whom I am grateful.

tigation of primate dominance systems. Particular emphasis will be given to the genus *Macaca*, as this is perhaps the best studied of all primate genera, and as the regularities of rank attainment (if not the underlying mechanisms) are known for several macaque species. The nature and occurrence of human status hierarchies will be discussed in light of the data from non-human primates.

DOMINANCE: CONCEPT AND MEASUREMENT

The terms status, social rank, and dominance rank are used inter-changeably throughout the primate literature. This fact, coupled with the use of a multitude of behaviors to measure the above phenomena, has led to confusion among researchers and laymen alike (see review by Bernstein 1970). Of the three terms, dominance rank is preferable when referring to non-human primates.

The view that the organization and behavior of a primate group revolve around its dominance network is untenable, although widely accepted. Intragroup dominance is but a single feature of the multi-faceted phenomenon of society and is understandable and useful only when considered in the light of all types of interactions and relation-ships. Several workers (Gartlan 1968; Rowell 1972) have reacted to the failure of a linear hierarchy model to explain primate social organ-ization by questioning the value of the entire concept of dominance. They, along with others, prefer to treat aggressive interactions within the larger framework of "roles" within the social group. (A role is a social position within the group defined by the role-player's relation-ships and behavior; e.g. control animal, secondary animal, peripheral male). Rowell (1972:163) even suggested that a dominance hierarchy may be a "... pathological response of a social system to extremely stressful environmental conditions" (e.g. captivity, overcrowding, provisioning). This appears to be somewhat of an overreaction. To label dominance hierarchies as pathological implies that primate groups exhibiting such arrangements are utterly abnormal in behavior and organization.

It appears to be more correct to view the ABILITY to form complex dominance systems (including, but not limited to, linear hierarchies) as being well within the capabilities of all primate species. This ability may be expressed by some species under only certain conditions, and by other species under all conditions. Thus, for some primate groups an analysis of dominance relations will be critical to an understanding of behavior and organization; for other groups, dominance analysis may reveal few useful data (see Rowell 1967). While dominance relationships and dominance-submissive behavior are apparently intensified in some "stressful" situations, they are also commonly found in relatively unstressed feral primate groups.

The least equivocal measure of dominance is the winning or losing of aggressive interactions. If A defeats B in a fight, then A is said to be the dominant individual. This appears to have been the original meaning of the term dominance as developed in relation to peck orders among chickens (Schjelderup-Ebbe 1922, as cited in Klopfer and Hailman 1967), and many primate researchers still follow this classical usage (Sade 1967; Bernstein 1970; Loy and Loy 1974). Some workers, however, have emphasized priority to commodities (e.g. food, water, sexually receptive females) in their dominance measures. For example, Carpenter (1964a:350) said: "An individual is said to be dominant over another when it has priority in feeding, sexual and locomotor behavior and when it is superior in aggressiveness and in group control to another or other individuals." Although priority to commodities is to some extent correlated with aggressive success, the former is a much less certain measure of dominance rank among free-ranging animals. Bold animals, though low in the hierarchy of aggressive dominance, may do well on food tests, for example, and conversely, highly dominant animals may occasionally be unreceptive to the stimulus objects (or the test situation) and thus appear low-ranking. (Hall [1968] agreed that the food test is an inadequate indicator of rank.) Bernstein (1969) reported on correlations between rank orders determined from measures of priority to incentives (feeding order) and agonistic interactions among pigtail macaques. Bernstein (1969:455) found that ". . . whereas feeding order is certainly related to dominance, it is not a direct measure of it," and concluded that agonistic interactions provide the most direct measure of dominance.

Agonistic interactions among primates are by no means a simple matter, however, and the investigator who chooses to measure dominance in terms of these exchanges must still decide which motor patterns fall within that category and which are to be emphasized as rank indicators. It is well known that the majority of primate agonistic interactions do not involve actual physical punishment, but rather are composed of motor patterns which THREATEN physical contact. The staring, open-mouth face of the rhesus macaque is an easily recognizable threat pattern, and Sade (1967) has shown that this pattern often grades into a biting attack. Several researchers working with squirrel monkeys have regarded penile displays to be threats and the direction of these displays to be a good dominance indicator (DuMond 1968; Baldwin 1968). Kaufmann (1967) regarded single mounts among rhesus monkeys as agonistic acts, but found mounting to be a poor indicator of dominance.

Loy and Loy (1974) have recently completed a study of dominance behavior among juvenile rhesus monkeys contained in a large outdoor corral. In this study, dominance rank was determined by the use of a combination of data from agonistic encounters and supplantations. The following rules were observed.

1.   Only data from dyadic interactions were utilized in assessing dominance.
2.   Rank depended on what animals another animal dominated; not on the frequency of successful agonistic encounters.
3.   Three types of behavior were defined as dominance interactions.
a.   Type 1: FIGHTS. Fights were defined as an attack of any intensity followed by a flight of any intensity. This definition followed Sade (1967), as did the catalog of attack and flight behaviors, with minor exceptions.
b.   Type 2: UNPROVOKED SUBMISSIVE GESTURES. For example, if monkey A grimaced at monkey B, although B had not clearly threatened the first animal, it was considered a good indication of B's dominance.
c.   Type 3: DISPLACEMENTS. One animal moves away from the approach of another prior to any noticeable directed threat from the latter monkey.
4.   Interaction types 1 and 2 were considered equally strong dominance indicators. Type 3 was considered to be slightly less reliable since it was based on the observer's interpretation of the motivation-prompting movement.
5.   Types 1 and 2 interactions, in which neither animal was clearly the dominant, were either not scored, or were scored as a "probable" win for one monkey. "Probable" wins were considered low-reliability dominance indicators.

The dominance matrix presented in Loy and Loy (1974) reflects the strong agreement between the three rank measures. Success in aggressive interactions and in displacements *vis-à-vis* the same subordinate monkeys were particularly highly correlated. Of a total of 148 displacements, in only two instances did an animal supplant an individual observed, at some point in the study, to defeat it in a fight.

BASIC AND DEPENDENT RANK

The concept of dominance rank is complex, and not only from the standpoint of having to choose the most reliable indicators from a large selection of possible dominance measures. The investigator must also recognize and deal with the influence of other animals upon dominance rank. In other words, he must distinguish between the "basic" and "dependent" ranks of the animals in his group. The concepts of basic and dependent rank were introduced by Japanese researchers (Kawai 1965a). Basic rank is that order determined through a series of dyadic dominance interactions unaffected by the actions or presence of other animals. Dependent rank is best described by a quote from Kawai (1965a:70): "Let us assume that basically A ranks socially higher than B. Now, when another monkey C is nearby, or when a particular situation S prevails, B becomes superior to A." Numerous examples of dependent rank within a group of Japanese monkeys were reported in another paper by Kawai (1965b).

There is no doubt that dependent rank affects an animal's behavior during the period of rank increase. On occasion, a low-ranking monkey can rise in basic rank through repeated agonistic support by a high-ranking individual (Loy and Loy, unpublished data). In most instances, however, it appears that an animal's rank reverts to its prior basic level after the period of dependence. Dependent rank may also be viewed as an "extension" of rank from the higher to the lower-ranking monkey during their association. Basic ranks are more easily identifiable in a free-ranging situation than in a confined group, where the effects of dependent rank become intensified (Bernstein 1969).

Most observers attempt to discover the basic ranks within their study groups, and to do so they utilize strictly dyadic encounters. An exception is Hall's and DeVore's (1965) description of savannah baboon social organization in which they utilized a combination of data from dyadic agonistic encounters and inter-male support patterns to determine a male's overall dominance rank.

CATEGORICAL RANK ABSTRACTIONS

Dominance relationships within a primate group are often reported as subsets of the total dominance matrix (e.g. the adult males, the adult females). While the determination of rank relations within age-sex categories provides valuable information concerning troop structure, and is extremely useful in the analysis of certain problems (e.g. the relationship between dominance rank and mating frequency among adult males), it has been correctly pointed out that these subsets are often abstractions rather than true organizational components (Alexander and Bowers 1969; but see later discussion of adult female hierarchy among macaques). In a monkey group with N members, there are $N \frac{N-1}{2}$ dominance relationships (Carpenter 1964a), and animals of different age-sex classes are interdigitated in the overall troop dominance structure (Kawai 1965a; Sade 1967). In daily interactions, the effects of dependent rank act to complicate further the already complex dominance arrangements. There are, however, certain general rules to which macaque monkeys, for example, appear to conform, as they move from a (basic) rankless infant state to their position(s) within the troop dominance structure. In order to understand these established courses for dominance attainment, age and/or sex class dominance abstractions must be made.

DOMINANCE AMONG MACAQUES

Japanese Monkeys (Macaca fuscata)

All macaque species studied to date conform to a multi-male heterosexual grouping pattern (Imanishi 1963; Southwick, Beg, and Siddiqi 1965; Simonds 1965; Sugiyama 1968; Bertrand 1969; MacRoberts 1970). In a troop of Japanese macaques the supremely dominant monkey is typically an adult male (Kawai 1965a; Alexander and Bowers 1969), although cases of supremely dominant females have been reported (Kawamura 1965). Dominance relations within the subsets of adult males (over six years) and adult females (over three years) typically form linear hierarchies (Imanishi 1963; Kawai 1965a; Kawamura 1965). Young males (five to six years) do not conform to a linear arrangement, but rather show numerous triangular relationships (A>B>C>A) (Kawai 1965a).

The phenomenon of dependent rank strongly affects daily dominance interactions. A monkey can, in the presence of a basically higher-ranking animal, take unwarranted privileges or actually attack the more dominant animal because of the proximity of a still higher-ranking individual whose support can be enlisted if necessary. Dependence may be based on kin bonds or on friendly bonds with non-relatives (Kawai 1965a, 1965b). The offspring of high-ranking adult females tend to attain high basic rank within the troop (Kawai 1965a; Alexander and Bowers 1969). This tendency is usually explained as an effect of dependence upon the mother's rank, transmitted via agonistic support by the mother (Kawai 1965a).

Partial rules of rank attainment have been worked out for Japanese macaques within the Minoo-B troop (Kawamura 1965) and the Arashiyama troop (Koyama 1967). The Minoo-B troop (twenty-nine monkeys total) contained four matrilineal genealogies, and the adult female matriline heads were arranged in a linear hierarchy. Adult female offspring ranked immediately below their mothers and above all members of lower-ranking genealogies. Among adult female siblings there was an inverse relationship between age and rank (i.e. the younger siblings rose to rank above the older). There were a few exceptions within the Minoo-B troop to these generalizations about female rank. Lulu, the four-year-old daughter of the head of matriline 2, was in the process of rising above the head of matriline 3, who had outranked Lulu since birth. The five-year-old daughter of the head of matriline 4 had risen in rank above her mother. In the Minoo-B troop, two three-year-old males were found to rank roughly according to their matriline rank. They were in the process of becoming peripheral to the "central" part of the troop, and rank changes among peripheral males are unpredictable (Kawamura 1965).

Koyama (1967) studied the Arashiyama troop of 125 Japanese monkeys and reported that (1) "within age class" ranks appeared by one year of age, and paralleled the mothers' ranks; (2) among adult female siblings, the dominance rank was in an inverse relationship to age; (3) the youngest female offspring comes to rank immediately below her mother as an adult; and (4) immature offspring of high-ranking females often outrank older animals whose mothers are lower-ranking than their own.

Rhesus Monkeys (Macaca mulatta)

Many of the dominance generalizations found among Japanese monkeys apply equally well to rhesus macaques. Adult males are arranged in a linear dominance hierarchy (Kaufmann 1967; Lindburg 1971; Loy 1971; Missakian 1972), as are adult females (Sade 1967; Loy

1971). Dependent rank often affects access to environmental commodities (Koford 1963a), and an offspring is frequently given agonistic support by its mother (Sade 1968).

Rhesus monkeys begin to engage in aggressive encounters (fights) while still less than one year of age (J. Loy, personal observation; Sade 1968), and have soon established their initial basic dominance relationships with many of their groupmates. Of course, the infant probably has many of its dominance relationships settled for it without a mutual testing of fighting ability, as when an older, stronger animal suddenly attacks it and sends it screeching. The most meaningful and stable dominance relations are those developed within a monkey's age class (Sade 1967).

From the age of about one year, the rank of immature rhesus monkeys WITHIN THEIR AGE CLASS (regardless of sex) parallels their mothers' ranking in the hierarchy of adult females. That is, the youngsters defeat age-mates whose mothers are ranked below their own mother, and are defeated by age-mates whose mothers outrank their own (Sade 1967).

The relationship between maternal rank and offspring rank was recently tested by Loy and Loy (1974) in a group of thirty-three juvenile rhesus monkeys (twenty-one yearlings and twelve two-year-olds) removed from a single social group. Basic rank relationships within the two age classes were predicted on the basis of knowledge of relative ranking of the juveniles' mothers in the natal group. Dominance interactions (described earlier) were seen between 229 likeaged dyads, and of that total, 219 relationships (95.6 percent) were as predicted.

The age class hierarchies established among rhesus monkeys are very stable, and indeed often last a lifetime for females, who come to rank directly under their mothers as adults (Sade 1967). Maturing males tend to rank near their mothers, but the situation is more complex than that of females. At puberty a male may become peripheral to the natal group and eventually change groups completely. If he remains in his natal group, he may experience rank changes in relation to peers. It is possible that the physiological changes and growth associated with puberty become the major determinants of agonistic success among males, outweighing the influences of maternal rank (Sade 1967). Nevertheless, maternal rank may well affect the probability that a male will remain with his natal group after puberty, and that he will attain high rank within the hierarchy of adult males (Koford 1963b).

Dominance between individuals of different age classes is highly variable, although it follows certain vague guidelines. Loy and Loy (1974) found the following relationships in their group of yearlings and two-year-olds. Two-year-olds (regardless of sex) tended to be able to defeat yearlings in all genealogies ranked below their own, to defeat occasionally a yearling of their own genealogy whose mother outranked their own, and to defeat occasionally a yearling belonging to the genealogy ranked immediately above their own. Yearlings (regardless of sex) tended to be able to defeat two-year-olds from genealogies more than one rank below their own.

Concerning the intragenealogical aspect of dominance relationships, the phenomenon of adult female siblings being ranked inversely to their ages holds true for rhesus as well as for Japanese macaques (Sade 1972; Missakian 1972). Rhesus females tend to remain dominant to their daughters all through life, and to their sons until the male is about six years of age, when he MAY rise over his mother if he is still with the natal group (Missakian 1972). Brother-sister rank depends on age, with the older sibling being the dominant, until typically the male becomes the permanent dominant at about three to four years of age (Missakian 1972). Brother-brother rank is also typically age dependent, with the older brother being the higher-ranking. A few rank reversals among brothers have been reported, these usually occurring among adult siblings, but occasionally among juveniles (Sade 1972; Missakian 1972; Loy and Loy 1974).

Apparently the dominance patterns of rhesus monkeys are not significantly affected by group size. Sade's (1967) observations were from a group of less than forty animals, while Missakian studied a group with over 200 members.

Other Macaques

The behavior and organization of the Barbary ape (*Macaca sylvana*) has recently been reported by MacRoberts (1970). Adult females exhibit a linear dominance hierarchy, and appear to support offspring in agonistic interactions. The lack of known genealogical relations prohibits a definite statement concerning the relations between maternal rank and offspring rank. However, the scanty data available at least do not disagree with the dominance patterns characteristic of rhesus and Japanese monkeys, and the overall similarities in behavior and organization among the three species tempt one to speculate that further research on *Macaca sylvana* will reveal just such patterns.

Bonnet macaques (*Macaca radiata*) are characterized by a linear dominance ranking among the adult males (Simonds 1965; Sugiyama 1971). Simonds was unable to rank completely the adult females in his study group, but Sugiyama observed a linear hierarchy among adult females at a feeding ground.

Bernstein (1969) found a stable dominance hierarchy within a captive group of pigtail macaques (*Macaca nemestrina*). In this group, there also appeared to be some positive correlation between maternal rank and offspring rank.

Stable dominance orders, based upon the direction of agonistic interactions, have recently been reported for captive crab-eating macaques (*Macaca fascicularis*) and Celebes monkeys (formerly *Cynopithecus niger*, but now considered to be a macaque [Fooden 1969; Bernstein 1970]).

GENERALIZATIONS CONCERNING MACAQUE DOMINANCE

The following regularities appear in a survey of dominance relationships among the macaque monkeys (an asterisk [*] designates rules applicable only to rhesus and Japanese monkeys, according to present knowledge).

1.   Several subsets within a macaque social group tend to form linear dominance hierarchies. These include (a) adult males, (b) adult females, and *(c) age classes of immatures.

2.   Maternal rank affects offspring rank among rhesus and Japanese monkeys, and possibly among pigtail macaques and Barbary apes as well.

*3.   As adults, female offspring rank immediately below their mothers.

*4.   Among adult female siblings rank is inversely related to age.

*5.   Rank among immature age-mates (regardless of sex) parallels that among their mothers.

*6.   Immature male age-mates rank in relation to their mothers' rank until they near puberty, when rank changes become unpredictable and the male may become peripheral or change groups.

*7.   Rank among dissimilarly-aged immatures is affected by sex, genealogy rank, and age.

*8.   The above rules appear to operate independently of group size.

MECHANISMS OF DOMINANCE SYSTEMS AND RANK ACQUISITION

Merely noting the observable regularities in macaque dominance relationships does not provide full understanding of the phenomenon. The latter depends on the elucidation of the mechanisms producing and/or controlling the observed behavior.

It is inevitable that aggressive interactions will occasionally occur within a primate social group owing, for example, to invasions of personal space or competition for desired commodities. In a newly-formed group, the winners of the initial fights are determined by several factors including fighting ability, physical condition, and temperament. The early fighting soon leads to the establishment of dominance relationships, and, once formed, these relationships appear to be maintained by a system of positive and negative reinforcements. Dominant animals are rewarded with freedom of movement, freedom from aggression, and priority to commodities. Subordinate animals are rewarded with freedom from aggression provided they display proper behavior *vis-à-vis* dominants, and they are punished if they fail to do so. (In this regard, Rowell [1972] suggests that the behavior of subordinates is of major importance in hierarchy maintenance.) All animals are rewarded with a predictable system of inter-animal communications.

The effect of maternal rank on the rank of her offspring has been explained in terms of social learning. Hall (1968:388) said that "the confidence or security, or simply the example of successful assertiveness afforded by the mother's behavior, serve to build up similar habits in the social behavior of the young. These habits then supposedly transfer to the interactions with age-mates . . ." This hypothesis is a restatement of the "identification" theory earlier presented by Japanese workers (Imanishi 1965; Kawai 1965a), and is based ultimately upon the existence of the strong mother-offspring bond which characterizes the mammalian biogram (Count 1958).

Although the possibility of direct genetic effects on offspring dominance rank has not been adequately investigated, and although the more complex features of dominance acquisition are not fully explained by the "identification" or "social dynamic" theory (Sade 1972), many of the theory's propositions appear to be correct. Undoubtedly the young monkey learns through observation and experience which individuals, and also importantly, which COALITIONS OF INDIVIDUALS, act in a dominant or submissive manner toward its mother (the latter is important because a single monkey is but a part of an agonistic support unit which must be dealt with in a fight [Marsden 1968]). At the same time, the immature monkey is learning which are the members of its own agonistic support unit. For the immature these learned relationships are translated within the age class as a hierarchy of basic rank paralleling that found in the subset of mothers. Outside the age class, the "mother-dominant" relationships often do not transfer directly to the young monkey (or at least not immediately). For example, although macaque adult female A dominates adult female B, the latter may initially dominate A's young offspring. However, A's offspring (at least the females) will ultimately rise to rank above B (see the example of Lulu, given earlier).

The social dynamic theory thus provides an adequate explanation for the "within-age-class" dominance alignments of young macaques. Support for the theory was provided by Marsden (1968), who showed that the rank of an offspring who acts independently of its mother and kin group in agonistic interactions may be less affected by changes in maternal rank than an agonistically supportive offspring.

Several dominance phenomena are not fully explained by the social dynamic hypothesis. These include the orderly rise in rank of females to an adult level immediately below their mother and above their older sisters, and dominance acquisition among orphaned monkeys. Sade (1972) treated these inadequacies in detail, and he pointed out that at least two mechanisms are needed to explain the general rise of females — one initiating the rise, and another determining the monkey's final rank level. Age and reproductive state have been suggested as explaining the initial rise in rank, but neither seems entirely satisfactory. The mechanism limiting rank increase is elucidated by the behavior of naturally orphaned monkeys. A rhesus female orphaned at nine months of age interacted most frequently with an older sister. The orphan did not experience a rank-limiting identification, however, but rather predictably rose in rank over her older sister, who was, in effect, her foster mother (Sade 1972). This suggests that among females the constraints on certain future dominance relationships may be formed early in life (Sade 1972) and may then be relatively inflexible.

TRADITION OR PHYLOGENY

The patterns of dominance ordering and the courses of dominance acquisition characteristic of the living species of *Macaca* appear to comprise a phylogenetically acquired complex of processes. This deduction is supported by the occurrence of the complex in species widely separated geographically. The possibility that the dominance patterns constitute a behavioral "tradition" (see Kummer 1971a) which has undergone repeated invention or widespread (and interspecific) diffusion is diminished by the intricacy of the total pattern, and by the striking similarities found in well-studied species. Longitudinal studies (see Sade 1972) of additional macaque species are needed to test the above hypothesis. Further work must also be done on macaque groups in varying environmental conditions in order to assess the relationships between environment and dominance patterning.

The possibility exists, of course, that the dominance complex described for macaques may not be limited to that genus. Longitudinal studies of non-macaque cercopithecoids may well reveal that the patterns are widespread throughout the family, and may show correlations with ecological adaptations, grouping tendencies, or other parameters. An ongoing study, by the author, of patas monkeys (*Erythrocebus patas*), held in a large outdoor corral, has revealed similarities to portions of the macaque dominance complex. With the outcome of agonistic interactions and displacements as the measures of dominance, it has been found that the adult patas females display a linear hierarchy, and that the dominance relations among the group's four infants (two males and two females, and all less than one year of age) all parallel the relative rankings among their mothers.

Similar data from a study of wild savannah baboons (*Papio cynocephalus*) have recently become available. Hausfater (1973 and personal communication) discovered a linear hierarchy among adult female baboons and correlations between the ranks of juveniles of known parentage and their mothers' ranks in the female hierarchy. Unlike the situation in macaques, dominance rank among immature baboons appears to be influenced by gender differences at an early age. Hausfater reported that the rank of immatures correlates with their mother's rank only within the offspring's age-SEX class. Males are apparently dominant to like-aged females very early in life.

FUNCTIONS OF DOMINANCE SYSTEMS

As noted earlier, the notion of dominance systems as providing the single basis of primate social organization appears unfounded. It is undeniable, however, that dominance relations do affect individual and group behavior in many ways for many species. An example cited earlier is that dominant animals often have priority of access to limited or prized environmental commodities (Crook 1970). One of the commodities presumably controlled by dominant adult males is sexually receptive females (Carpenter 1964b; Hall and DeVore 1965; Altmann 1962). This assertion, coupled with the widespread belief that sexual activity (estrus) in non-human primate females consistently signals ovulation, has led some writers to the conclusion that "only dominants propagate" (Tiger and Fox 1971:31). However, recent reports indicate that rhesus monkey females can exhibit estrous behavior proximal to menstruation as well as at mid-cycle (Loy 1970), and that rhesus males of all dominance ranks tend to concentrate their mating activity in the central portion of a female's estrus (Loy 1971). These reports cast grave doubts upon the validity of the "only dominants propagate" theory.

An oft-repeated maxim is that dominance hierarchies serve to reduce aggression. Gartlan (1968) argued against, but failed to disprove, this hypothesis. It is certain, however, that dominance relations do serve to control the DIRECTION of agonistic interactions. In so doing they fulfill their major and supremely important function: providing part of the network of social relationships which make inter-animal communications effective and their outcome predictable, and thus make life in a social group possible (Kummer 1971b). Effective communications allow animals of different ranks to cooperate in such essential activities as mating, infant care, and group defense. (The dominance relations within a group need not form a linear hierarchy for communication to take place. Triangular relationships are confusing to researchers, but have little effect on the animals, whose communications are primarily dyadic.)

It has been proposed that dominance may affect group organization though the orientation of the attention of subordinates (Chance and Jolly 1970). This is an interesting hypothesis, which has yet to be adequately tested.

Finally, as the longitudinal studies of rhesus and Japanese macaques are beginning to indicate, dominance relations often have the important function of providing one parameter for the orderly integration of new individuals into the total social group. Contrary to the conclusions of Alexander and Bowers (1969), certain subsets of individuals appear to be valid, functioning components of macaque societies. The subset of adult females is a prime example. The rank relationships within this subset function to determine the hierarchical alignments within the age classes of immature monkeys, and the adult dominance positions of maturing females.

COMPARATIVE DATA

One of the objectives of this essay is to investigate the hypothesis that dominance systems, including hierarchies, are a commonly occurring feature of the general primate biogram. To that end, a brief and highly selective review of the primate literature will be presented.

Prosimians

Jolly (1966) reported the occurrence of a linear dominance hierarchy within a wild troop of *Lemur catta*. Based upon the winning and losing of aggressive interactions, "there was a clear dominance order among males, a fairly clear one among females, and females were dominant over males" (1966:104). In significant contrast to the usual conclusions concerning primate dominance functioning, the male dominance hierarchy did not allow unchallenged access to sexually receptive females. During periods of mating, otherwise subordinate males successfully chased dominant ones, and subordinate males accomplished several matings (Jolly 1967).

In a laboratory group of *Galago crassicaudatus*, a linear dominance hierarchy was found among the females, but not among the males nor in the group as a whole (Roberts 1971).

The males of several species of tree shrews (genus *Tupaia*) display linear dominance hierarchies when in captive groups (Sorenson 1970). *Tupaia longipes* exhibits both male and female hierarchies, with the latter being the more stable (Sorenson and Conaway 1966).

New World Monkeys

Adult male squirrel monkeys (*Saimiri sciureus*) form a linear dominance hierarchy during the species' mating season. This hierarchy is established through the use of stereotyped penile displays. Position in the hierarchy, however, has no apparent effect on other types of social interaction or upon priority of access to commodities. During

the non-mating season, adult males become socially inactive (Du-
Mond 1968; Baldwin 1968). Castell and Heinrich (1971) concluded
that there was no overall rank order among the subadult females in
their captive squirrel monkey group.

Eisenberg and Kuehn (1966:59) reported that within groups of
spider monkeys (genus *Ateles*) dominance hierarchies are "not strongly expressed and a classical, linear hierarchy appears to be absent."

Separate dominance hierarchies appear to be present among the
adult males and the adult females of a wild howler monkey (*Alouatta
palliata*) group. The slope of the dominance gradient among males
appears to be somewhat steeper than that of the females (Carpenter
1965).

Old World Monkeys

Several non-macaque species of Cercopithecoidae exhibit dominance
hierarchies. Dominance among wild male baboons (*Papio cynocephalus*) has been mentioned previously. A linear dominance ordering
is complicated by the tendency of males to form supportive coalitions. The alpha male tends to possess females swollen to the maximum, although an individual male's frequency of copulation is often
unrelated to high rank (Hall and DeVore 1965; Saayman 1971). The
variability possible in baboon social behavior and organization is
demonstrated by Rowell's (1972) report on the feral baboons near
the Ishasha River in Uganda. Rowell found no evidence of a hierarchical rank ordering among the males of her study groups. Hall and
DeVore (1965) reported an inability to determine clearly hierarchical
positions among baboon females. In contrast, Hausfater (1973) found
a stable, linear hierarchy among the adult females of the group he
studied in Kenya's Amboseli Game Reserve.

Jay (1965) observed multi-male groups of Hanuman langurs (*Presbytis entellus*) in northern India and was able to determine a hierarchical rank ordering among the adult males, but not among the
adult females. Yoshiba (1968) studied *Presbytis entellus* living in one-
male groups near Dharwar, India, and agreed with Jay that langur
females do not show a recognizable dominance hierarchy. Yoshiba
found a dominance hierarchy among the males of all-male langur
groups.

Nilgiri langurs (*Presbytis johnii*) of south India exhibit stable, well-
defined, linear dominance hierarchies among adult males (when more

than one is present) and among adult females, even though dominance interactions occur infrequently (Poirier 1970).

Chalmers and Rowell (1971) reported a linear hierarchy (based on
supplantation data) within a small captive group of mangabeys
(*Cercocebus albigena*). Similarly, Bernstein (1970) found a stable
dominance order, based on the direction of agonistic interactions,
within a captive group of *Cercocebus atys*.

Struhsaker (1967) stated that a distinct dominance hierarchy occurred within each of the wild vervet monkey (*Cercopithecus aethiops*)
groups he studied. In contrast, Gartlan (1968) found the entire concept of dominance unusable in his study of vervet behavior, and turned to role analysis as an alternative.

The occurrence of a linear hierarchy among the adult females in a
captive group of patas monkeys (J. Loy, unpublished data) was mentioned previously, and confirms an earlier report by Hall (1968).

Apes

The most dominant animal in a wild group of mountain gorillas
(*Gorilla gorilla beringei*) is generally a silver-backed male. If there
are several silver-backed males, they exhibit a linear dominance hierarchy. Silver-backed males are dominant to all black-backed males,
females and young. Black-backed males dominate young animals, but
are occasionally defeated by adult females. Adult females appear to
lack a stable dominance hierarchy among themselves, with rank possibly changing with the presence or absence of dependent young
(Schaller 1963, 1965).

The social organization of wild chimpanzees (*Pan troglodytes*) is
characterized by small groups of temporarily associated individuals
(Goodall 1965). Within these groups, dominance interactions are
infrequent and permanent hierarchies appear to be absent (Reynolds
and Reynolds 1965).

Gibbons occur in monogamous families of one adult male and one
adult female and their offspring. Within the family, the adults are
about co-equal in dominance (Carpenter 1964c).

These references support the contention that the ABILITY to form
complex dominance systems featuring linear hierarchies is found
throughout the non-human primates. The fact that some species fail
to display hierarchical rank orders does not disprove this hypothesis.

Sade (1973) has pointed out that particular features of a system may remain latent until elicited by a certain set of conditions. The conditions which elicit dominance hierarchies in primates are imperfectly understood at present. Rowell (1972) suggested that dominance hierarchies are caused by stressful environmental conditions. However, this suggestion appears inadequate to explain the array of dominance orders found in feral primate groups.

Man

Numerous researchers have remarked on the occurrence of hierarchical status arrangements in human cultures. Count (1958: 1075) said: "In man, dominance-subordination and social hierarchicalism are even more strongly motivated than among other animals. . ." Tiger (1970: 287) discussed man's "apparent general tendency to form hierarchies." The examples in the following section are intended to provide support for the hypothesis that hierarchical status (power, dominance) arrangements are a common characteristic of human societies, and that the ability to produce such arrangements should be viewed as part of man's phylogenetic heritage.

Tiger (1970) has discussed in detail the dangers inherent in revealing the biological roots of systems of social inequality. It should suffice to say here that while non-human primate dominance hierarchies and human status hierarchies seem to be behavioral homologues, human hierarchies operate within a milieu of moral awareness lacking among the lower primates. Thus human hierarchies are to some extent qualitatively different from those of the non-human primates. The study of human hierarchical structures should lead to a recognition of both the good and harmful effects of these systems, and to the understanding necessary to minimize the latter. Therefore, this essay cannot be interpreted as a moral justification for human hierarchical systems, but rather as an attempt to explain man's ability to form such arrangements.

Human hierarchies take a wide variety of forms. Some are almost purely STATUS hierarchies, wherein position lacks an equivalent amount of social power (the ability to make other people do one's will [Beattie 1964]). Others are more nearly true POWER hierarchies, wherein rank is loaded with physical control over subordinates. Most of us are quite familiar with the endless varieties of both status and power hierarchies found in modern Western cultures (in business, the

military services, religion, fraternal orders, government, etc.). A summary of human social and political stratification was given by Coult
and Habenstein (1965). Using data from 565 cultures from all parts
of the world (compiled by Murdock [1957]), they reported the following varieties of stratification among freemen (percent of total sample
is shown in parentheses).

1. Absence of significant social stratification among freemen. Purely
political and religious statuses are not treated as classes. (38.6 percent)
2. Formal age classes without other significant stratification among
freemen. (4.1 percent)
3. Wealth distinctions of importance, based on possession or distribution of property, without definite crystallization into hereditary
social classes. (15.9 percent)
4. Hereditary aristocracy or noble class differentiated from ordinary
freemen. (20.2 percent)
5. Complex stratification into three or more social classes or castes
(exclusive of slaves). (18.1 percent)
6. No information. (3.2 percent)

Several examples of the varieties of human status systems are presented below. They are primarily taken from the political sphere of
non-Western cultures.

The Blackfoot Indians of North America were organized into
bands, which were segments of the tribe. Bands lacked a formal
chief, but had recognized leaders selected for qualities such as gener-
osity, prowess in hunting and war, etc. The leaders of large and
powerful bands were generally accepted as tribal leaders during the
summer tribal gathering, one among them being pre-eminent. Tribal
leadership tended to remain within one family of one band for several
generations (Ford 1961).

The political control within the societies of certain East African
peoples (e.g. the Masai and the Nandi) was in the form of a hierarchical age-set system combined with an allocation of authority based
on seniority. Membership in an age set was limited to men, and depended upon year of birth. The age set moved as a unit through various
role grades (childhood, junior warriorhood, senior warriorhood, junior elderhood, senior elderhood). Each grade performed particular
duties within the society. Senior elders occasionally constituted coun-
cils which made community decisions (Beattie 1964).

Among the Nootka and Kawakiutl Indians of British Columbia
there was relatively little organized political power. Rank was evident,

however, and every village had a few noble families which possessed rights to certain fishing and hunting grounds and claimed certain social privileges (e.g. the right to display particular crests). There were commoners and slaves dependent on each noble household. High rank depended on the possession of riches, and was shown by giving great feasts for the village. Commoners who achieved wealth could rise to noble rank, and likewise, nobles could lose rank through a lack of show of wealth (Ford 1961).

The Yoruba of southwestern Nigeria are an example of an elaborate African state. The king (*alafin*) resided in Oyo, the capital city of the largest of the tribal divisions. The *alafin* was a priest-chief with both religious and secular authority. Advising the *alafin* were district chiefs, each of whom ruled a large town plus its dependent villages. Each village had a separate chief, and within the village, each compound (containing a group of related families) had a headman. The death of the *alafin* was usually followed by the killing of his wives, slaves, and eldest son. The district chiefs then selected the next king from a different branch of the royal family. The various rulers could call upon their subjects for limited periods of public labor or for warfare (Ford 1961).

The Aztecs of the valley of Mexico were organized into twenty non-totemic clans united by patrilineal descent. Each clan had a headman (elected, but usually the title remained in a family for generations), a war chief, and a speaker. Above the clansmen ranked the class of honorary lords (rank conferred for public service, prowess in war, etc.) and the class of priests. The classes of workers and slaves ranked below the clansmen. The twenty Aztec clans were grouped into four phratries, each with its own leader. Affairs of state were conducted by a council composed of the clan speakers. For exceptionally important matters, a "great" council (including clan speakers, headmen, and war leaders, phratry leaders, and other high officials and ranking priests) would be called. Among the duties of the "great" council was the election of the Aztec king (the *tlacatecutli*). The kingship remained within a single lineage, and was passed to a younger brother on the king's death. The Aztec king was the tribal war chief, levied taxes throughout his kingdom, and exercised summary judicial powers in times of war. The council of speakers, however, was actually the supreme authority within the tribe (Murdock 1934).

The native state of Cochin of southwestern India provides an example of a state with a caste organization. The principles of land-holding and secular authority were complexly interwoven with the caste divisions. The political organization included a royal house (the state's largest landholder), district chiefs, and local chiefs. When a chief at any level owned the land he ruled, he could tax the residents. Obligations of those low in the political hierarchy toward higher rulers who were not landowners were limited to support in war and participation in ceremony. The hierarchy of Cochin castes (high to low) was as follows:

1. The royal house, which belonged to the Khshatriya group of castes, but which had a special rank as a sacred ruling family.
2. The Nambudiri Brahmins.
3. The Nayars (landowning freemen).
4. High-ranking castes which performed personal services to the Brahmins and Nayars.
5. "Untouchable" castes including low castes of artisans, fishermen, serfs, and members of hill tribes (Ford 1961).

These examples, plus knowledge of the political and social hierarchies common among Western cultures, indicate the widespread occurrence of human status hierarchies and the multitude of forms they may take. Tiger (1970) has noted two general tendencies cross-cutting the varieties of human hierarchies: older persons tend to have higher status positions than younger ones, and men tend to attain higher status than women.

The occurrence of status hierarchies within human cultures can be viewed as a behavioral and organizational homologue of non-human primate dominance hierarchies. However, the methods of status acquisition among humans (e.g. by age-set promotion, the accumulation and dispersal of wealth, the demonstration of valued personality traits, and the inheritance of position) are cultural analogues of the phylogenetically-based rank attainment rules characteristic of the macaques.

STATUS HIERARCHIES AMONG EARLY HOMINIDS

The fragmentary nature of the data regarding the anatomy, locomotion, and ecological adaptations of the earliest hominids limits speculations about so specific a feature of social organization as dominance systems. The evidence from living primates suggests that *Ramapithecus* and *Australopithecus* had the ability to form dominance hierarchies.

However, whether such arrangements were in fact part of their social organization remains unknown. *Ramapithecus* was a forest dweller who may have exhibited a social organization similar to living chimpanzees (Pilbeam 1972), and therefore may have lacked stable dominance networks. *Australopithecus africanus* was adapted to life in more open country than *Ramapithecus* (Pilbeam 1972). Is it therefore legitimate to infer the baboon-macaque type of dominance hierarchies for *Australopithecus africanus*? Even if one is so inclined, one thing appears certain: any dominance systems exhibited by the australopithecines were beginning the transition toward the cultural status arrangements of true man.

SUMMARY

Complex dominance systems are characteristic of many social primate species and function primarily to insure effective, predictable communication among the members of a social group. Hierarchical dominance systems occur so commonly among the primates that the ability to produce them should be considered a feature of the general primate biogram. The conditions which elicit dominance hierarchies are as yet poorly understood.

Among non-human primates, dominance is best measured in terms of the winning and losing of aggressive interactions. Using these criteria, intricate dominance systems have been discovered within the social groups of macaque monkeys. These systems include established courses for initial rank attainment and for many rank changes. The dominance complex of *Macaca* appears to be a phylogenetically acquired characteristic of that genus.

Many human cultures exhibit hierarchical status systems. In contrast to the dominance hierarchies of non-human primates, human status hierarchies are cultural in nature, and the hierarchy varieties, as well as the methods of status measurement and attainment, have increased in number and complexity. Man's ability to form hierarchical power and status arrangements is an expression of the primate biogram.

REFERENCES

ALEXANDER, B. K., J. M. BOWERS
  1969 Social organization of a troop of Japanese monkeys in a two-acre enclosure. *Folia Primatologica* 10:230–242.

ALTMANN, S. A.
  1962 A field study of the sociobiology of rhesus monkeys, *Macaca mulatta. Annals of the New York Academy of Sciences* 102:338–435.

ARDREY, R.
  1966 *The territorial imperative.* New York: Dell.

BALDWIN, J. D.
  1968 The social behavior of adult male squirrel monkeys (*Saimiri sciureus*) in a seminatural environment. *Folia Primatologica* 9:281–314.

BEATTIE, J.
  1964 *Other cultures.* New York: The Free Press.

BERNSTEIN, I. S.
  1969 Stability of the status hierarchy in a pigtail monkey group (*Macaca nemestrina*). *Animal Behavior* 17:452–458.
  1970 "Primate status hierarchies," in *Primate behavior: developments in field and laboratory research,* volume one. Edited by L. A. Rosenblum, 71–109. New York: Academic Press.

BERTRAND, M.
  1969 The behavioral repertoire of the stumptail macaque. *Bibliotheca Primatologica* 11. Basel: S. Karger.

CARPENTER, C. R.
  1964a "Societies of monkeys and apes," in *Naturalistic behavior of nonhuman primates.* Edited by C. R. Carpenter, 342–357. University Park, Pennsylvania: Pennsylvania State University Press.
  1964b "Sexual behavior of free-ranging rhesus monkeys (*Macaca mulatta*): periodicity of estrous, homosexual, autoerotic and nonconformist behavior," in *Naturalistic behavior of nonhuman primates.* Edited by C. R. Carpenter, 319–341. University Park, Pennsylvania: Pennsylvania State University Press.
  1964c "A field study in Siam of the behavior and social relations of the gibbon (*Hylobates lar*)," in *Naturalistic behavior of nonhuman primates.* Edited by C. R. Carpenter, 145–271. University Park, Pennsylvania: Pennsylvania State University Press.
  1965 "The howlers of Barro Colorado island," in *Primate behavior: field studies of monkeys and apes.* Edited by I. DeVore, 250–291. New York: Holt, Rinehart and Winston.

CASTELL, R., B. HEINRICH
  1971 Rank order in a captive female squirrel monkey colony. *Folia Primatologica* 14:182–189.

CHALMERS, N. R., T. E. ROWELL
  1971 Behaviour and female reproductive cycles in a captive group of mangabeys. *Folia Primatologica* 14:1–14.

CHANCE, M. R. A., C. J. JOLLY
1970   *Social groups of monkeys, apes and men.* New York: E. P. Dutton.

COULT, A. D., R. W. HABENSTEIN
1965   "Cross tabulations of Murdock's world ethnographic sample." University of Missouri, Columbia, Missouri.

COUNT, E. W.
1958   The biological basis of human sociality. *American Anthropologist* 60:1049–1085.

CROOK, J. H.
1970   "The socio-ecology of primates," in *Social behaviour in birds and mammals.* Edited by J. H. Crook, 103–166. London: Academic Press.

DU MOND, F. V.
1968   "The squirrel monkey in a seminatural environment," in *The squirrel monkey.* Edited by L. A. Rosenblum and R. W. Cooper, 87–145. New York: Academic Press.

EISENBERG, J. F., R. E. KUEHN
1966   *The behavior of* Ateles geoffroyi *and related species.* Smithsonian Miscellaneous Collections 151(8). Washington, D.C.

FOODEN, J.
1969   Taxonomy and evolution of the monkeys of Celebes. *Bibliotheca Primatologica* 10. Basel: S. Karger.

FORD, C. D.
1961   *Habitat, economy and society.* London: Methuen.

GARTLAN, J. S.
1968   Structure and function in primate society. *Folia Primatologica* 8:89–120.

GOODALL, J.
1965   "Chimpanzees of the Gombe Stream Reserve," in *Primate behavior: field studies of monkeys and apes.* Edited by I. DeVore, 425–473. New York: Holt, Rinehart and Winston.

HALL, K. R. L.
1968   "Social learning in monkeys," in *Primates: studies in adaptation and variability.* Edited by P. C. Jay, 383–397. New York: Holt, Rinehart and Winston.

HALL, K. R. L., I. DE VORE
1965   "Baboon social behavior," in *Primate behavior: field studies of monkeys and apes.* Edited by I. DeVore, 53–110. New York: Holt, Rinehart and Winston.

HAUSFATER, G.
1973   "A new look at the baboon group: dominance relations in baboons (*Papio cynocephalus*)." Paper presented at the Forty-second Annual Meeting of the American Association of Physical Anthropologists, April 12-14, 1973, Dallas, Texas.

IMANISHI, K.
1963   "Social behavior in Japanese monkeys, *Macaca fuscata*," in *Primate social behavior.* Edited by C. H. Southwick, 68–81. Princeton: D. Van Nostrand.

1965   "Identification: a process of socialization in the subhuman society of *Macaca fuscata*," in *Japanese monkeys: a collection of translations*. Edited by S. A. Altmann, 30–51. Published by the editor. Atlanta.

JAY, P.
1965   "The common langur of north India," in *Primate behavior: field studies of monkeys and apes*. Edited by I. DeVore, 197–249. New York: Holt, Rinehart and Winston.

JOLLY, A.
1966   *Lemur behavior: a Madagascar field study*. Chicago: University of Chicago Press.
1967   "Breeding synchrony in wild *Lemur catta*," in *Social communication among primates*. Edited by S. A. Altmann, 3–14. Chicago: University of Chicago Press.

KAUFMANN, J. H.
1967   "Social relations of adult males in a free-ranging band of rhesus monkeys," in *Social communication among primates*. Edited by S. A. Altmann, 73–98. Chicago: University of Chicago Press.

KAWAI, M.
1965a   "On the system of social ranks in a natural troop of Japanese monkeys, part one. Basic rank and dependent rank," in *Japanese monkeys: a collection of translations*. Edited by S. A. Altmann, 66–86. Published by the editor. Atlanta.
1965b   "On the system of social ranks in a natural troop of Japanese monkeys, part two. Ranking order as observed among the monkeys on and near the test box," in *Japanese monkeys: a collection of translations*. Edited by S. A. Altmann, 87–104. Published by the editor. Atlanta.

KAWAMURA, S.
1965   "Matriarchal social ranks in the Minoo-B troop," in *Japanese monkeys: a collection of translations*. Edited by S. A. Altmann, 105–112. Published by the editor. Atlanta.

KLOPFER, P. H., J. P. HAILMAN
1967   *An introduction to animal behavior: ethology's first century*. Englewood Cliffs, New Jersey: Prentice-Hall.

KOFORD, C. B.
1963a   "Group relations in an island colony of rhesus monkeys," in *Primate social behavior*. Edited by C. H. Southwick, 136–152. Princeton: D. Van Nostrand.
1963b   Rank of mothers and sons in bands of rhesus monkeys. *Science* 141(3578):356–357.

KOYAMA, N.
1967   On dominance rank and kinship of a wild Japanese monkey troop in Arashiyama. *Primates* 8:189–216.

KUMMER, H.
1971a   *Primate societies: group techniques of ecological adaptation*. Chicago: Aldine-Atherton.

1971b   "Spacing mechanisms in social behavior," in *Man and beast: comparative social behavior.* Edited by J. F. Eisenberg and W. S. Dillon, 219–234. Washington: Smithsonian Institution Press.

LINDBURG, D. G.
1971   "The rhesus monkey in north India: an ecological and behavioral study," in *Primate behavior: developments in field and laboratory research,* volume two. Edited by L. A. Rosenblum, 1–106. New York: Academic Press.

LORENZ, K.
1963   *On aggression.* New York: Bantam Books.

LOY, J.
1970   Peri-menstrual sexual behavior among rhesus monkeys. *Folia Primatologica* 13:286–297.
1971   Estrous behavior of free-ranging rhesus monkeys (*Macaca mulatta*). *Primates* 12(1):1-31.

LOY, J., K. LOY
1974   Behavior of an all-juvenile group of rhesus monkeys. *American Journal of Physical Anthropology* 40:83–96.

MAC ROBERTS, M. H.
1970   The social organization of Barbary Apes (*Macaca sylvana*) on Gibraltar. *American Journal of Physical Anthropology* 33:83–100.

MARSDEN, H. M.
1968   Agonistic behavior of young rhesus monkeys after changes induced in social rank of their mothers. *Animal Behavior* 16(1): 38–44.

MISSAKIAN, E. A.
1972   Genealogical and cross-genealogical dominance relations in a group of free-ranging rhesus monkeys (*Macaca mulatta*) on Cayo Santiago. *Primates* 13(2):169–180.

MURDOCK, G. P.
1934   *Our primitive contemporaries.* New York: Macmillan.
1957   World ethnographic sample. *American Anthropologist* 59:664–687.

PILBEAM, D.
1972   *The ascent of man.* New York: Macmillan.

POIRIER, F. E.
1970   Dominance structure of the Nilgiri langur (*Presbytis johnii*) of south India. *Folia Primatologica* 12:161–186.

REYNOLDS, V., F. REYNOLDS
1965   "Chimpanzees of the Budongo Forest," in *Primate behavior: field studies of monkeys and apes.* Edited by I. DeVore, 368–424. New York: Holt, Rinehart and Winston.

ROBERTS, P.
1971   Social interactions of *Galago crassicaudatus. Folia Primatologica* 14:171–181.

ROWELL, T. E.
1967   A quantitative comparison of the behaviour of a wild and a caged baboon group. *Animal Behavior* 15(4):499–509.
1972   *The social behaviour of monkeys.* Harmondsworth: Penguin.

SAAYMAN, G. S.
1971   Behaviour of the adult males in a troop of free-ranging chacma baboons (*Papio ursinus*). *Folia Primatologica* 15:36–57.

SADE, D. S.
1967   "Determinants of dominance in a group of free-ranging rhesus monkeys," in *Social communication among primates*. Edited by S. A. Altmann, 99–114. Chicago: University of Chicago Press.
1968   Inhibition of son-mother mating among free-ranging rhesus monkeys. *Science and psychoanalysis* 12:18–38.
1972   "A longitudinal study of social behavior of rhesus monkeys," in *The functional and evolutionary biology of primates*. Edited by R. Tuttle, 378–398. Chicago: Aldine-Atherton.
1973   "Theory on the fringe." Unpublished symposium held at the State University of New York, Oswego.

SCHALLER, G. B.
1963   *The mountain gorilla: ecology and behavior*. Chicago: University of Chicago Press.
1965   "The behavior of the mountain gorilla," in *Primate behavior: field studies of monkeys and apes*. Edited by I. DeVore, 324–367. New York: Holt, Rinehart and Winston.

SCHJELDERUP-EBBE, T.
1922   Beiträge zur Sozialpsychologie des Haushuhns. *Zeitschrift für Psychologie* 88:225–252.

SIMONDS, P. E.
1965   "The bonnet macaque in south India," in *Primate behavior: field studies of monkeys and apes*. Edited by I. DeVore, 175–196. New York: Holt, Rinehart and Winston.

SORENSON, M. W.
1970   "Behavior of tree shrews," in *Primate behavior: developments in field and laboratory research,* volume one. Edited by L. A. Rosenblum, 141–193. New York: Academic Press.

SORENSON, M. W., C. H. CONAWAY
1966   Observations on the social behavior of tree shrews in captivity. *Folia Primatologica* 4:124–145.

SOUTHWICK, C. H., MIRZA AZHAR BEG, M. RAFIQ SIDDIQI
1965   "Rhesus monkeys in north India," in *Primate behavior: field studies of monkeys and apes*. Edited by I. DeVore, 111–159. New York: Holt, Rinehart and Winston.

STRUHSAKER, T. T.
1967   Behavior of vervet monkeys and other cercopithecines. *Science* 156(3779):1197–1203.

SUGIYAMA, Y.
1968   The ecology of the lion-tailed macaque (*Macaca silenus* [Linnaeus]) — a pilot study. *Journal of the Bombay Natural History Society* 65(2):283–292.
1971   Characteristics of the social life of bonnet macaques (*Macaca radiata*). *Primates* 12(3-4):247–266.

TIGER, L.
   1970   Dominance in human societies. *Annual Review of Ecology and Systematics* 1:287–306.
TIGER, L., R. FOX
   1971   *The imperial animal.* New York: Holt, Rinehart and Winston.
YOSHIBA, K.
   1968   "Local and intertroop variability in ecology and social behavior of common Indian langurs," in *Primates: studies in adaptation and variability.* Edited by P. C. Jay, 217–242. New York: Holt, Rinehart and Winston.

The Influence of Hormonal and Ecological Factors upon Sexual Behavior and Social Organization in Old World Primates

GRAHAM S. SAAYMAN

INTRODUCTION

Free-ranging monkeys and apes normally associate in relatively permanent groups containing one or more adult males, a number of adult females, and immature animals. This form of social organization has long been considered as typical only of the primates, and investigators have attempted to identify the factors responsible for it. The proposition, first elaborated by Zuckerman, that the possibility of prolonged sexual activity, associated with the menstrual cycle characteristic of Old World primates, is a primary determinant of their social organization has formed an important — and controversial — point of reference:

The factors underlying associations of monkeys and apes are characterised by their continuous, rather than intermittent, sexual nature. The male primate is always sexually potent, while the female is also always to some extent receptive. In the lower mammal, on the other hand, the female, as a rule, accepts the male only during isolated periods of heat, and this intermittent character of the sexual bond is reflected in the transitory nature of their social unions (Zuckerman 1932: 313).

It is now known that permanent associations between adult males and females may also occur in nonprimate mammals such as the social carnivores (Schaller and Lowther 1969), the plains zebra and the mountain zebra (Klingel 1969; 1972), and possibly some delphinid species (Caldwell and Caldwell 1972; Tayler and Saayman 1972). Furthermore, recent research has identified a variety of cohesive factors other than sexual attraction. The survival value of primate social structure as an adaptation to ecological pressures is considered particularly important (Hall 1965). Nevertheless, the extent to which Zuckerman's hypothesis continues to generate debate (Imanishi 1960; Washburn and DeVore 1961; Hall 1965; Lancaster and Lee 1965; Washburn and Hamburg 1965; Washburn, Jay, and Lancaster 1965; Rowell 1972a, 1972b; Vandenbergh 1971) indicates that its impact upon contemporary speculation is far from spent. More recent evidence concerning the occurrence of prolonged periods of sexual activity in nonhuman primates is examined in this review and an attempt is made to place Zuckerman's hypothesis in perspective.

HORMONAL FACTORS AND SOCIAL ORGANIZATION

Estrous and Menstrual Cycles

The term "estrus" implies a circumscribed period of behavioral receptivity in the female mammal correlated with characteristic endocrine activity and a particular condition of the reproductive tract. Estrus generally succeeds a prolonged "anestrus" or nonbreeding season, during which time sexual receptivity is completely absent (Eckstein and Zuckerman 1956). Ovulation usually takes place during estrus. However, Eckstein and Zuckerman (1956) note that sexual receptivity or "heat" may occasionally occur during gestation in a number of forms such as rabbits, cats, and horses.

The differential effects of the estrous and menstrual cycles upon the frequency and duration of copulatory behavior were originally elaborated by Zuckerman:

The matings of the lower mammal are confined to short periods that appear to be circumscribed by activity of the follicular hormone. The matings of the primates are diffused over the entire cycle, coinciding with the continued action of the follicular hormone, but varying in frequency according to the varying degrees of activity of that hormone (Zuckerman 1932: 116).

Although the hormonal control of sexual behavior in the catarrhine monkeys has been shown to be considerably more complex than was previously thought (see reviews by Herbert 1970; Michael 1972), it remains true that sexual behavior in many of the species studied varies throughout the phases of a true menstrual cycle. Some primatologists, however, continue to employ the terms "estrous," "non-estrous," and "partially estrous" to describe the sexual status of nonhuman primates (Saayman 1969) and, since sexual activity is said to be restricted to the circumscribed period inherent in the definition of the term, it has sometimes, perhaps not surprisingly, been concluded that sexual attraction cannot function as a cohesive factor in social organization since adult males and females do not leave the primate group during "anestrus."

The Mating System of Cynocephalus Baboons

The sexual activity of adult male baboons is expressed most frequently in interactions with adult females with fully swollen sexual skins at the height of the turgescent phase of the menstrual cycle (Bolwig 1959; Hall 1962; Hall and DeVore 1965). Since ADULT males may sometimes form exclusive consort relationships with females for a few days at midcycle, the contention that copulation is limited to a circumscribed "estrous period" appears, at least for *Papio* sp., to receive some support. Quantitative analysis, however, indicates that this view, de-emphasizing as it does the additional, although more sporadic, sexual interactions which occur between females and juvenile and subadult males during the early follicular and luteal phases of the menstrual cycle, is an oversimplification which fails to take account of the role which the rotating system of mating may play in promoting troop cohesion.

In free-ranging baboons female sexual invitations to adult and immature males and mounting of females by juvenile, subadult, and adult males occur throughout the menstrual cycle, although sexual interactions are significantly elevated in the follicular phase, particularly during the swollen cycle state (Rowell 1967; Saayman 1970). This means, in effect, that females may be receptive and attractive to males for a minimum of the first half of the menstrual cycle, a period which averages 19.45 days in an average cycle length of 35.6 days (Gillman and Gilbert 1946). In exceptional cases, an adult male may associate with a swollen female for as long as 15 consecutive days (Saayman 1970) — a finding which indicates that phases of heightened receptivity and attractiveness may be considerably more prolonged in free-ranging individuals than normative data on cycle length, derived from small samples of captive animals, would suggest. In addition, female chacma baboons show the full pattern of copulatory behavior, including consummatory sexual responses, during the early luteal phase, when the sexual skin has begun to deturgesce.

As females enter the follicular phase of the menstrual cycle, an increase occurs in the frequency with which they make characteristic sexual approaches to males. The female is primarily responsible for initiating mounting activity with a variety of juvenile and subadult male partners (Saayman 1970). Although adult males may monopolize some females at the height of the turgescent phase, it is not necessarily overt competition by males for females which determines the establishment of consort bonds. The females themselves may play an active role in the selection of partners at specific stages of the menstrual cycle, since swollen females, in particular, invite copulation significantly more frequently from adult males. The survival value of such selection in the choice of mate by the female has been emphasized by Goss-Custard, Dunbar, and Aldrich-Blake (1972).

Whatever the selective factors involved, however, aggressive competition between adult males for females is a rare event in normally constituted groups of baboons (Tayler and Saayman 1972), and in a review of other species, Rowell notes that ". . . direct evidence of competition for females by potent males, which might lead to sexual selection, is limited" (1972a:87). Furthermore, receptive female chacma baboons were seldom involved in aggressive incidents, either as initiators or as recipients of attack (Saayman 1971b). There is little evidence, therefore, to support the suggestion that the formation of consort bonds introduces a major disruptive element into the social life of free-ranging chacma baboons. The mating system, comprising rotating sexual partners, may well be adapted for the periodic reinforcement of social bonds between adult females and partners selected from those age classes of males which are capable of integrated copulatory responses. It is likely that such a system functions to promote, rather than to disrupt, friendly social relationships and consequently may contribute toward the maintenance of troop cohesion. It may well be relevant, in this connection, that the pattern of copulatory behavior in the chacma baboon consists of a prolonged series of mounts which is associated with intermittent bouts of grooming by both partners; grooming by adult males is confined almost entirely to their swollen female consorts, whereas flat females, in the late luteal phase, continue to maintain particularly prominent grooming relationships with the adult males, as well as with other troop members (Saayman 1971c). The protracted sexual associations inherent in this mode of copulation may very well, therefore, operate to reinforce bonds between males and females which may have originated during their social development and which may persist beyond the context of primary sexual behavior.

The polygamous mating system does not necessarily exclude the possibility of partner preferences. Indeed, the observations of Marais (1939) originally suggested that sexual preferences might occur in chacma baboons, and this impression was supported by an analysis of the behavior of individual adult males in a free-ranging troop (Saayman 1971c). The least aggressive and most sexually active male, which was generally closely associated with females and their offspring and frequently intervened on their behalf during agonistic encounters, was presented to proportionately more often by receptive females and was groomed significantly more frequently than the other adult males by females in all stages of the reproductive cycle. At night this male often formed a distinct subgroup at a separate sleeping site in the company of lactating females, infants, and juveniles (Stoltz and Saayman 1970). His relationship with females and their young undoubtedly reinforced his leadership potential, thereby contributing to the prominent role he assumed in the direction of troop maintenance activities. Ransom and Ransom (1971) found that strong pair bonds between adult male and female olive baboons persisted irrespective of the cycle state of the female. Close affinitive relationships were sometimes extended to include "paternal" responses by the male to the infant of the female. The strength of the preferential relationship between the adult pair affected the degree of protection afforded infants and the nature of their early experiences with adult males. Further long-term research on individually recognizable animals is necessary to investigate the origins of individual sexual preferences and to determine the extent to which they influence the social systems of free-ranging groups.

Interspecific Comparison

There is a wide range of variation in the patterns of copulatory behavior and in the extent to which the menstrual cycle influences female receptivity and mating behavior in catarrhine monkeys under normal, free-ranging conditions (Saayman 1969). Marked individual differences may also occur within species, for example in the responses of ovariectomized baboons treated with known doses of estrogen (Saayman 1972, 1973). It is not possible to enter here into details, particularly as much of the information must necessarily be extracted from many field studies in which the collection of data on sexual interactions was often incidental to the major aims of the investigation. A comprehensive review by Rowell (1972a) is available but a number of investigations, designed specifically for the quantitative analysis of mating behavior, are directly relevant to the present concern with the distinction between the estrous and the menstrual cycles.

In those species which display fluctuations in the size of the sexual skin in relation to the phases of the menstrual cycle, true copulation with insemination is unlikely under free-ranging conditions during the late luteal phase, since in chacma baboons insertion rarely occurs when males mount females in the flat cycle state (Saayman 1970). Eckstein and Zuckerman (1956) report that chimpanzees with quiescent sexual skins permitted copulation but note that this may have been due to captive conditions. However, investigators have confirmed that copulation occurs throughout the menstrual cycle in a number of species although, in some cases, the frequencies of behavioral components measuring the sexual receptivity and attractiveness of females fluctuate rhythmically to reach maximal levels at midcycle.

In free-ranging rhesus monkeys (*Macaca mulatta*), females displayed peaks of mating and receptive behavior not only at midcycle, but also prior to, during, and after menstruation; behavior at these times was so similar that it was ". . . impossible to differentiate conclusively between the two without the observation of external bleeding" (Loy 1970: 291). Further, Michael, Herbert, and Welegalla (1967) observed peaks of mounting activity in some of their pairs of oppositely sexed rhesus monkeys, not only at midcycle, but also in the late luteal phase immediately prior to menstruation. In a captive colony of rhesus monkeys, Rowell found that mating occurred ". . . throughout the cycle except the days preceding and during menstruation; there was, however, a steady rise in mating frequency through the cycle until a sudden drop just before the next menstruation" (Rowell 1967: 29)

Hanby, Robertson, and Phoenix (1971) recorded repeated mating throughout the breeding season in a colony of captive macaques *(Macaca fuscata)* but observed no rhythmic fluctuations in the frequency of copulatory activity. The observations of these authors are pertinent:

We have not observed cyclic copulatory behavior that warrants the term "estrous cycle"; certainly, not as the expression has been used to describe cycles of receptivity in rodents. Aside from the seasonal factor, we have observed no coincidence between ovarian or menstrual cyclicity and restricted periods of receptivity. Therefore, we avoid using the term "estrous" or "estrous cycle" to describe periods of copulatory behavior in the Japanese macaque for the same reasons we would avoid the term to describe cycles of sexual behavior in the human female (1971: 140).

Rowell's comments on her studies of vervet *Cercopithecus aethiops* and Syke's monkeys *C. mitis (albogularis) kolbi* are similarly important:

... it has been stated that all monkeys show a mid-cycle oestrus period. We now have, not only an example of a species, the vervet, in which females emphatically do not have a mid-cycle oestrus, or any cyclicity of oestrus/ non-oestrus behavior, but also in Sykes' monkeys, a species whose females do show periodic mating but not at a consistent, specific stage of the menstrual cycle. We must, because of this last finding, query a great deal of earlier work in this area. Unless menstrual cycles were followed by histological methods, or records of visible menstrual bleeding, we cannot accept observation of limited periods in which mating periodically occurs as evidence of oestrus periods associated with ovulation and limited to the stage of the menstrual cycle in which it occurs (1971: 643).

Loy (1970, 1971) has called for a redefinition of "estrus":

Under field conditions, it is often impossible to ascertain whether estrous behavior exhibited by a non-pregnant rhesus female is inter-menstrual or peri-menstrual. Thus if field workers are to use the term "estrus," the occurrence of ovulation must be dropped from its definition and the term extended to include peri-menstrual behavior (1970: 294).

The occurrence of estrus proximal to menstruation necessitates changes in conceptual thinking and terminology for researchers working with rhesus monkeys. Measures such as "estrous cycle length" and "estrous duration" must be redefined and re-interpreted. "Estrous cycle length" is no longer equivalent to "menstrual cycle length," and the two must be carefully differentiated (1971: 25).

Conditions of observation may influence the behavior encountered, while experiments with small groups of monkeys indicate that social factors, in addition to endocrine state, influence sexual interactions and partner choice. Eaton (1973) found that female sexual receptivity and male intromission frequencies remained constant across the menstrual cycle in pigtail macaques (*Macaca nemestrina*) when single females were paired with males, whereas Goldfoot (1971) demonstrated signif- icant increases in indices of receptive behavior and in male copulatory behavior when maximally swollen female pigtail macaques were tested in a social group comprising three females and a male. Marked partner preferences, shown by male rhesus monkeys tested with a pair of fe- males (Herbert 1967, 1968) were modified by treatment with estrogen and progesterone (Herbert 1970). However, in Goldfoot's study (1971) the social dominance of females was an important determinant of inter- actions between females and males and, under certain conditions, exerted a more significant effect upon receptive behavior and the frequency of copulation than did the endocrine state of the female.

In summary, the evidence presently available does not support the generalization that the expression of sexual activity in Old World primates is strictly limited to abruptly initiated and terminated periods of "heat" of "estrus"; consequently, the concept of "estrus" is of little value in the assessment of factors responsible for their characteristic social organization.

Pregnancy and Sexual Receptivity

The female baboon is thought to be sexually inactive during gestation and the lactation interval, a period which may total some eighteen months to two years. However, copulation occurs during pregnancy in a variety of other species: rhesus monkey (Conaway and Koford 1964; Kaufmann 1965), vervet monkey *Cercopithecus aethiops* (Struhsaker 1967), chimpanzee *Pan troglodytes schweinfurthi* (van Lawick-Goodall 1968), Japanese macaque (Hanby, Robertson, and Phoenix 1971). Further reports of copulation in pregnant gorillas, Sykes' monkeys, vervet monkeys, and langurs *(Presbytis entellus),* are reviewed by Rowell (1972a).

The limited duration of many field studies of baboons has often excluded the possibility of long-term observations upon specific females throughout the course of the reproductive cycle, and there is the additional problem of reliable identification of an adequate sample of females in large and unmarked troops. However, Gillman and Gilbert (1946) described small swellings of the sexual skin of chacma baboons during the first three months of gestation. Rowell (1972a) reported swellings in pregnant baboons but commented that these were too small to be associated with copulation. It should be noted in this connection, however, that some free-ranging females copulated frequently although displaying only very small amounts of sexual skin turgescence when ovariectomized baboons were treated with implants of ovarian hormones (Saayman 1972, 1973). Kriewaldt and Hendrickx (1968) recorded turgescence in pregnant baboons which was apparently confused with perineal reactions during the menstrual cycle. A female chacma baboon, caged together with an adult male, exhibited maximal turgescence of the sexual skin and copulated frequently during the first month of pregnancy (Saayman, unpublished observation). Van Lawick-Goodall (1968) noted large sexual swellings in four of ten pregnant chimpanzees which were receptive and copulated frequently during the first four to six months of gestation; smaller swellings were seen in two of the other females. Turgescence of the sexual skin in the pregnant chimpanzee, particularly during the first two to three months of gestation, is well documented (Eckstein and Zuckerman 1956).

Rowell (1972a, 1972b) has commented that it is difficult to reconcile the occurrence of copulation in pregnant monkeys with the finding that progesterone antagonizes the stimulatory effect of estrogen upon female sexual attractiveness and receptivity (rhesus monkey — Michael, Saayman, and Zumpe 1968; chacma baboon — Saayman 1972, 1973). This question is particularly pertinent in the case of the baboon and the chimpanzee since turgescence of the sexual skin in both species is estrogen-dependent, whereas deturgescence is stimulated by a substance with progesterone-like activity (baboon — Gillman and Gilbert 1946; chimpanzee — Graham et al. 1972). Data on circulating levels of progesterone in the pregnant baboon are lacking, and Graham (1970) notes that this question requires further study in the chimpanzee. However, there were marked quantitative differences in plasma progesterone concentrations in individual menstrual cycles of rhesus monkeys (Neill, Johansson, and Knobil 1967). Individual variations in the concentrations of estradiol and progesterone in peripheral plasma were also recorded in pregnant rhesus monkeys, and the levels of both hormones fluctuated asynchronously during the first forty days of gestation (Hodgen et al. 1972). There were similar individual differences in the progesterone profiles of bonnet macaques *(Macaca radiata)* during the menstrual cycle and pregnancy (Stabenfeldt and Hendrickx 1972). Furthermore, Graham et al. (1972) have speculated that the partial turgescence of the sexual skin sometimes observed to precede menstruation in the chimpanzee might be due to a high estrogen to progesterone ratio. The occurrence of copulation in a proportion of individuals, in the late luteal phase of the menstrual cycle as well as during early pregnancy, may therefore be associated with quantitative differences in the hormonal patterns of individual females and with fluctuations in the balance of circulating levels of estrogens and progesterone. Further research is clearly essential, but the behavioral evidence already available is not compatible with the generalization that the intervention of pregnancy necessarily excludes all possibility of sexual expression in Old World primates.

ECOLOGICAL FACTORS AND SOCIAL ORGANIZATION

Population Dynamics

Statistical estimates of the duration of the discrete stages of the reproductive cycle are generally derived from analyses of captive animals, studies of small colony groups, and small samples of free-ranging populations. The contention that the intervention of pregnancy and lactation interrupts sexual activity presupposes that reproductive processes take place in a system characterized by static states in which the adult females of the population are EITHER receptive OR pregnant OR lactating. The norm is a statistical abstraction; it is also necessary to consider the wide range of variability in individual responsiveness to numerous variables inherent in the dynamic socioecological system characteristic of free-ranging populations of monkeys.

One such variable is the fertility of individual females. Gillman and Gilbert (1946) found that a high percentage of matings were infertile in captive chacma baboons, even when optimally timed for conception. Kriewaldt and Hendrickx (1968) reported that as many as 15 percent of a captive sample of 133 female baboons from East Africa appeared to be barren and a very low rate of births was calculated by Altmann and Altmann (1970: 60) on the basis of data on East African baboons presented by DeVore. At least 10 percent of the free-ranging adult females studied by Saayman (1970) continued to show consecutive menstrual cycles despite frequent copulation with adult males. Similarly, seven of twenty-one females failed to give birth during Loy's (1971) study of rhesus monkeys. In a laboratory study of reproductive patterns of three species of macaque (*M. mulatta, M. arctoides* and *M. fascicularis*), 58 percent of the females became pregnant when exposed to a potent male for limited periods near midcycle and 43 percent produced live young (MacDonald 1971). Variations in the rate with which individuals conceive may therefore ensure the availability to males of a requisite number of receptive females.

Similar considerations apply to suggestions that the lactation interval necessarily limits the supply of cycling females. Menstrual cycles recommence within two to three weeks after the death or removal of an infant from the female baboon (Rowell 1972b; but see also discussion by Altmann and Altmann 1970: 59–62). In their studies of yellow baboons, Altmann and Altmann found that the deaths of infants accounted for much of the overall death rate. A high rate of infant mortality was recorded for free-ranging chacma baboons (Stoltz and Saayman 1970) and Washburn (quoted by Lancaster and Lee 1965) reported similar findings for East African baboons. Yoshiba (1968) observed marked increases in sexual activity in the Indian langur after changes in group composition which were sometimes associated with the killing of infants by new group leaders. Koford (1965) reported that the infant mortality rate of the Cayo Santiago rhesus monkeys ranged from 5.9 to 10.7 percent over a period of four years. It is therefore likely that a proportion of females become fully sexually receptive considerably earlier in free-ranging populations than would be predicted on the basis of normative data on the duration of gestation and the lactation interval derived from the captive situation.

There is also evidence that the menstrual rhythm is not suppressed throughout lactation. Gillman and Gilbert (1946) noted that turgescence of the sexual skin might commence during the process of weaning, and, in exceptional cases, turgescence occurred within 33 days postpartum in the presence of a suckling infant (Gilbert and Gillman 1951). However, Altmann and Altmann (1970) observed no sexual skin turgescence in mothers with infants during postpartum intervals 60, 71 and 327 days or more in duration. Nevertheless, Rowell (1972a) remarks that cycling commences in all monkey species prior to the completion of the weaning process. Female vervet monkeys may copulate within five weeks of giving birth (Rowell 1970). Four of five Japanese macaques with recent infants became pregnant (Hanby, Robertson, and Phoenix 1971), and David and Ramaswami (1969) reported that lactation persisted through eight menstrual cycles in the Indian langur, even in the absence of an infant. By terminating weaning at an optimum time, it was possible to increase the birthrate in a breeding colony of hamadryas baboons, and females were capable of producing two infants in the course of fourteen months (Asanov 1972). Similar results were obtained with the Japanese macaque (Nomura et al. 1972).

The evidence suggests that under free-ranging conditions adult males are not necessarily deprived of all sexual expression for prolonged periods due to reproductive processes in the female. If sexual attraction does indeed function as a cohesive factor in primate social organization, it is likely that its effect would be to retain adult males in the company of adult females and their offspring, which develop enduring bonds during the slow maturation process characteristic of the higher primates. It is noteworthy that, in the first instance, bisexual reproductive groups generally contain more adult females than adult males, although exceptions may occur, notably in the yellow baboons studied by the Altmanns. Secondly, many of the catarrhine monkeys are polygamous and display systems of mating which resemble that of the cynocephalus baboons. If potent males were deprived of adequate sexual outlet for prolonged periods, however, they might move to a neighboring group. Lindburg (1969) found that migration of adult male rhesus monkeys in India corresponded with the mating season and migratory males copulated more frequently than nonmigratory males. Migration in the baboon is largely confined to the adult male class (Altmann and Altmann 1970), although exceptions may occur (Saayman 1971d; Rowell 1972a). It is of interest, therefore, that L.P. Stoltz (personal communication) has found that a high rate of migration is characteristic of adult males among marked troops in a population of chacma baboons in the Transvaal. Whether or not mobility of males is determined primarily by sexual attraction or by variations in their long-term social relationships in their troop of origin remains to be determined.

Annual Reproductive Cycles

The discovery that many species of monkeys do not breed at an equal rate throughout the year has implications not only for reproductive physiology, but also for the generalization that sexual attraction influences the permanency of the heterosexual unit. If females are entirely nonreceptive during a long birth season, sexual attraction becomes an inadequate explanation for the permanent association between adult males and females.

In a widely quoted review, Lancaster and Lee (1965) drew attention to the important distinction between the "birth peak" and the "birth season"; the former implies a fluctuating distribution of birth and mating frequencies throughout the year, whereas the latter signifies a clear-cut restriction of births to a limited period of the year, associated with a similarly restricted mating season which precedes it. Data were reviewed on three species of the genus *Macaca,* the Indian langur, and four populations of African baboons, derived from a total of eleven studies on monkeys ranging in duration from two months to six years. In two of the populations (the Takasakiyama Japanese macaques and the rhesus monkeys of Cayo Santiago), there was a marked birth season, and mating activity was also restricted to a circumscribed part of the year. Similar seasonal restrictions in the distribution of births were not conclusively confirmed for the other nine monkey populations (Indian rhesus, bonnet, and langur monkeys and the African baboons) although birth peaks were apparent and copulation, in the majority of cases, occurred throughout the periods of study. The question of seasonality was left open in the case of the African apes because of low birth rates, small samples of populations, and limited observations of copulation, although it was suggested that birth peaks might occur. These data confirm the existence of rhythms in the annual reproductive cycle, suggested earlier by the work of Hartman (1932) on the rhesus monkey, but they are not incompatible with the interpretation that many Old World primates copulate throughout the year although mating frequencies may be inversely correlated with a peak in the birth rate during part of the year. Indeed, Washburn, Jay, and Lancaster have commented on the data reviewed as follows: ". . . probably the most common situation is a birth peak, a time of the year at which births tend to be concentrated, rather than sharply limited mating and birth seasons" (1965: 1543).

The factors responsible for seasonal variations in the birthrate remain obscure, and a causal relationship between environmental variables associated with seasonal fluctuations in reproductive characteristics of nonhuman primates and humans has yet to be demonstrated (Vandenbergh 1971). Several other variables may influence the annual reproductive cycle. The onset of seasonal sexual behavior was delayed by the presence of an infant in the rhesus monkey (Kaufmann 1965) and possibly in the Japanese macaque (Eaton 1972). In the latter case, pregnancy also limited the duration of the breeding season. Asanov (1972) reported that the timing of weaning affected the onset of sexual activity in captive hamadryas baboons, creating the impression of a breeding season, which could, however, be altered in relation to the time of year by experimentally manipulating the time of weaning. Seasonal cyclicity in male rhesus monkeys may contribute to the breeding rhythm, since testis size (Sade 1964) and spermatogenesis (Conaway and Sade 1965) increased during the mating season. The incidence of ejaculation in male rhesus monkeys under constant laboratory conditions showed an annual rhythm (Michael and Keverne 1971), suggesting that factors other than ecological variables are also implicated. It has long been known that ovulation does not always occur during the irregular menstrual cycles characteristic of the rhesus monkey during the summer months (Hartman 1932). A decrease in the rate of conception due to anovulatory cycles and to a decline in spermatogenesis might well partially account for a decrease in the birthrate, and the demonstration of birth peaks or birth seasons alone does not necessarily confirm the complete suppression of mating activity at certain times of the year.

The complexities are further compounded by ambiguities inherent in the interpretation of behavioral components generally used to measure sexual responsiveness (Herbert 1970; Saayman 1973), and the importance of using multiple behavioral indices in the analysis of primate sexual behavior has previously been discussed (Michael and Saayman 1968). Altmann observed associations between consort pairs of rhesus monkeys on Cayo Santiago which persisted during the pregnancy of the female; although copulation did not occur; these associations

... so closely resembled mating consort pairings that they at first were mistaken for such. In no case, either during pregnancy or at any other time, was a male seen attempting to force coition. Indeed, perhaps more striking was the fact that adult males who were closely associated with pregnant females were on several occasions seen to masturbate manually to the point of ejaculation (1962: 391–392).

More recently, Loy (1971), using a variety of behavioral indices generally employed to measure sexual attractiveness and receptivity, demonstrated cyclical fluctuations in affinitive relations betweeen males and nonpregnant femaies thoughout the year in the Cayo Santiago colony, and true copulatory mounting series and insemination were observed in a small proportion of females in every month of the year. These findings are in contrast to those reviewed by Lancaster and Lee (1965) on this rhesus monkey population and recall the speculations of Kaufmann who wrote as follows on his observations of the Cayo Santiago colony:

If the females' physiologic cycles, with accompanying behavioral changes, do persist throughout the year, the behavioral estrus of the mating season could be viewed as an intensification of an ever-present phenomenon. Estrous behavior in primates might then be viewed simply as sexually orientated behavior in females resulting chiefly from hormone fluctuations, without regard to the possibility of conception. This is purely speculative, but it would tie together the different situations observed in the laboratory and in the field, and would be consistent with the great variation in reproductive timing of primate populations all over the world. As is true of many mammals, every gradation exists from rigidly seasonal breeders to populations which may produce young in any month, and there is much variation in different populations of the same species. Some form of seasonal effect, even if it is only a seasonal peak in births, seems to be the rule in the populations already studied [referring to work of Lancaster and Lee] (1965: 511).

Thus, the cyclical, affinitive, and sexual behavior reported by Loy (1971) during the nonmating season might have been due to the maintenance of a measure of sexual attraction by comparatively low levels of estrogen which periodically achieved levels sufficient to facilitate increases in the sexual capacity of males. This possibility is supported by the findings of Vandenbergh (1969) who demonstrated that increased testicular activity, associated with increased copulatory behavior, might be stimulated by the exposure of sexually inactive adult male rhesus monkeys to ovariectomized females rendered sexually attractive by treatment with estrogen.

In the Japanese macaque, however, amenorrhea persisted throughout the summer months, and levels of urinary estrogen were very low and showed no cyclicity (Nomura et al. 1972). It is nevertheless noteworthy that in the Oregon colony a marked seasonal increase occurred in the play and affiliative behavior (including gross bodily contact and grooming activity) of adult males with adult females and other adult males during the period of gestation and the birth season (Alexander 1970). It would be interesting to determine whether similar changes in social behavior accompany the decline in primary sexual activity in other species, such as the talapoin monkey *(Miopithecus talapoin)*, which are said to show discrete mating and birth seasons (Gautier-Hion 1970).

DISCUSSION

Whereas theories concerning the factors responsible for the social organization of Old World primates are still very much at the level of hypothesis, the evidence presently available does not invalidate Zuckerman's (1932) distinction between the differential effects upon behavior of the estrous and menstrual cycles. Moreover, the capacity for increased sexual expression in the higher primates is correlated with relatively permanent social bonds between males and females which may extend beyond the context of primary sexual behavior. The influence of sexual attraction upon social organization is perhaps most dramatically illustrated in some of the pinnipeds, which have adapted to the ecological requirements of an amphibious way of life: bulls establish and maintain territories and harems during the breeding season, but the animals disperse in less structured herds during the remainder of the year. Factors other than sexual attraction, however, are implicated in the regulation of primate social structure and behavior (genealogical relationships — Imanishi 1960; Sade 1965; van Lawick-Goodall 1968; mother-infant affectional systems — Harlow and Harlow 1965; ecological factors — Crook 1970; the influence of learning and social tradition — Hamburg 1965; Washburn and Hamburg 1965; Frisch 1968). Furthermore, there is a wide range of variation in the nature of mating systems and in the extent to which sexuality is expressed in different primate species (Washburn, Jay, and Lancaster 1965; Jay

1968; Rowell 1970, 1971, 1972a, 1972b). It is clear, therefore, that generalizations emphasizing the exclusive importance of any one cohesive factor are inadmissible. Nevertheless, as Rowell has commented: "If the cohesive function of sexual interaction is denied, we are left with the task of explaining why monkeys and apes are receptive proportionately more of the time than are other mammals — even other social mammals" (1972b: 132).

In recent years academic research has focused increasingly upon the social organization and behavior of nonhuman primates, possibly because these animals are considered important for theories concerning the evolution of man. Indeed, Zuckerman (1932) first elaborated the proposition that studies of physiological mechanisms regulating the sexual cycle of nonhuman primates are relevant for theories concerning the evolutionary development of human social systems. However, Schaller and Lowther (1969) have indicated that the study of bisexual groups characteristic of some social carnivores, such as the wolf, lion, wild dog, and hyena, may yield insights into the social system of the early hominids, in which efficient methods of cooperative hunting may well have represented an important determinant of social organization. Similarly, Eisenberg (1973) has drawn attention to the significance of comparative studies of large-brained, long-lived, nonprimate mammals, and has challenged the assumption that complex behavioral repertoires, communication systems, social traditions, and an advanced form of social organization are unique to the higher primates.

Particularly fruitful insights may perhaps be derived from comparisons of the social organization of the higher primates and the phylogenetically unrelated Delprinidae, a group of animals whose terrestrial links were severed some sixty-five million years ago, but which nevertheless show a number of markedly similar features in common with primates such as the baboon (Tayler and Saayman 1972). In the captive bottlenose dolphin (*Tursiops aduncus*), primary sexual behavior occurs throughout the year, although frequencies may be elevated in spring and early summer; pregnant cows accept the bull for the first ten months of a gestation period which lasts approximately one year. The complete pattern of copulatory behavior occurs some six weeks after parturition and continues throughout lactation which, in captivity, may continue for more than three years. Furthermore, sexual behavior is a prominent feature of the social behavior of free-swimming bottlenose dolphins (Saayman, Tayler, and Bower 1973), and observations of both captive and free-ranging groups suggest that courtship-like activity, comprising homosexual and heterosexual interactions between adults, juveniles, or combinations of these age-classes, may well form part of the normal behavioral repertoire of these highly social marine predators (Saayman and Tayler 1973a, b).

Current systematic studies of free-ranging humpback dolphins (*Sousa* sp.) indicate that schools of these inshore dolphins have a home-range which is at least semipermanent (Saayman, Bower, and Tayler 1972), and more recent observations suggest that bulls are permanent members of resident schools, since primary sexual behavior is seen during all seasons of the year. The members of a large school, some of which are identifiable by virtue of prominent scars and color patterns, disperse in diversely constituted groups which range independently over the habitat, occasionally reuniting at the feeding ground. Vigorous social interactions, closely resembling primary sexual behavior, are often stimulated when subunits combine, and it is possible that these courtship-like interactions operate as a form of "greetings ceremony" which functions to reinforce social bonds. The animals may then depart in newly composed subunits, which frequently alter in composition from one sighting to the next. The availability of reef-dwelling fish, which apparently form a major prey item of humpback dolphins, may represent an important ecological correlate to their social organization (Saayman and Tayler 1973b.).

These observations indicate striking similarities in the social organization of a delphinid and the relatively flexible or, in the terminology of Nishida (1968), "extensible" social systems characteristic of the chimpanzee (Reynolds and Reynolds 1965; van Lawick-Goodall 1968; Nishida 1968, 1970), social carnivores (Schaller and Lowther 1969), and hunter-gatherers such as the Bushman (Tobias 1964). The scientific merit of such comparisons of animals which are only distantly related in their behavioral evolution must be assessed against traditional attempts to develop a phylogeny of behavior with the higher primates located at the upper end of the scale. Attempts to reconstruct the nature of the social organization of the early hominids may very well be broadened in scope by investigations of the socioecology of animals other than the more closely related living species of nonhuman primates.

REFERENCES

ALTMANN, S. A.
   1962   A field study of the sociobiology of rhesus monkeys, *Macaca mulatta. Annals, New York Academy of Science* 102:338–435.

ALTMANN, S. A., J. ALTMANN
  1970   *Baboon ecology*. Chicago and London: The University of Chicago Press.

ALEXANDER, B. K.
  1970   Parental behavior of adult male Japanese monkeys. *Behaviour* 36:270–285.

ASANOV, S. S.
  1972   "Comparative features of the reproductive biology of hamadryas baboons (*Papio hamadryas*), grivet monkeys (*Cercopithecus aethiops*) and rhesus monkeys (*Macaca mulatta*)," in *The use of non-human primates in research on human reproduction*. Edited by E. Diczfalusy and C. C. Standley, 458–472. Stockholm: WHO Research and Training Centre on Human Reproduction.

BOLWIG, N.
  1959   A study of the behaviour of the chacma baboon (*Papio ursinus*). *Behaviour* 14:136–163.

CALDWELL, D. K., M. C. CALDWELL
  1972   *The world of the bottlenosed dolphin*. Philadelphia and New York: J. B. Lippincott.

CONAWAY, C. H., C. B. KOFORD
  1964   Estrous cycles and mating behavior in a free-ranging band of rhesus monkeys. *Journal of Mammalogy* 45:577–588.

CONAWAY, C. H., D. S. SADE
  1965   The seasonal spermatogenic cycle in free ranging rhesus monkeys. *Folia Primatologica* 3:1–12.

CROOK, J. H.
  1970   "The socio-ecology of primates," in *Social behaviour in birds and mammals*. Edited by J. H. Crook, 103–166. London: Academic Press.

DAVID, G. F. X., L. S. RAMASWAMI
  1969   Studies on menstrual cycles and other related phenomena in the langur (*Presbytis entellus entellus*). *Folia Primatologica* 11:300–316.

EATON, G.
  1972   Seasonal sexual behavior: intrauterine contraceptive devices in a confined troop of Japanese monkeys. *Hormones and Behavior* 3:133–142.
  1973   "Social and endocrine determinants of sexual behavior in simian and prosimian females," in *Primate reproductive behavior*. Edited by C. H. Phoenix, 20–35. Basel: S. Karger.

ECKSTEIN, P., S. ZUCKERMAN
  1956   "The oestrous cycle in the mammalia," in *Marshall's physiology of reproduction*. Edited by A. S. Parkes, 226–396. London: Longmans, Green.

EISENBERG, J. F.
  1973   "Mammalian social systems: are primate social systems unique?" in *Precultural primate behavior*. Edited by E. W. Menzel, 232–249. Basel: S. Karger.

FRISCH, J. E.
  1968   "Individual behavior and intertroop variability in Japanese ma-
         caques," in *Primates: studies in adaptation and variability*. Edited
         by P. C. Jay, 243–252. New York: Holt, Rinehart and Winston.

GAUTIER-HION, A.
  1970   L'Organisation sociale d'une bande de talapoins (*Miopithecus
         talapoin*) dans le Nord-Est du Gabon. *Folia Primatologica* 12:
         116–141.

GILBERT, C., J. GILLMAN
  1951   Pregnancy in the baboon (*Papio ursinus*). *South African Journal
         of Medical Science* 16:115–124.

GILLMAN, J., C. GILBERT
  1946   The reproductive cycle of the chacma baboon *Papio ursinus* with
         special reference to the problems of menstrual irregularities as
         assessed by the behaviour of the sexual skin. *South African Jour-
         nal of Medical Science* 11 (Biology supplement): 1–54.

GOLDFOOT, D. A.
  1971   "Hormonal and social determinants of sexual behavior in the
         pigtail monkey (*Macaca nemestrina*)," in *Normal and abnormal
         development of brain and behaviour*. Edited by G. B. A. Stoelinga
         and J. J. van de Werff ten Bosch, 325–342. Leiden: Leiden Uni-
         versity Press.

GOSS-CUSTARD, J. D., R. I. M. DUNBAR, F. P. G. ALDRICH-BLAKE
  1972   Survival, mating and rearing strategies in the evolution of primate
         social structure. *Folia Primatologica* 17:1–19.

GRAHAM, C. E.
  1970   "Reproductive physiology of the chimpanzee," in *The chimpan-
         zee*, volume three. Edited by G. H. Bourne, 183–220. New York:
         University Park Press.

GRAHAM, C. E., D. C. COLLINS, H. ROBINSON, J. R. K. PREEDY
  1972   Urinary levels of estrogens and pregnanediol and plasma levels
         of progesterone during the menstrual cycle of the chimpanzee:
         relationship to the sexual swelling. *Endocrinology* 91:13–24.

HALL, K. R. L.
  1962   The sexual, agnostic and derived social behaviour patterns of the
         wild chacma baboon, *Papio ursinus*. *Proceedings Zoological So-
         ciety of London* 139:283–327.
  1965   Social organisation of the Old-World monkeys and apes. *Sym-
         posium Zoological Society of London* 14:265–289.

HALL K. R. L., I. DE VORE
  1965   "Baboon social behavior," in *Primate behavior*. Edited by I. De-
         Vore, 53–110. New York: Holt, Rinehart and Winston.

HAMBURG, D. A.
  1965   "Observations of mother-infant interactions in primate field stud-
         ies," in *Determinants of infant behaviour IV*. Edited by B. M.
         Foss, 3–14. London: Methuen.

HANBY, J. P., L. T. ROBERTSON, C. H. PHOENIX
1971 The sexual behavior of a confined troop of Japanese macaques. *Folia Primatologica* 16:123–143.

HARLOW, H. F., M. K. HARLOW
1965 "Effects of various mother-infant relationships on rhesus monkey behaviors," in *Determinants of infant behaviour IV*. Edited by B. M. Foss, 15–36. London: Methuen.

HARTMAN, C. G.
1932 Studies in the reproduction of the monkey *Macaca (Pithecus) rhesus* with special reference to menstruation and pregnancy. *Contributions to Embryology* 134(23):1–161. Carnegie Institute of Washington.

HERBERT, J.
1967 "The social modification of sexual and other behaviour in rhesus monkeys," in *Progress in primatology*. Edited by D. Starck, R. Schneider and H.-J. Kuhn, 232–246. Stuttgart: Fischer.
1968 Sexual preference in the rhesus monkey *Macaca mulatta* in the laboratory. *Animal Behavior* 16:120–128.
1970 Hormones and reproductive behaviour in rhesus and talapoin monkeys. *Journal of Reproduction and Fertility* Supplement 11: 119–140.

HODGEN, G. D., M. L. DUFAU, K. J. CATT, W. W. TULLNER
1972 Estrogens, progesterone and chorionic gonadotropin in pregnant rhesus monkeys. *Endocrinology* 91:896–900.

IMANISHI, K.
1960 Social organisation of subhuman primates in their natural habitat. *Current Anthropology* 1:393–407.

JAY, P.
1968 "Primate field studies and human evolution," in *Primates: Studies in adaptation and variability*. Edited by P. C. Jay, 487–503. New York: Holt, Rinehart and Winston.

KAUFMANN, J. H.
1965 A three-year study of mating behavior in a freeranging band of rhesus monkeys. *Ecology* 46:500–512.

KLINGEL, H.
1969 The social organisation and population ecology of the plains zebra *(Equus quagga)*. *Zoologica Africana* 4:249–263.
1972 Social behaviour of African Equidae. *Zoologica Africana* 7:175–185.

KOFORD, C. B.
1965 "Population dynamics of rhesus monkeys on Cayo Santiago," in *Primate behavior*. Edited by I. DeVore, 160–174. New York: Holt, Rinehart and Winston.

KRIEWALDT, F. H., A. G. HENDRICKX
1968 Reproductive parameters of the baboon. *Laboratory Animal Care* 18:361–370.

LANCASTER, J. B., R. B. LEE
  1965   "The annual reproductive cycle in monkeys and apes," in *Primate behavior*. Edited by I. DeVore, 486–513. New York: Holt, Rinehart and Winston.

LINDBURG, D. G.
  1969   Rhesus monkeys: mating season mobility of adult males. *Science* 166:1176–1178.

LOY, J.
  1970   Peri-menstrual sexual behavior among rhesus monkeys. *Folia Primatologica* 13:286–297.
  1971   Estrous behavior of free-ranging rhesus monkeys (*Macaca mulatta*). *Primates* 12:1–31.

MAC DONALD, G. J.
  1971   Reproductive patterns of three species of macaques. *Fertility and Sterility* 22:373–377.

MARAIS, E. N.
  1939   *My friends the baboons*. London: Methuen.

MICHAEL, R. P.
  1972   "Determinants of primate reproductive behaviour," in *The use of non-human primates in research on human reproduction*. Edited by E. Diczfalusy and C. C. Standley, 322–363. Stockholm: WHO Research and Training Centre on Human Reproduction.

MICHAEL, R. P., J. HERBERT, J. WELEGALLA
  1967   Ovarian hormones and the sexual behaviour of the male rhesus monkey (*Macaca mulatta*) under laboratory conditions. *Journal of Endocrinology* 39:81–98.

MICHAEL, R. P., E. B. KEVERNE
  1971   An annual rhythm in the sexual activity of the male rhesus monkey, *Macaca mulatta*, in the laboratory. *Journal of Reproduction and Fertility* 25:95–98.

MICHAEL, R. P., G. S. SAAYMAN
  1968   Differential effects on behaviour of the subcutaneous and intravaginal administration of oestrogen in the rhesus monkey (*Macaca mulatta*). *Journal of Endocrinology* 41:231–246.

MICHAEL, R. P., G. S. SAAYMAN, D. ZUMPE
  1968   The suppression of mounting behaviour and ejaculation in male rhesus monkeys (*Macaca mulatta*) by administration of progesterone to their female partners. *Journal of Endocrinology* 41:421–431.

NEILL, D. D., E. D. B. JOHANSSON, E. KNOBIL
  1967   Levels of progesterone in peripheral plasma during the menstrual cycle of the rhesus monkey. *Endocrinology* 81:1161–1164.

NISHIDA, T.
  1968   The social group of wild chimpanzees in the Mahali Mountains. *Primates* 9:167–224.
  1970   Social behavior and relationships among wild chimpanzees of the Mahali Mountains. *Primates* 11:47–87.

NOMURA, T., N. OHSAWA, Y. TAJIMA, T. TANAKA, S. KOTERA, A. ANDO, H. NIGI
  1972   "Reproduction of Japanese monkeys," in *The use of non-human primates in research on human reproduction.* Edited by E. Diczfalusy and C. C. Standley, 473–482. Stockholm: WHO Research and Training Centre on Human Reproduction.

RANSOM T. W., B. S. RANSOM
  1971   Adult male-infant relations among baboons (*Papio anubis*). *Folia Primatalogica* 16:179–195.

REYNOLDS, V., F. REYNOLDS
  1965   "Chimpanzees of the Budongo Forest," in *Primate behavior.* Edited by I. DeVore, 368–424. New York: Holt, Rinehart and Winston.

ROWELL, T. E.
  1967   "Female reproductive cycles and the behavior of baboons and rhesus monkeys," in *Social communication among primates.* Edited by S. A. Altmann, 15–32. Chicago: University of Chicago Press.
  1970   Reproductive cycles of two *Cercopithecus* monkeys. *Journal of Reproduction and Fertility* 22:321–338.
  1971   Organisation of caged groups of cercopithecus monkeys. *Animal Behavior* 19:625–645.
  1972a Female reproduction cycles and social behavior in primates. *Advances in the Study of Behavior* 4:69–105.
  1972b *Social behaviour of monkeys.* Harmondsworth: Penguin.

SAAYMAN, G. S.
  1969   Endocrine factors and behaviour in the Old World monkeys. *South African Journal of Science* 65:121–126.
  1970   The menstrual cycle and sexual behaviour in a troop of free-ranging chacma baboons (*Papio ursinus*). *Folia Primatologica* 12:81–110.
  1971a Behaviour of the adult males in a troop of free-ranging chacma baboons (*Papio ursinus*). *Folia Primatologica* 15:36–57.
  1971b Aggressive behaviour in free-ranging chacma baboons (*Papio ursinus*). *Journal of Behavioral Science* 1:77–83.
  1971c Grooming behaviour in a troop of free-ranging chacma baboons (*Papio ursinus*). *Folia Primatologica* 16:161–178.
  1971d Behaviour of chacma baboons. *African Wild Life* 25:25–29.
  1972   Effects of ovarian hormones upon the sexual skin and mounting behaviour in the free-ranging chacma baboon (*Papio ursinus*). *Folia Primatologica* 17:297–303.
  1973   "Effects of ovarian hormones upon the sexual skin and behaviour of ovariectomised baboons (*Papio Ursinus*) under free-ranging conditions," in *Primate reproductive behavior.* Edited by C. H. Phoenix, 64–98. Basel: S. Karger.

SAAYMAN, G. S., C. K. TAYLER
  1973a Some behaviour patterns of the southern right whale *Eubalaena australis. Zeitschrift für Säugetierkunde* 38:172–183.
  1973b Social organisation of inshore dolphins (*Tursiops aduncus* and

Sousa sp.) in the Indian Ocean. *Journal of Mammalogy* 54:993–996.

SAAYMAN, G. S., D. BOWER, C. K. TAYLER
1972 Observations on inshore and pelagic dolphins on the south-eastern Cape coast of South Africa. *Koedoe* 15:1–24.

SAAYMAN, G. S., C. K. TAYLER, D. BOWER
1973 Diurnal activity cycles in captive and free-ranging Indian Ocean bottlenose dolphins (*Tursiops aduncus* Ehrenburg). *Behaviour* 44: 212–233.

SADE, D. S.
1964 Seasonal cycle in size of testes of free-ranging *Macaca mulatta*. *Folia Primatologica* 2:171–180.
1965 Some aspects of parent-offspring and sibling relations in a group of rhesus monkeys, with a discussion of grooming. *American Journal of Physical Anthropology* 23:1–18.

SCHALLER, G. B., G. R. LOWTHER
1969 The relevance of carnivore behavior to the study of early hominids. *Southwestern Journal of Anthropology* 25:307–341.

STABENFELDT, G. H., A. G. HENDRICKX
1972 Progesterone levels in the bonnet monkey (*Macaca radiata*) during the menstrual cycle and pregnancy. *Endocrinology* 91:614–619.

STOLTZ, L. P., G. S. SAAYMAN
1970 Ecology and behaviour of baboons in the northern Transvaal. *Annals of the Transvaal Museum* 26(5):99–143.

STRUHSAKER, T. T.
1967 *Behavior of vervet monkeys (Cercopithecus aethiops)*. University of California Publications in Zoology. Berkeley and Los Angeles: University of California Press.

TAYLER, C. K., G. S. SAAYMAN
1972 The social organisation and behaviour of dolphins (*Tursiops aduncus*) and baboons (*Papio ursinus*): some comparisons and assessments. *Annals Cape Province Museum* (*Natural History*) 9:11–49.

TOBIAS, P.
1964 "Bushman hunter-gatherers: a study in human ecology," in *Ecological studies in Southern Africa*. Edited by D. Davis, 67–86. The Hague: W. Junk.

VANDENBERGH, J. G.
1969 Endocrine coordination in monkeys: male sexual responses to the female. *Physiology and Behavior* 4:261–264.
1971 "Reproductive adaptations in macaques," in *Advances in reproductive physiology*, volume five. Edited by M. W. H. Bishop, 103–118. Logos Press.

VAN LAWICK-GOODALL, J.
1968 *The behaviour of free-living chimpanzees in the Gombe Stream Reserve*. Animal Behavior Monographs 1:161–311.

WASHBURN, S. L., I. DE VORE
1961 The social life of baboons. *Scientific American* 204:62–71.

WASHBURN, S. L., D. A. HAMBURG
1965 "The implications of primate research," in *Primate behavior*.

Edited by I. DeVore, 607–622. New York: Holt, Rinehart and Winston.

WASHBURN, S. L., P. C. JAY, J. B. LANCASTER
1965   Field studies of Old World monkeys and apes. *Science* 150:1541–1547.

YOSHIBA, K.
1968   "Local and intertroop variability in ecology and social behavior of common Indian langurs," in *Primates: studies in adaptation and variability*. Edited by P. C. Jay, 217–242. New York: Holt, Rinehart and Winston.

ZUCKERMAN, S.
1932   *The social life of monkeys and apes*. London: Kegan Paul, Trench, Trubner.

Social Behavior and Ecological Considerations of West African Baboons (Papio papio)

GILBERT K. BOESE

INTRODUCTION

Studies of *Papio anubis* and *P. cynocephalus* in Kenya by Washburn and DeVore (1961), *P. cynocephalus* in Kenya by Altmann and Altmann (1970), and *P. ursinus* in South Africa by Hall (1962a, 1962b) suggested similar forms of social organization. The basic, stable social unit was found to be the multi-male group of forty to eighty individuals (DeVore and Hall 1965) which contains no apparent subgrouping.

Further studies of the anubis baboon (Rowell 1966; Crook and Aldrich-Blake 1968) and the chacma baboon (Saayman 1971a, 1971b) indicated that variations in social organization occur within a species in response to specific ecological conditions. However, data suggested that the multi-male group is still the basic social unit.

Kummer (1968b) reported that the most constant social unit of the hamadryas baboon (*P. hamadryas*) in Ethiopia is the one-male unit. These harem-type units gather in "unconstant troops of up to 750 animals" at specific sleeping cliffs (Kummer 1968b).

Kummer (1968a, 1971) compared the hamadryas baboon to the cynocephalus baboon as defined by Hill (1967). Although all the

Richard Soderlund and Wilma B. Boese participated in the field study. David Manske, Kate Scow, and Margaret Von Ebers collected portions of the 1972 data. Many members of the Brookfield Zoo staff contributed in many ways. Dolores Fisera typed and proofed the manuscript. To all these individuals I am deeply grateful.

This study was supported by the predoctoral National Institute of Mental Health Traineeship, NOMH–11110–02–04, through the Johns Hopkins University and the Chicago Zoological Society.

species of *Papio* have vocalizations and communicative gestures in common, cynocephalus baboons do not have stable subgroups. Only temporary consort relationships develop between a male and female during estrus. This relationship lasts from several hours to a few days; the female moves freely throughout the group during anestrus (DeVore and Hall 1965).

Hamadryas baboons form permanent male-female bonds which persist during estrus, anestrus, pregnancy, and lactation (Kummer 1968b). This form of bond exists between one male and several "bonded" females.

It is within this comparative framework that I will describe the social organization of the Guinea baboon and the interaction of the species with its environment.

Previous reports supported the premise that *P. papio* lived in multi-male groups lacking any apparent stable or permanent subgrouping (Bert et al. 1967a, 1967b; Dunbar and Nathan 1972).

Per contra, I concluded that the most constant unit of social organization of *P. papio* is the single-adult-male subgroup. These subgroups are an integral part of a larger multi-male group (Boese 1973).

This conclusion is based on more than 1,200 hours of observation of a captive group of *P. papio* at the Chicago Zoological Park (Brookfield Zoo) between June, 1968, and September, 1970. Further support for this conclusion is based on nine weeks of field observations in Senegambia between January and March, 1971.

The single-adult-male subgroups observed in captivity consisted of one adult male, one to four adult females, offspring infants, and juveniles that were two to four years old. During the study, certain subgroups included a subadult associate male which became an integral part of the subgroup. The subadult associate joined the group when he was approximately four years old and remained with it for up to two years before forming his own subgroup.

Thirty subgroups observed and analyzed in the field revealed a mean composition of 1.1 adult males, 2.9 adult females, 0.9 subadult males, 2.97 juveniles, and 2.4 infants (Boese 1973). These subgroups or parties separated from the group exhibited the same basic composition as the subgroups of known individuals studied in captivity. The study of the captive group is still in progress.

The main body of data presented in this paper was collected from June through December, 1972, during which time the study focused on grooming interactions, spatial relationships, sexual interaction, and subgroup-specific communication. These data will be compared with earlier results to assess the permanence and exclusiveness of the captive sub-groups and will be discussed in reference to my field observations and those of others.

STUDY SITES AND METHODS

The Guinea baboon group at the Brookfield Zoo lives on a complex of large artificial rocks and outcroppings separated from the public by a dry moat. The facility dimensions are 120 by 90 feet. The animals have access to approximately 70,000 square feet of multilevel surfaces. Included in the facility are foraging pits, ponds, streams, and a network of interconnected cement trees.

During the 1972 study period the baboon group consisted of six adult males, seventeen adult females, one subadult male, eight juvenile males, ten juvenile females, five infant males, and five infant females, for a total of fifty-two animals.

All animals were processed on an annual basis from 1969 through 1973, including body measurements, weight, eye tests, and permanent tattoo. Animals were processed biannually from 1965 to 1969. Data cards were kept for each animal stating date of birth, parents, sibs, tattoo, body measurements, and other pertinent data.

Field observations were conducted mainly on groups in Parc National du Niokolo Koba in Senegal, West Africa, at the camps of Niokolo Koba and Simenti. Another site of concentrated observations was a *réserve du faune* near Seleti, Senegal, which is twenty-five kilometers south of Bathurst, Gambia. Detailed habitat descriptions are presented elsewhere (Boese 1973).

Field observations concentrated on group organization, group movements, and social interactions. The data collected were based on seventy-two visual contacts with baboons and represent seventy-four man-hours of observation.

Specific data collection methods will be described with the resultant data.

RESULTS

As I watched the Brookfield Zoo baboons and became acquainted with all individuals, it became apparent that certain individuals spent the bulk of their time together. Thus, in 1969 and 1970 methods were

Table 1. Summary of spatial relationships for the Brookfield Group 1972 representing fifty-two hours of "nearest neighbor" (NN) scores for the adult and subadult males

Adult male		High frequency (NN) females				Female sub-total	Subadult associate male	Juvenile (NN) score	Infant (NN) score	Juvenile and infant subtotal	Other adults as (NN)	Total
B	♀	15A	45A	11A	121							
	Number	198	168	137	56	559		71	65	136	191	886
	Percent	22.3	19.0	15.6	6.3	63.1		8.0	7.3	15.3	21.6	100.00
S	♀	2A	125	+	N		Y♂					
	Number	176	145	120	70	551	112	62	73	135	178	936
	Percent	18.8	15.5	12.8	7.5	54.6	12.0	6.5	7.9	14.4	19.0	100.00
+	♀	H1	X	121	26A		IH					
	Number	151	113	87	46	397	37	118	29	147	127	671
	Percent	22.6	16.7	13.0	6.7	59.0	4.7	18.0	4.0	22.0	19.0	100.00
N	♀	I	Y	F1	26A							
	Number	136	104	75	64	379		70	82	152	213	781
	Percent	17.4	13.3	9.6	8.2	48.5		9.0	10.5	19.5	27.3	100.00
Z	♀	142										
	Number	287				287		55	111		157	610
	Percent	46.4				47.1		9.0	18.2		25.7	100.00

Adult subgroup ♂

Subadult male							Adult subgroup ♂					
Y♂	♀	+	125	2A	N		S♂					
	Number	85	75	72	68	300	127	77	117	194	247	868
	Percent	9.7	8.6	8.3	7.9	34.5	14.6	8.9	13.5	22.4	28.5	100.00

Plates

Ecology, Diet, and Social Patterning in Old and New World
  Primates   ii–vi
  by *C. M. Hladik* (pp. 3–35)

Population Dynamics of the Toque Monkey, *Macaca sinica*   vii
  by *Wolfgang P. J. Dittus* (pp. 125–151)

The Learning and Symbolizing Capacities of Apes and Monkeys   viii
  by *Duane M. Rumbaugh* (pp. 353–365)

Plate 1.   A group of *Presbytes senex* in the forest of Polonnaruwa. This group, located in H on Figure 1, lives in a very small territory (one hectare). The resources available are the minimum for survival

Plate 2. Gray langurs (*Presbytis entellus*) feed on leaves in the canopy; but they choose species that differ in some ways from those eaten by *P. senex*. Corresponding to this ecological pattern, they live in larger groups and show lower population density

Plate 3.   *Lepilemur leucopus*, a "solitary" folivorous primate. When leaves are no longer available, it feeds on the flowers of *Alluaudia procera*. The total amount of these flowers determines the minimum size of the individual territory

Plate 4. A group of howlers moving in the canopy of the rain forest of Barro Colorado. These monkeys have a frugivorous diet including a fairly high proportion of leaves

Plate 5.   Chimpanzees in the rain forest of Gaboon, catching ants (*Polyrhachis*) in a hollow trunk. These fruit-eating primates have a particular social patterning, with very large home ranges for regional populations, in correlation with this habit of complementing their diet with small animal prey

Plate 1. An adult male *Macaca s. sinica*

Plate 1.   Lana's computer-controlled language training situation. The overhead bar must be pulled for the console to be activated. Facsimiles of the lexigrams on the surfaces of the word-keys are portrayed on the projectors above the keyboard, from left to right, as the selected keys are pressed. Juice and water dispensers are immediately below the console; banana and M&M dispensers are shown in the lower right of the photograph. (Additional keyboards will be added to the right of the one shown, the only one that was operative at the time of the studies reported here)

developed to quantify these relationships.

The method used by Kummer (1968b) was modified in order to score the "nearest neighbors (NN)" to the adult males in the zoo group. Data sheets were devised on which the NNs of each male were scored every ten minutes for one-hour time blocks. Observations were scattered throughout the day, but all hours between 7:00 A.M. and 7:00 P.M. were covered at least four different times. The four adult individuals nearest to the subject male were scored, the activity of the male recorded, and any infants or juveniles present between the subject male and the fourth NN were recorded. It should be noted that not all males were observed for every ten-minute time block because of movements of the animals and because the animals could enter a holding facility under the rock work. This method allowed males to be nearest neighbors to one another or to have nearest neighbors in common.

The results of the 1972 spatial relationship data are shown in Table 1. They are based on fifty-two hours of NN scores recorded between June and September, 1972. Two important facts are shown in Table 1: (1) the bonded females and subadult associate account for the majority of the NN scores for all adult males of the Brookfield group; and (2) the majority of the juveniles and infants scored for the adult males were offspring of the subgroup. The spatial relationship showed a significant degree of spatial cohesiveness for subgroups throughout the day. For example, in both the B and S subgroups, each female would account for 16.72 and 17.68 NN scores respectively if the spatial relationship were random. The subgroup females in either subgroup would have accounted for a total of 7.56 percent versus the 63.1 percent scored for B subgroup and the 54.6 percent scored for S subgroup.

The subadult associate male Y scored 427 of the 868, or 49.1 percent, of the scores with his attached subgroup. It should also be pointed out that ninety-two of the 177 NN infant scores for male Y were with infants of the S subgroup females.

Grooming Interactions

One method used to show social relationships of the Brookfield group focused on dyadic grooming interactions. Grooming interactions were selected as this behavior indicated a friendly (if only for the bout) encounter between the two interactants.

The data shown in Table 2 are the results of grooming bouts observed during ninety-six hours of observation between June 10 and

December 31, 1972.

Two methods were employed for gathering the grooming data. One method consisted of recording all grooming bouts observed during a ten-minute period. Six ten-minute periods were conducted per hour. The grooming individuals were scored only once during each period. Individuals were identified as groomer or groomee.

The second method consisted of taking elaborate notes on a single adult male for a thirty-minute period, noting all social interactions between the subject animal and all other animals of the group. The grooming interactions that occurred between the subject animal and others of the group are totaled with the data of the first method.

It was apparent that the adult grooming matrix showed very definite clustering of grooming bouts between members of specific subgroups. The percentage range of grooming bouts conducted between subgroup members varied from 100 to 67 percent, meaning that most of the adult grooming bouts occur between subgroup members.

Adult males rarely groomed animals other than subgroup members. In the case of male S, the low subgroup percentage (61.5 percent) can be explained because (1) male S had a low grooming score and therefore a few deviations or grooming bouts outside the subgroup would have a great effect on the percentage; and (2) more important, three grooming bouts initiated by male S were with female 26A. She had been a member of the S subgroup for two years and had shifted to the N subgroup during the 1972 observations. Those three bouts and the one bout with male Y, the subadult associate to the S subgroup, would give eleven subgroup interactions, or 85 percent subgroup interactions.

I conclude that Guinea baboon males groom their subgroup females frequently. In fact, males have higher grooming scores than many of the females. One cause of these high grooming frequencies for males is the inclusion of "rapid grooming" in the total scores. Rapid grooming is used, particularly by males, during times of potential conflict. Rapid grooming is further described below.

The high grooming scores for the males of the Brookfield group indicate that (1) close social ties exist between the subject male and particular females and (2) the male-female bond that is the basis of the subgroup organization is continually reinforced by both the adult male and the female. The matrix also shows that adult males rarely groom non-subgroup members, but that adult females do groom animals outside the subgroup. The grooming data indicate further that individual females interact with females from other subgroups, but they do not interact with adult males of other subgroups.

The high grooming scores could be the result of the one-way openness of subgroups as males maintain constant proximity and practice positive reinforcement to this close proximity between themselves and their bonded females.

Herding Behavior

Cohesion within the one-male unit of hamadryas baboons is maintained by the aggressive herding of unit females by the male leader (Kummer 1968b). Ransom (1971) also reported herding behavior by *P. anubis* males during the consort relationship between a male and an estrous female. He further described "resident males" herding anestrous females when new, young males were present in the troop.

I interpreted male herding behavior as signifying a special social relationship between a particular male and a particular female. Herding behavior of the Brookfield baboons was analyzed (1) to show whether or not it was specific to subgroup members and (2) to catalogue the types of herding behavior observed.

Herding behavior was defined as the inhibition of a female's behavioral interactions by a male, through either physical intervention or signaling the female in such a way that she stopped her involvement in the interaction and moved away.

The Guinea baboon males showed consistent herding of particular females. This consisted of a number of different behavioral patterns ranging from the subtle to the overt, but all met the requirements for the definition of herding behavior.

The different types of herding behavior are listed (in Table 3) and described as follows:

1. Move between: The male places himself between his subgroup female and the other interactant. This usually occurs when females are threatening each other at a distance or when the female is moving in the direction of another male. The subgroup male, by moving between, stops the interaction, which results in the female moving away from the interaction.

2. Run at: This behavior occurs when a subgroup female is sitting with or near members of a different subgroup. The bonded male runs directly at the female, but stops ten to twelve feet from her. The "run at" is usually enough to induce the subgroup female to return to her subgroup. The female often grimaces and screams as she returns.

3. Chase: The chase differs from the "run at" by the male continuing

Table 3. List of herding behaviors observed in the Brookfield baboon group. Behaviors are listed according to the frequency observed and the percent of total herding behavior each specific behavior represents. The herding behaviors marked with an asterisk are those observed in Senegambia. Males also inhibited a female's behavior by rapid mounting and, at times, copulation

		Frequency	Percent total herding
* 1.	Chase	43	21.7
* 2.	Rapid mount	29	14.8
* 3.	Run at	20	10.1
4.	Hand push or pull	17	8.6
5.	Move between	15	7.6
* 6.	Neck bite	14	7.0
* 7.	Attack	11	5.6
* 8.	Prance-kick	9	4.6
* 9.	Rump push	7	3.5
10.	Rapid groom	6	3.0
*11.	Cover	6	3.0
12.	Hand hold-down	5	2.5
13.	Neck grab	5	2.5
14.	Long look	4	2.0
15.	Kick-press	4	2.0
16.	Body push	3	1.5
Total:		198	100.0

to run after the female as she flees, and usually catching her. He then punishes her, grooms her, signals her to follow him, or pulls her, which results in another chase. The male also runs past the female, giving her a slap or pulling her leg or arm out from underneath. She then grimaces, screams, and runs after the male. The male then usually runs back to the subgroup with the punished female in pursuit, until she has also rejoined the subgroup. Males end the flight with puffed cheeks and a gutteral growl.

4.   Rapid mount: The subject male rapidly approaches a subgroup female and quickly mounts in copulatory fashion. This behavior can occur when the subject male and female are approached by another adult male or when the subgroup female is in conflict with an extra-subgroup female.

5.   Rapid groom: Subject male quickly approaches a subgroup female and grooms her in a rapid and exaggerated fashion. This usually occurs when the male or female is being threatened by another male or female. This behavior was considered as herding because in all cases observed the groomee moved from the interaction. The groomer followed bipedally and continued grooming. The result was the separation of the interactants. The grooming interaction, coupled with movement

away from the other interactants, did not stimulate continued threatening and the original interaction ceased. Females were observed to rapid-groom their subgroup male in similar situations.

6.   Cover: The subgroup male stands over the subgroup female in conflict, covering her with his body. In many instances of conflict, mothers stand over or cover their infants. The covering behavior inhibits the continued threats of the interactant toward the subject female and offers her protection. After the interaction ceases, the male usually walks away from the interaction and the female follows. The cover was also observed in the initial shaping interactions between an adult male and a young menarchial female in the formation of a developing subgroup (Boese 1973).

7.   Hand push or pull; body push: These actions are used quite frequently by adult males to stop interactions. Either the male moves directly to the side of his subgroup female and grabs her by the hair, usually around the back of the neck or shoulders, and pulls her from the interaction, or he approaches the female and pushes her. The pull is used mostly in overt conflict interaction. The hand push and body push are used mostly in response to the approach of another male. The subject male pushes with his hand or body to get the female moving. As the subject male and female(s) move away, the subject male usually walks very close to the female, crowding her and controlling the speed and direction of her movement.

8.   Rump push: The Guinea baboon communicates a state of high arousal through a "prancing" display. When executed on the branch of a tree, this prancing display constitutes a specific form of branch shaking. Branch shaking and prancing were reported by Anthoney (1969), Hill (1970), and Dunbar and Nathan (1972). I reported on the message responses to prancing, the display modification of prancing, and the social specificity of the message as the display becomes more complex (Boese 1973). The rump push of the subject male begins with a prance display. He then pushes his rump into the subgroup female, usually driving her from the place or interaction in which she was previously involved (see Figure 1).

9.   Prance-kick: This is a modification of the prance. The male extends both legs and delivers a mule-kick to the subject female. It is very effective in stopping conflict.

10.   Kick-press: This is a prancing display on top of the female, driving her into a crouched position.

11.   Hand hold-down: The male runs to the female and pushes her into a crouched position with his hand. The female responds with a

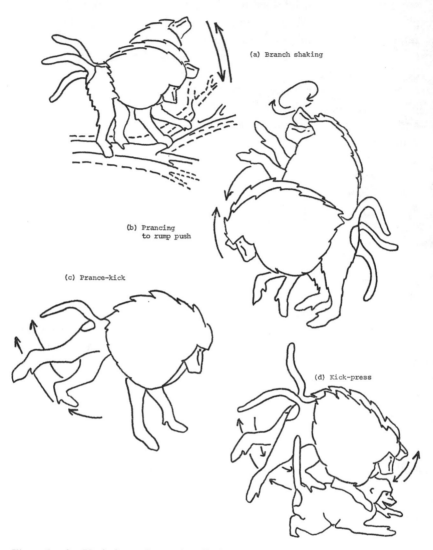

(a) Branch shaking

(b) Prancing
to rump push

(c) Prance-kick

(d) Kick-press

Figure 1a–d.   Variations of prancing display (Boese 1973)

grimace and then follows the male.

12.   Neck grab: This behavior was used by one male in the Brookfield group. During a conflict between females, male + ran at female 121 and hand pushed her away from the interaction. If she turned as she started to walk away, male + stood over her, grabbed her by the hair at the nape of the neck, and held her in place.

13.   Neck bite: The male may bite the female on the nape of neck or

shoulder to stop an interaction. This pattern is similar to that described for the hamadryas baboon by Kummer (1968b).

14.   Long look: The male often sits on a vantage point and continually looks at the female. The female initially "looks away" from the male's gaze, but finally she responds with a grimace and moves away from the non-subgroup animals.

15.   Attack: The attack occurs infrequently and at times of high stress, i.e. when all-out fighting breaks out in the group. Males attack and herd their females vigorously. In many cases it appears that males redirect attacks to subgroup females from male-male interactions.

Guinea baboon males display some very specific types of behavior and especially direct these behaviors to control the movements or the social interactions of certain females. As Table 4 shows, those behaviors listed as herding were used exclusively by the subgroup male and were directed toward particular females.

Table 4 demonstrates the variability in the amount of herding carried out by particular males. For example, male + was scored with sixty-three herding interactions; the established subgroup males ranged from thirty-six to twenty-eight. Male Z scored thirty-five herding interactions, all but one of which were directed toward female 142. The data suggest that males of developing subgroups are not as secure in their relationship with the female and monitor her behavior more severely.

Another possible explanation for increased herding as observed in the Brookfield group is the concept of "females of contest." Female 121 was formerly of the male B subgroup. Male + was constantly watching for male B and herded 121 away when the male B subgroup appeared. Also, female 121, being from the male B subgroup, attempted to continue interactions with B subgroup females.

The mature subgroup did not have female members "of contest," and this, along with the strong bonds that kept the mature subgroup together, could account for reduced herding.

It should be pointed out that female X of the + subgroup was formerly from the S subgroup. Female H1 received fewer and less severe herding responses than did X or 121 (Table 4). Female H1 had not been a member of a subgroup prior to bonding with male +.

Subadult associate male Y of the S subgroup, although showing a low frequency of herding, concentrated herding behavior on the S subgroup females. He kept the females of this subgroup together when the lead male was not present (Boese 1973).

Females 26A and 121 appear in the scores with different males because of their social status at the time of data collection. Female 26A

Table 4.   Summary of herding behavior for the Brookfield Zoo group showing the herding behavior of each adult and subadult male of the group during 1972 and the recipient females. Table represents fifty-two hours of observation

Behavior	Male + to females					Male N to females							Male B to females				Male S to females					Male Y to females					Male Z to females	
	HI	X	26A	121	142	Y	I	121	26A	J	136	F1	11A	15A	45A	125	2A	125	+	N	26A	2A	+	X	125	K	142	121
1. Chase	4	11			1	3	1						2		2	2	6	5	2	2		1	1	1		2	2	
2. Rapid mount	1	2	1	5		2	2						2	3	2		1	2									10	
3. Run at	2	2		4		2	2						2	2	1		1	1		1					1		4	
4. Hand push or pull		1		2		1							2	3	2		1	1	1	2					1	1	5	
5. Move between	2		1	5	1								3	1													2	
6. Neck bite				3					1	1			1		1					2	1					1	4	1
7. Attack		1						1	1	1			1		1			1		1	1	1		1	1	1	2	1
8. Prance-kick								1		1		1			1			1		1	1			1	1	1	1	
9. Rump push				2			2										1	1	1									
10. Rapid groom		1	1	1											2			1									1	
11. Cover		2									1				1			1					1					
12. Hand hold-down				1		1				1									1	1							1	
13. Neck grab				5		1													1	1								1
14. Long look	1						1																					
15. Kick-press		1		1		1				1						1												
16. Body push						1								1													1	
Individual totals	11	18	3	29	2	9	9	2	4	1	1	1	11	9	12	1	10	10	4	10	2	1	1	3	3	5	33	2
Subgroup totals	63					28							33				36					13					35	

had left S subgroup and had associated with male + for three weeks. When she came into estrus, male N started to follow 26A and to copulate with her. She joined the N subgroup in late July, 1972, and remained with this subgroup until now (July, 1973). Female 26A gave birth to a male infant on July 14, 1973, which made her the center of grooming bouts in the subgroup.

Female 121 appears in the data under males +, N, and Z. Female 121 attempted, on two occasions, to take infant 45 from its mother, female F1. Male N inhibited female 121 from getting the infant with one prance-kick and one attack (Table 4). Male Z directed a kick-press and neck bite to 121 when his herding of 142 away from 121 was not successful in stopping their interaction. Both 142 and 121, as mentioned, originally were members of the B subgroup. Male Z appeared very tense during this episode.

The general conclusion is that Guinea baboon males herd the females of their subgroups. The behaviors used in herding are specific responses to conflicts between females of different subgroups or to the close proximity of subgroup females to other adult males.

In our field observations, behaviors that could be classified as herding were observed infrequently. I described group rendezvous as marked by high frequencies of chases and punishing of females by males as well as conflicts between males (Boese 1973). As in the Brookfield group, herding observed in the field was used to keep the females with the subgroup and to inhibit them from engaging in interactions of possible negative consequences.

SELETI 1:05 P.M.
Group arrives at observation site: one adult male, two three-year-old juveniles, one two-year-old juvenile, one adult female and transition infant, one estrous female with brown infant riding dorsally. Group sights us. Adult male moves to termite mound, delivers hand slap in our direction and wahoo-bark; females groom. Male moves out of sight. Female with transition infant stops grooming, stands, starts walking in our direction; adult male appears, runs at female; female crouches, grimaces; male runs in direction opposite us; female with transition infant follows male. The rest of group follows.

The immediate response and control of the female and her following response suggest that she was accustomed to herding behavior and the appropriate responses.

DIABUGU 2:00 P.M.
The large group we observed this morning was spread over a large outcrop. There was much chasing and screaming. Most interactions observed were

males chasing females. Observed adult male run at young female, catch her, and pull her leg out from underneath. The female fell and then chased the male. The male moved away from area when he started to chase female. Male stopped, sat down; female sat next to him.

This kind of situation was observed on four different occasions. Gatherings of subgroups could provide the opportunity for younger males to start the interactions necessary to develop the subgroup male to female bond. The data suggest that when subgroups gather, subgroup males spend considerable time herding subgroup females.

However, as observed in the field and at Brookfield Zoo, the majority of subgroup gatherings do not involve constant and increased herding. Males maintain surveillance over the subgroup by maintaining what we called "a point of view." During periods of group interaction, adult males move to positions from which the behavior of the subgroup members can be monitored.

On the Brookfield facility, the adult males move to the outermost rock areas which provide the most panoramic view of the island. If a female moves too close to another male, the subject male will carry out some form of herding behavior and then return to the "point of view" or to his subgroup.

The "point of view" behavior also was observed during group movements. Guinea baboons move at times in a group column (Bert et al. 1967a, 1967b; Dunbar and Nathan 1972; Boese 1973). As the subgroups moved into the column formation, adult males were observed on four different occasions to move to the side of the columns, where they sat and watched the columns pass. The males then quickly moved to the side of a female and traveled with her through the column.

It was observed that when subgroups joined, there was social interaction between juveniles and adult females of different subgroups. Adult males tended to sit widely spaced and watch the ongoing behavior. However, as the group started to move, it appeared that males positioned themselves with the subgroup members.

The herding data show that *P. papio* males tolerate interactions of subgroup females with non-subgroup individuals, with the exception of inter-subgroup agonistic interactions and interactions with other adult males. Both the subject male and other males follow this behavioral pattern. For example, when a subgroup female is within ten to fifteen feet of another male, the subgroup male attempts to herd her, while the other male also moves to increase the distance between himself and the subject female. At times, a male herds his subgroup away from the approach of a non-subgroup female.

Sexual Behavior

Descriptions of baboon sexual behavior include details on the consort relationships that develop between a particular male and a particular female when she is in the turgescence phase of perineal swelling. In cynocephalus type baboons, this consort relationship lasts from a few hours to a few days, depending on the ratio of adult males to females in the group and on the number of females in estrus at any given time (DeVore and Hall 1965). In groups with several males and a ratio of 1:2 adult females, consort pairs form for two or more days. The consort pair remains some distance from the group. Groups having few females show constant interruption of sexual relations (DeVore and Hall 1965; Ransom 1971).

DeVore and Hall (1965) concluded that high-ranking females in a group copulate with low-ranking males during the early phases of perineal swelling, and upon turgescence become the consorts of the dominants males. The dominant male inhibits, through attacks and threats, any subordinate males from having access to the consort female. The consort relationship ends with deflation, and the female again interacts freely with other members of the group. This lack of permanent male-female bonds contrasts dramatically with the social system of hamadryas baboons (Kummer 1968b).

Copulatory behavior can be used as a measure of the degree of exclusiveness of male-female bonding between members of a group. The behavior can range from "promiscuous" to very exclusive mating behavior. The Brookfield baboons showed an exclusiveness in copulatory behavior similar to that described by Kummer (1968b). Table 5 shows the 274 copulations recorded during the 1972 study period. Data in-

Table 5. Copulations recorded from June 10 to December 31, 1972, for the adult and subadult males of the Brookfield Zoo group. Female 121 transferred from the male B subgroup to the male + subgroup

Males		Females																		Total
		45A	15A	11A	121	2A	4A	112	125	N	26A	Y	I	K	HI	X	142	136	J	
	B	27	44	17	1															89
	S					23	5	2	2		6									38
	N								1		21	12	7	3						44
	+				15						1				3	6				25
	Z				3												35			38
	Y	6			1	6	4	12	1		2			2		2		1	3	40

cluded the individual male and female, number of pelvic thrusts, presence of copulation call, and any use of mouth or hands during all copulations observed. The important point in Table 5 is the exclusiveness of copulations between the subgroup male and female.

Male B, male S, and male N did not copulate with females outside the subgroup. But certain females did copulate with males outside the subgroup. As stated previously, female 121 had been with the B subgroup since 1968. During the summer of 1972, she left the B subgroup and stayed with male +. Male + had been the subadult associate to the B subgroup since 1969. When male + split from the subgroup and started on his own, female 121 moved with him. The copulation scores show the shift from male B to male +. Male Z also copulated with female 121 during this transition.

The mature subgroups of 1972 showed very little copulation outside the subgroup. Males + and Z were in the developing subgroup phase. By the end of December, male + had a subgroup of three females: 121, H1, and X. Female X came from the S subgroup and H1 was a young female with a newborn infant. Female H1 was with male + from the start of the 1972 study. Male Z succeeded in gaining female 142 from the B subgroup and remained very close to 142 throughout the study period.

Male Y was the subadult associate to male S. Although his copulations were concentrated on S subgroup females during the early stages of turgescence, he did copulate with other adult females of the group. Copulation with females of other subgroups occurred when the subgroup male was not in sight. Male Y would immediately return to the S subgroup when he sighted an adult subgroup male. Male Y was very cautious, constantly looking around as he copulated, and ran from the female after dismounting. The female was also apprehensive, looking around immediately, and running ten or more feet from male Y. The female copulation call usually brought the subgroup male, ending the sexual interaction.

The copulatory behavior appeared very similar to that of the hamadryas baboon, i.e. adult males copulating only with females of their own units. Hamadryas females, like Guinea females, copulate with young males outside the subgroup (Kummer 1968b).

Subgroup copulations are enhanced by subgroup exclusiveness in the Brookfield group, as the adult males ignore or actively avoid the sexual presentations of estrous females outside their subgroup. Kummer (1968b) reported this for hamadryas baboons. Data on cynocephalus type baboons, i.e. *P. anubis*, *P. cynocephalus*, and *P. ursinus*, show a

Table 6. Copulations observed between male B and females of the Brookfield Zoo group. R = removed from group; L = lactating during observation period; D = died during study; T = transferred to another subgroup; P =pregnant during observations. In 1968 male B associated closely with females 154, 142, 11A, and 45A. Females 142, 11A, and 45A were nursing infants and started cycling at the end of study period. Female 15A became a member of the subgroup in 1971. As of July, 1973, the male B subgroup consisted of 11A, 45A, and 44. Female 121 transferred in 1972

	Male B 115	154	142	11A	45A	121	26A	15A
1968	1	12	1	2	L		L	
1969		14	13	2	4	2	35	
1970	R	D	33	L	15	17	T	
1972			T	17	27	1		44

Table 7. Copulations observed between male S and females of the Brookfield Zoo group. The male S subgroup consisted of females N, 4A, 2A, and 125 during the 1972 study period. Females 4A, 2A, and X were incorporated into the subgroup in late 1969. The 1973 data show that the S subgroup consisted of females N, 4A, 2A, 125, and X. Female X returned to S subgroup

	Male S 121	111	156	112	126	114	26A	157	N	4A	2A	125	X
1968	1	2	1	1	4	1	1		1				
1969		D	2		1	2	7	5	9			P	
1970			R		D	1	26	4	8	L	P	L	L
1972				2		R	T	R	6	5	23	2	T

pattern of short, temporary sexual consorts between one adult male and the one estrous female. The Guinea baboon and hamadryas baboons exhibit sexual exclusiveness based primarily on the behavior of the adult male.

How exclusive is the sexual relationship between a male and female? The permanent bond between a male and certain females is shown by reviewing the copulation records of the Brookfield group from 1968 to 1972.

Tables 6 and 7 show the copulations recorded for males B and S. In 1968 both males were subadults and their sexual behavior was similar to that of subadult male Y in 1972. Copulations were infrequent and included a number of different females. Tables 6 and 7 show the trend for the copulations to become limited to certain females and to increase in number. (The absence of copulatory data for a particular female indicates pregnancy or lactation during a particular study period.)

When I focused on male B in 1968, there were nineteen adult females in the Brookfield group. Male B was observed to copulate with only four females. One female, 45A, was lactating throughout the 1968 study period. Female 11A weaned her infant toward the end of the study period, which explains the low frequency of copulations recorded for male B and female 11A. Since 1968 male B has interacted with eight females. Two of these females have died, and three others have shifted from his subgroup to another. The subgroup was considered mature in 1969. Three females remained with male B at the end of 1972, and two of these have been with male B since 1968, when he was a young adult forming his subgroup.

The lack of overlap between females on the part of the males is very interesting. Male S and male B did not interact agonistically or compete for females. The only exception was the transfer of female 26A to the S subgroup in 1970. Female 26A moved from male B and copulated with male S. When male S started to herd 26A, she followed, and male B avoided both S and 26A.

A principal discovery in my research on Guinea baboon sexual behavior is the very limited and exclusive nature of the interaction between the adult subgroup males and their bonded females. Sexual interactions of the Guinea baboon clearly differ from those reported for the cynocephalus type baboon and appear to be closer behaviorally to those of the hamadryas baboon as described by Kummer (1968b).

DISCUSSION

The study of the Brookfield Zoo baboon group has provided insights into the dynamics involved in the development of social bonds. As Ransom and Ransom (1971) point out, factors such as death, exchanges of animals among troops, births, and maturation all must affect the development of social bonds. These factors also have a definite impact on the individual's social role and in turn the social behavior and organization of the group.

In the Guinea baboon the dynamics of social development result in a basic form of social organization, the subgroup-group two-level form of group organization. Data from our captive study show that although subgroups vary according to individual differences of their members, this form of organization is based on long-term male-female bonds. Data now being analyzed indicate that the filial subgroup is a social base from which juveniles orient as they develop social roles in peer groups. Data also indicate that adult male-subadult associate male relationships develop between infant and juvenile males and that this relationship is continued in later years.

Studies in the field by Bert et al. (1967a, 1967b), although concentrating on behavior at sleeping sites, concluded that one consistent form of group organization was the longitudinal social organization. Longitudinal social organization was observed as groups approached the sleeping site and comprised the group moving in a column formation consisting of adult males, adult females, and infants. The column was headed by a halo of juveniles.

Our observations indicate that the column is one type of group formation which occurs during GROUP movement to and from sleeping sites and approaches to water sources in dense bush. We observed the juvenile halo only as the group approached the sleeping site. Perhaps the juvenile halo is the result of younger members of the group moving rapidly into a known area where a period of play precedes movement into the sleeping trees.

Bert et al. (1967a, 1967b) did not always observe the column formation. They reported that some groups arrived at sleeping sites in scattered parties, separated in time. Although the composition of the scattered parties was not given, these could have been subgroups which, instead of gathering and moving as a column, gathered at the sleeping site.

Of the ten observations we made at sleeping sites, subgroups gathered there on three occasions. The remaining seven sleeping site observations indicated that the group moved in a column to the sleeping site, suggesting possible group rendezvous at an earlier time.

DuPuy and Gaillard (1969) reported their observations of a *P. papio* group near Dar es Salaam in Senegal. The group was described as homogenous in appearance, showing no nuclear families or harems. Their observations and those of Bert et al. support the multi-male group level of organization for *P. papio*. Dunbar and Nathan (1972) generally support these findings, but they indicate subgrouping of some form during the daily activity pattern and at the sleeping sites.

In his report on the mammals of Niokolo Koba National Park in Senegal, DeKeyser (1956) reported that Guinea baboons lived in bands of 50 to 100 individuals. He further stated that the adult males had at their disposal a harem of three to four females. The "harem" also contained a tolerated subadult male. Although DeKeyser did not provide data or counts in his report, it appears that the group separated into subgroups during portions of the daily activity pattern.

Based on our observations in Senegambia, the generalized activity pattern (Figure 2) is suggested for *P. papio* in habitats varying from

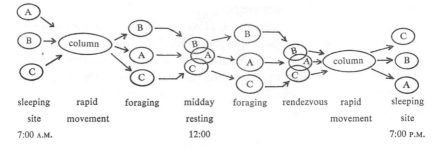

Figure 2. Generalized representation of the diurnal activity pattern of a hypothetical Guinea baboon group consisting of three subgroups. Column movement is shown when it occurs at highest frequency. The column can also form before and after midday rest or during midday as a group assembles and approaches a water source. Each subgroup represents the average subgroup encountered in the field, consisting of one adult male, three adult females, one subadult male, three juveniles, and three infants (Boese 1973)

evergreen forest (Seleti) to wooded savanna (Simenti and Niokolo Koba). This generalized activity pattern shows the "fusion-fission" pattern described by Kummer (1968a).

At Seleti and Simenti, the adult male of a subgroup was often observed moving ahead and looking over an area before the subgroup continued. As the adult male moved ahead, the subgroup with the subadult associate remained behind, sitting quietly or occasionally grooming. Juveniles and infants remained within four to five feet of the subgroup. On four occasions the adult male returned to the subgroup and then led it in another direction. In two other instances the adult male paused and then continued; the subgroup then followed.

As subgroups moved through the bush, the adult males gave the two-phase bark vocalization. This was answered by other males in the vicinity. The barking increased in frequency toward evening as the subgroup rendezvoused before or at the sleeping sites.

It is my impression that the frequency and intensity of the bark differed depending on whether it was used as a contact call or an alarm call. The barking male was relaxed and continued his walking or other activity while giving the contact bark. This was in contrast to the tense stance and concentrated stare of the male when giving the alarm bark.

I infer that the subgroup-group form of social organization is well adapted to the habitat of *P. papio* where bush is thick and observation impaired. It would be difficult to maintain the group positioning presented by DeVore and Hall (1965) and to provide equal protection for all members of the group. The subgroup level provides male protection for all members of the subgroup, and the subadult associate provides continued protection in the absence of the adult male. The group was observed to function as a unit on open areas specifically after the tall dry grass had been burned and the new dry season growth had started. The group level of organization provides opportunities for subadult males to start subgroups with young nonbonded females during periods of group movement and interaction.

The effect of the subgroup organization on the individual can only be revealed through experimentation and manipulation. Two experiments have been carried out with the Brookfield Zoo group to elucidate the social dynamics of the subgroup level of organization. These will be presented only briefly to provide insights into the organizational function.

In one experiment a group of baboons was separated from the island group, and after twenty-two months of residence in the primate house facility, the female K was released back onto the island. Female K was considered to be bonded to the male of the primate house subgroup and was pregnant at the time of release. A control female and her 6.5-month-old male infant were taken from the island group and held with female K for two days.

Upon release, the control female, 2A, and her offspring, male 36, ran to male S, the subgroup male, and moved from the introduction site. Male S led female 2A to the high rock portion of the island and the two animals remained within four feet of each other the entire day. Female K attempted to follow 2A but was constantly mounted, kicked, or investigated by juveniles and adult females. Adult males herded their females away from the approach of female K. After two hours, female K was no longer followed by the juveniles and was following male Z and female 142.

Female K was not incorporated into a subgroup, and when she gave birth, her infant was kidnaped by female 121 and the infant died within ten days. A similar situation occurred in 1969: when a non-subgroup primiparous female gave birth, her infant was kidnaped but managed to survive.

Observations during the summer of 1973 showed female K to be peripheral to the male N subgroup. Bonded primiparous females were closely watched by the subgroup male and potential kidnapers were driven away.

The introduction experiment using female K, although only one trial, indicated that the Brookfield subgroup was closed to social strangers and that introduced animals were not readily incorporated into the society as in the cases reported by Kummer (1968b). The experiment also revealed the protective nature of the subgroup organization to the female members.

The second experiment involved reducing the Brookfield group by one subgroup. In the removal, female H1 of the male + subgroup was removed and placed in a cage with adult male Z, two menarchial females, one juvenile male, and two male and two female infants. One infant male belonged to female H1. (A major portion of the data was collected by K. Scow during March 21 through June 21, with a total of twenty-five hours of observation.)

Table 8 shows the basic social avoidance of male Z by female H1.

Table 8.   Shows grooming interaction recorded for 1973 primate house group from March 21 through June 21, 1973. The table shows lack of grooming directed by H1 (the bonded female to male +) to male Z. H1 groomed her offspring, male 38, and the male 41, which was separated from his mother. Table also shows the concentrated grooming of female H1 by male Z

		Groomee								
		Z♂	H1	J	18♂	E	35	38♂	41♂	31
	Z♂	–	34	7					1	
	H1	1	–	1	2	5		48	45	1
	J	38	7	–	9	6	7			
Groomer	18♂	3	1	21	–	7	2			
	E	7	7	5	19	–		8	1	4
	35	1	1	2	2		–	2	1	1
	38♂	2	5	5				–	1	
	41♂	1	7	8					–	
	31			1	10	15				–

The data suggest that she did not readily transfer to another adult male. This also suggests that the bond carries over for some individuals and that it can carry over some months after social separation.

The female member of a subgroup has a special type of relationship with the subgroup male. As the data show, this bond provides a source of protection and support which helps to ensure successful raising of offspring.

This male-female bond is a relationship developed over time, with certain critical periods when specific interactions and reinforcements are necessary. The bond is not based solely on presence and constant reinforcements, as data, although limited, suggest bond carry-over. Certainly, the relationship carried over for short periods, as we observed in our introduction controls and in the longer separation experiment.

The subgroup bond is also maintained through subgroup-specific forms of communication. Herding behavior has been shown to be basically subgroup specific.

Another sociologically specific form of communication observed is the tail wrap. This occurs as a subgroup male and female move from a conflict. The male places his tail over the female's hind quarters as they walk. Tail wrapping has been observed in various forms between mothers and infants, and was first noted among black infants, who wrap their tails around the tails of their mothers. During the weaning period, very frequently the infant wraps its tail around the mother's leg. Further observation showed that bonded males and females use the tail in subtle forms of communication — e.g. running the tail under the chin as one subgroup animal passes another. The response to this is grooming, nuzzling, or following.

CONCLUSION

The Guinea baboon subgroup-group form of social organization is similar to that of *P. hamadryas*, with subgrouping based on male-female bonds and adult-offspring bonds. This suggests an intermediate form of social organization in the genus *Papio* between the multi-male group lacking permanent subunits and the closed units of the hamadryas baboon.

The closed nature of the hamadryas unit is one of the major differences noted between *P. papio* and *P. hamadryas*. One possible explanation for the closed versus the "one-way" openness could be the age at which the female becomes incorporated into the subgroup or unit. Kummer (1968b) reported that many initial units began with young adult males and females twelve to eighteen months old. At this age, the social development of the female would be limited, especially in the closed unit organization. Our studies on captive subgroup infants show that peer interactions become part of the infant's behavioral profile at three to four months of age. However, peer interactions do not become prominent in the profile until the age of ten to twelve months, for at that age captive infants spend 35 percent of daily observations with their mothers.

Guinea baboon females which were three and one-half to four years old would have a more complex social background and would have developed strong peer bonds. This could explain the extra-subgroup interactions allowed by the adult male.

Observations in the field indicate reduced social interaction for infants and juveniles as subgroups separate and move.

Conditions in the natural habitat dictate a much longer period to develop peer bonds. Thus, in the case of hamadryas baboons, the social experience of an eighteen-month-old female could be considerably reduced. It is evident that to show the existence of subgrouping within baboon groups, either groups must be separated and closed (as *P. hamadryas*) or they must be subject to long-term studies involving individual recognition. Long-term studies would also provide data on the social dynamics and changes of social roles that result in a form of social organization.

Through long-term captive studies of groups large enough to provide all age/sex classes and in numbers approaching those of wild groups, the complexities of a society can be studied. The genealogies can show the effects of filial bonds and peer relationships on adult social roles.

The forms of sociologically specific communication can provide a valuable tool for assessing the possible relationship between two interactants. For example, the various forms of herding behavior indicate the Guinea baboon subgroup bond.

My data show the existence of permanent subgroups in a captive group of *P. papio*. Data collected in the field support this subgroup-group form of social organization. It appears that one of the adaptive characteristics of the genus *Papio* is the variability of bonding that occurs between the males and females of the different species.

However, the variability may not be as great as present data suggest. The interplay between the two-level form of social organization and the habitat could result in greater expression of the group level of organization. The subgroups, if not closed, would be difficult to ascertain.

REFERENCES

ANTHONEY, T. R.
  1969　Threat activity in wild and captive groups of savannah baboons. *Proceedings of the Second International Congress of Primatology* 1:108–114.

ALTMANN, S. A., J. ALTMANN
  1970　*Baboon ecology: African field research.* Chicago: University of Chicago Press.

BERT, T., H. AYATS, A. MARTINO, H. COLLOMB
  1967a Le sommeil nocturne chez le babouin *Papio papio. Folia Primato-logica* 6:28–43.
  1967b Note sur l'organisation de la vigilance sociale chez le babouin *Papio papio. Folia Primatologica* 6:44–47.

BOESE, G. K.
  1973 "Behavior and social organization of the Guinea baboon (*Papio papio*)." Unpublished doctoral dissertation, Johns Hopkins University, Baltimore. Ann Arbor: University Microfilms.

CROOK, T. H., P. ALDRICH-BLAKE
  1968 Ecological and behavioral contrasts between sympatric ground dwelling primates in Ethiopia. *Folia Primatologica* 8:192–227.

DE KEYSER, P. L.
  1956 Mammifères. *Mémoires de l'Institut Français d'Afrique Noire* 48:35–79.

DE VORE, I., K. R. L. HALL
  1965 "Baboon ecology," in *Primate behavior: field studies of monkeys and apes*. Edited by I. DeVore, 20–53. New York: Holt, Rinehart and Winston.

DUNBAR, R. I., M. F. NATHAN
  1972 Social organization of the Guinea baboon, *Papio papio. Folia Primatologica* 17:321–334.

DU PUY, A., D. R. GAILLARD
  1969 Capture d'un cynocephales présentant une anomalie de coloration. *Mammalia* 33:732–733.

HALL, K. R. L.
  1962a Numerical data, maintenance activities and locomotion of the wild chacma baboon, *Papio ursinus. Proceedings of the Zoological Society of London* 139:181–220.
  1962b The sexual, agonistic, and derived social behavior patterns of the wild chacma baboon, *Papio ursinus. Proceedings of the Zoological Society of London* 139:283–327.
  1965 "Baboon social behavior," in *Primate behavior: field studies of monkeys and apes*. Edited by I. DeVore, 53–110. New York: Holt, Rinehart and Winston.

HILL, W. C. O.
  1967 "Taxonomy of the baboon," in *The baboon in medical research*, volume two. Edited by H. Vagtborg, 3–12. Austin: University of Texas Press.
  1970 *Primates: comparative anatomy and taxonomy*, volume eight: *Cynopithecinae*. Edinburgh: Edinburgh University Press.

KUMMER, H.
  1968a "Two variations in social organizations of baboons," in *Primates: studies in adaptation and variability*. Edited by P. Jay, 293–312. New York: Holt, Rinehart and Winston.
  1968b *Social organization of hamadryas baboons*. Chicago: University of Chicago Press.

1971   *Primate societies: group techniques of ecological adaptation.* Chicago: Aldine.

RANSOM, T. W.

1971   "Ecology and behavior of baboons *Papio anubis* in the Gombe National Park." Unpublished doctoral dissertation, University of California, Berkeley.

RANSOM, T. W., B. S. RANSOM

1971   Adult male-infant relations among baboons, *Papio anubis. Folia Primatologica* 16:179–195.

ROWELL, T. E.

1966   Forest living baboons in Uganda. *Journal of Zoology (London)* 149:344–364.

SAAYMAN, G. S.

1971a Behavior of the adult males in a troop of free-ranging chacma baboons (*Papio ursinus*). *Folia Primatologica* 15:36–57.

1971b Aggressive behavior in free-ranging chacma baboons (*Papio ursinus*). *Journal of Behavioral Sciences* 1:77–83.

WASHBURN, S. L., I. DE VORE

1961   The social life of baboons. *Scientific American* 204:62–71.

Discussion

TUTTLE: In suggesting this topic I hoped to generate discussion on the extent to which ecology and subsistence behaviors can influence or even determine social patterning in monkeys and apes.

DITTUS: In assessing the ecological determinants of primate social organization, a general underlying pattern appears to be emerging even though it is now very remnant. A principal causal factor, which I noted in my own fieldwork of three-and-one-half years on the Ceylon toque monkey, is the effect of the spatial and temporal dispersion of food sources on the grouping patterns of macaques. Hans Kummer has expressed a similar view noting that in hamadryas baboons, animals group themselves so as to minimize conflict in a foraging context. If food sources are concentrated and widely dispersed, small widely spaced foraging parties might be expected, each party clustering about one food concentration thereby minimizing overall conflict. I was very pleased to note that Klein and Klein have noticed a similar spatial pattern in the South American *Ateles belzebuth*. Small groups of spider monkeys predominate when food sources are concentrated in small packages and widely spaced; but larger groups predominate when the resource substrate is spatially and temporally more spread. The situation is not as simple as I have just stated it. A more general statement might be made here. Animals group themselves in such a manner as to minimize energy expenditure in carrying out primary life supporting processes of food acquisition, reproduction, and avoidance of death, mainly through predation. This very general consideration can lead to more specific considerations. I submit the following basic factors for consideration: (1) the spatial and temporal dispersion of food sources, (2) the animal's locomotor abilities, including not only its anatomy but also the substrate on which the animal moves, (3) the potential for group cohesion in the species, nocturnal species having less potential for cohesion because communication for cohesion is impeded, and (4) phylogenetic considerations as outlined by Eisenberg in his 1972 article in *Science*. In addition the influence of each of these factors can be modified by the habitat type, predation pressure, and other factors. In delimiting the determinants of the size of groups, all of these factors must be considered. Which factor or combination of them is most influential will depend on the exact circumstances. Now I would direct a question to Dr. Boese. He indicated that in *Papio papio* the social organization is very much akin to what Kummer and Kurt observed in *Papio hamadryas*. Dr. Boese, what was the nature of the habitat in which you studied the species in the wild? Please indicate the pattern of dispersion of the food sources on which these animals fed.

BOESE: We conducted a preliminary survey for nine weeks in three areas. One was in a coastal extension of evergreen forest, south of Bathurst in Gambia. This was a disturbed forest with considerable secondary growth, characterized by thick tangles of lianas. We did not conduct an extensive survey of food sources. Food appeared to be concentrated in trees, such as oil palms and acacias, and in the open fields. The baboons would move into these agricultural fields and feed on grass seeds and shoots. We also studied baboons in wooded savanna habitat at Niokolo Koba National Park. This is a highly variable habitat, consisting of tall grass, wooded shrub, and large, open clearings. Because the park was subject to burning, grass was available throughout our observations. The animals would move from thick bush to the burned areas and feed on grass shoots. Baboons also fed in trees on the pods of certain acacia and other plants. In the wooded or evergreen forest the group tended to separate into subgroups. The subgroups appeared to forage independently of one another. But near Simenti, in an area of new grass growth following burning, the entire group foraged in the open area. We followed them from their sleeping site to the foraging area.

DITTUS: Was the subgrouping pattern less marked when they were foraging in the grasslands than in the thick bush?

BOESE: Yes, it was. In the thick bush and in the forest the subgroups were separated. However, on the grassland there was more group cohesion. The subgroups foraged closer together and there was mixing of juveniles and certain females between subgroups. This is the same pattern that we saw on some evenings prior to moving to sleeping sites.

DITTUS: Would you agree then that this species conforms to our postulate that the spacing or at least the grouping or subgrouping is affected by the nature of the dispersion of the sources?

BOESE: There is an adaptation to the habitat. But there is a flexibility within this adaptation. In the area in which we studied there is a variable type of habitat. The animals have a flexibility to move into these particular variabilities. It allows that subgroups in forests still have an adult male and many times a subadult male. There is a reproductive potential and a protective factor. In the open many animals group together. But we do not have very good evidence on the relationship to food sources. So I can only say that there is a gross relation to the type of habitat. In thick, heavy bush the group separated into subgroups. In short grass the group was more cohesive, with subgroups interacting as they did at sleeping sites and in the morning before foraging.

DITTUS: Did they feed on shrubs in the bush?

BOESE: The animals feed on many things. As the animals moved they would take handfuls of grass seeds. Fecal samples showed that they were feeding about everything that was available: fromage flowers, palm fruit, pods and grass. But these observations were cursory.

DITTUS: Would anyone else like to comment on grouping patterns relative to the feeding substrate based on their own observation of primates?

STRUHSAKER: Would you apply your ideas to make predictions on other species based strictly on food habits? For instance, what would you predict if we had a species that fed primarily on clumped food sources as opposed to a species that fed primarily on a food item that was both dense and widely and uniformly distributed? Would you predict anything about group size and composition based on these two different types of diet?

DITTUS: Given that all other factors are equal, which they rarely are, I would predict that with clumped sources there would be small group sizes whereas with evenly and widely dispersed food there would be larger groups. And I would predict that this would hold not only for primates but also for other mammals. Generally in ungulates, the browsing species occur in very small groups whereas grazers occur in large groups. Now I admit that there is a difference between ungulate and primate social organization. Grazing ungulates have an open social system. But this openness, or flexibility, in group size is probably an adaptation to the variability in the dispersion of the grazers' food substrate. The nature of the strategy for the avoidance of predation is also influential in determining the size of social groups, especially in ungulates.

STRUHSAKER: In two species of colobus monkeys in Uganda, John Oates and I have found a situation which apparently would not conform to your prediction. The black-and-white colobus, *Colobus guereza*, lives in relatively small groups, averaging about ten members per group and having one fully adult male in each group. The major component of their diet comes from one particular tree species, *Celtis durandii*. Our extensive tree enumerations and studies of crown size in these trees indicate that it is a uniformly distributed species, one of the most common trees in the forest. When one considers the density of the species and the crown size, it has a very high cover index, indicating that it is a widely distributed common food species. The red colobus is in sharp contrast to this. They live in large groups, averaging about fifty animals, with more than one fully adult male in each group. In a group of fifty they generally have six or seven fully adult males. Their diet is much more diversified and therefore they encounter a much greater diversity of food distribution patterns. In other words, in any given day they can be feeding on both highly clumped food sources and uniformly distributed food sources which are either dense or sparse. Your suggestion that subgrouping sizes vary with the type of food that they are feeding on may be applicable to the red colobus situation but it would seem not to apply to the interspecific comparison of these two Colobinae.

DITTUS: There are factors other than the distribution of the food sources involved. For instance, we might compare *Presbytis senex*, an Asian langur which occupies the top canopy and that has a food distribution pattern very similar to what you just described for *Colobus guereza*, to *Presbytis entellus*, which is a ground living langur. Both are folivorous, *P. senex* more so than the *entellus*. We must consider here especially the species' ability to get around, to get at the food sources. Now *P. senex* lives in very small groups in a discontinuous canopy of emergents. In order for *P. senex* to get from one food tree to another they must expend a considerable amount of energy because arboreal routes of travel are frequently circuitous and indirect. For some groups of *senex* in Ceylon access to some food trees necessitated a descent to and travel over the ground. If they lived in large groups, single food trees would soon be exploited so that the group as a whole would have to shift to another. Probably because this shifting pattern takes up too much of their energy budget, their small group sizes and home ranges are attributable to difficulties in arboreal mobility. In contrast, *P. entellus* live in very large groups and home ranges, three or four times larger than those of *senex*. But for them mobility from one food source to another is not so much a problem because they can move directly on the ground. So, more than just the dispersion and concentration of the food source has to be taken into consideration.

GLANDER: Is it possible that aspects of the phenology of the trees could be related to the group sizes? The Kleins (see Klein and Klein, this volume) found a definite relationship between food availability, viz. clumping of resources, and the localization of large groups or the aggregation of several subgroups into a large feeding group and then dispersion as those sources of food disappeared.

DITTUS: Yes, the Kleins' paper substantiates my point very nicely. Here you have a species which in seasons when food is very clumped in small packages and dispersed, the animals are found singly or in small groups very frequently. And when food is dispersed over a larger area of the canopy larger group sizes occur. Well, the flexibility that is shown in this *Ateles* species is exactly similar to what one would find in an omnivorous situation, like a macaque for instance. Even during different times of the day when toque macaques encountered concentrated food sources, say mushrooms growing on termite mounds, the troop would fragment into small clusters, scattering according to the distribution of the termite mounds with mushrooms. At a different time of day when the macaques feed in fig trees the whole group fuses again and spreads evenly in the canopy. Now if a species is adapted chronically to feed on a food source that is concentrated one would expect to find it in smaller group sizes, in contrast to a group that chronically feeds on more dispersed food sources. In most of the omnivorous or eclectic species we would expect to find a much greater variability in the dispersion of the foods, and probably larger group sizes are an adaptation permitting greater flexibility in exploiting such resources.

RUMBAUGH: Perhaps we should also take cognizance of the basic social needs of the various species, the tendency for strong bonds of attachment to develop between members of various taxa. Hence the degree to which they disperse and cluster in accordance with the distribution of food can also be a reflection of basic psychological needs. Thus we have a very complex interaction in addition to just the type of food and the distribution of food.

BECK: Dr. Dittus, in your framework how do you explain the patas monkey which is a highly mobile animal, presumably feeding on widely dispersed food sources, presumably with considerable predation pressure, and yet exhibiting quite small groups, usually with only one adult male?

DITTUS: First, to answer Dr. Rumbaugh's question about the influence of psychological or let us say social factors. I would think that psychology, behavior and the social needs of the species is a secondary adaptation to primary life requirements of which the foraging pattern is one. The animal first needs to feed and to reproduce. Its whole psychology and social structure is adapted to that. On an average, social bonds will not interfere or run counter to the basic adaptation to the environment. The psychology and the social organization are the result of the nature of the adaptive syndrome to the environment. Regarding the patas monkey, Hans Kummer has addressed himself to the problem you pose. Their food sources are more or less similar to that found for the hamadryas. The smaller groupings can be explained by similar food dispersion patterns. The major difference is how they adapt to predators. Patas tend to run away or hide in the tall grass. The male has an extreme form of vigilance behavior. Hamadryas, in contrast, are protected from predation by using sleeping cliffs.

GLANDER: For too long we have been concentrating on social behavior and ignoring ecological effects or looking at them in a cursory fashion. It is time (and the papers presented in this session are encouraging) for a change in emphasis to ecology while keeping social behavior in mind. A balanced combination of the two can produce much clearer and more thorough answers to our questions and probably also generate many more interesting questions.

BECK: Dr. Dittus, the notion that patas tend to hide and flee from predators has to be tempered by the observations of patas males attacking jackals that had picked up juveniles. Now it is very rare that predation on monkeys is actually observed. Here we have very clear cases of successful attacks on predators by the patas group. Thus we should not overemphasize the fact that patas tend to run. I am not sure they are greatly different from other terrestrial cercopithecines in this regard.

STRUHSAKER: Let me also try to clarify the patas situation. Although they live in small unimale groups the patterns of dispersion are often very wide even within these groups. Sometimes a group of ten or fifteen will be dispersed over a very large area, which is quite in contrast with the hamadryas single male groups. In addition, mode of predator defense probably depends on the type of habitat. Patas range from habitats with savanna woodland and very high grass to the open sahel savanna where there is hardly any grass at certain times of the year. Where we saw the patas attack jackals there was virtually no cover for hiding.

KLEIN: You cannot treat the food resource situation independent of the physiology of the animal, i.e. what it can, in fact, digest. One of the important points that emerges from this discussion is that the more eclectic the primate's diet is, the more difficult it will be to correlate a stable social structure with ecological patterns. Although we found consistent and frequent breakups of the spider monkeys' social units, and extreme flexibility of social spacing, it was much more difficult to find similar phenomena in those animals whose diets were more eclectic because they appeared to be buffered from major kinds of seasonal and daily changes in source, abundance, and desirability of food resources. It must be understood that we are referring to dietary eclecticism in terms of daily variety. We found that the number of dietary items that conspecifics can in fact feed on in any one day, particularly in sight of one another, was critical. Characteristic of capuchin monkeys in our study area was their utilization of many more food items in a single day than either *Ateles* or *Alouatta*. On most occasions of our observations, different items were fed on simultaneously by different members of the group. The group remained cohesive and relatively constantly aware of one another's positions. In animals like spider monkeys, whose diet is considerably more specialized, social patterning is much more obviously responsive to changes of food concentration, abundance, and dispersion pattern. It is not inconceivable, however, that some primates who are, in fact, quite capable of utilizing an extraordinarily diverse spectrum of food items might inhabit, in part of their range, areas in which the variety of food items was extremely limited and concentrated. Under these circumstances a physiologically generalized feeder might be forced to pattern its social structure to most effectively utilize a few major types of crops. Hamadryas baboons, dependent upon small acacia trees for most of their sustenance, have to a degree developed social patterns of fission-fusion similar to some extent to the specialized evergreen forest frugivores.

DITTUS: The diversity of food items available at one point in space and time is a function of the forest type, season, and dietary ability of the species; animals spatially arrange themselves accordingly. Hamadryas as you say, is an eclectic feeder in a relatively invariable habitat, therefore you cannot quote the hamadryas situation as the exemplar of a typically more variable omnivore food base.

KLEIN: There are several kinds of specialists. Because one is a special feeder on ripe fruits of a certain sort does not mean that one adheres to a consistent pattern throughout the year or from month to month. The abundance and dispersion of ripe fruits even in tropical evergreen forests show considerable amounts of variability from week to week and month to month, even though not in the sort of regular seasonal patterns we associate with major fluctuations of seasonal rainfall and temperature. Howler monkeys illustrate the fact that another type of specialization is possible with considerably different effects on the social system. In our area, a considerable portion of their diet was composed of mature leaves. This resource enables them to utilize many parts of the habitat almost independently of the patterning of most fruits. Social changes need not be coordinated with changes in the abundance and pattern of fruit, even though the animals will eat many of these items when available. This is quite different from the type of specializations which require an animal to radically change its ranging and feeding habits as a consequence of a dependency upon mature fruits of several types. This type of specialization is characteristic of spider monkeys; it results in extreme spatial flexibility in which the animals of any single group may disperse over one-half square mile.

DITTUS: I did not designate *Ateles* an omnivore, I only used *Ateles* to illustrate the idea that animals show different group sizes in accordance with the dispersion of food sources.

KLEIN: That is correct.

DITTUS: There are also many other factors that must be taken into consideration. But food dispersion is one of the major ones. *Ateles* are so specialized that if there is a limited number of clumped food sources one or two dominant individuals may dominate the food source and other individuals do not have anything else on which to feed. Therefore they have to disperse. Macaques may (but do not always) have an alternative food source near by.

KLEIN: But most of the time macaques do. I was really talking about capuchin monkeys. Dominance is a very difficult topic in the spider monkeys and it is not accurate to say that one animal can dominate a food source.

DITTUS: I was using "dominate" in the sense of priority of access to a resource.

GLANDER: In the literature, the howling monkey has been considered to be an eclectic feeder. However, I found that the words specialist and generalist have to be carefully used in regards to howling monkeys at Finca La Pacifica (see Glander, this volume). The howlers were not as eclectic as previous studies would suppose them to be. For instance, of the ninety-six tree species in their range my study group utilized only twenty species as primary food sources. They fed on a total of fifty species but in most cases it was only a leaf here and a fruit there. They got most of their food from the twenty basic species. Phenology was very important. Seasonality limited the utilization of the twenty primary resource species to a few individuals of a species or to a few species at any one time.

KLEIN: I agree that the terms have been misused. You have given very interesting information. And in our experience usually all the members of a howler group were observed feeding on the same substance at the same time and for lengthy periods during the day. This too, is frequently the case for spider monkeys. On that parameter both taxa are similar and definitely not eclectic feeders, in comparison, for example, with capuchins and macaques. Another factor, of course, is the nature of the diet itself. Apparently howler monkeys are specialized for eating mature leaves and certain types of green fruit. In our study area fig fruit was a relative specialty of the howler monkeys. More fig fruit was probably eaten by howler monkeys than by any of the other sympatric taxa, including the generally frugivorous spider monkey.

GLANDER: The fig is an important food source on Barro Colorado Island. This is not true in many of the other habitats of howlers. For instance there were three fig trees in my study area, but they produced no fruit. Mature leaves of the various tree species may be an important part of the diet in certain areas. But my study group consumed mature leaves during less than 10 percent of their total feeding time and then only from selected individual trees. They mostly ate new growth, flowers and fruit.

KLEIN: It is impossible to understand these things unless we pay a great deal of attention to interspecific competition. What other species of primates in fact existed in your forest?

GLANDER: There were no other primates in the forest. However, in a neighboring area where there were other primates, much the same foraging pattern was seen by another observer.

KLEIN: Our impression of why the howler monkeys ate in quantity some of the things they did eat was that other animals may have been preventing them from utilizing as much ripe fruit of certain varieties as they would have liked, and perhaps the same might be true of buds in the few trees in our area in which a total leaf fall and regrowth occurred. Although we did not systematically collect feeding data for *Alouatta* as we did for *Ateles*, we did make some observations which indicated that, in general, the howler, as the spider monkey, did prefer young leaves and buds over mature, dying, and insect-riddled ones when they were available, and at times even appeared to be selecting the younger leaves within a tree in which a selection was possible. In the same vein, they may have eaten more green fig fruit as a consequence of intertaxa competition than they might have if given free access to the less abundant fruits which appeared to be highly desirable to spider monkeys and capuchins. However, I agree with you that variability in any taxon's diet in different habitats is to be expected and it is interesting that in your particular area fig fruit and mature leaves do not appear to be utilized as heavily by the howler monkeys there as in other areas such as Barro Colorado Island and our study site. But again, interspecific competition and feeding differences relative to sympatric taxa is what I suggest ought to be emphasized because there is going to be a great deal of room for a broader spectrum of diet where competition is limited or circumscribed. I'm not just talking about intertaxa primate competition; at least in the South American tropics some of the more important food competitors with primates are birds.

GLANDER: That is very true. In my study area lizards, birds, and leaf-cutter ants are very important competitors with the howlers.

[Mr. Glander summarized his paper and illustrated it with slides.]

[Dr. Wolfgang Dittus summarized his paper and illustrated it with slides.]

RICHARDS: Dr. Dittus, you said that the males migrate because they are attracted to estrous females in other groups, and that because all males migrate there is no inbreeding. If it is the attraction of estrous females that pulls them to the other group, why are they not attracted to the estrous females of their own group?

DITTUS: The adolescent males left their troop not only because they were attracted to estrous females in other groups but also because in their own troops they were pushed toward the periphery by competition with older males for food sources and estrous females in the same troop. They did not stand a chance in the established hierarchical pattern.

RICHARDS: In the period of transition do juvenile males go directly from one troop to another troop?

DITTUS: By going directly, I assume you mean are they accepted into the host troop without problem. They went directly all right. The physical migration may have taken only ten minutes or so; social acceptance or integration took very much longer, however. Some wandered back and forth for a period of several months. They were progressively less accepted by the members of their own troop. The migration process or becoming attached to another troop is a gradual process. It is not an overnight event.

BOESE: As these young males are migrating is there a peer association? Is there any competition between the juveniles to get access to another group? Are they acting in a solitary way or are they acting in a cooperative way?

DITTUS: Sometimes they were solitary and occasionally they went in pairs or even trios. They may have been very good buddies in the troop. The older members generally chased younger followers back to the troop. Within the host troop (on the few observations I have of trios or pairs migrating), they still remained buddies for a period of time. They also established new liaisons. Usually both of them were so harrassed by others that they were almost forced to remain buddies.

BOESE: And those that do not successfully join the host group, do they move back into their maternal group? Do they stay for another year until the next cycle and then move again? Is there a "peripheral period" when these young males are quite vulnerable to the possibility of being pushed out?

DITTUS: They did not return to their maternal troop permanently. They may have returned for a few minutes or hours, perhaps even a week or more. Then they left again. Usually after a period of a few months they never returned to their maternal troop. It became progressively more difficult for them to re-enter their troop because peers or younger members in the troop ganged up on them and did not allow them in. Some migrants left never to be seen again.

TUTTLE: What is the mechanism of their acceptance in a new troop? Why would they be accepted in another troop and not in their own?

DITTUS: I am using the term acceptance figuratively here. They can establish a position in the hierarchies whereby they have access to food. The established host members try to keep them away from these sources. Unless a male can assert his dominance over others he maintains a peripheral position. So entrance into a troop means establishing a position in the hierarchy. As my mortality records for adolescent males indicate, however, most died and never achieved a position of membership.

[Dr. Boese summarized his paper and illustrated it with slides. Dr. Struhsaker summarized his paper.]

BECK: Dr. Struhsaker, do red colobus neonates have a natal coat that is as conspicuous as the guereza?

STRUHSAKER: Yes. The four subspecies of red colobus that I have studied have a conspicuous natal color. To me it is not as striking as the black-and-white colobines. In the black-and-white colobus the neonate is completely white with a pink face; no black on it whatsoever. But the neonate red colobus which I studied had no red or brown at all. It is completely black. Let me elaborate on what we think the handling of neonates by other members of the group means. Looking at several other species, particularly the langurs, it seems that there is a fair correlation between the attention given to newborn infants and the presence of group territoriality. In other words, this may strengthen the inter-group bonding, which would of course be essential for a kind of territoriality in which all members of the group participate. Exceptions are provided however by some populations of *Presbytis entellus*.

VOGEL: Dr Struhsaker, did you see ground licking in red or in black-and-white colobus such as described by Ullrich and as we observed in langurs in India?

STRUHSAKER: John Oates did quite an interesting study on this. It is common knowledge in East Africa that black-and-white colobus come to the ground and eat soil. I once encountered them in a tunnel that they had excavated into the bank of a river. It went into the bank about three meters and they were actually inside this small excavation. They came out covered with dirt. It could be related to mineral deficiencies in their diets. In the Kibale Forest we have never seen ground-eating.[1] John Oates saw guerezas enter a pond and eat aquatic plants. They waded up to their armpits in the water. We had mineral analyses done on some of these aquatic plants. They were high in sodium. Thus the aquatic plants that they fed on were high in a certain mineral in which their common food item was low. Perhaps in other areas they make up for this mineral deficiency by eating soil, but in the Kibale it is possible they make up for this by eating aquatic plants.

TUTTLE: Elaine Morgan would be delighted with the latter.

DITTUS: Both species of langurs in Ceylon, *Presbytis entellus* and *P. senex*, eat earth from termite mounds. In *P. senex* which are very arboreal and very rarely come to the ground, I have seen a group sit around a termite mound and consume the tops of freshly constructed turrets.

---

[1] Since September 1973, we obtained evidence of soil-eating in the Kibale Forest (Struhsaker, personal communication).

Meat-Eating and Behavioral Adaptations to Hunting

Meat-Eating and Hunting in Baboons

ROBERT S. O. HARDING

INTRODUCTION

A field study of free-ranging olive baboons *(Papio anubis)* was made near the village of Gilgil, Kenya, between September 1970 and October 1971. The first three months of this period were spent surveying baboon populations in the area and habituating one particular troop to the observer. During the last eleven months, 1,032 hours were spent in close observation of this troop, with two principal objectives in mind: (1) to record as accurately as possible the way in which the troop utilized its home range, and (2) to collect information on the behavior of adult male baboons.

During the preliminary phase of this study, 496 baboons, divided into seven troops ranging in size from 35 to 121 animals, were seen in an area of 44 square kilometers. Median troop size was 49, and population density was 11.3 baboons per square kilometer. The troop selected for intensive study varied in size and composition throughout the year, but on the average it consisted of 4 adult males, 18 adult females, 2 subadult males, 15 juveniles, and 10 infants, or 49 animals in all.

The study troop's home range centered on a large cattle ranch on the floor of the Rift Valley and consisted of a series of parallel valleys separated by tall cliffs, up to 90 meters in height. There were very few large trees of the sort used as sleeping sites by baboons elsewhere in Africa, and as a result all but one of the seven troops observed retired to sleep on the cliffs at night. The valley floors over which the baboons ranged during the day were open grassland, for the most part, interspersed with patches of mixed bush and assemblages of a large, crown-sprouting shrub called locally *leleshwa (Tarchonanthus camphoratus)*.

There have been humans in this part of Kenya for a long time: the Acheulian site of Kariandusi (Cole 1963) adjoins the study troop's home range, and several Kenya Capsian (=Elmenteitan) sites are only a few kilometers away. In this century, however, the large-scale introduction of domestic livestock has had a significant effect on the baboon's environment. First of all, predator control programs, undertaken to protect the cattle, have reduced the numbers of large felines in the area, although no records have been kept to document this fact. Lions are only occasional visitors, and leopards, while known to exist in the study troop's home range, have been periodically live-trapped for removal to national parks. (Leopards and cheetahs may have been objects of poaching as well.) Second, water has been piped to cattle troughs all over the ranch, where it is available throughout the year. Third, large areas of *leleshwa* scrub have been cleared to make room for grasslands.

The process of making this area fit to raise cattle has also caused local ungulate populations to expand. Thomson's gazelles *(Gazella thomsoni)*, which prefer an open habitat, are capable of lambing twice a year (Robinette and Archer 1971) and have greatly increased their numbers over the past fifteen years, keeping pace with the range-clearing program. Reduced predator pressure may also have contributed to the increased number of ungulates; at any rate, at the time of this study an estimated 2,000 Thomson's gazelles and 800 impala *(Aepyceros melampus)* lived in the area used by the baboon study troop as its home range (L. Blankenship, personal communication).

Although the habitat in which baboons may have evolved might be open to discussion (e.g. Rowell 1966), there is no doubt that human intervention in the recent past had changed some crucial aspects of the Gilgil baboons' habitat. At the same time, they were relatively free from human harassment because the country on all sides was used for raising cattle and there were few human crops to serve as a point of conflict with local people. In addition, trapping of baboons for medical research, which has put heavy pressure on baboon populations elsewhere in Kenya, had not been permitted on the ranch.

During the course of the field study, baboons of the study troop were seen to catch, kill, and consume an unusual number of small vertebrates. These events can be compared with similar behavior seen in other nonhuman primates, and the implications of meat-eating and hunting in the lower primates for the origin of hunting in the Hominidae can be considered.

DISCUSSION

It is important to understand at the outset that baboons, whatever their carnivorous propensities (Dart 1963), subsist primarily on vegetable matter. Data from this study show that the adult male baboons of the study troop spent 79.9 percent of their feeding time procuring and eating grass seeds, blades, and roots, 18.1 percent on fruits, seeds, and flowers, and only 2 percent on sources of animal protein, including invertebrates. While similar figures are not now available for other age-sex classes, meat-eating was a relatively unimportant behavior for the Gilgil baboons in terms of time.

Nonetheless, during the 1,032 hours that were spent in detailed observations of this troop, I observed 47 small vertebrates being killed and eaten by the baboons. This figure, which includes neither several unsuccessful predatory attempts nor instances of predation observed in nearby troops, represents a predation rate far higher than has been reported for any other nonhuman primate group. Chimpanzees of the Gombe National Park are known to have killed and eaten 95 small animals, but these observations stretch over a decade (Teleki 1973).

The preferred prey of the Gilgil baboons was the Thomson's gazelle infant. Sixteen of these animals were killed and eaten, and antelope in general (including also eight dik-dik [*Rhynchotragus kirki*] of various ages, five infant antelope whose species could not be determined, one impala infant, and one steinbok [*Raphicerus campestris*]) made up two-thirds of the baboons' prey. Twelve cape hare (*Lepus capensis*), one button quail (*Turnix sylvatica*), and three small mammals of indeterminate species constituted the remaining third of the prey.

There was some evidence that local, learned tradition played a role in the selection of prey animals, for the study troop did not try to catch and kill every small vertebrate of a suitable size, and nearby baboon troops were seen to capture and eat different kinds of prey. Rock hyrax *(Procavia habessenica)*. for instance, lived on most of the cliffs where the study troop went to sleep at night, and although baboons and hyrax encountered each other regularly. no baboon was ever seen trying to catch a hyrax. Subsequent observers of the same troop have evidence indicating that other troops in the area prey on hyrax (W. Malmi, personal communication), and elsewhere in East Africa baboons are reported to eat hyrax (Kingdon 1971).

Helmeted guinea fowl (*Numida mitrata*) flocks were frequently seen wandering through the study troop as it sat eating grass, and although guinea fowl were often within easy reach of baboons, they were always ignored. However, a large troop of baboons, whose home range overlapped that of the study troop, caught and ate guinea fowl on several occasions. It is clear that different baboon troops have different notions as to what constitutes an attractive prey animal. In the near future, some light may be shed on how these preferences are acquired because three adult males emigrated into the study troop after this study ended, at least one of which came from the troop that ate guinea fowl (W. Malmi and S. Strum, personal communication). It is entirely possible that those now observing the study troop will see the troop alter its predatory habits to include guinea fowl.

Adult female baboons were seen to catch only three of the forty-seven small animals killed by the study troop, and on two of these occasions, the female was chased by an adult male and dropped her prey before she could eat it. The third female was also chased by a male, but her pursuer was distracted when she dropped part of her kill, and she was able to hide behind a bush and finish the rest. As it was very difficult for an observer to anticipate a kill, the actual capture of a prey animal was seen only ten times. Nevertheless, adult males probably caught the remaining forty-four animals, because the prey was usually still alive when the observer first detected the incident, indicating that the capture had taken place only seconds earlier.

The newborn antelopes, hares, and other animals that the study troop killed and ate were all animals that defend themselves against predators by remaining immobile, using whatever cover is available to conceal themselves. It is not surprising, therefore, that most of the baboons' kills were made apparently by chance. In one typical example, fifteen minutes after the troop had settled in a grassy field to feed, a small, newborn Thomson's gazelle struggled to its feet from its hiding place in the long grass and began to wander off. An adult male promptly seized and killed the antelope, which had been left behind when the herd to which its mother belonged left the area before the baboons arrived.

Yet killings were not always fortuitous: adult male baboons were seen to leave the troop as it made its way across an open field, move over to a herd of grazing antelope, and begin to walk a crisscross pattern through the herd, eyes directed at the grass on either side (see Bartlett and Bartlett [1961] for comparable behavior among baboons in the Serengeti National Park). The male baboons of the study troop also made similar excursions into brushy areas, typical dik-dik habitat. These appeared to the observer to be conscious efforts to look for suitable prey, and each type of search resulted in a kill on occasion. Although male baboons were seen to take up the chase of a prey animal already being pursued by another baboon, there was no indication that the monkeys were cooperating with each other by doing so.

Once the prey animal had been caught, the baboons made no deliberate attempt to kill it before beginning to eat it, just as some mammalian carnivores do not deliver a killing bite, but begin to eat their prey as soon as it is under their control. In the case of neonatal antelope, the baboons usually began eating the soft underside of the animal, and death ensued quickly. Smaller animals, such as the button quail, virtually disappeared in a mouthful, but young antelope were carefully eaten. The baboons tore off chunks of meat by gripping the flesh with their incisors, grasping the prey with two or more limbs, and pulling their heads back. A baboon occasionally stripped the skin from an antelope limb with its incisors, but in general, the meat was eaten from the inside of the skin and no attempt was made to skin the prey. Examination of several kill sites after baboons had finished eating revealed that very little was left at the end of a feeding bout, usually only scraps of skin and occasionally a long bone or a mandible. At the end of a bout, the skull was often punctured with a canine and the brain cleaned out with a finger.

Once a prey animal had been captured, the usual reaction of its conspecifics was to stand at a distance and watch; however, on six occasions female antelope were seen trying to rescue their young. On one of these occasions, a female impala successfully defended her infant, apparently unable to get to its feet, from repeated attacks by at least two adult male baboons. In the course of chasing the baboons to the sleeping cliffs, she incited other impala herds in the same valley, first an all-male herd of fifteen animals, and then a herd of one male and twenty-three female impala, with the result that impala chased baboons in all directions and the study troop soon moved on.

It has already been mentioned that female baboons were never seen to keep all of their catch if an adult male were aware that a prey animal had been captured. Adult females were able to pick up scraps dropped by adult males on only five occasions, and these scraps consisted mostly of bits of hide with very little flesh adhering to them. As a result, adult female protein intake from this source was practically nonexistent.

There was an unequal distribution of meat among the adult males as well, however. Adult male Carl, who was the largest animal in the troop and ranked first in almost every measurement of dominance taken, caught and ate eighteen small animals, almost twice the number killed by the next most accomplished male, Sumner, who caught ten. Males Radcliffe, Alger, and Moses caught five, three, and two animals respectively, while three were caught by females and six by males who could not be identified at the time. These figures are deceptive, however, because Carl was able to add considerably to the amount of meat he ate by confiscating animals killed by other baboons immediately after they had been taken. Carl obtained an additional nine animals in this way, making him the primary meat consumer of the troop, with twenty-seven animals eaten, or 57 percent of those caught. No other baboon came close to Carl in this regard, and Moses, at the other end of the scale, was forced to give up his two captures to Carl and finished with no animals to his credit. Adult males often acquired substantial amounts of meat by being the first to grab the carcass once the original eater had abandoned it; females, however, never got access to a carcass until the adult males had finished with it. In other words, while Moses got less meat to eat than any other male, he was still able to obtain more than any female.

No baboon of any age-sex class was ever seen to share meat voluntarily with another baboon, unless abandoning the carcass when satiated can be described as voluntary sharing. On the contrary, the killing and eating of a prey animal generally caused aggression levels in the troop to rise markedly. The most common reaction of other male baboons was the "vulture response" (Altmann and Altmann 1970), which consisted of sitting within five meters of an animal eating meat and staring at him. This behavior was usually punctuated by yawns and outright threats, directed both at the meat eater and at other males who were watching him eat. While dominance ranking sometimes appeared to determine which baboon consumed most of a prey animal, this was not always the case: for instance, adult male Carl was often seen watching a less dominant animal eat meat without making any overt attempt to acquire it. In another such incident, several days after he had been wounded in a fight and had become the least influential male in the troop, Radcliffe presented to Carl, then turned with a snarl and drove Carl from the carcass of an infant Thomson's gazelle. Thus, dominance ranking in males was not always a reliable predictor of behavior around a kill.

Baboons were only seen to eat meat when either they or another baboon of the same troop had killed it. The study troop ignored the carcass of a newly dead steinbok on one occasion, although several baboons passed within one meter of it during a troop movement. Similarly, a juvenile baboon drove a Verreaux's eagle (*Aquila verreauxi*) from the remains of an infant antelope, and although the juvenile and several other baboons pawed the dead antelope, they made no attempt to eat it. Yet an adult male baboon was observed early in the morning picking up and gnawing the hide of an antelope that had been killed and eaten by another male of the same troop just before nightfall on the previous evening.

It was not always possible to watch every meat-eating bout until the last scrap of hide had been chewed by the last baboon involved, but most bouts probably lasted less than an hour, a hare lasting only fifteen minutes and the larger antelopes proportionately longer. The longest meat-eating bout observed lasted just under two hours, but this occasion included a complex set of aggressive interactions which resulted in four adult males and several other animals gaining access to the meat.

These data were analyzed to see whether the killing of small animals by baboons could be correlated in any way with external factors. For example, rainfall in Gilgil is usually limited to two distinct seasons, and it seemed likely that killing would increase with the dry weather, when other sources of baboon food were scarce and little cover was available for prey animals. No such correlation was found, however. Similarly, Thomson's gazelles are known to have birth peaks in other parts of East Africa (Robinette and Archer 1971; Brooks 1961), but in contrast to what might have been predicted, there were no significant peaks found in the killing and eating of infant Thomson's gazelles. Evidence from other data indicated that the study troop moved significantly farther during the hours beginning with 10:30 A.M. and 3:30 P.M. than at any other time, and increased movement during these periods should have resulted in more fortuitous killing of small animals. It did not. Finally, there were some occasions where kills followed one another closely, but there were not enough examples of this kind of clustering in time to indicate that a successful kill was a major factor in stimulating additional killing.

Many nonhuman primates thrive in captivity on diets that include meat, and the fact that baboons in particular kill and eat small animals in the wild has been known for some time. Dart (1963) has prepared a convenient summary of references in the early literature to the predatory habits of baboons, combining reports of attacks upon South African domestic stock by baboons (Sclater 1900-1901; Marais 1939) with incidents where baboons had been seen to kill wild game. Dart's purpose in collecting this sort of information was to show "that predatory behaviour in a large terrestrial primate other than man was natural and that such behaviour was consistent with the insectivorous origin and diet of Primates" (1963:49). If a nonhuman primate such as a baboon could be shown to have a "perpetual" and "instinctive need" for animal protein, of course the hominid *Australopithecus* could be expected to have had at least as pressing an "instinctive need."

The implications of Dart's conclusions will be discussed later, but his work is introduced at this point to show that when the first modern field studies of nonhuman primates began in the late 1950's, the fact that baboons occasionally ate meat was known. DeVore and Washburn (1963), combining the results of studies in Rhodesia, Nairobi Park, and the Masai-Amboseli Game Reserve, described the killing of two infant Thomson's gazelles, two hares, one juvenile vervet monkey (*Cercopithecus aethiops*), and several fledgling birds. Altmann and Altmann (1970), working in the Masai-Amboseli Game Reserve several years later, saw eighteen animals caught and eaten by baboons in over a year's observation, prey animals including vervets, hares, infant antelope, and fossorial mammals. Rowell (1966) observed four hares being caught by Uganda forest-living baboons at times when the baboons ventured into open grassland, an average of one kill for every thirty hours of observation in this habitat. Stolz and Saayman, working in the northern Transvaal, saw one hare and one small antelope taken by baboons in 1,285 hours of observation, and mentioned a 1967 investigation by the Nature Conservation Division in which 46 of 120 farmers interviewed claimed that they had lost stock to baboons. One farmer was said to have lost an average of seventeen lambs a month during the dry season, and on one day, two troops of baboons were reported to have killed twenty-three and seventeen lambs respectively (Stolz and Saayman 1970:123).

Among the other nonhuman primates, the chimpanzee (*Pan troglodytes*) also makes meat from small mammals a regular part of its diet in some parts of its range. This tendency has been described in several reports by van Lawick-Goodall (1967, 1968, 1971), and summarized most recently by Teleki (1973). In the first ten years of personal observation of the approximately fifty chimpanzees that frequent the van Lawicks' research station in the Gombe National Park, Tanzania, ninety-five mammals were known to have been killed by chimpanzees and another thirty-seven unsuccessful predatory attempts were recorded. Other primates, such as baboon infants, red colobus, blue monkey, and redtailed monkey, made up 65 percent of the prey animals, while bushbuck and bushpig young accounted for the rest.

In both baboons and chimpanzees, the killing of small animals appears to be an activity carried on only by adults and almost exclusively by males. In contrast to the Gilgil baboons, however, the Gombe chimpanzees will cooperate with one another in obtaining a prey animal: both Teleki (1973) and van Lawick-Goodall (1971) report having seen several chimpanzees blocking escape routes of a young baboon while one of their number advanced slowly on the intended prey animal. Chimpanzees have also deliberately wrung or bitten the neck of their prey before beginning to eat it, whereas the Gilgil baboons were never seen to do this.

The Gombe chimpanzees seemed to treat a prey animal as common property for the first few minutes after a kill, and interference with any other ape trying to obtain meat was rare. After several minutes had gone by, however, the chimpanzees with major portions of the prey established what Teleki (1973:38) called "hoarders' rights," and others wanting meat had to beg for it from the hoarder. Nonetheless, sharing almost always occurred: in ten years of observation, only two unshared kills were seen, and these were the simultaneous killings of two small bushpigs by two adult female chimpanzees. No other apes were present at the time. When a Gilgil baboon killed a small animal, however, intense aggression was the rule and competition over the prey animal sprang up immediately. Some of this activity resulted in depriving the captor of his prey, but in no case was a baboon seen to share meat voluntarily. This is in sharp contrast to Teleki's personal observations: in forty-three hours spent watching meat-sharing, chimpanzees were never seen to fight over possession of meat (Teleki 1973:42).

The Gombe chimpanzees also spent a great deal of time consuming their prey: Teleki observed one consumption period of nine hours and stated that the mean duration of the predatory episodes he personally witnessed was just under four hours. The shortest episode was one hour and forty-five minutes, roughly the same amount of time as the longest feeding bout of the Gilgil baboons. At least part of the difference in time taken to consume a prey animal may have been the result of the chimpanzees' habit of alternating mouthfuls of leaves with mouthfuls of meat, a habit the Gilgil baboons did not share. At the same time, the relatively tense atmosphere obtaining at a baboon kill site would encourage rapid consumption of meat, while the relaxed chimpanzees were free to eat their prey at whatever rate they chose.

CONCLUSIONS

No complete analysis has yet been made of the protein content of baboon or chimpanzee foods in the wild, but it is apparent that protein from freshly killed animals is a minor part of the diet of these primates. Moreover, in spite of the unusually high predation rate that this article describes in one troop of baboons, it should be emphasized that adult female, juvenile, and infant baboons of the Gilgil troop were virtually excluded from this food source, while adult males spent only 2 percent of their time eating animal protein from all sources. Meat was more widely distributed in one chimpanzee group, but it remained a relatively unimportant part of their diet.

Dart's conclusion that predatory behavior in terrestrial primates is consistent with the presumed insectivorous origin of the order is supported by the nonhuman primate data. However, because so little is known about the nutritional requirements of free-ranging primates and because meat from small mammals has been shown to make up a small proportion of the diet of only one age-sex class of baboons, it is highly unlikely that baboons have a "pressing, instintive need" for animal protein.

Among living primates, furthermore, meat is important as a source of protein only for man, and for modern, "civilized" man in particular. The !Kung Bushmen derive two-thirds of their calories and 63 percent of their protein from vegetable sources, for example, while only one-sixth of the hunting and gathering peoples listed in a recent survey were found to emphasize hunting, all of them living in high altitudes where vegetable food sources are rare or nonexistent (Lee 1968). Similarly, Woodburn (1968) estimated that the diet of the Hadza of Tanzania was 80 percent vegetable, 20 percent meat and honey by weight, despite "an exceptional abundance of game."

Yet even though meat is a minor factor in the diet of most living primates, the social importance to baboons, chimpanzees, and humans of catching and eating small animals is striking. Among the Gilgil baboons, intense aggression invariably developed at the scene of a kill if more than one baboon were aware that freshly killed meat was available. Competition over a kill was the norm, and the presence of other baboons interested in the meat probably contributed to the fast rate at which a prey animal was consumed. Although chimpanzees were not observed to fight over meat, there was no doubt that they prized it highly: there were seldom fewer than five chimpanzees around a kill, some of them coming from as far as a mile away. The view that meat-eating in chimpanzees has a highly social aspect is reinforced by Teleki's (1973) observation that many predatory episodes started soon after the apes had eaten large quantities of fruits or other vegetable matter.

Similarly, the capturing and eating of meat is apt to have an importance in human societies out of proportion to the part that it actually plays in their nutrition. The fact that the Hadza eat relatively little meat despite an abundance of game has already been mentioned, yet Woodburn (1968:52) reports that they regard themselves and describe themselves as hunters:

Moreover, the Hadza place such emphasis on meat as proper food and treat vegetable foods as so thoroughly unsatisfactory in comparison that they are apt to describe themselves as suffering from hunger when they have less meat than they would like.

The resemblance to Gombe chimpanzees hunting for meat when their bellies are full of fruit is striking. Lee (1968) also observes that hunting involves a great deal of prestige among the !Kung Bushmen, although in this case game is far from abundant.

The nonhuman primate data, then, lend support to observations of human groups which show that eating meat may be something more than just a way of acquiring protein because meat is a high-priority item no matter what proportion of the diet it comprises. What are the implications of these data for reconstructing the origin of hunting behavior in the Hominidae?

First, note that at least two extant nonhuman primate species are capable of catching and consuming substantial numbers of small animals without any particular anatomical specialization. Nonhuman primates have brains capable of cooperative hunting, locomotor anatomy suitable for catching small prey, teeth able to prepare animal food for ingestion, and a digestive apparatus well equipped to make use of animal matter, including small amounts of bone. I know of nothing to indicate that these are recent evolutionary developments; indeed, as Teleki (1973) has suggested, it is likely that our prehominid primate ancestors were omnivores, making small mammals, and particularly other primates, a regular part of their diet.

It is possible to use the nonhuman primate data to construct models for the evolution of hunting behavior in humans, but these models are necessarily highly speculative, given the lack of supporting data from the archaeological record (Isaac 1971) and the need to postulate hypothetical interventions such as environmental changes conferring selective advantages on animals eating large amounts of meat. The real importance of this information lies elsewhere: i.e. the demonstration that at least two species of nonhuman primates, specifically the two species most often used as hominid surrogates in theories of human evolution, have a lively interest in meat-eating and an ability to acquire substantial amounts of meat blurs the line dividing human and nonhuman primate behavior. Because it does so, it is less likely that predatory behavior was a major shaping force in human evolution (e.g. Ardrey 1961; Morris 1967) On the contrary, the characteristic human diet, a mixture of meat and vegetable foods, is probably a continuation of an ancient primate pattern.

REFERENCES

ALTMANN, S. A., J. ALTMANN
   1970   *Baboon ecology.* Basel: S. Karger.
ARDREY, R.
   1961   *African genesis.* New York: Atheneum.
BARTLETT, D., J. BARTLETT
   1961   Observations while filming African game. *South African Journal of Science* 57:313–321.
BROOKS, A. C.
   1961   A study of Thomson's gazelle (Gazelle thomsoni *Guenther*) in *Tanganyika.* Colonial Research Publications 24:1–147.
COLE, S.
   1963   *The prehistory of East Africa.* New York: Macmillan.
DART, R. A.
   1963   Carnivorous propensities of baboons. *Symposium of the Zoological Society of London* 10: 49–56.
DE VORE, I., S. L. WASHBURN
   1963   "Baboon ecology and human evolution," in *African ecology and human evolution.* Edited by F. C. Howell and F. Bourlière, 335–367. Viking Fund Publications in Anthropology 36. New York: Wenner-Gren Foundation.
ISAAC, G. LL.
   1971   "The diet of early man: aspects of archaeological evidence from Lower and Middle Pleistocene sites in Africa," in *World Archaeology,* volume two, number three. Edited by Derek Roe, 278–289. London: Routledge and Kegan Paul.
KINGDON, J.
   1971   *East African mammals.* London: Academic Press.
LEE, RICHARD B.
   1968   "What hunters do for a living, or, how to make out on scarce resources," in *Man the hunter.* Edited by R. B. Lee and I. DeVore, 30–48. Chicago: Aldine.
MARAIS, E.
   1939   *My friends the baboons.* London: Methuen.

MORRIS, D.
1967   *The naked ape.* New York: McGraw-Hill.
ROBINETTE, W. L., A. L. ARCHER
1971   Notes on ageing criteria and reproduction of Thomson's gazelle. *East African Wildlife Journal* 9:83–98.
ROWELL, T. E.
1966   Forest living baboons in Uganda. *J. Zool. Lond.* 149:344–364.
SCLATER, W. L.
1900–1901   *The mammals of South Africa.* London: Porter.
STOLZ, L. P., G. S. SAAYMAN
1970   Ecology and behaviour of baboons in the northern Transvaal. *Annals of the Transvaal Museum* 26(5):99–143.
TELEKI, GEZA
1973   The omnivorous chimpanzee. *Scientific American* 228(1):32–42.
VAN LAWICK-GOODALL, J.
1967   *My friends, the wild chimpanzees.* Washington: National Geographic Society.
1968   The behaviour of free-living chimpanzees in the Gombe Stream Reserve. *Animal Behaviour Monographs* 1(3):161–311.
1971   *In the shadow of man.* London: Collins.
WOODBURN, J.
1968   "An introduction to Hadza ecology," in *Man the hunter.* Edited by R. B. Lee and I. DeVore, 49–55. Chicago: Aldine.

The Origin of Hominid Hunting:
A Primatological Perspective

AKIRA SUZUKI

INTRODUCTION

The ancestors of man might have possessed hunting techniques and cooperative division of labor even before the acquisition of erect posture. These social advances might have preceded those elements commonly cited as key factors in the evolution of the early hominids, namely erect posture, release of the hands, bipedal walking, and the making and use of tools. Hunting behavior required release of the hands from locomotive functions and was, therefore, one of the driving factors which led to the evolution of such high-level faculties as erect posture, big brain, and tool use.

Wild-living chimpanzees eat meat and make and use simple tools;

The research for this artiicle was financed by the Scientific Research Fund of the Ministry of Education, Japan, and in part by the Wenner-Gren Foundation for Anthropological Research.

The article is a summary of the results of the author's studies from 1964 to 1973 as a member of the Kyoto University Africa Primatological Expedition and a participant in the overseas primate field studies of the Primate Research Institute, Kyoto University.

I thank Professor Kinji Imanishi, Gifu University; Professor Shiro Kondo, Primate Research Institute, Kyoto University; Dr. Junichiro Itani, The Laboratory of Physical Anthropology, Kyoto University; Professor Masao Kawai, Primate Research Institute, Kyoto University; Professor W. B. Banage, Department of Zoology, Makerere University, and National Research Council of the Government of Uganda. I received assistance from the members of the expedition and the staff of the Primate Research Institute, Kyoto University, and of the Department of Zoology, Makerere University. I am greatly indebted to Mr. and Mrs. J. S. Kingdon, School of Fine Arts, Makerere University and in Budongo Forest to Mr. D. Baggaley and Mr. and Mrs. Sim. I thank my wife, Takako, for her help in observing the chimpanzees in the field throughout the study period.

thus it is now recognized that chimpanzee behavior includes some important patterns (albeit in unskilled states) which were formerly thought to be specifically human. It was thought that "meat-eating probably does not occur among forest living chimpanzees" (Reynolds 1967), but I observed six cases of meat-eating among chimpanzees living in Budongo Forest. Predatory behavior is therefore found in both forest- and savanna-living populations. Carnivorous behavior in otherwise frugivorous chimpanzees derives from social excitement, which is caused by particular situations confronted by the group in its nomadic life (Suzuki 1971).

The author has been investigating the ecology and social life of chimpanzees in two areas of East Africa since 1964; one study area is in Budongo Forest, Uganda (October 1965, May 1967 to September 1968, October 1970 to February 1971, August 1972 to the present); the other one is in the area between the Malagarashi and Lugufu rivers in western Tanzania (May 1964 to September 1965, August to October 1970).

This article discusses and compares the life of forest-living chimpanzees (in Budongo) with those in the savanna woodlands of western Tanzania from the viewpoint of hominid evolution. The problem of the hominoids' adaptation to life in the savanna is one which cannot be avoided in discussing the origin of the human species.

The author compares the home ranges, food composition, social composition, nomadic patterns, etc., of chimpanzees in both forest and savanna woodland areas and discusses the significance for hominid evolution of those behavior patterns, social organization, and the nomadic life that are peculiar to the chimpanzee but are not found in other nonhuman primates.

At the same time chimpanzee hunting behavior can be seen against the background of large-scale hunting, which the early hominids developed, and this view will make clear the role of open habitats in human evolution.

OBSERVATIONS OF HUNTING AND MEAT-EATING IN CHIMPANZEES

In the Budongo Forest my first observation of chimpanzees eating meat was when Ropoka, the largest male in the group, held a mutilated baby chimpanzee by its remaining leg (Suzuki 1971). Since that observation in November 1967 I have observed five cases of chimpanzees' predatory behavior in Budongo Forest; in three cases the prey were black-and-white colobus monkeys (May 1968, September 1972, February 1973); in one case it was a blue monkey (May 1968), and more recently a blue duiker (September 1972).

In addition to these observations predatory behavior has been observed in all the chimpanzee habitats that have been subject to long-term studies in East Africa. Eleven species of mammals have been observed to fall prey to chimpanzees (see Table 1). The chimpanzees' prey were neither carrion nor small animals, such as birds and mice, but were middle-sized animals which the chimpanzees themselves hunted.

Table 1. The prey of chimpanzees

Name of prey	Scientific name	Habitat		
		Budongo forest	Gombe Stream[1]	Western Tanzania excluding the Gombe Stream
Chimpanzee	*Pan troglodytes*	O	O[2]	
Baboon	*Papio anubis*		O	
Black-and-white colobus	*Colobus abyssinicus*	O		
Red colobus	*Colobus badius*		O	
Red-tailed monkey	*Cercopithecus ascanius*		O	O[3]
Blue monkey	*Cercopithecus mitis*	O	O	
Galago	*Galago crassicaudatus*			O[4]
Bushbuck	*Tragelaphus scriptus*		O	
Blue duiker	*Cephalophus monticola*	O		
Suni	*Nesotragus moschatus*			O[4]
Bushpig	*Potamochoerus porcus*		O	

[1]   J. van Lawick-Goodall (1971).
[2]   David Bygott, personal communication.
[3]   Kawabe (1966), *Primates* 1: 393–396.
[4]   T. Nishida, personal communication.

Eating Blue Duiker

I have already reported on meat-eating among chimpanzees (Suzuki 1971). Here I will describe in detail chimpanzees in Budongo Forest eating a blue duiker, *Cephalophus monticola*, and discuss some remarkable points in the hunting and meat-eating behavior of the chimpanzees. Hitherto the chimpanzee prey in Budongo Forest were all arboreal primates, but the killing of a duiker makes it clear that forest-dwelling chimpanzees also hunt on the ground.

On the 28th of September, 1972, four adult chimpanzees were observed spending two and a half hours (11:15 A.M. to 1:43 P.M.) eating a subadult blue duiker. This group of chimpanzees had returned the previous day to the center of their nomadic area or home range after a week's travel to the southern edge of their range. There had been very few suitable items of food available at this time, and the chimpanzees of this group had been observed on the move during the earlier part of the morning (9:30 A.M. and 10:10 A.M.). At 11:05 A.M. a blue duiker was heard screaming about 200 meters from me, in the area where the chimpanzee group was walking. After ten minutes, I found the four big males in a tree crying and struggling with one another for the spoils of the duiker. Ropoka, who is at present the top-ranking male in this group (which has been under observation since 1967), was holding the body of the duiker which had lost a hindleg and had been torn open. Kim, the oldest male, and Mkubwa, the second-ranking male in the group, were sitting closest to Ropoka and were sharing the meat, while Labuda was sitting five meters away on the same branch. Several furious struggles then took place between the four animals; these were followed by silent periods of eating the meat. Figure 1 shows how the prey came to be divided.

Until 12:10 A.M. Ropoka had almost monopolized the body and had been eating from it voraciously. At this time Mkubwa took over the head, neck, and some body skin, while Ropoka continued to eat the last remaining forelimb, finishing it at 1:23 P.M.; at that time he appeared to lose interest in eating meat, did not attempt to take anything away from the other individuals, and only picked up in his hand a piece of skin left on a branch by Kim. Ropoka was still carrying this skin at 1:45 P.M. when he descended to the ground with the other three males who were still carrying pieces of duiker.

During the two and a half hours of observation four big chimpanzees had almost entirely consumed the meat of a small duiker. A young male chimpanzee, eight or nine years old, seemed to have been allowed to share a bit of meat by Ropoka in the early stages of the incident before I arrived; he was sitting about twenty meters away in a neighboring tree licking blood off his hand.

When I first arrived ten minutes after the killing, the four adult males were all very excited and struggling for a share of the meat. The climax was reached at 1:45 when Ropoka and Labuda divided the whole duiker into two parts. At this time Labuda, who had been sitting in the next tree, rushed up to Ropoka and, bodies touching

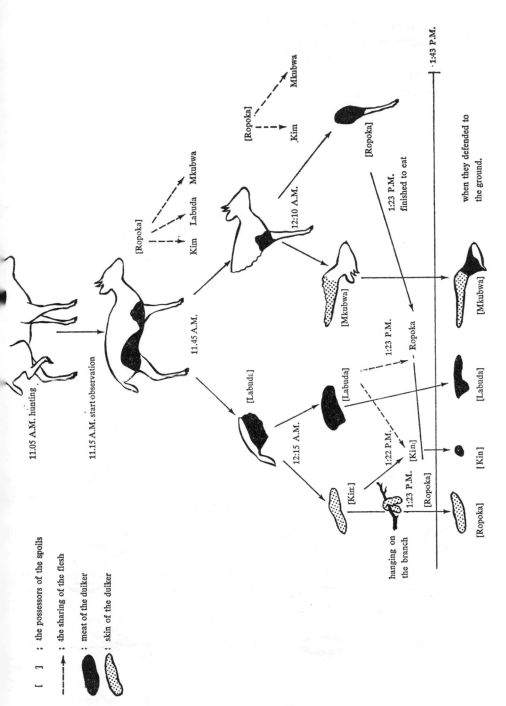

Figure 1.   The sharing of the meat of the blue duiker

momentarily, Labuda patted Ropoka's face with his right hand. Descending to a lower branch, Labuda took hold of the duiker's hindleg and pulled. As the two chimpanzees pulled the animal in opposite directions, I could hear at thirty meters the sound of tearing meat and bone. The tearing was done only with the hands. Mkubwa, who took the head and neck, broke open the skull with his teeth and ate the brain.

Notes on Hunting and Meat-Eating

I will now discuss several points arising from my observations of wild-living chimpanzees that may be relevant to the reconstruction of early hominid evolution.

LIKING FOR MEAT   From the tense reactions of the chimpanzees toward the possession of the prey, which are shown Figure 2, it is obvious that a taste for flesh is common to all members of the group, although they normally do not try to hunt animals even within easy reach. It should also be noted that in all of the observed cases car-nivorousness did not involve dead flesh or small-sized animals, but only the flesh of middle-sized living animals the chimpanzees had captured.

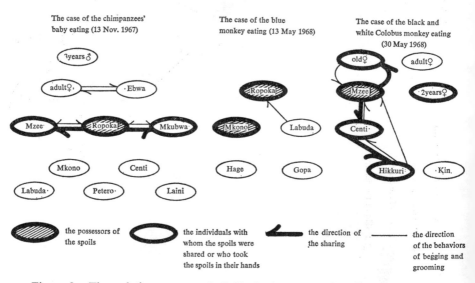

Figure 2. The relations among individuals in meat-eating and cannibalism (Suzuki 1971)

BEGGING GESTURES AND FOOD-SHARING   The fact that the possessors of the prey were limited to only several chimpanzees produced fascinating and tense relationships between the possessors and others in this group (see Suzuki 1971). Some individuals offered to groom or made begging gestures to the possessors of the meat. Some were fortunate enough to be allowed to share a piece of flesh, but others failed to gain a share.

The possessors of the prey are generally high-ranking individuals in the group; the hunting and killing also seem to be performed by these high-ranking chimpanzees. It is very interesting to note the way in which the prey is divided into pieces and shared with neighboring individuals.

CARRYING BEHAVIOR   The chimpanzees did not always eat up their prey on the spot where they had hunted it; generally they carried part of the carcass a considerable distance, holding it in their mouths or hands or putting it between their upper thighs. Carrying valuable food, such as meat, in the hands may signify the recognition by the chimpanzee of the value of the carried object. The chimpanzees, however, not only carry meat but also large-sized fruits, such as *Trecullia africana, Myrianthus arboreus, and Desplatzia lutea.*

I observed one chimpanzee carry a piece of dry vine stem for about 500 meters. This piece (which was about twenty-five centimeters long) was chewed by the chimpanzee as he was walking along a path. Chimpanzees also carry "fruit balls," which have been made by chewing fruits such as *Ficus mucuso.* These balls are shaped and hardened in the mouth and lips. I observed one mother chimpanzee carry a hardened fruit ball from a fruiting fig tree into another tree where her two-year-old baby begged for it. The mother gave part of the ball to her baby.

Carrying behavior is thought to have a very important relationship to erect posture, bipedal walking, and the release of hands in human evolution. The urge to carry an object implies the recognition of a value in the object. I think this recognition was a condition already possessed before the acquisition of such physical characteristics.

COOPERATIVE WORKING   In the blue duiker hunting, I could not observe the hunting and killing but can guess that the four males who were eating this prey might have hunted cooperatively because cooperative hunting has been reported in the cases where a black-and-white colobus monkey and a red colobus monkey were the prey (van

Lawick-Goodall 1971; Suzuki 1971). Van Lawick-Goodall (1971: 254) sair that:

The hunting seems to be much more deliberate, purposeful activity, and often at such times the different individuals of the chimpanzee group show quite remarkable co-operation as when different chimpanzees station themselves at the base of trees offering escape routes to a cornered victim.

In the case of blue duiker eating, the act in which Ropoka and Labuda tore the prey into pieces could be interpreted as a case of cooperative working for the division of the spoils.

Judging from the facts which have emerged from recent studies on hunting in carnivores, for whom cooperation is common to most species, it can be said that hunting behavior improves the faculty of cooperation (Schaller and Lowther 1969; van Lawick and van Lawick-Goodall 1970).

TOOL-USING   There have been no observations of the use of tools associated with hunting by chimpanzees. While eating the blue duiker, the chimpanzees frequently ate young leaves of *Cynometra*. They wiped the blood of the duiker off their hands and mouths with leaves and after doing so, they ate or threw the leaves away. I once observed a male wiping sperm off his penis with leaves after copulating. Chimpanzees use leaves for wiping other sticky materials off their bodies.

Chimpanzees frequently broke large dead branches from tall trees above me. This behavior was found much more in the chimpanzees of western Tanzania, and was a deliberate and purposeful activity. They looked for suitable dead branches in advance and, while shouting at me, they rushed into the branches and knocked them down in my direction. In the same way they used to drop their excrement down onto me. This occurred when they were frightened. This behavior suggests that chimpanzees are very close to using weapons against enemies.

I also observed instances during which the chimpanzees hid themselves behind leaves for ten to fifteen minutes when they were surprised by people in the forest. If these behavior patterns operated as a coordinated whole, the result could work progressively toward technical skills improving hunting ability.

A well-known example of the use of tools by chimpanzees is their collecting and stripping grass and twigs for termite-fishing. Since the first observation in Gombe Stream in Tanzania, this behavior has been observed in Kasakati and Kasoge, also in western Tanzania

(Goodall 1963; Suzuki 1966; Nishida, personal communication). The tool-making exhibited by chimpanzees illustrates the earliest stages of tool manipulation in hominoid evolution.

WHAT TRIGGERS THE MEAT-EATING? Van Lawick-Goodall (1971) suggested that meat-eating behavior in the chimpanzees occurs in cycles. She said:

It may be that a chance hunting success, when, for instance, a chimpanzee accidentally comes across a baby bushpig in the undergrowth, starts off a craze for meat in the group as a whole. While this craze lasts, for one or even two months, the adult and adolescent males may set out to hunt deliberately. Then, either because their craving is satisfied, or because a succession of hunts results in failure and they lose interest, the chimpanzees return to a diet of fruit, vegetables and insects. Until a few months later, something triggers off another meat-eating craze.

Chimpanzees are often observed unconcernedly sitting on the same branches close to arboreal monkeys such as blue monkeys, red-tailed monkeys, and colobus monkeys, and eating fruits with them. They are generally not hostile toward the monkeys. In the midst of the dry season in western Tanzania, in August 1964, I observed three adult male chimpanzees moving in procession in open land. A subadult bushbuck (*Tragelaphus scruptus*) came out just in front of them and came within one or two meters of them; however they did not hunt it. In the Budongo Forest (January 1973) I observed a young black-and-white colobus monkey, frightened by approaching chimpanzees, run into a tree where there was an adult female chimpanzee who stretched out her hand and touched the colobus without attempting to catch it. So chimpanzees are not always on the hunt whenever game comes near them.

I have pointed out that the hunting and meat-eating of chimpanzees seems to be related to some socially excited situation in their nomadic life that is dependent on changes in their food seasons (Suzuki 1971).

The case of eating a baby chimpanzee, which was observed in November 1967, occurred at the end of the *Celtis* season which had continued for more than one month; the cases of eating blue monkeys and a colobus monkey, which were observed in May 1968, took place in the transition from the *Maesopsis* season to the *Pseudospondias* season. In these three cases the hunting occurred when the groups of chimpanzees were very excited and moving very widely and rapidly over their nomadic area.

When the blue duiker was eaten, on the 28th of September, 1972, the group had just returned from a long safari to the southern edge of their territory. The day before the kill (on the 27th of September) they had been very noisy while visiting a ground nest of honey-bees, and on the 30th of September five adult male chimpanzees spent three hours eating a lump of gum from a *Khaya anthotheca* tree. At this time there were very few suitable foods in the forest, and the feeding habits of the chimpanzees from September to the beginning of October 1972 were abnormal. On September 7th an adult male chimpanzee was observed carrying a young colobus monkey in his mouth, and on the 9th of October I encountered a site where the chimpanzees had brought down a bird's nest and eaten the eggs.

The relation between eating meat and the physical and mental states of the chimpanzees in their nomadic life should not be overlooked. The motive force which drives them to hunt animals is not the mere fact that the prey happens to be within their easy reach, but it is also related to social excitement caused by the situation of the group in their nomadic life.

THE NOMADIC LIFE OF CHIMPANZEES: COMPARATIVE STUDY BETWEEN FOREST AND SAVANNA WOODLAND AREAS

Study Area

Chimpanzees are distributed widely in the tropical rain forest and along the outer margins adjoining the savanna environments. The vegetation of the Budongo Forest is described as *Cynometra - Celtis*, medium-altitude moist semideciduous forest, and was divided by Eggeling (1947) into five types of vegetation, namely colonizing woodland forest, colonizing *Maesopsis* forest, mixed forest, *Cynometra* forest, and swamp forest. Dry *Combretum* savanna is distributed outside the forest, but chimpanzees have scarcely ever been observed taking foods there.

My other study area is in the Kigoma and Mpanda districts of Tanzania. The vegetation here is *Brachystegia - Isoberlinia*, savanna woodland. The vegetation in this study area is divided into three main types: (1) grassland and savanna, (2) open forest or woodland, and (3) riverine forest and thicket; these are subdivided into twenty vegetation subtypes (Table 2). The open forest or dry woodland type is

Table 2.   Vegetation types in the Kasakati area, western Tanzania

Vegetation type	Symbol	Area percent	Square kilometers
Grassland and Savanna		31.23	62.8
Grassland	(Sg)	15.68	
Diplorhynchus savanna	(Sd)	2.31	
Combretum savanna	(Sc)	7.97	
Brachystegia longifolia savanna	(Sb)	0.33	
Mixed savanna	(Sm)	3.04	
Herb bush	(Sh)	0.72	
Arundinalia bush	(Sa)	1.18	
Open Forest or Woodland		58.88	118.3
Julbernardia open forest	(Og)	41.74	
Brachystegia bussei open forest	(Ob)	2.04	
B. allenii open forest	(Oa)	0.44	
Isoberlinia open forest	(Oi)	9.73	
Pericopsis open forest	(Op)	4.13	
Monotes open forest	(Om)	0.63	
Uapaca open forest	(Ou)	0.17	
Riverine Forest and Thicket		9.89	19.9
Albizzia riverine forest	(Ra)	2.82	
Cordia riverine forest	(Rco)	2.10	
Cynometra riverine forest	(Rcy)	2.90	
Syzygium riverine forest	(Rs)	0.24	
Vitex riverine forest	(Rv)	0.30	
Thicket	(Rt)	1.53	
Total		100.00	201.0

Source: Suzuki (1969).

Table 3.   The number of kinds of vegetable foods of chimpanzees in savanna woodland

Vegetation type	1964								1965							Total
	May	June	July	August	September	October	November	December	January	February	March	April	May	June	July	
Savanna			3							1						4
Open forest	1	5	7	5	7	7	1			1	1	2	4	3	2	19
Riverine forest	14	12	10	3	10	14	11	10	13	8	9	13	17	12	10	55
Rt	3	5	6	3	2	3	1	1	2	3	4	5	7	5	4	15
Rv	2	2	1						1	1	1	1	2	1		3
Rco	4	5	2		5	4	4	4	1	1	1	5	8	6	4	14
Rcy														1		1
Rs	1				1											2
Ra	4		1		2	7	6	5	9	3	3	1			1	21
Total	15	17	20	8	17	21	12	10	13	10	10	15	21	15	12	78

Source: Suzuki (1969).

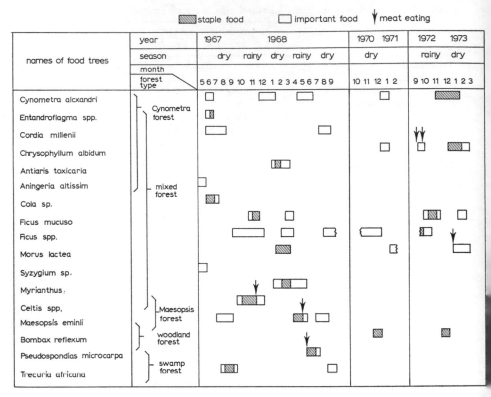

Figure 3. The correlations between the meat-eating and the food seasons of chimpanzees in Budongo forest, 1967–1973

most widely distributed, occupying about 60 percent of the study area; the riverine forest and thicket type occupy only 10 percent. The evergreen forest is distributed only narrowly along rivers.

Food Adaptation

Seasonal changes in the main foods of chimpanzees in the Budongo Forest are shown in Figure 3. Figure 4 shows equivalent data for the savanna area, according to vegetation types. Seventy-eight plants were eaten by chimpanzees in the savanna area during the seventeen months of study in 1964–1965, while in the forest area only about fifty species of plants were eaten during 1967–1972.

The characteristics of the chimpanzees' food habits in both areas are as follows (Table 3):

Scientific name (native name)	vegetation type	%	Dry season 1964	Rainy season 1965	Dry season	%
			May Jun. Jul. Aug. Sept. Oct.	Nov. Dec. Jan. Feb. Mar. Apr.	May Jun. Jul.	
Julbernardia sp. Brachystegia sp. (Miombo)	0	10.77				50 / 0
Pilostyles sp. (Binsonpufu)	0	1.36				
Vitex doniana (Bufuru)	0	0.91				
Parinari curatellifolia (Mbura)	0	2.84				
Strychnos innocua (Kankundu)	0	1.26				
Uapaca kirkiana (Kakusufinya)	0	0.93				
Garcinia huillensis (Kasorio)	0	0.98				
Brachiaria brizantha (Kanpandanpanda)	Rt	1.34				
Aframomum sp. (Matunguru)	Rt	6.98				
Uragoga cyanocarpa (Dafurafu)	Rt	1.46				
Canthium gueinzii (Buti-1)	Rt	1.65				
Tarenna friesiorum (Fubira)	Rt	1.72				
Canthium hispidium (Buti-2)	Rt	4.78				
Strychnos sp. (Fefiye)	Rt	1.54				
Vitex ferruginea (Kaburanpako)	Rv	7.64				
Uvaria angolensis (Bonko)	Rv	2.85				
Ficus sp. (Hambwa)	Rco	6.84				
Cordia abyssinica (Mukibu)	Rco	1.93				
Canarium schweinfurthii (Shigomfi)	Rco	2.46				
Morus sp. (Sapara)	Rco	3.28				
Saba sp. (Ribufu)	Rco	3.78				
Saba sp. (Ifukura)	Rco	0.94				
Linociera nilotica (Murengere)	Ra	0.83				
Landolphia sp. (Katimba)	Ra	1.53				
Saba florida (Ilombo)	Ra	12.89				
Sp-indet (Kajara)	Ra	1.17				
Pseudspondias microcarpa (Ipepeti)	Ra	2.61				
Uvaria sp. (Satuke)	Ra	3.14				

Figure 4.   Seasonal changes of chimpanzees' foods in Kasakati, western Tanzania in 1964–1965. Percent is volume of contents of droppings during a year (Suzuki 1969)

1.   The number and types of food taken by chimpanzees in each food season are fewer in the forest habitat than in the savanna woodland. In the forest habitat chimpanzees restrict themselves to a few abundant foods for long periods (a month or more). Typical of such seasonal food supplies are *Ficus* species, *Maesopsis*, *Pseudospondias*, *Cynometra*, etc. In the savanna an average of seven or eight kinds of vegetable foods can be found in the chimpanzees' feces in any season.

2. Forest-living chimpanzees habitually eat the leaves of trees such as *Celtis, Cynometra, Morus,* and *Ficus,* especially when other foods are scarce but even at times when fruit is abundant. In the savanna, however, chimpanzees rely on hard fruits, nuts, and seeds that are found in thickets during times of scarcity.

3. The reliance on the seeds of *Caesalpinaceae* in both habitats is striking; the savanna chimpanzees eat large numbers of seeds in the open forest while the forest chimpanzees feed intensively on *Cynometra alexandri* seeds at the beginning of the dry season.

4. The savanna-living chimpanzees took insects (mainly ants and termites) during the rainy season much more than those living in the forest (Suzuki 1966). Meat-eating was observed in both areas.

A most important point about the adaptations of chimpanzees' food habits is that in the dry season, when food supplies are low in the forest area, the savanna-living chimpanzees move out on a large scale into the open land and use the rich foods of savanna woodland (Suzuki 1969). Characteristic food sources in the savanna woodland during the dry season are (1) hard seeds of *Caesalpinaceae* and *Papilionaceae*, (2) fleshy half-dried fruits of *Vitex, Uapaca, Parinari,* and *Garcinia* and fruits of *Strychnos*, and (3) grain of *Brachiaria*. Also it is noteworthy that during the dry season in the savanna area the chimpanzees found a lot of dried fruits such as *Canthium, Tarenna, Uragoga,* etc. in the thickets. So during a long dry season, for the five months from May to October, the main food resources for the chimpanzees are in open forest or woodland.

Nomadic Area and Land Utilization

It is characteristic of the chimpanzees' nomadic life that they use each vegetation type by season, moving about widely. In order to survive in a radically fluctuating food situation, it is essential for chimpanzees to seek out a wide variety of foods over extensive areas.

In Budongo Forest a social unit, which consists of seventy to eighty individuals, has a nomadic area ranging about fifteen to twenty square kilometers. Comparing this with the nomadic ranges of each kind of monkey in Budongo Forest, that of the chimpanzees is far wider than the ranges of any species of monkey in the same forest (see Figure 5).

In the savanna the number and size of social units of chimpanzees and the nomadic ranges of each group have not been established

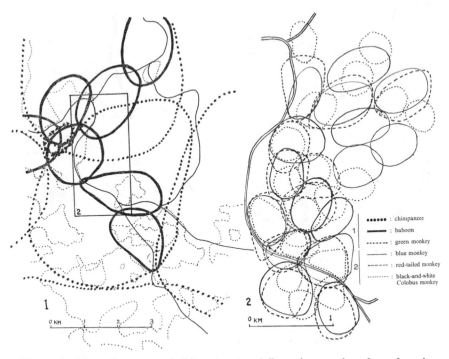

Figure 5. Nomadic ranges of chimpanzees and five other species of monkeys in Budongo forest

(Suzuki 1969; Kano 1971). I estimate that a social unit consists of forty to fifty individuals and has a nomadic area of about 200 square kilometers, which consists of both mountainous and flat areas. According to the author's surveys in the savanna area in 1965 and 1970, nine unit groups of chimpanzees could be estimated in an area of about 2600 square kilometers (see Figure 6).

The extent of the nomadic ranges of chimpanzees in the savanna woodland is far greater than that of any nonhuman primates studied so far. Even the nomadic range of mountain gorillas covers only ten to twenty square kilometers (Schaller 1963). The range of savanna-living chimpanzees is remarkable for being of similar extent as the home ranges of hunting and gathering peoples such as Bushmen.

Social Adaptation

There are three modes of existence for each chimpanzee nomadic group. These are (1) concentration, (2) linkage, and (3) dispersal;

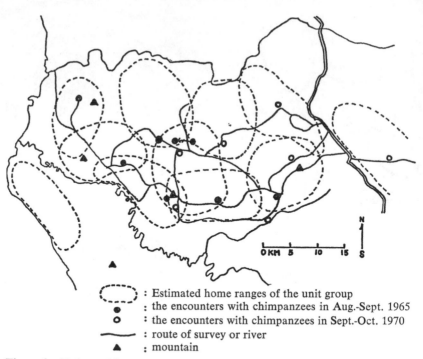

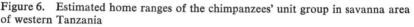

- - - : Estimated home ranges of the unit group
● : the encounters with chimpanzees in Aug.-Sept. 1965
○ : the encounters with chimpanzees in Sept.-Oct. 1970
—— : route of survey or river
▲ : mountain

Figure 6. Estimated home ranges of the chimpanzees' unit group in savanna area of western Tanzania

they are dependent on the conditions of the vegetation, the amount and distribution of food supply, and whether the chimpanzees are stationary or traveling (Suzuki 1969). Chimpanzees have large-sized groups or social units which consist of thirty to eighty individuals with several males in the group (Itani and Suzuki 1967; Nishida 1968). However, a characteristic which cannot be found in other nonhuman primates is that the chimpanzees have such an elastic social organization that membership of the nomadic group can change inside the social unit according to their situation.

Table 4 shows a comparison of types of nomadic groups with observations drawn from Goodall (1965), Reynolds and Reynolds (1965), and Suzuki (1969). The differences that can be observed between the composition of nomadic groups in forest and savanna habitats pose very interesting problems.

In the savanna mixed nomadic groups containing individuals of both sexes and of sundry ages centering around one or more adult males is most frequent, while in forest areas (in Budongo and Gombe Stream) many nomadic groups consist solely of adults, mothers, and

Table 4. Nomadic groups of chimpanzees in each habitat in East Africa

Habitat	Budongo forest	Gombe Stream	Savanna area in western Tanzania
Observer	Reynolds and Reynolds (1965)	Goodall (1965)	Suzuki (1969)
Type of unit	Percent	Percent	Percent
Mixed nomadic group	37.2	30.0	77.9
Adults nomadic group	30.2	18.0	4.8
Mothers nomadic group	16.8	24.0	2.8
Males nomadic group	15.8	10.0	1.0
Lone individual	–	18.0	13.5

Source: Suzuki (1969).

males respectively. In the forest, which provides a rich and stable environment, chimpanzees of similar age and sex classes tend to come together. In the savanna woodland, where chimpanzees are used to moving much more widely and face greater dangers, they form a mixed group, in which males can lead the group in their nomadic life. In the forest mothers and infants generally stay scattered near the feeding trees, while the males or adults of the nomadic group move around looking for new feeding trees. Mothers and infants learn of new feeding trees through the crying of males or adults of the nomadic group. Such an elastic organization in chimpanzee society is thought to be more developed than in the societies of other nonhuman primates, which have strong ranking systems in the group and must always move in one party. The acquisition of the elastic social organization might have involved the acquisition of a certain degree of individuality, in which an animal can fend for itself without being totally dependent on the ranking system which exists within its society. This could mean that chimpanzee society already exhibits some elements of the division of labor, which would be necessary for a hunting life.

DISCUSSION

Based on observations of the food habits of chimpanzees in savanna woodland, I offer the following hypothesis: some of the groups of precarnivorous hominoids came to live partly in open land, feeding mainly on vegetable foods, and then gradually turned carnivorous (Suzuki 1969). At the same time from the viewpoint of morphology Jolly (1972) points out the importance of "small-object feeding" in open land on the formation of hominid dentition. He thinks that hominid evolution may have been accomplished in two stages; the first stage is the acquisition of hominid dentition through small object feeding in open land; the second stage is the acquisition of meat-eating, erect posture, bipedal walking, big brain, language, etc. Simons and Ettel (1970) suggested that *Gigantopithecus* might have fed on seeds and roots in dry open land. Some early hominoids might have adapted to life in the open before they began to hunt on a large scale. I have shown how open savanna woodland provides an abundant source of food for these anthropoid apes. Today fruits of *Uapaca, Strychnos, Vitex, Garcinia, Parinari*, etc. are relished by people in this habitat. Even in the drier *Acacia* savannas and *Combretum* woodland, the fruits of *Balanites* are a common food for many African tribes. Kingdon (1971) stated that:

Climatic changes in the Miocene and Pliocene are thought to have converted vast areas of land to drier more open vegetation types. There is no evidence that such habitats were less rich in food resources for primates than forests even if these resources were more dispersed. Apes were the dominant primates of the period so that there is nothing essentially problematic about the groups' invasion of savanna.

The factors that are considered necessary for man to hunt animals on a large scale are (1) the faculty of long-distance locomotion to get his animals, (2) a high-level social relationship with division of labor, and (3) a high-level technical faculty such as the making and use of tools. Chimpanzees have already acquired the first two elements. They evolved some social sharing of foods and have a flexible social organization, which provides the base for division of labor and large-sized social units, which cannot be found among other living anthropoid apes. They are also able to travel long distances and thus use many vegetation types scattered over the mosaic of their nomadic range. This range can be readily compared with the home ranges of hunting and food-gathering peoples that have been studied in similar habitats.

Schaller (1964) said that the life of the mountain gorilla "was a life of leisure, of eating and sleeping and rambling about with little to break the rhythm of daylight and darkness." How much variety the chimpanzees' life has in comparison with the monotonous life of the mountain gorilla!

Chimpanzees have a very much wider nomadic range which includes a mosaic of many types of vegetation; they move about more widely, and they use more varied vegetation types according to the seasons than do the gorillas. Furthermore, the chimpanzees use the outer margins of the African forest blocks much more than the gorillas do. These differences between two clearly related anthropoid apes might throw a most important light on the process of hominid evolution.

I observed several times that chimpanzees run down steep slopes on hillsides by bipedal walking with their hands swinging above their heads. The topography that provided a rich variety of vegetational habitats with good water resources and easy hunting would also have provided a combination of physical contrasts such as escarpments and plains, and this might also have allowed the early hominids to find ample opportunities for bipedal walking as they adapted to open country.

I believe that in the first stage of hominid evolution some of the earliest hominoids had wide home ranges. The topography of their ranges may have been greatly varied both physically and ecologically. Having some omnivorous traits but living mainly on vegetable resources, these early bands may have had similarities with the groups of chimpanzees that I studied in the savannas of western Tanzania.

It is interesting that meat-eating and very extensive ranges are found among baboons living in open country. This can be understood as an adaptation to more arid environments.

It is not enough to explain hunting behavior as a simple adaptation to living in open country because some species of arboreal monkeys have also been observed eating small animals (K. Hayashi and P. Waser, personal communication). The origin of meat-eating must be considered in the whole rhythm of a nomadic life in a wide area with a great variety of habitats. This environment encourages tension and excitement, a condition that allows us to contrast the mental situation of chimpanzees and baboons with that of the mountain gorilla's stable life.

The origins of hunting behavior in human evolution should be related to a developing mental mechanism, which preceded the acquisition of erect posture; in the second stage of hominid evolution hunting behavior required the release of the hands and was, therefore, one of the driving factors which led to the evolution of such high-level faculties as erect posture, big brain, and tool use.

REFERENCES

EGGELING, W. J.
    1947   Observations on the ecology of the Budongo rain forest, Uganda. *Journal of Ecology* 34:28–87.

GOODALL, J.
1963   My life among wild chimpanzees. *National Geographic* 124(2): 272–308.
1965   "Chimpanzees of the Gombe Stream Reserve," in *Primate behavior*. Edited by I. DeVore, 425–473. New York: Holt, Rinehart and Winston.

ITANI, J., A. SUZUKI
1967   The social unit of chimpanzees. *Primates* 8:355–381.

JOLLY, A.
1972   *The evolution of primate behavior*. New York: Macmillan.

KANO, T.
1971   The chimpanzee of Filabanga, Western Tanzania. *Primates* 12(3–4):229–246.

KINGDON, J.
1971   *East African mammals*, volume one. London and New York: Academic Press.

NISHIDA, T.
1968   The social group of wild chimpanzees in the Mahali Mountains. *Primates* 9:167–224.

REYNOLDS, V.
1967   *The apes*. London: Cassel.

REYNOLDS, V., F. REYNOLDS
1965   "Chimpanzees of the Budongo forest," in *Primate behavior*. Edited by I. DeVore, 368–424. New York: Holt, Rinehart and Winston.

SCHALLER, G. B.
1963   *The mountain gorilla*. Chicago: University of Chicago Press.
1964   *The year of the gorilla*. Chicago: University of Chicago Press.

SCHALLER, G. B., G. R. LOWTHER
1969   The relevance of carnivore behavior to the study of early hominids. *Southwestern Journal of Anthropology* 25(4):307–341.

SIMONS, E. L., P. C. ETTEL
1970   Gigantopithecus. *Scientific American* 222(1):76–87.

SUZUKI, A.
1966   On the insect-eating habits among wild chimpanzees living in the savanna woodland of Western Tanzania. *Primates* 7(4):481–487.
1969   An ecological study of chimpanzees in a savanna woodland. *Primates* 10:103–148.
1971   Carnivority and cannibalism among chimpanzees. *Journal of the Anthropological Society of Nippon*. 79(1):30–48.

VAN LAWICK, H., J. VAN LAWICK-GOODALL
1970   *Innocent killers*. London: Collins.

VAN LAWICK-GOODALL, J.
1971   *In the shadow of man*. London: Collins.

Behavioral and Intellectual Adaptations of Selected Mammalian Predators to the Problem of Hunting Large Animals

ROGER PETERS and L. DAVID MECH

In the course of their evolution, many different mammals, including hominids, particularly early man, came to depend on large animals for food. Because problems faced in the detection, apprehension, and consumption of large mammals are the same for various types of predators despite diverse phylogenetic backgrounds, it is useful to compare the different behavioral solutions that they have evolved to these physical problems. Furthermore, such a comparison may help to provide valuable insight into certain human traits that may have been fostered by the dependence of hominids upon a hunting economy.

Our comparisons will be based on three social carnivores: the wolf *(Canis lupus)*, the African hunting dog *(Lycaon pictus)*, and the lion *(Panthera leo)*; on two living primates: the chimpanzee *(Pan troglodytes)* and the baboon *(Papio* spp.); and on inferences about hunting by early hominids. We will not attempt to establish the importance of hunting at any given stage of human evolution (for which we need, not more words, but more fossils), but rather we will analyze the problems encountered by early hominids when they did hunt and the solutions they evolved, compared with those of other species using similar resources.

The behavioral solutions to the problems of detection, apprehension, and use of large prey, like the morphological ones, vary from species to species, but there are some common dimensions. Atz (1970) and Lockhard (1971) have discussed the difficulties of comparing behaviors in different animals on the basis of phylogeny and homology. We try to

Peters was supported by a fellowship from the Danforth Foundation during the preparation of this paper. Field observations of wolves hunting deer in Minnesota were financed by a New York Zoological Society grant to Mech.

avoid these difficulties by using categories of behavioral traits based on function rather than on phylogeny. The traits we have found useful in comparing the behavior of various hunters are persistence, cooperation, strategy, and cognitive mapping. We have *a priori* judged these traits to be of significant value to any organism dependent on the capture of large prey.

We define persistence as the extent to which an organism allocates time, energy, or information-processing capacity to a particular task. Cooperation refers to behavior by one animal that consistently increases the probability of success at a task by its associates. Strategy is future-oriented behavior involving a progressive series of acts, some of which performed alone would not contribute toward achieving the ultimate goal. Cognitive mapping is the mental storage of the spatial organization of locations perceived by an animal (Kaplan 1973); in several mammals such memories are organized into representations of the physical environment that preserve major topological and geometric relationships.

A comparison of the importance of persistence, cooperation, strategy use, and cognitive maps in various species will be made for each of the three major problems faced in depending on large prey, that is, detection, apprehension, and use. In analyzing the degree of development of the behavioral traits shown by various hunters, we will seek to define those that may have developed to a high degree in predatory mammals, especially in primates (including early hominids), and that thus may have formed a behavioral substrate that fostered the evolution of human intelligence.

PERSISTENCE

Persistence is demonstrated in varying degrees by the hunters we are comparing, and functions in various ways in the different phases of the hunt.

Wolves display a relatively high degree of persistence during the detection phase, as indicated by the proportion of their time spent in search activity and by the length of a typical search. Wolves begin to search for prey as soon as they leave a kill, and continue to search whenever they are traveling, which they do for eight or more hours a day, with local and seasonal variations (Mech 1970). Mech (1966a) observed wolves hunting on Isle Royale for a total of sixty-eight hours, during which they detected moose *(Alces alces)* sixty-six times, for an average of a little more than an hour per search. On Isle Royale, prey density is higher than in most areas where moose are hunted, so this persistence time probably represents a minimal figure.

During the pursuit of prey, wolves are also relatively persistent. Although they are not the extremely long-distance coursers that Young (1944) claimed, they do pursue their prey with greater persistence than do most predators. To the extent that there is such a thing as a typical pursuit by wolves, it consists of a slow stalk, a quick rush at top speed, followed by a chase that covers less than two kilometers and lasts no more than a few minutes (Mech 1970).

In about 75 percent of the close pursuits observed by Mech (1970) on Isle Royale, the wolves gave up within a kilometer and usually quit within ten or fifteen seconds if the moose could maintain a hundred-meter lead. However, such observations seem to document the wolves' ability to judge when a chase is useless more than they attest to any lack of persistence, for under the right conditions, wolves do persist during the pursuit. Mech (1966a) reported a few cases in which wolves ran at or near top speed for up to twenty minutes, and we saw a single wolf chase a deer (*Odocoileus virginianus*) for over fifteen minutes running at top speed much of that time. On open tundra, where wolf packs follow caribou (*Rangifer tarandus*) herds, there are records of ten-kilometer-long chases (Crisler 1956).

During the attack and kill, persistence is also evident. Generally wolves kill quickly after once catching and wounding their prey, but there are some notable exceptions. In several kills observed by Mech (1966a), wolves held onto the nose, throat, or rump of a moose for over a minute, and once for ten minutes, while the moose struggled violently. Persistence at this time is obviously adaptive when other pack members can attack the victim elsewhere or when a predator can tire or incapacitate its prey in this manner. Smaller packs of wolves may even rely on their persistence to help them finally kill a wounded moose, allowing it to weaken from earlier wounds before continuing the attack. In such a case, the wolves rest near the wounded animal and keep it standing until it weakens, which may take more than a day (Mech 1966a).

The African hunting dog (*Lycaon pictus*), which is the ecological homologue of the wolf (Mech 1975), seems to be much less persistent during its hunts, at least on the flat, open Serengeti plains and in Ngorongoro Crater, where its favorite food, gazelles (*Gazella* spp.), occur in relatively high densities. Packs of hunting dogs are active for only about two hours a day, and Kuhme (1965a) and Estes and Goddard (1967) agreed that the average search lasts only about twenty minutes. In Ngorongoro Crater the dogs usually begin pursuit with an unconcealed stalk, giving chase only when they get within 300 meters of the Thomson's or Grant's gazelles which are their principal prey. Outside the crater, on the Serengeti plains, the dogs hunt the same animals but begin with a rush as soon as the quarry is sighted. The gazelles bolt when the dogs are 600 to 800 meters away, but the dogs are almost always able to overtake them. The typical chase lasts three to five minutes and covers two to three kilometers. In observations of forty-eight hunts on the Serengeti plain, Schaller (1972) found the average time elapsed from the beginning of travel to the kill to be about one-half hour. Once hunting dogs contact their prey, a kill ensues immediately. Although these observations do not indicate that hunting dogs are persistent, we must emphasize that circumstances in the study areas did not require them to be so; maybe with lower densities of prey, the hunting dog would be just as persistent as the wolf.

Perhaps the abundance of prey also explains the lion's leisurely hunting schedule. Prides of lionesses spend about two hours a day actively searching for food, remaining inactive for twenty to twenty-one hours a day (Schaller 1972). Prides are seldom active for more than an hour at a time. Lionesses do spend some of their resting time alert for passing prey, and sometimes lie in ambush for up to eight hours, which demonstrates their ability to persist when necessary. However, Schaller's observations indicate that generally they do not need to persist in their searches as long as wolves do, but rather seem to fit the hunting dog pattern.

To apprehend their prey, lionesses depend on a stealthy stalk followed by a short rush which brings them into contact with the victim. They have not been observed chasing prey more than 200 meters (Schaller 1972). Although they usually give up if their rush fails, they frequently stalk their quarry for more than sixty meters.

The size and strength of lions usually render even their largest victims immobile almost as soon as attacked. However, when required, a lioness will persist in the struggle for as long as thirteen minutes (Schaller 1972).

Baboons (*Papio* spp.), for whom hunting is an occasional, rather than daily, occupation, have not been observed actively searching for prey other than insects, and they pursue vertebrates only "in passing" (DeVore and Washburn 1963). They often pass up opportunities to eat animal food. For example, they frequently rest among flocks of guinea fowl, neither species paying much attention to the other.

Baboons seem almost as casual in their pursuit of prey as they are in search of it. The most persistent pursuit on record was observed by DeVore and Washburn (1963), who saw a baboon chase a hare for sixty meters, after which the hare "froze" and was immediately devoured. Unsuccessful chases lasted only a few meters at most.

Chimpanzees also regularly eat animals, but they do not search for or pursue them. Although Teleki (1973) says that baboons and chimps "actively seek out" their prey, his observations, as well as those of van Lawick-Goodall (1971), indicate that they do not. The most common prey of chimpanzees is young baboons, and according to Teleki, most "hunts" begin with the chimpanzees relaxed and dozing or grooming one another near young baboons or colobus monkeys *(Colobus* spp.) until they are aroused by cries of alarm or aggression by the nearby animals. They then begin their pursuit with a stalk, a chase, or an "immediate seizure" of the baboon or monkey.

In twenty-two of the thirty successful predatory episodes witnessed by Teleki, the pursuit phase consisted of a sudden lunge followed by "instantaneous capture." Teleki saw eleven chases that involved "a dash of 100 yards or more." Six of these were successful. He also observed four "stalks," which are slow and cautious and which "can last more than an hour." None of these was successful. In both of the two successful hunts observed by van Lawick-Goodall (1971), there was a cautious stalk lasting less than a minute, followed by seizure after a short rush on the order of meters in length.

In neither the baboon nor the chimp does persistence in the hunt seem to be well developed except in the unsuccessful stalks by chimps. However, it is also true that neither of these species is dependent on hunting; rather, they are only opportunistic meat eaters.

We may never know the extent to which it was necessary for early hominids to persist in their search for game. Some contemporary hunter-gatherers, for example the Australian aborigines described by Gould (1968), persist in search to a greater extent than any of the animals considered here (Laughlin 1968), but they are confined to marginal areas where prey is less easily detected than it was in the savanna environment of our earliest ancestors. Moreover, cross-cultural variation in human hunting habits is high. However, the importance of foraging in the life of !Kung tribesmen (Lee 1965) and Australian aborigines, together with the comparative evidence above, suggests that early hominids probably would not have needed to persist in search for much more than a few hours at a time. This assumes that their environment was not radically different from what it is generally believed to have been — a forest-savanna mosaic not very different from that found in South and East Africa today (Clark 1970).

The above analysis suggests that although a certain degree of persistence is necessary for hunting, particularly in the detection stage, several species show a relatively high degree of success without an unusual development of this trait.

COOPERATION

Cooperation during all stages of the hunt seems to characterize the social carnivores and is also apparent in some hunting primates.

All of the species we are considering cooperate more often, more obviously, and in more ways during pursuit than in search. There are, however, important differences among them in both the degree and the forms of cooperation.

Our observations of packs of wolves hunting in northern Minnesota, as well as those previously summarized by Mech (1966a, 1970), indicate a high degree of cooperation during the search for prey. Pack members retain a loose association, and when prey is seen or scented, it is often impossible to tell whether one wolf has detected it and the others are reacting to the detector, or whether they have all located the prey simultaneously.

The search phase commonly terminates with a group ceremony, in which animals excitedly mill, touch noses, wag their tails, and then begin pursuit (Mech 1966a). It is possible that in the group ceremony the degree of excitement of each animal is transmitted or raised, ensuring that all members are aware of the detection or aroused for the impending pursuit.

Wolf packs following caribou herds face the problem of detecting suitable prey out of a milling mass of animals, most of which are capable of outrunning their pursuers. They test the herd by rushing, and if an animal falls behind the rest of the herd, they concentrate their efforts on it (Murie 1944; Crisler 1956).

Although single wolves can kill deer and caribou alone, cooperation is often important during pursuits by groups of wolves, for both these ungulates can usually outrun wolves (Mech 1970). With moose, also, packs no doubt are more successful than singles, for a healthy adult moose is a formidable opponent, and even packs have a low success rate (Mech 1966a).

There are several forms of cooperation evident in pursuits of all three of these ungulates. Wolves allegedly use strategy when they "cut corners" during a chase, but this is an example of cooperation that does not require strategy. It results from each wolf orienting toward the prey as the latter veers to one side, and it requires no anticipation.

Nevertheless, this cooperative behavior is still adaptive because it does decrease the distance between the wolves and their quarry. An extreme form of this behavior has been described in chases of deer (Rutter and Pimlott 1968) and caribou (Kelsall 1968), in which the prey fleeing the lead wolves made a circle and encountered others resting or lagging behind. On several occasions we have watched wolves that were chasing deer alternately slow down, then speed up, seemingly in response to one of the number who finds the energy for an extra spurt of running. This spurring to further effort results in greater persistence, and possibly in more successful pursuits than would be made by a single wolf of average motivation.

A pack of wolves can separate young animals from defending adults, whereas it would be most difficult for a single predator to do this. On Isle Royale, Mech (1966a) observed several cases in which some wolves chased a cow or held her at bay while others killed the calf that she was attempting to defend.

Cooperation is seen most strikingly during the kill itself. This is especially apparent with wolves killing moose (Mech 1966a). After several animals grab the running moose by the rump, slowing it down and sometimes tripping it, one wolf bites the moose in the nose and holds on. This occupies the moose and controls it while the remaining pack members slash at the hindquarters until their quarry falls. Because the nose hold itself is not mortal, its function would seem to be valuable only in cooperation with the more deadly holds of the other pack members.

Cooperation in use of prey, whether in wolves or the other species we are comparing, refers to behavior by one animal that increases the probability that an associate will be able to consume at least part of the prey. Thus, submission, respect for possession, and et-epimelesis are examples of cooperation in use.

While it is true that subordinate wolves defer to dominants in feeding, our observations of captive animals (Mech 1970; Peters 1974) indicate that even when wolves have been deprived of all food for three or more days, an animal that obtains possession of a large piece of fresh red meat will not be successfully challenged, even by those dominant over him. There seems to be a zone of "ownership" just in front of a wolf's face within which food is safe. But if the owner turns away, even while remaining close to the food, it will be snatched instantly. This zone of ownership is the area within which possession can most easily be defended, and respect for this zone reduces conflict and increases the probability that a wolf who has obtained food will be able to consume it in peace.

For several weeks after the birth of pups, other pack members provide the mother with much of her food, and for at least five more months they feed the pups by regurgitation. They also cache food near the den and move the pups to kills if they are not too far away (summarized by Mech 1970). All of these activities may continue, with reduced frequency, throughout the rest of the year.

Hunting dogs cooperate in hunting much as wolves do. During the search, they may approach a herd of gazelles, for example, and spread out along a front. Each dog rushes a single gazelle or a particular group; those animals slowest in escaping are then pursued by several dogs (Schaller 1972; Kuhme 1965a). The dogs cooperate in the detection of single animals as well. Schaller (1972) reported that they set out to hunt in single file but soon spread out across the line of travel, "a useful formation for finding a crouched gazelle."

During the pursuit they cut corners, fanning out during both the stalk (Estes and Goddard 1967) and the chase (Kuhme 1965a). Kuhme noted that a kill was more likely when several dogs, rather than one, chased an antelope. When killing, they attack from several directions at once, allowing some animals to wound the prey while avoiding its hooves. The very high rate of success in pursuit (70 percent according to Schaller; 100 percent according to Kuhme) is attributable to this cooperation as well as to their great speed.

An equal or even greater degree of cooperation seems to characterize the use of prey by hunting dogs. Kuhme (1965a) described an elaborate ritual of meat-sharing at a den: the dogs "returned to the burrow and disgorged the meat in front of the begging pups and the guards who had stayed behind. The guards could also disgorge in their turn, and . . . a piece of meat could wander through several stomachs before finally being digested."

According to Kuhme, the roles of guard and hunter pass freely from dog to dog, and neither he, Estes and Goddard (1967), nor Schaller (1972) saw either agonistic competition for food or evidence of a dominance hierarchy. Rather, the dogs "tried to outdo each other in submissiveness" (Kuhme 1965b). All four observers noted that pups are allowed to take precedence at a kill.

Lionesses show several of the same forms of cooperation in hunting, and a few of their own. Kuhme (1965b) stated that lionesses always travel at least somewhat spread out across the line of travel, which, especially in the dense cover where they do most of their hunting, would increase the probability of detecting prey. According to Schaller (1972), they generally travel single file on roads, but elsewhere they travel loosely scattered or in an irregular line. Lionesses seem to cooperate in search to the extent that the presence of other lionesses may increase the probability of flushing prey, but neither Schaller nor Kuhme mentioned special cooperative search behaviors as highly developed as those of the canids.

Prey that circles or doubles back on a pride of lionesses is often caught by those who trail behind the rest. Prides frequently fan out and approach prey in a broad front, sometimes 200 meters across their line of travel (Schaller 1972). They sometimes converge on prey in a way that suggests (but does not require) strategy, for each lioness heads more or less toward the prey. Cooperative driving, in which several lionesses trot toward their prey with no attempt at concealment, often results in the prey bolting into dense brush where a capture may result (Schaller 1972). The significance of these forms of cooperation is shown by Schaller's figures on predation efficiency, which reveal that pursuits by more than one lioness are successful more than twice as often as pursuits by singles. There are some prey, like buffalo (*Syncerus caffer*) and giraffe (*Giraffa camelopardis*), that are almost never pursued by single lionesses.

Lions do not seem to depend on cooperation as much as wolves or hunting dogs, however. About half of the hunts Schaller observed were by single lionesses, and in three-quarters of these, other lionesses were present without participating. Although cooperative hunting allows a pride to capture prey more easily, almost all the killing itself is performed by a single member of the pride (Guggisberg 1960), which, unlike a canid, rarely needs help in this process.

Despite the cooperation lions show during pursuit, they cooperate little in their use of prey. They possess neither a hierachical system like that in wolves, which reduces conflict, nor rituals of submission, like those in wolves and hunting dogs, which inhibit aggression. Outcomes of conflicts are determined by size and strength. Male lions monopolize kills until gorged, and females feed next, often striking cubs and taking food from them.

Lionesses sometimes cooperate by attacking a male and putting him to flight (Schaller 1972). Nevertheless, a kill made by a single lioness generally feeds several animals. Regurgitation in the feeding of young has not been observed, but lionesses do sometimes lead cubs to a kill.

Hunting by baboons, as witnessed by DeVore and Washburn (1963), is an individual activity. For most of the game they pursue (hares, infant gazelles, fledglings), cooperation is unnecessary. Consequently, during all stages of the hunt, including the use of prey, cooperation is slight or nonexistent in this animal.

Chimpanzees also generally hunt alone, but they do cooperate at times. In twenty-two of the thirty hunts by chimpanzees that Teleki (1973) observed, one chimp simply lunged at a young baboon or vervet monkey (*Cercopithecus aethiops*) who was nearby. However, Teleki did state that two or more chimpanzees may "coordinate their action," and once he saw a hunt by five in which "the movements of the chimpanzees were plainly cooperative."

Three forms of cooperation are evident from Teleki's description: (1) when prey climbs a tree to escape, several chimps may surround the tree, blocking possible escape, (2) the chimpanzees, ordinarily very vocal, remain silent during a stalk, and (3) priority on the basis of dominance is suspended during pursuit, the leading position shifting from one chimp to another regardless of rank. Van Lawick-Goodall (1971) described four pursuits involving two chimps and two other pursuits involving at least four. She saw chimpanzees surround the tree to which the prey had fled and, in at least one pursuit, noted that the leading position was held by an animal of low rank. These observations indicate that what Teleki witnessed has been common at Gombe for some time.

In using their prey, chimpanzees may also engage in complicated interactions centered about the division of prey. These have been described in detail by Teleki (1973). Immediately after capture, the kill is "up for grabs" and any chimp who gets there in time can try to take meat without interference. Soon thereafter, chimpanzees become proprietors of whatever part of the kill they have taken, and newcomers do not attempt to grab at any part already held. Instead they form "sharing clusters," in which groups of chimps sit close together, sometimes picking up fallen particles of meat, sometimes taking meat from the possessor's hand or mouth, and sometimes begging with gestures, over one-quarter of which are rewarded. High social rank is no guarantee of success in begging, and Teleki observed no fighting over meat.

Cooperation among modern primates in active search for prey thus seems to be confined to humans. Human searching is almost always cooperative not only in technique but also in its use of language and religious ceremony. It involves degrees of cooperation orders of magnitude greater than those found among other predators (Lee 1965; Laughlin 1968).

We have no information about cooperative search among early hominids, but it can be assumed that they must have developed systems of communicating the location of big game that could not be successfully pursued by an individual. Presumably, early hominids could have imitated or independently developed all the forms of cooperation observed in the other hunting species. If the bones found with australopithecine remains are from their prey, some form of cooperation would have been likely, for many of the bones come from animals much larger (buffalo), faster (gazelle), and more formidable (saber-toothed tiger [*Smilodon* spp.] than the australopithecines (Dart 1959). Some of these animals, even weakened by age or disease, would be more than a match for a single australopithecine. If these remains are the result of scavenging rather than hunting, cooperation would have been equally essential, for then the early hominids would have been competing not only with the predator that killed the animal but with other dangerous scavengers, like hyenas (*Crocuta crocuta, Hyaena hyaena*) and lions, as well.

We may never know the extent to which early hominids cooperated in their use of prey. If their bands were small, the corpse of one of their larger prey could well feed them all. Australopithecines probably weighed well under forty kilograms (Campbell 1966), and if their capacity for gorging was in proportion to their weight, a large gazelle, which could provide one to two kilograms of meat apiece, might feed as many as ten.

The above comparison of the use of cooperation among various hunters indicates that this trait probably has been well developed for a long period, as it is found in most of the diverse species discussed and is of significant value to each species in securing prey.

STRATEGY

In discussing strategy in any stage of the hunt, it is difficult to avoid the problem of intention. To guard against unwarranted anthropomorphizing, we tried to adhere to "Morgan's canon" and use the word "strategy" only when any explanation not involving anticipation would be either incongruent with known behavior patterns or less parsimonious. (We apply words like "anticipation" and "foresight" in a strictly behavioristic sense to any behavior adapted to future conditions, without assumptions about the subjective experience of the animal exhibiting the behavior.)

When this criterion is applied to the behavior of wolves, the only suspected example of strategy during the search state of the hunt is the use of vantage points to locate prey visually. On four occasions, we have seen tracks in northern Minnesota where a wolf detoured from its travel route to an open ledge that afforded a clear view of a large area, stood there briefly, and then returned to its original course. In each case, fresh deer signs were plentiful, and the wolf tracks had been following fresh deer trails both before and after the presumed visual reconnaissance.

Our interpretation of these tracks is supported by observations by Murie (1944) and Cowan (1947), who have observed wolves searching for caribou, Dall sheep (*Ovis dalli*), and elk *(Cervus elaphus)* by traveling along the tops of ridges, from which they are more likely to see prey.

Twice we have found tracks of a wolf following a deer in which the wolf made several sweeps perpendicular to the line of travel upon crossing the top of a hill. Each of these sweeps was at least twenty meters long and in both cases pursuit followed by a kill resulted.

During the pursuit stage of the hunt, strategy is more apparent. The simplest form seen in wolves is the termination of a chase that probably will be unsuccessful. When wolves give up after a short chase with the prey still in sight, foresight is a more likely reason than fatigue. Quitting is adaptive when the energy expended in chase or attack may approach that realized from consumption of the prey, or when the probability of a kill is very low. Mech (1970) observed that wolves can run at or near top speed for up to twenty minutes, covering as much as five to ten kilometers (see above), but usually they gave up within one or two minutes, having covered less than a kilometer. This was the case in thirty-four of forty-one instances of close pursuit of moose observed by Mech on Isle Royale.

Mech concluded that wolves can tell when the moose they are chasing is likely to be vulnerable and that the wolves would have gone on to attack if they had judged that they "could overcome their prey with a minimum of risk." The fact that none of the thirty-six moose that stood their ground when rushed were attacked certainly supports the notion that wolves evaluate risks. In Crisler's (1956) observations of wolves hunting caribou, she was impressed with "how quickly the wolves had judged when a chase was useless." Observations by Murie (1944) suggest that wolves quickly realize when pursuit of Dall sheep, which are quick, agile climbers, will be useless. Our observations of wolves chasing deer in northern Minnesota indicate that the same strategic judgment is used there, but we have observed too few complete chases to quantify the results.

A second type of possible strategy that wolves use conforms more closely to the usual use of the word. Kelsall's (1968: 252) description affords the clearest example:

At Winter Lake, September 15, 1952, a pack of five wolves watched a small band of caribou move into a small clump of stunted spruce. Once the caribou were out of sight an adult wolf, presumably the "killer" in the pack, moved just uphill from the spruce and secreted itself directly in the path in which the caribou were traveling. The other four circled the spruce, spread out along its downhill side, and commenced a stealthy "drive" through it. The object was clearly to move the caribou toward the wolf waiting uphill. The hunt was foiled through one wolf, a pup of the year judging from its size, nearly stepping on a bull caribou, prematurely dashing after it, and putting all the prey to flight

Haber (1968) described a similar form of strategy in wolves hunting caribou.

Estes and Goddard (1967) and Schaller (1972) observed several cases in which it was clear that hunting dogs employed a simple form of strategy during the pursuit. They sometimes began running before they topped a hill, and at least once did so when no prey was on the other side, which eliminates, or at least reduces, the possibility that they were following a scent.

Lions display at least as great a variety of strategies during the pursuit as do wolves. Schaller (1972) observed them ambushing prey in ways that strongly suggest anticipation. Lionesses sometimes wait in thickets by waterholes while game moves nearby. They rush only when the prey approach to within five or ten meters, and sometimes wait until several animals have passed so that they can burst on them from behind. Presumably a rear attack is advantageous when a lioness rushes from concealment because it gives her a head start before she is detected. An even simpler form of strategy occurs during the chase. Lionesses generally aim their charge well ahead of running prey, orienting to its future, rather than present, position. Stalking, followed by rushing, is the most common tactic used by lionesses and occurred in 88 percent of the pursuits observed by Schaller.

Strategy is evident in three forms during this type of hunting: (1) During the stalk, according to Schaller, a lioness "is fully aware of the advantage that cover confers" — and often relies on occultation to get within rushing distance. (2) A stalking lioness usually watches her prey intently and freezes immediately at any sign of alertness. (Ear position is one excellent cue in ungulates.) This tactic seems adapted to preventing premature flight of prey, because lionesses do not use it when stalking groups of animals in which some are nearly always attentive. Neither occultation nor attention to alertness are employed sterotypically, and stalks often fail when lionesses do not use these techniques. (3) By far the most complex and clearest form of strategy is slow, coordinated encirclement, in which some lionesses, usually at least two, detour around a herd, while the others wait until they have blocked avenues of escape. Then an advance by one lioness sometimes drives the herd toward the others. Schaller noted that the lionesses integrated their actions "by observing each other's posture and movements." His diagrams illustrating this type of hunt leave little doubt that the lionesses' actions are well adapted to block the most probable routes of escape and that they involve a high degree of coordination among several lionesses.

Lions occasionally resort to simple strategies in their use of prey. They often drag a kill into a thicket where they can consume it without competition from scavengers, or possibly other lions. This latter possibility is suggested by several cases in which Schaller saw a lioness make a kill, then sit down and look around casually, as though nothing had happened, until other lions could no longer observe her; then she began to eat.

In baboons, DeVore and Washburn (1963) observed no strategy, or even anything like a stalk during a hunt, and in chimpanzees hunting generally is also opportunistic, requiring no strategy. However, Teleki did observe a few chases and stalks by chimps that "clearly involve a strategy and maneuvers aimed at isolating or cornering the selected prey." Van Lawick-Goodall's (1971) descriptions supported this claim. On one occasion she watched a chimpanzee creep toward a juvenile baboon in a fig tree. Simultaneously, "the chimpanzees who had been resting and grooming peacefully on the ground had got up and stationed themselves close to trees that would act as escape routes for the intended victim." With the level of foresight demonstrated by chimpanzees in the laboratory, the use of simple strategy is not surprising. Given the largely vegetarian diet of chimpanzees and the frequent social interactions among chimpanzees and their prey, however, it is unlikely that degrees of strategy and cooperation beyond those demonstrated here are often necessary to secure food.

Chimpanzees show only one form of strategy in their use of prey, but it is of interest because it involves the use of a tool. Teleki observed chimps sopping up liquids from the cranial cavities of prey using a wad of leaves, which is then chewed. Goodall (1962) also observed them sponging water from depressions in trees in the same manner.

It has been suggested that in early hominid evolution the necessity for cooperative strategy in pursuit of big game played an important role (Read 1920; Dart 1953; Campbell 1966). It certainly is true that today human beings in a hunting economy do employ complex strategies. This includes quartering, or the systematic scanning of an area strip by strip; the use of vantage points; lying in ambush in places where game is likely to appear; cooperative driving of game by noise or fire; the use of dogs; and moving spread out across the line of travel. Furthermore, the behavior of the species we are comparing suggests that it would not have been unusual for early hominids to have been capable of using most of these techniques, although in the absence of archaeological evidence this statement must be purely conjectural.

Dart (1957) has suggested that *Australopithecus* used bones and jaws from one prey animal to kill and dismember others; his statistical analysis of bones found in association with australopithecines is highly suggestive. While it is true that the forms of many of the "tools" described by Dart are mimicked in detail by bones gnawed by wolves and dogs, none of the carnivores or primates we have considered amass bones in the proportions described by Dart; however, it appears that hyenas do so (Sutcliffe 1970). Existence of other probable agencies of collection does not eliminate the use of bone tools by australopithecines but does make it more conjectural.

In summarizing our comparison of the use of strategy by diverse predators, it is apparent to us that strategy, like cooperation, has long been an important factor in successful predation by a diversity of social species, particularly those preying on large animals.

COGNITIVE MAPPING

A well-organized memory for routes, locations, and spatial relationships would be useful for any animal that must search for scarce prey within a range that is large relative to its scanning capacity but restricted enough to permit repeated visits to the same places. Such a cognitive map would enable him to travel to and search intensively some areas, while avoiding others where prey is scarce, invulnerable, or wary. Cognitive maps would be particularly useful for hunters whose prey tend to remain in certain areas because of territoriality, clumped distribution of resources, or other reasons.

Peters (1973) discussed evidence suggesting that wolves, like some other mammals, possess cognitive maps. We have several reasons for believing that cognitive maps are important in wolves' search for prey: (1) Wolves often take shortcuts through dense cover to eliminate a bend in a road or other travel route, or to get to another route, which they then follow. In tracking wolves over approximately 180 kilometers on fifty-eight separate occasions, Peters (1974) found six cases where wolves displayed this apparently "insightful" behavior under conditions which precluded any explanation other than that the wolves knew where they were going. (2) Wolves are known to return to denning or rendezvous sites from many different directions, even after prolonged absences during which they traveled considerable distances and pursued various prey, which would make it unlikely that they merely retraced their own trails. (3) Sometimes several members of a pack will split off and then rejoin the others kilometers and hours away. It is likely that the separated members know in a general way where the others are headed and depend on this knowledge to get them at least within howling distance. (4) Wolves can hold a straight course, detouring around blowdowns, boulders, and other obstructions, and returning to their original direction. In northern Minnesota, Peters (1974) recorded three cases in which wolves traveled over two kilometers and three more cases in which they traveled over one kilometer while their direction of travel remained within 15° of their original bearing, all in dense brush that prevented orientation by distant landmarks.

Knowledge of geography and topography can be useful to each of the subject predators in their use of prey as well as during their search for and pursuit of it.

Data from radio-tagged wolves (Mech, unpublished material) indicate that they often travel five miles or more to return to a kill made several days previously. Wolves are known to have carried food over nineteen kilometers to a den (Dixon 1934) and to have hunted as far away as thirty-two kilometers from the den (Murie 1944; Kelsall 1957). Returning to a point this far away after a chase involving many turns and switchbacks would be difficult, even with a compass, unless the hunter had at least a general notion of the lay of the land. Backtracking by sight or smell is a possible alternative to the use of cognitive maps, but would place the animal at the mercy of rain, snow, and wind which could obliterate its trail. It seems that wolves must be highly dependent upon the ability to remember routes and locations in bringing food to pups, as well as in pursuit of prey.

Hunting dogs, too, must be able to find their way back to the den, but at least on the open veldt they could depend on long-distance vision more than could animals inhabiting the forest. We would expect hunting dogs to have well-developed cognitive maps, but theirs need not be as detailed as those of wolves.

Serengeti lions spend most of their search time in cover, where they are most likely to approach game without being observed (Schaller 1972) The area within which they hunt is relatively large (200 to 400 square kilometers), so cognitive maps would be useful to them. Prides do sometimes travel through bush in straight lines for more than a kilometer at a time as though they did possess such maps. Furthermore, Schaller observed what appears to be a very systematic and regular quartering of a rectangular area about one kilometer long and half a kilometer wide, involving eight successive one-kilometer-long, parallel sweeps which effectively covered the entire rectangle.

The average area of range for each of ten lion prides studied by Schaller was about 130 square kilometers, which is considerably smaller than the typical wolf territory studied by Mech (1972), which covered about twice as much area. Thus lionesses bringing their cubs to food (or *vice versa*) would not have to remember so large a piece of terrain as wolves, but like wolves, they would probably need some mechanism to help them avoid getting lost.

Baboons and chimpanzees cover a much more restricted range than do any of the other predators. They generally do not travel to hunt live prey, but may use cognitive maps in their search for other food, particularly in the case of the regular returns by baboons to the group of trees forming the nucleus of their range (Altmann and Altmann 1970).

Early hominids, according to Kuhme (1965a), probably hunted in a manner similar to hunting dogs, the majority roving in groups while a few remained with the young to protect them. The hunters would then have had to find their way back home with the meat they had obtained. DeVore and Washburn (1963) and Washburn (1968) believed that these hominids must have hunted over large areas. Their opinion is supported by the experiment of Schaller and Lowther (1969), whose success in hunting and scavenging depended on being able to cover large areas, as do the social carnivores we have described. These areas probably consisted largely of a forest-savanna mosaic, which would have reduced scanning capacity considerably. If this was the case, cognitive maps would have been as important to hominids as they are to wolves, hunting dogs, and lions.

It should be apparent from the above that memory for spatial relationships, that is, the possession of cognitive maps, would be important for any predator of large animals that covers extensive areas, and indeed such predators, including early hominids, probably had them.

DISCUSSION AND CONCLUSIONS

In our foregoing comparisons of the importance of persistence, cooperation, strategy, and cognitive mapping in diverse species of mammalian meat eaters, we have tried to put each of these traits into a perspective from which we could judge its possible contribution to the evolution of intelligence in *Homo sapiens*.

We have seen that persistence, while useful in predation, does not seem to be of overriding value. Given the assumption of a relatively high density of prey animals on the early Pliocene savanna, predators should have been able to locate prey quickly.

Krantz (1968) suggested that persistence in pursuit by early hominids selected for increased attention span in australopithecines, leading to an expansion of the brain which resulted in the emergence of genus *Homo*. It is true, as Krantz pointed out, that many hunting cultures have depended on chases lasting more than a day to exhaust their prey. However, the high success rate of relatively short chases by chimpanzees reported by Teleki (1973), the favorable results of experimental hunting and gathering by Schaller and Lowther (1969), and the larger number of hunting and gathering cultures who do not chase prey for days all indicate that it probably was not always necessary or efficient for early hominids to persist in pursuit to the extent described by Krantz.

Cooperation, strategy, and cognitive mapping, however, seem to us to have several significant properties of prime candidates for behavioral precursors or contributors to the evolution of at least some aspects of intelligence. All are found to some extent in all species we are comparing, all are valuable in most phases of hunting, and all are developed in some species in degrees that border on genuinely "insightful" activity.

It does not seem unreasonable to postulate that early hominids and their precursors showed these traits. Furthermore, there seems to us to be good reason to believe that selection for these traits and their extended development into intelligence would have been a necessity in such creatures. The meat-eating species already competing for the large-animal resource on the Pliocene savanna were the forerunners of the modern carnivores; they probably had evolved long before into species highly adapted to such an economy. The protohominid or early hominid was a latecomer, poorly adapted to securing large live prey. He had neither the fleetness, the dentition, nor the claws for a predatory life. How was he to compete with those that did?

By evolving intellectually. Through developing increasingly progressive degrees of cooperation and strategy, the early hominids would find their niche, for the role of the intellectual hunter was the only exploitive role in the large-animal economy that had not yet been filled. The early hominid, away from his previous economy, had either to adapt or face extinction. No doubt many species took the latter course, but some, like the ancestor of the australopithecines, adapted.

It would be a small step from developing a predisposition for a high degree of strategy to evolving the ability to use tools, and later the ability to make tools. What is tool-using but the ability to see how an object can be employed in a strategic manner? Toolmaking would require just a second similar insightful step, plus the physical ability in the form of digits with high manipulability.

No doubt the need for evolving the ability to employ a high degree of strategy also fostered the ability to use and make tools, and as each trait was utilized successfully in competing in the new economy, it would have been strongly selected for. Furthermore, if tool-using became weapon-using, and if cannibalism resulted, a double selection pressure could have taken place, with the weapon users directly causing the demise of those who had not yet learned to use weapons, as Mech (1966b) has pointed out.

The contribution of the cognitive map in the process of intellectualization may be high, but it is difficult to assess. Nonhunting species (e.g. rats [*Rattus norvegicus*]) also possess cognitive maps, but these mental constructs may not be so important to browsers and grazers whose resources are available at the turn of the head. However, the increased need of early hominids to compete for a mobile resource with carnivorous species already highly adapted in other ways for such competition could have fostered a much increased ability in these early hominids to remember more aspects of the environment, including spatial relationships.

In addition, cognitive mapping may be closely allied to strategy use. Kaplan (1973) has described the formal similarity between mental representations of relationships among locations in space (cognitive maps) and representations among events in time (plans) with the phrase "what leads to what." The cortical basis of cognitive maps which allows an animal to use alternate routes might well also be what allows him to use alternate strategies of pursuit, for the two tasks are similar in logical structure. If this is so, cognitive mapping, cooperation, and strategy could all be different adaptive manifestations of a common cortical mechanism that hominids evolved to a degree higher than that of their carnivorous competitors to compensate for their relative lack of physical features adapted to carnivorousness.

One final point is also apparent. Even with a high degree of cooperation, strategy, cognitive mapping, and the use of primitive weapons, the early hominids would still have been at a relative disadvantage if their manner of harvesting large animals was through direct hunting. Most prey species possess formidable physical and behavioral means of defense. The mere tricking through strategy only brings the predator closer to the prey. Killing must then take place, and primitive weapons would not be very effective, at least not on larger species.

However, with strategy developed to a high degree, an alternative method would have existed. Instead of hunting large animals, hominids could have trapped them. Trapping could have consisted of merely running a herd over a cliff or into a mudhole, or it could have employed special devices such as primitive snares, nets, deadfalls, or pits. None of these devices would have lasted long enough to be discovered archaeologically, but they could have been used, and they would have greatly aided an intellectual predator in killing his prey. Furthermore, success with this method would have been highly adaptive and would have strongly selected for increased intellectualization, for trapping is far more of an intellectual process than is hunting.

REFERENCES

ALTMANN, S. A., I. ALTMANN
  1970   Baboon ecology. *Bibliotheca Primatologica* 12.
ATZ, J. W.
  1970   "The application of the idea of homology to behavior," in *The development and evolution of behavior*. Edited by L. R. Aronson, E. Tobach, D. S. Lehrman, and J. S. Rosenblatt, 53–74. San Francisco: Freeman.
CAMPBELL, B. G.
  1966   *Human evolution*. Chicago: Aldine.
CLARK, J. D.
  1970   *The prehistory of Africa*. New York: Praeger.
COWAN, I. M.
  1947   The timber wolf in the Rocky Mountain National Parks of Canada. *Canadian Journal of Research* 25:139–174.
CRISLER, L.
  1956   Observations of wolves hunting caribou. *Journal of Mammalogy* 37:337–346.
DART, R. A.
  1953   The predatory transition from ape to man. *International Anthropological and Linguistic Review* 1:201–219.
  1957   *The Osteodontokeratic culture of* Australopithecus prometheus. Transvaal Museum Memoir 10. Pretoria.
  1959   *Adventures with the missing link*. New York: Harper and Brothers.
DE VORE, I., S. L. WASHBURN
  1963   "Baboon ecology and human evolution," in *African ecology and human evolution*. Edited by F. C. Howell and F. Bourlière, 335–367. Viking Fund Publications in Anthropology 36. Chicago.
DIXON, J. S.
  1934   The timber wolf in California. *California Fish and Game* 2:125–129.

ESTES, R., J. GODDARD
1967   Prey selection and hunting behavior of the African wild dog. *Journal of Wildlife Management* 31:52–70.

GOODALL, J.
1962   "Feeding behavior of wild chimpanzees," in *Primates,* 39–47. Zoological Society of London Symposia 10.

GOULD, R. A.
1968   Living archaeology: the Ngatajara of western Australia. *Southwestern Journal of Anthropology* (Summer): 14–37.

GUGGISBERG, C. A. W.
1960   *Simba.* Bern, Switzerland: Hallwag.

HABER, G.
1968   "The social structure and behavior of an Alaskan wolf population." Unpublished master's thesis, Northern Michigan University, Marquette, Michigan.

KAPLAN, S.
1973   "Cognitive maps in perception and thought," in *Cognitive mapping: images of spatial environments.* Edited by R. M. Downs and D. Stea. Chicago: Aldine.

KELSALL, J. P.
1957   *Continued barren-ground caribou studies.* Canadian Wildlife Service, Wildlife Management Bulletin Series 1 (12).
1968   *The migratory barren-ground caribou of Canada.* Ottawa: Queen's Printer (Canadian Wildlife Service).

KRANTZ, G.
1968   Brain size and hunting ability in earliest man. *Current Anthropology* 9:450–451.

KRUUK, H.
1972   *The spotted hyena.* Chicago: University of Chicago Press.

KUHME, H.
1965a Communal food distribution and division of labor in African hunting dogs. *Nature* 30:443–444.
1965b Freilandstudien zur Soziologie des Hyänenhundes. *Zeitschrift für Tierpsychologie* 22:495–541.

LAUGHLIN, W. S.
1968   "Hunting: an integrating biobehavior system and its evolutionary importance," in *Man the hunter.* Edited by R. B. Lee and I. DeVore, 304–320. Chicago: Aldine.

LEE, R. B.
1965   "Subsistence ecology of !Kung bushmen." Unpublished doctoral dissertation, University of California, Berkeley, California.

LOCKHARD, R. B.
1971   Reflections on the fall of comparative psychology. *American Psychologist* 25:168–179.

MECH, L. D.
1966a *The wolves of Isle Royale.* Washington, D.C.: Government Printing Office.
1966b Some comments concerning Hockett and Ascher's contribution on the human revolution. *Current Anthropology* 7:200–201.

1970   *The wolf.* New York: Doubleday.
1972   Spacing and possible mechanisms of population regulation in wolves. *American Zoologist* 12:9. (Abstract.)
1975   "Hunting behavior in two similar species of social canids," in *Ecology and social behavior of canids.* Edited by M. W. Fox. New York: Van Nostrand.

MURIE, A.
1944   *The wolves of Mount McKinley.* Washington, D.C.: Government Printing Office.

PETERS, R.
1973   "Cognitive maps in wolves and men," in *Environmental design research,* volume two (EDRA 4). Edited by W. F. E. Pressier. Stroudsburg, Pennsylvania: Dowden, Hutchinson, and Ross.
1974   "Hunting and the evolution of intellect." Unpublished doctoral dissertation, University of Michigan, Ann Arbor, Michigan.

READ, C.
1920   *The origins of man.* Cambridge: Cambridge University Press.

RUTTER, R. J., D. H. PIMLOTT
1968   *The world of the wolf.* Philadelphia: J. P. Lippincott.

SCHALLER, G.
1972   *The Serengeti lion.* Chicago: University of Chicago Press.

SCHALLER, G., G. LOWTHER
1969   The relevance of carnivore behavior to the study of early hominids. *Southwestern Journal of Anthropology* 25:307–341.

SUTCLIFFE, A. J.
1970   Spotted hyaena: crusher, gnawer, digester, and collector of bones. *Nature* 227:1110–1113.

TELEKI, G.
1973   The omnivorous chimpanzee. *Scientific American* 228(1):32–47.

VAN LAWICK-GOODALL, J.
1971   *In the shadow of man.* Boston: Houghton Mifflin.

WASHBURN, S. L.
1968   Behavior and the origin of man. *Rockefeller University Review* (January-February): 3–17.

YOUNG, S.
1944   *The wolves of North America,* part one. Washington, D.C.: American Wildlife Institute.

Discussion

[Dr. Roger Peters summarized his paper.]

KORTLANDT: The predatory carnivorous, hunting, and similar cultural behavior which we see in chimpanzees has a rather different character from what we observe in monkeys and many carnivores. The cardinal concepts of this issue are much too simplistic. Let us look at some of the facts. In captive monkeys, baboons, and gibbons complete predatory behavior occurs in all the taxonomic groups and is more frequent than incomplete predatory behavior. *Per contra*, in the great apes, incomplete predatory behavior, i.e. catching without killing and eating, or killing without catching and eating, or eating without catching and killing, or two of the three items, occurs more often than the complete sequence. Regular occurrence of complete predatory behavior is known only in the chimpanzee among the great apes in captivity. In the wild, complete predatory behavior has been observed in most families or genera of monkeys, baboons, and gibbons, and in chimpanzees; but not in gorillas or orangs. In this respect there is a clear difference between the great apes and all other primates.

There is something special about hunting, killing, predatory, carnivorous, meat-eating behavior in the great apes. The slide shown here is the only picture available of actual killing by a chimpanzee in the literature.[1] In this male chimpanzee we see very aggressive facial and gestural expressions. Now everybody who is familiar with chimpanzees will at once recognize that this is the type of behavior that you will

[1] J. van Lawick-Goodall, 1967, *My friends the wild chimpanzees*, p. 64. National Geographic Society.

observe in socially aggressive intercourse when for example they batter trees or destroy any sort of objects. Phenomenologically this is SOCIAL aggression rather than the kind of behavior that you see in the true carnivores. The Carnivora do not show any such intimidation behavior while hunting and killing prey. Secondly note that the onlookers are terrified by the showing off by this male. This clearly demonstrates that it has intimidation effects. A plausible interpretation of this episode is that it is a case of redirected aggression toward group members, redirected against a semi-conspecific (i.e. a baboon) with which they have normal social intercourse. The killing technique here is the same one as is often used in child killing in concentration camps. Third, we might consider this behavior as a form of racism since, to chimpanzees, baboons are a sort of semi-conspecific as shown by social intercourse with them. A fourth factor here is that according to Teleki's data we can compute that approximately 50 percent of the baboon population input of Camp Troop was killed by chimpanzees. My conclusion is that so-called predatory behavior as performed by these apes is actually to a large extent intimidation behavior, that is showing off toward insiders, redirected towards outsiders, and, at the same time, extermination of food competitors. It is interesting that chimps mainly eat baboons, monkeys, bushbuck (which is to some extent a food competitor) and bushpig (which is not a food competitor). They do NOT eat frogs, toads, lizards, chameleons, birds, gallinacious fowl, small mammals, duiker antelopes, and other small to medium-sized vertebrates which are easily accessible to them. I suggest, therefore that such so-called predatory behavior is predominantly a form of pest control or guerilla warfare against food competitors. On the basis of the complete data available in Jane Goodall's and Teleki's papers and from my research team we find that only six categories of behavioral data provide evidence that this complex of behavior should be regarded as predatory and carnivorous, whereas twelve categories of evidence suggest that it is some form of food competitor control. Three categories of evidence show that it is optional behavior. So apparently the phenomenon has several roots, of which food competitor control is the most important one.

BECK: Dr. Kortlandt's hypothesis is very stimulating. Comparing Teleki's work with Harding's work I too felt that there was something more than a nutritive function in chimpanzee predation. Robert Harding hinted at this in his paper (see Harding, this volume). But let me give you some figures which might demonstrate this. The period of prey consumption by chimpanzees averages about four hours and may last up to nine hours. The period of prey consumption by baboons lasts less than one hour on the average even though baboon prey tend to be relatively larger than chimpanzee prey. Second, aggression surrounding prey consumption is surprisingly low in chimpanzees whereas it is markedly high in baboons. Third, the correlation of dominance, if we can use the term, to the amount of meat actually consumed by individuals is quite low in chimpanzees whereas it is quite high in baboons. Fourth, the amount of cooperation and food-sharing during the consumption of prey is quite high among chimpanzees and markedly low or absent in baboons. Fifth, the chimpanzees use a curious behavior which Teleki calls wadging, which is consuming leaves with meat tissue. Little bits of meat, especially brain, are wrapped in leaves. This mass is kept in the mouth for a long period of time and masticated slowly. Teleki suggests that this might be a way of savoring or prolonging the flavor of the tissue that is ingested. No such behavior is seen in baboons; they gobble the stuff right down as fast as they possibly can. But probably most compelling is Teleki's observation that chimpanzees usually hunt or kill vertebrates after a long period of feeding on vegetable material, i.e. they are quite sated. This is not true for baboons. These lines of evidence lead me to believe that killing of vertebrates by chimpanzees has more than a nutritive function. I do not mean to imply that nutrition is not operative. Oxnard and his associates have shown that vitamin B_{12} is essential to the normal functioning of the peripheral nervous system. In primates without B_{12} peripheral neuropathy develops to the point of paralysis. Vitamin B_{12} is not present in any significant amount in vegetable material. However, it is notably present in meat protein, especially viscera like liver. Thus I suspect that all primates must ingest a certain amount of meat protein. Usually it is quite inconspicuous. Larvae may be ingested with fruit or leaves. So we certainly have a common underlying denominator of nutritive need for meat protein in the primates but the evidence that I presented above indicates that there is more than a nutritive function occurring in chimpanzee predation. Whether it is, as Dr. Kortlandt suggested, the elimination of a semi-conspecific or a food competitor, or is simply related to some sort of social bonding, I do not know.

PETERS: We who study carnivores in particular feel that the differences are so great that it is really misleading to call these hunting behaviors. I hope that the differences would emerge from what I said, in particular the anomalous things such as a chimpanzee brushing other baboons aside, i.e. physically coming into contact with baboons, in order to attack a specific baboon. The chimpanzee may chase him for a while and then sit down next to him. This just does not look like predation. It looks more like redirected aggression or something else.

RUMBAUGH: Food preferences as such have not been mentioned in any of the discussions thus far. Food preferences, as for brain tissue, might be very influential in determining the prey both in terms of size and the species.

PETERS: It may be that hominid hunting began in something very much like this redirected aggression that has been observed in chimpanzees or it may have been something much more calculated as we see in the aggressionless hunting by the social carnivores. It should be noted that the facial signals, body postures, and so forth associated with aggression are entirely absent in social carnivores in all stages of the hunt up until use phase, when we see them directed towards conspecifics.

KORTLANDT: With regard to hominids we should distinguish between small-game and large-game hunting. I could imagine that small-game hunting started as food-getting behavior and that large-game hunting started as intimidation behavior and warfare.

VOGEL: I should like to point out another sort of killing among monkeys that has nothing to do with nutritional function but clearly relates to social function alone. In langurs spectacular infant killing is done by the new male leader of a group during high social excitement (Sugiyama, Mohnot). This may be a form of redirected aggression. The new leader wants to have access to the females. A female carrying a small infant wants to protect her infant and does not react as she should to a new leader. In high excitement, the male is threatening to the female but his aggression is directed towards the infant.

PETERS: There remain a few cases that do not quite fit the redirected aggression model. I think of two cases. One is a case cited by Goodall. She saw a slow coordinated stalk. Teleki also reports stalks that last up to one hour in which several chimpanzees systematically place themselves at exit routes and move very silently. In neither of these cases was a kill in fact made. Nevertheless it appears that they were doing something like real hunting without this excitement.

BECK: Another point might argue against the redirection of aggression hypothesis: Teleki observed no wounds inflicted by baboons on chimpanzees during the killing of baboon young. Further, chimps have not been observed to wound any baboons except the infants that they eat.

YAKIMOV: Mr. Peters, what is the influence of meat-eating on intergroup relations, particularly on dominance relations in apes and monkeys?

PETERS: In the coordinated hunts, that is, the stalks in which there seems to be some intentionality rather than excitement, the key or pivot position seems to switch back and forth from chimp to chimp without regard to dominance position. Apparently dominance is quite important in predicting and understanding the clusters that form about the use of prey. However, although many of the spontaneous killings are by dominant animals, in particular males, it seems that there are episodes during these slower, more considered hunts in which more strategic considerations seem to outweigh dominance. Teleki reported two cases in which subordinate animals held the critical position and initiated the final charge.

YAKIMOV: Goodall's observations show that in chimpanzees, there are special changes in the social relations among group members during hunting. When catching prey a nondominant male can be in the role of a dominant male. The otherwise dominant male will ask him for part of his catch just like any other member of the group. This is very important for understanding the change in intragroup relations of our early ancestors. Clearly in these groups selection would be not only along the line of the powerful males but also among the clever and capable males that were the best qualified members of the groups in certain skills, and who thereby earned the right to temporary leadership. These chimpanzee studies elucidate the change in the intragroup behavior of our early ancestors and show the impact of the hunting of animals on intragroup behavior.

Self-Awareness and Capacities for Perceptual Integration Across Sensory Modalities, Learning, Symbolizing, and Intelligence

Towards an Operational Definition of Self-Awareness

GORDON G. GALLUP, JR.

The purpose of this paper is two-fold. First an attempt will be made to review the literature on the psychological properties of mirrors as determined by research on a variety of species, and then to show how such surfaces may provide a means by which an objective assessment of self-awareness can be accomplished.

Since most organisms rarely look at sources of direct light, for perceptual purposes most light can be characterized as reflected light. Mirrors can be distinguished from ordinary reflecting surfaces by the fact that they reflect almost as much light as they receive. Moreover, depending on their surface characteristics, mirrors can provide fairly accurate or wildly distorted visual reproductions of other reflecting surfaces.

While there are a few naturally occurring mirrors, such as the surface of calm water under conditions of appropriate incident light, for most organisms it is reasonable to assume that this is an atypical or at least infrequent type of reflected light. However, with the advent of fabricated mirrors, this has become a common visual experience for man. Written records show that men have been contriving mirror-like surfaces for purposes of self-inspection for well over 3,000 years (Swallow 1937). The ancient Chinese, who were the first to use artificial mirrors, believed that supernatural powers emanated from mirrors and they were used to diagnose and even treat many physical ailments and diseases. Currently one still finds much of the modern literature laced with subtle, recurring, and sometimes superstitious references to the mystical properties of mirrors.

In recent times mirrors have had many applications in the behavioral sciences, ranging from such things as learning to cope with reversed visual cues in mirror drawing tasks, to the use of the one-way or half-silvered mirror as a device for obscuring the observer in clinical and social experimentation, and they continue to be used in a variety of settings. The principal concern of this study will be with what is called mirror-image stimulation (MIS), which refers specifically to situations in which an organism, human or otherwise, is confronted with its own reflection in a mirror.

SOCIAL STIMULUS PROPERTIES

Since much of the earlier work on the psychological properties of mirrors has been reviewed elsewhere (Gallup 1968), only a brief overview will be presented here.

In front of a mirror an observer is in the rather peculiar position of being able to modify and control certain aspects of his visual environment without coming into direct physical contact with it; i.e. manipulating the reflected image of one's self in the mirror. Since the behavior of an animal can, and frequently does, serve as a source of stimulation for the responses of another, this ability to effect changes at a distance is true of many types of social behavior and can be thought of as one of its distinguishing characteristics.

Indeed, for many animals with adequate visual sensitivity MIS does seem to function in the capacity of a social stimulus, despite the fact that the reflection only mimics the behavior of the observer. Many organisms, when confronted with their own reflection in a mirror for the first time, respond as if in the presence of another animal of the same species, and mirrors have been used to simulate a variety of social situations in animal research (e.g. Simpson 1968; Yerkes and Yerkes 1929). For example, aggressive displays are readily obtained using MIS with fish (Lissmann 1932), birds (Ritter and Benson 1934), sea lions (Schusterman, Gentry, and Schmook 1966), and primates (Schmidt 1878).

There is even a report that chaffinches and hedge sparrows will occasionally fight with their reflected images in stationary automobile hubcaps, sometimes to the point of physical exhaustion (Smythe 1962). Other evidence that the image is initially interpreted as another organism comes from the finding that isolated pigeons will not normally lay eggs unless given the opportunity to see other pigeons or, as the previous example might suggest, view their own reflection in a mirror (Matthews 1939). Lott and Brody (1966) observed a similar effect of MIS on ovulation in ring doves.

A well-established finding in social psychology is that organisms behave differently in the presence of other organisms than they do in isolation. An example of such an effect is social facilitation, which refers to a behavioral enhancement due to the mere presence of others. For instance, it is known that chickens will eat appreciably more food in the presence of other chickens than they will in isolation. As evidence for the idea that a mirror may carry the same psychological significance as another organism, this same enhancement effect has been obtained on the feeding behavior of chicks by substituting a mirror for the presence of a companion (Tolman 1965). Exposure to mirrors even causes the adult males of certain strains of squirrel monkeys to show pronounced penile erections (MacLean 1964), which might appear to be a case of extreme narcissism, but is not, because this is a typical aggressive gesture to the presence of another male.

As further support for the proposition that the reflection is initially interpreted as representing another individual, many animals, including human infants (e.g. Dixon 1957), frequently try to look behind mirrors when presented with a reflection of themselves.

In summary, many responses to mirrors could be characterized as other-directed behaviors since the subject acts as if it were viewing another animal. In all instances of other-directed responsiveness the reflection operates as the referent for, or object of, the behavior. In view of their profound social stimulus properties mirrors are ideally suited as a laboratory technique for studying visually induced and visually guided social responses because they eliminate the presence of confounding cues in other modalities. To study the degree to which social activities are solely dependent on visual cues would otherwise require cumbersome and elaborate controls. On the other hand, human behavior in the presence of mirrors is typically self-directed in the sense that the self becomes the referent, and the reflection is used to respond to or inspect personal features. Humans, unlike many animals, seem capable of realizing the dualism implicit in a mirror surface and show the ability to identify and recognize correctly their own reflections.

AN UNFAMILIAR OTHER

In addition to its social stimulus properties, for an inexperienced organism MIS ought to also simulate the presence of a new or unfamiliar companion. That is, when an animal views itself in a mirror for the first time it should be confronting the image of an animal it has never seen before, and one would therefore expect to find responses typical of those emitted in the presence of a stranger. In support of this expectation consider the case of the pigtailed macaque (*Macaca nemestrina*). Anyone familiar with adult male pigtailed monkeys knows that they show a distinctive social gesture during courtship or in the presence of another unfamiliar male which consists of crouching and protruding the lips while retracting the scalp. By presenting a caged pigtailed monkey with a small pocket mirror you can readily elicit immediate and intense gesturing, whereas responsiveness in a well-established colony typically occurs at a rather low and infrequent level.

The behavior of domestic chickens (*Gallus gallus*) provides another good illustration of the fact that the mirror image is perceived as not only another animal, but an unfamiliar one. Domestic fowl are notorious for establishing stable dominance hierarchies or peck orders. The initial formation of the hierarchy and attainment of status positions within the flock is based on overt aggression, but once complete, individual rank is maintained largely through threat postures and appeasement signals. On the other hand, presenting a dominant or alpha chicken from a well-established flock with a mirror elicits considerable hostility accompanied by attempts to attack the reflection, whereas aggression in the original group is minimal. Thus, when confronted with a mirror the chicken appears to make an attempt to establish status lines with this "new" bird.

MOTIVATIONAL PROPERTIES OF MIRRORS

Another well-established characteristic of MIS is that it carries incentive value for many animals. One of the most frequent demonstrations of this effect has been to show that brief access to the mirror will serve as a reward for learning to make new responses which are instrumental in the production of such stimulation. Reward or reinforcing-like effects of MIS have been reported in Siamese fighting fish (Thompson 1963), paradise fish (Melvin and Anson 1970), fighting cocks (Thompson 1964), squirrel monkeys (MacLean 1964), pigtailed monkeys (Gallup 1966), and rhesus monkeys (Gallup and McClure 1971).

Figure 1, for instance, depicts data gathered (Gallup, Montevecchi, and Swanson 1972) on baby chicks which were required individually to run down a narrow six-foot runway in order to obtain thirty seconds of exposure to themselves in a small mirror. As shown in Figure 1, the birds receiving brief access to their reflection were running about four times faster by the sixth trial than control chicks not receiving the mirror reward. This indicates that MIS can be a potent visual incentive for young chicks.

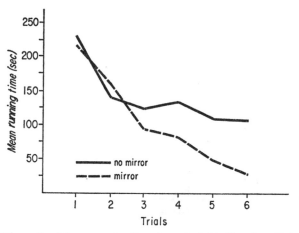

Figure 1. Mean running time in a straight alley for chicks receiving either thirty seconds of MIS in the goal box or no mirror exposure as a function of trials (Gallup, Montevecchi, and Swanson 1972)

SUPERNORMAL STIMULUS EFFECTS

Not only will animals learn to make novel responses to seeing themselves in a mirror, but there is recent evidence that a mirror may be more effective than a live companion for eliciting and sustaining certain classes of motivated behavior. In other words, in some species MIS seems to be what the ethologists call a SUPERNORMAL STIMULUS, or a contrived stimulus situation which is more effective than the natural stimulus for eliciting a particular pattern of behavior.

As an illustration of the possible supernormal stimulus properties of MIS, Baenninger, Bergman, and Baenninger (1969), using male Siamese fighting fish, found that a mirror was more effective than visual access to another live male for eliciting the elaborate aggressive display characteristic of this species. Similarly, adolescent chickens show aggressive behavior to their own reflection at rates that are four to five times higher than they are to other, like-sexed, unfamiliar chickens (Gallup, Montevecchi, and Swanson 1972). In much younger three-week-old chicks, which are momentarily separated from their brooder mates, MIS is better than a live companion for reducing distress vocalizations (see Figure 2).

The tendency for mirrors to elicit exaggerated social responses may also extend to certain species of primates. In an unpublished study (by M. K. McClure and myself) using six adult male patas monkeys (*Erythrocebus patas*), which show a peculiar aggressive gesture consisting of what appears to be a deceptively harmless yawn, a higher inci-

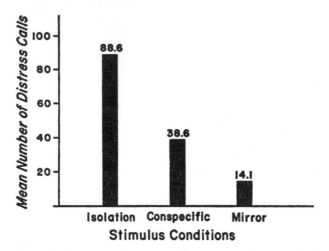

Figure 2.   Mean number of distress calls as a function of the conditions in effect during a three-minute period of separation from brooder mates (Gallup, Montevecchi, and Swanson 1972)

dence of threats directed to a mirror was found as compared to threats toward another unfamiliar male, and yawning reactions to the mirror did not habituate nearly as fast over a five-day period as they did to the other male.

PREFERENCE FOR MIRRORS

Related to the notion of supernormal stimulation is an increasing number of reports which show that when given a choice between viewing their own reflection in a mirror or looking at another conspecific, some animals seem to prefer MIS in the sense that they spend more time in association with the reflection. Baenninger (1966), for example, found that when given a continuous choice between MIS and visual access to another male, Siamese fighting fish spent up to three times more time orienting in front of their own image.

More recently, Gallup and Hess (1971) found a similar effect of MIS in goldfish (*Carassius auratus*). Using ten goldfish in an underwater alley, provided with a continuous choice between viewing a mirror or another conspecific behind plexiglas, a significant preference for MIS was obtained. Figure 3 shows that much like Siamese fighting fish the goldfish spent about three times more time in association with the reflection. Recently, Ternes, Jemail, and Laborde (1972) report finding that mirrors produce a more potent social facilitation effect on the extinction performance of goldfish than does the presence of a live companion.

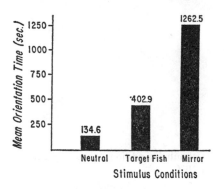

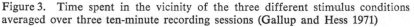

Figure 3. Time spent in the vicinity of the three different stimulus conditions averaged over three ten-minute recording sessions (Gallup and Hess 1971)

Using birds, Gallup and Capper (1970) found evidence of a preference for mirrors in weaver finches (*Passer domesticus domesticus*) and domestic parakeets (*Melopsittacus undulatus*). The birds were tested in a square plywood box containing four small perches, one on each wall. Each perch was associated with a different visual incentive: on one wall hanging immediately in front of the perch was a mirror, in front of the opposite perch was a comparably dimensioned window through which the bird could view a like-sexed conspecific contained in a small wire cage, and the remaining two perches provided access to food and water or a blank piece of cardboard attached to the wall. Each perch was designed so that the weight of a small bird would activate a switch and start an electric clock, thereby providing an estimate of the amount of

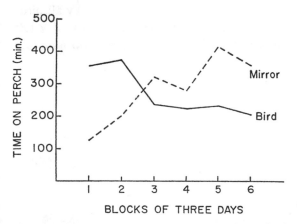

Figure 4. Mean time spent in front of a mirror (broken line) and in front of a target bird (solid line) by two adult finches as a function of blocks of three days (Gallup and Capper 1970)

Figure 5.   Mean times spent in front of four stimulus conditions by adult parakeets averaged over five days (Gallup and Capper 1970)

time a bird spent in association with the different stimuli.

Starting with two adult male finches, each bird was left alone in the box for eighteen consecutive days. Recording was carried out during daylight hours for approximately twelve and one-half hours each day, and to obviate the possible influence of extra-apparatus cues the test box was rotated ninety degrees every other day. Figure 4 shows the average time spent by both birds on the mirror perch and the perch which provided visual access to another finch as a function of days. Although there was an initial preference for the other bird, after the ninth day of testing both subjects were spending significantly more time in association with their own reflections.

As a check on the generality of these findings, two female and three male parakeets were tested sequentially in the same apparatus for five days each. Figure 5 shows the results for the parakeets averaged over days, and reveals a highly reliable preference for the mirror perch. Figure 6 depicts the average amount of time spent per day by all birds on the two perches, providing social stimulation over the five-day test period. In concert with the finch findings, it is interesting to note that

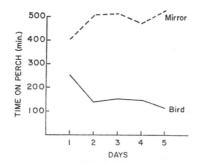

Figure 6.   Mean time spent in front of a mirror (broken line) and in front of a target bird (solid line) by parakeets as a function of days (Gallup and Capper 1970)

the mirror preference potentiates over days, with birds initially spending about one and one-half times more time in the mirror perch and four and one-half times more time by the fifth day. On the sixth day, as a control for possible perch or position preferences related to extraneous intrabox cues, the mirror was transferred to the perch previously associated with cardboard and remained in that position for an additional three days. In spite of the change, all subjects still preferred the mirror and spent most of their time on the new perch.

Although it appeared that a clear demonstration of a mirror preference in birds had been achieved, the testing situation might have been confounded. Since the target animal was confined in a cage the preference could simply have been based on the greater attractive potential of a noncaged companion. So finally, as an additional control procedure, small metal bars were placed across the surface of the mirror in a pattern similar to that used in the construction of the target bird cage. Then, in an attempt to assess preferences for the "caged" image, two additional parakeets were tested for three days with no bars, followed by two days with bars. The introduction of bars over the mirror surface produced virtually no effect on perch time, with both birds still spending four times more time in front of the mirror.

Unlike finches and parakeets, in domestic chickens and turkeys a preference for mirrors may be dependent on early social experiences. Schulman and Anderson (1972) found that group-reared fowl preferred orienting toward other conspecifics, while those raised in the presence of a mirror preferred mirror-image stimulation. On the other hand, chicks and turkeys raised in social isolation showed no consistent preference for either mirrors or conspecifics. One interpretive problem with the Schulman and Anderson study, however, was that the testing situation required subjects to choose between seeing their own image versus looking at TWO conspecifics behind glass. Due to the unequal levels of social stimulation associated with the visual alternatives, an equally tenable interpretation of their findings might be that the rearing conditions simply influenced a preference for viewing multiple companions, and the data may not, therefore, reflect on the attractive potential of a mirror.

More recently, in an attempt to determine whether primates might show a preference for mirrors, Gallup and McClure (1971) conducted a study using differentially reared rhesus monkeys (*Macaca mulatta*). The apparatus consisted of two cages mounted end to end. One cage was designated the experimental cage and the other the target cage. Both ends of the experimental cage were fitted with plywood partitions, and built into each partition was a guillotine door. A nylon rope was attached to each door and was threaded through a series of pulleys, so that the end of each rope, which was tied to a metal ring, hung down into the respective ends of the experimental cage. Pulling one rope enabled the subject to look at another monkey in the target cage, while pulling the opposite rope gave him access to his reflected image in a mirror. Micro-switches attached to the guillotine door runners, and wired to clocks and counters, provided measures of the number and duration of responses to the two visual incentives.

Fourteen preadolescent rhesus monkeys were employed as subjects. Six animals were feral (i.e. born in the wild) and eight were laboratory-born and reared in social isolation on artificial surrogate mothers. Each monkey was placed in the experimental cage by itself for two hours every day for five consecutive days, and was provided with a target mon-key in the adjoining cage which had been subject to a rearing history comparable to its own. Figure 7 shows the average amount of time spent viewing the target animal and the mirror by feral monkeys as a function of days. It is interesting to note that unlike goldfish and parakeets, the wild-born rhesus show a clear and consistent preference for viewing an-other monkey. Figure 8 shows the same comparison for laboratory-reared isolates who, contrary to their feral counterparts, exhibit a revers-ed preference and spend more time viewing the mirror. Unfortunately, data gathered on isolate monkeys represent responses for only three of the subjects, since the other five animals never pulled either rope.

As a check on the apparent preference for MIS shown by some of the isolate animals, both guillotine doors were permanently raised to elimi-nate the instrumental component and the same eight animals were

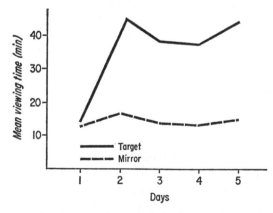

Figure 7.   Average time spent viewing target animal and mirror by feral monkeys for a two-hour session each day (Gallup and McClure 1971)

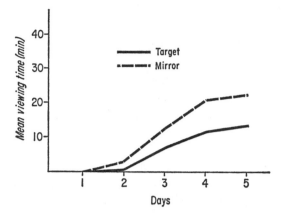

Figure 8. Average time spent viewing target and mirror by surrogate-reared monkeys for five two-hour sessions (Gallup and McClure 1971)

re-tested two months later. The test consisted of placing a monkey into this free-choice situation for one hour, during which time its behavior was monitored from another room through a one-way wide angle lens. Data were gathered by time-sampling their behavior once every sixty seconds for the first and last fifteen minutes of each hour. Records were made on whether the monkey was viewing the mirror or the target animal, as well as the nature of the interaction with the stimulus. Data obtained using this procedure are presented in Figure 9. As can be seen the isolate rhesus monkeys were all found to view the mirror more frequently than the target animal while engaged in both passive looking and active interaction with the stimulus alternatives.

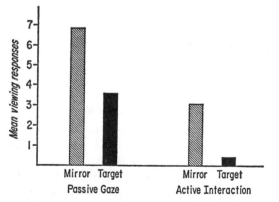

Figure 9. Average number of passive and active time-sampled viewing responses made to mirror and target animal by surrogate-reared monkeys (Gallup and Mc-Clure 1971)

AN INTERPRETATION

At this point at least two questions arise. First, why do feral monkeys show a preference for viewing a live companion while fish and birds prefer mirrors, and second, why do rhesus monkeys reared in isolation make visual choices which are the opposite of those shown by animals born in the wild? The answers to both questions may relate to the degree to which the social behavior of different species depends on learning and early socialization.

In rhesus monkeys, for example, a large proportion of their social behavior is acquired as a result of early experiences with other monkeys, as evidenced by the devastating effect of early social isolation on adult behavior (e.g. Harlow and Harlow 1962). Thus, for a normal rhesus monkey MIS would probably represent a highly atypical kind of social stimulation, since the image in the mirror never responds independently of the observer and as a consequence never initiates a social gesture, nor does it ever reciprocate.

On the other hand, the social behavior of fish and birds may be so rigidly preprogrammed and inflexible that reciprocal stimulation arising from a conspecific may be needed to progress through the interdependent chain of events inherent in a normal social episode, so as to reach an end point. In other words, the fish or bird may perseverate in front of its own reflection by way of trying to approximate a more natural exchange of social stimulation. In the absence of being able to achieve a normal outcome, which would be required to exit from the loop and terminate the encounter, the subject remains bound to the situation. Thus, the preference for MIS in fish and birds may be more apparent than real and could represent the effect of short-circuiting the natural sequence of reciprocal events imposed by genetic instructions.

Perhaps isolate rhesus monkeys, on the other hand, really do prefer watching their own reflections in mirrors. Pratt and Sackett (1967), for example, have shown that rhesus monkeys subjected to varying degrees of early social deprivation spent more time viewing comparably reared, but unfamiliar, conspecifics than others with different rearing histories. Since like-reared companions were used as target animals in the Gallup and McClure (1971) study it would appear that its own image in a mirror has more attention value for a social isolate than visual access to a comparably deprived peer. One way of conceptualizing these data is in terms of varying degrees of predictability in intraspecific encounters. The behavior of a live companion is usually never completely predictable, but, if confronted with a conspecific with a rearing history similar to its own, predictability ought to improve. In the case of MIS it would have to be perfect.

Because the image never initiates a social encounter, the enhanced predictability, and implicit element of control over the behavior or the image, may provide the isolate animal with a greater degree of initial security in a new social encounter. Also it may be that an isolate is less capable of responding to the initiative of another monkey, whereas in front of a mirror its own behavior is the sole determiner of the ingredients of any social episode. What could be more compatible with the atypical and aberrant behavior of a socially deprived rhesus monkey than a reflection of that behavior in a mirror?

SELF-RECOGNITION IN PRIMATES

Another point about mirrors, and probably the most obvious one for humans, is that MIS represents a potential source of information about the self. Mirrors are unique in that they enable visually capable organisms to see themselves as they are seen by other animals. In front of a mirror an animal is literally an audience to its own behavior. However, for most animals, confrontation with themselves in mirrors represents a form of social stimulation rather than a means of self-inspection. In this sense MIS might be characterized as an instance of self-sensation rather than self-perception. Although ostensibly stimulated by an image of itself (self-sensation) the animal responds as if in the presence of another organism.

To the extent that there exists some kind of underlying continuity between animals and man with regard to most basic biological and psychological processes, the absence of self-directed behavior in animals might appear discrepant from many findings in other areas. Interestingly, however, this pervasive other-directed orientation to mirrors shown by animals has also been reported for humans who are inexperienced with mirror surfaces, suggesting that self-recognition of one's reflection may be an acquired or learned phenomenon. For example, although there is a lack of consensus on this question, the best current estimate is that children initially respond to the image as though it were another child and do not learn to recognize their reflections until about twenty months of age (Amsterdam 1972).

Similarly, people born with congenital visual defects, which are eventually corrected, not only misinterpret their own reflections as representing other people, but tend initially to respond to the mirror space as though it were real: e.g. reaching for reflected objects in the mirror (von Senden 1960). There are also reports of mentally retarded children, ranging up to nineteen years of age, who seem totally incapable of learning to interpret mirrored information correctly, and persist in showing other-directed responses even after prolonged exposure to mirrors (e.g. Shentoub, Soulairac, and Rustin 1954).

Finally, it is known that certain mental patients with serious psychotic disorders cease to be capable of recognizing themselves in mirrors or photographs and often show signs of other-directed behavior in the presence of their own reflections (Faure 1956; Wittreich 1959).

In view of the preceding examples it would seem reasonable to conclude that the ability to recognize one's own reflection depends in part on learning, and the opportunity for such learning should in part be related to the amount of mirror exposure. Moreover, most of us are undoubtably given explicit verbal instructions by our parents and others with regard to the identity of the reflection.

A major difference between the natural environment of humans and animals is in terms of frequency with which we see ourselves in mirrors. Naturally occurring sources of MIS are probably only occasionally encountered by most organisms, whereas the human milieu tends to be permeated with such surfaces. The question arises, therefore, as to whether an animal could learn to recognize its reflection if given sufficiently prolonged confrontation with a mirror.

In an attempt to test this conjecture (Gallup 1970), two male and two female wild-born, group-reared preadolescent chimpanzees (*Pan troglodytes*) were each given individual exposure to a full-length mirror for eight hours per day over a period of ten consecutive days. To insure enforced self-confrontation with the reflection during the ten-day period each chimp was kept by itself with the mirror positioned in front of a small empty cage in an otherwise empty room. Observations were made by watching the chimp's reflection in the mirror through a small hole in the wall of an immediately adjacent room, and data were gathered by time-sampling the subject's behavior every thirty seconds for fifteen minutes each morning and afternoon. Two observers recorded data and periodically compared results as a reliability check.

Figure 10 portrays the average incidence of time-sampled social responses or other-directed behaviors given to the mirror image over the ten-day period. Only behaviors typically made in the presence of other chimpanzees were scored as social, such as bobbing, vocalizing, threatening, etc. In all instances of social behavior the reflection was judged to have been the referent for the behavior. As can be seen, other-directed

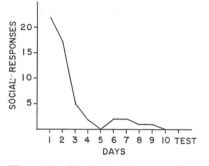

Figure 10. Number of time-sampled social responses directed to the mirror image over days (Gallup 1970)

tendencies were initially quite strong but waned rapidly and became almost nonexistent after the third day of mirror exposure.

Figure 11 depicts the development of what appeared to be self-directed responses to the reflection. In all instances of what were identified as self-directed behavior, the self (body, face, arms, hands, etc.) was the referent via the reflection. Under conditions of self-directed responding the mirror was used by the chimpanzee to gain visual and, as a result, precise manipulatory access to what would otherwise be inaccessible information about the self. Examples of behaviors scored as self-directed were attempts to groom parts of the body while watching the results and guiding the fingers in the mirror, picking bits of food from between the teeth, visually guided manipulation of anal-genital areas, identifying and then picking extraneous material from the nose with the aid of the mirror, manipulating food wads with the lips while inspecting the reflection, blowing bubbles, and making faces with the help of mirror feedback.

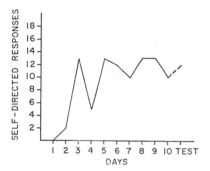

Figure 11. Total number of time-sampled responses directed toward the self through the mirror reflection over days (Gallup 1970)

The following description represents a few selected examples of the development of self-directed responding taken from notes kept on "Marge," one of the females (Number 1825):

Day 3.   Marge used the mirror to play with and inspect the bottom of her feet; she also looked at herself upside down in the mirror while suspended by her feet from the top of the cage.

Day 4.   She was seen using the reflection to manipulate a metal clip which was situated on the outside of the cage and could not be seen without the mirror.

Day 5.   Marge used the reflection to groom and remove fecal material from the underside of her left forearm. She was also observed to stuff celery leaves up her nose using the mirror for purposes of visually guiding the stems into each nostril, and then began playing with the protruding stems while watching the reflection and batting at the leaves with fingers. Later the same day she was seen vigorously splashing water in her water pan while watching the results in the mirror. At the end of the day when an experimenter entered the room she watched him indirectly in the mirror and occasionally glanced back as if to confirm what she saw in the reflection.

Day 6.   She watched herself eat in the mirror, and continued to spend considerable time watching the reflection during feeding periods on subsequent days. (Increased visual attention to the image during feeding was evidenced by all four animals). She also looked at herself upside down in the mirror again and began slapping her face while inspecting the reflection.

Day 7.   Marge used the mirror for the first time to manipulate her genital area, which had begun to show signs of pubertal swelling. (After the original incidence of visually guided genital manipulation this behavior was seen repeatedly in both females in subsequent sessions.)

Day 8.   She was seen to curiously manipulate a chewed banana peel for a long time with her lips while intently watching the reflections.

Day 9.   She actively inspected her mouth, lips, and teeth using her fingers to apparently make these structures more accessible in the mirror.

Post-test. Two days after the completion of testing the mirror was moved to within a few inches of the front of the cage and while viewing the reflection Marge identified a piece of white mucus in the corner of her right eye and then, using an index finger to remove it, ate the material.

It is important to note that self-directed responding seemed to supplant the social orientation to the mirror on about Day 3 (see Figures 10 and 11), which would be expected, since MIS would have to effectively lose its social stimulus overtones in order for self-recognition to occur. More importantly, the emergence of self-directed responding would suggest that the chimpanzee has correctly determined the identity of the reflection.

Figure 12 shows the average amount of time chimps spent viewing their own reflections averaged over the two fifteen-minute recording sessions each day. These data show that prior to having realized the significance of the reflection the animals show considerable interest in the mirror, but at about the time self-directed responses begin to appear, viewing time decreases and continues to remain at a relatively low level on subsequent days.

Even though these data were impressive, particularly those relating to self-directed responding, it was felt that other investigators might not be particularly convinced by the seemingly subjective interpretations of self-directed responsiveness in the presence of a mirror.

In an attempt to objectify these impressions a more rigorous procedure was instituted as a further test of self-recognition. Following the tenth day of mirror exposure, each chimp was completely anesthetized with a one-milligram-per-kilogram dosage of phencyclidine hydrochloride (Sernylan). The mirror was then removed from the room and

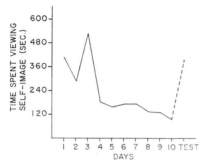

Figure 12. Average amount of time, during two fifteen-minute sessions, spent viewing the reflected image in the mirror over days (Gallup 1970)

the chimpanzee was lifted out of the cage. While the animal was unconscious, marks were applied to the uppermost portion of an eyebrow ridge and the top half of the opposite ear with a cotton swab dipped in a bright red alcohol-soluble dye (Rhodamine B base). After the marks were dry, the chimp was placed back into the small testing cage without the mirror and allowed to recover from the anesthesia.

It is important to realize that there were two special properties of this procedure. First, the chimpanzees would have no way of knowing they had been marked since the procedure was accomplished while they were unconscious, and the dye was selected because of its complete lack of tactile and olfactory properties, once dry. Second, the marks were carefully placed at predetermined points so that it would be impossible for them to be seen without the mirror after the subject recovered from anesthesia.

Following complete recovery, all subjects were fed and watered and then directly observed without the mirror for a thirty-minute pretest to determine the number of times any marked portion of skin was touched "spontaneously." After the pretest, the mirror was then reintroduced into the room for the first time since the marking procedure as a test of self-recognition, and each chimp's behavior was monitored in the presence of the mirror for an additional thirty minutes. Figure 13 shows the number of mark-directed responses (attempts to touch a marked area) made prior to mirror exposure and following the re-introduction of the mirror.

As can be seen, the number of mark-directed responses went up dramatically in the presence of the mirror, with a total of over twenty-five times more responses being shown when the reflection was made available for self-inspection. In terms of a chimpanzee's perception of its

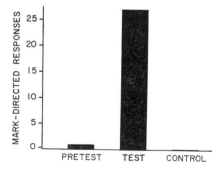

Figure 13.   Number of mark-directed responses made by experimental animals before being exposed to a mirror and by experimental and control animals during the test of self-recognition (Gallup 1970)

own facial features, it may be significant to note that of the mark-directed responses that occurred, over twice (2.36) as many visually guided responses were mad٤ to the eyebrows as compared to the marked ears. Occasionally a mark-directed response was also followed by direct visual inspection of the fingers which had been used to touch marked areas. In another case there were olfactory as well as visual attempts to inspect a finger which had made contact with a dyed spot.

Although seemingly unimportant, these instances of visual and olfactory inspection of the fingers are critically related to an interpretation of the data based on self-recognition. Given the demonstration of self-directed responding and even mark-directed behavior, the skeptic could still argue that these observations do not necessarily show that the subjects recognized themselves. However, if the reflection was still being interpreted as another animal there would be no reason for the chimps to smell or look at their own fingers on the test of self-recognition because these would not have been the fingers that made actual contact with the red spots. Only if the animals had correctly identified the dyed area in the mirror as pertaining to themselves, and not another chimpanzee, would there be a reason to inspect their OWN fingers.

Not only did the incidence of mark-directed behaviors increase with exposure to the mirror, but there was also a profound increment in the amount of time animals spent watching the reflection (see Figure 12). Visual access to themselves after having been marked with red dye produced over a threefold enhancement in average viewing time, which suggests that there was something about being able to inspect these spots which increased their visual attention to themselves in the mirror. Also, as Figure 10 reveals, other-directed responsiveness on the test day was completely absent, showing that the effect of the marking procedure was not to cause the subjects to revert to responding as though the reflection were another chimpanzee.

Although it seemed obvious on the basis of these data that the animals had learned to recognize their own reflections, it could still be argued that mark-directed responses might somehow have been an artifact or residual effect of anesthesia. To circumvent this objection a further check on the source of these reactions was instituted. One additional preadolescent male and female chimpanzee were anesthetized and marked with dye. Both animals were feral and neither had ever received prior exposure to mirrors. When given access to the mirror for the first time, the red dye was completely ignored and there were no mark-directed behaviors whatsoever (see Figure 13). Instances of self-directed response to the reflection were likewise absent. As was the case for the other chimps on the first day of MIS, their predominant orientation to the mirror throughout the test was unmistakably social, indicating that self-recognition must have been learned by the previous animals sometime during the eighty hours of mirror exposure antedating the test.

To investigate this capacity in other primates, four adult, wild-born, stumptail macaques (*Macaca arctoides*) and two adult male rhesus monkeys were given twelve hours of mirror exposure for fourteen consecutive days under conditions comparable to those employed with chimpanzees. Following the fourteenth day of mirror self-confrontation, the monkeys were anesthetized and marked with red dye. On the test of self-recognition all animals failed to show signs of self-directed behavior or self-directed responding and continued to maintain a distinct social orientation to the reflection. Moreover, informal observations of the monkeys during the fourteen-day period of mirror exposure indicated that all subjects persisted in showing more or less unabated other-directed responsiveness to the reflection.

Although these data could mean that monkeys do not have the capacity for self-recognition, it might be argued that the monkeys were simply not given enough time to learn to recognize themselves, even though they received over twice as much total mirror exposure (168 hours) before being tested. Also, both the stumptailed and rhesus monkeys were adults, and therefore not developmentally equivalent to the chimps who had just begun to show signs of sexual development.

To circumvent these latter two objections, three male and one female preadolescent cynomolgous monkeys (*Macaca fascicularis*) were given twenty-one consecutive days of mirror exposure, twelve hours each day, for a total of 252 hours, or over three times more time in front of the mirror over the twenty one days, and no mark-directed responses were seen on the tests of self-recognition. Thus, chimpanzees were the only mirror over the twenty-one days, and no mark-directed responses were seen on the tests of self-recognition. Thus, chimpanzees were the only ones capable of extracting this more abstract information from mirrors.

Following the initial report of self-recognition in chimps and negative findings with monkeys, there have been at least two additional attempts to demonstrate self-recognition in primates. In concert with our results M. Bertrand (personal communication) failed to find evidence of self-recognition in macaques and, perhaps more importantly, K. H. Pribram and his students (personal communication) were unable to demonstrate this capacity in gibbons, which are classified as apes rather than monkeys. To date, man and chimpanzee are the only species which have been found capable of recognizing themselves in mirrors. It is unfortunate that so far orangutans and gorillas have not been systematically tested for self-recognition, since it could contribute greatly to our knowledge of great ape mentality and might help to clarify our own taxonomic relationship to chimpanzees.

One of the most striking aspects of these findings is the apparent inability of monkeys to recognize themselves in mirrors. Although macaques can learn to use mirrors to manipulate objects (Brown, McDowell, and Robinson 1965; Tinklepaugh 1928) they do not seem capable of learning to integrate features of their own reflection sufficiently so that they can use mirrors to respond to themselves. When looking at an experimenter or a piece of food in the mirror they seem quite capable of recognizing the inherent dualism as it pertains to objects other than themselves, and after adequate experience do respond appropriately by turning away from the mirror to gain direct access to the object of reflection; but for some curious reason they fail to interpret correctly their own reflected image. Since other investigators (for a good review of the literature see Rumbaugh 1970) using more traditional behavioral tasks, such as learning set, have found only slight quantitative differences in learning and problem-solving performance between monkeys and chimpanzees, perhaps the deficiency is unrelated to learning *per se*.

Given the fact that there are no very profound or qualitative differences in learning ability between macaques and chimpanzees, maybe the deficit is due to the absence of an integrated self-concept in monkeys. Since the identity of the observer and the mirror image are one and the same, without a rudimentary identity of its own it would seem difficult, if not impossible, for an observer of a mirror to infer correctly the identity of the reflection. Thus, the deficiency may be much more cognitive than mechanistic.

The fact that chimpanzees appear rather unique in their ability to recognize themselves in mirrors would also seem to mesh quite nicely with other recent findings on chimpanzee mentality, such as the demonstration of intermodal equivalence of stimuli by Davenport and Rogers (1970), and the claims for language acquisition in chimps (e.g. Gardner and Gardner 1969; Premack 1971). It is important to point out, however, that since systematic attempts have not been made with monkeys, a claim CANNOT be made for the notion that language acquisition is a unique feature of human and chimpanzee mentality.

It remains a remote possibility that the demonstrations of language learning in chimps may be more a reflection of the expertise, patience and skill of the human trainers than of an intrinsic, higher mental process in the chimpanzee. Anytime an organism must be subjected to a complex training regime in order to demonstrate a particular effect, there is always the danger that the outcome may be more a function of the experimenter's capabilities than those of the subject. As is often the case, the real significance of any behavioral phenomenon may only come to light when viewed from a broad comparative perspective. The demonstration of language capability in chimpanzees will contribute very little to our understanding of the evolutionary relationship between man and other nonhuman primates until such time as the species limits of this phenomenon are established. As it stands, language in the chimpanzee may or may not have anything to do with biological or phylogenetic boundaries of learning.

SELF-RECOGNITION AS A CRITERION FOR SELF-AWARENESS

To the extent that self-recognition implies the existence of a self-concept, the data on chimpanzees would seem to qualify as one of the first experimental demonstrations of a self-concept in a nonhuman form. As already indicated, the ability to discern correctly the identity of the reflection would seem to necessitate an already established identity on the part of the organism making that inference. Indeed, these findings would seem to imply that man may not be the only creature who is aware of himself, and contrary to popular and contemporary dogma, humans may not have what heretofore has been assumed to be a monopoly on the self-concept.

Moreover, to the extent that consciousness refers to the ability to reflect on or be aware of one's own existence then these data might also be construed as evidence for consciousness in chimpanzees. Contrary to the claims of some (e.g. van Lawick-Goodall 1972), the fact that a chimp that has learned sign language can make symbolic gestures seemingly referring to himself, in the presence of MIS, does not necessarily implicate an unequivocal concept of self, but rather may simply represent an operant or instrumental response maintained by reinforcement, much like the behavior of a rat pressing a bar for food, and need not be accompanied by a state of explicit self-awareness. Labeling the reflection may be quite different from self-recognition (see following section on Self-Recognition in Man).

More recently, data have been obtained (Gallup et al. 1971) which give reason to suspect that the capacity for self-recognition in chimpanzees may be influenced by certain kinds of early experience. To the extent that one would require an already integrated concept of self before he could learn to recognize himself in a mirror, it seemed reasonable to suppose that the development of self-awareness could be influenced by early experience, and that it, too, might be an acquired phenomenon.

One of the early proponents of this view was Cooley (1912), who theorized that an individual's concept of self could arise only out of social interaction with others. For Cooley the self-concept was seen as an interpersonal phenomenon in the sense that the way other people react to an individual constitutes the primary source of information a person has about himself. Similarly, Mead (1934) held that it was the immediate social environment which prompted an individual to become aware of himself as a separate and distinct entity. In order for the self to emerge as an object of conscious inspection, from Mead's point of view, it requires the opportunity to examine one's self from another's point of view.

If, by chance, the speculations of Cooley and Mead bear on the development of self-awareness, it was reasoned that chimpanzees reared in social isolation might not have the necessary information to achieve self-awareness and acquire an identity, and therefore might be expected to show an inability to recognize their own reflections. In an attempt to assess the effects of early social deprivation, six additional preadolescent chimps were selected for testing. Two females and one male were born in the wild, and in captivity were usually kept in group cages containing at least one other companion. The remaining three chimps, also two females and one male, were born in captivity, separated from their mothers shortly after birth, and reared in individual cages which prevented physical contact with other animals and minimized visual contact.

The experimental procedure was the same as that employed in the original 1970 study. All animals were given eight hours of mirror exposure each day, followed on the tenth day by the test of self-recognition. In concert with the previous findings, social responsiveness to the mirror was initially quite high for feral chimps but disappeared after two to four days. Isolate chimpanzees, however, failed to show any of the typical other-directed responses to the reflection throughout the experiment; this should not be surprising since they had never been subject to normal social encounters.

The average amount of time the animals spent viewing themselves in the mirror during the thirty-minute recording session each day is presented in Figure 14. Very much like the animals in the initial study, feral chimps showed a gradual decline in the amount of time spent viewing the reflection, while isolates showed significantly higher and

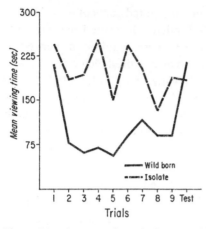

Figure 14.   Average time during ten thirty-minute sessions spent viewing their reflections in the mirror by wild-born and isolate chimpanzees (Gallup et al. 1971)

more stable levels of visual attention to the image over days. The accentuated interest in the mirror exhibited by deprived chimpanzees seems strikingly reminiscent of the preference for MIS shown by isolate rhesus monkeys (Gallup and McClure 1971), and could be taken to mean that isolate chimps resemble similarly reared rhesus monkeys more than they do feral monkeys. Curiously, there are also data which indicate that prolonged mirror gazing, often accompanied by an apparent loss of self-recognition, may be symptomatic of impending schizophrenia in man (Abély 1930; Delmas 1929; Ostancow 1934).

Figure 15 depicts the number of mark-directed responses made to dyed portions of the skin following recovery from anesthetization. In accord with the prediction from Cooley's theory, the feral chimps showed 13.5 times more mark-directed responses on the test for self-recognition than did the isolates. Moreover, the number of mark-directed responses made by isolate animals on the test was equivalent to the number shown by the ferals on the pretest, implying that the isolates were unable to infer correctly the identity of the mirror image (despite the fact that they spent more time watching their reflections).

It is also important to note that the wild-born chimps, much like previous animals, showed a substantial increase in viewing time (see Figure 14) when they saw themselves in the marked condition. However, as further evidence of their inability to determine the significance of the reflection the isolate chimps showed virtually no change in viewing time as a result of being allowed to see themselves after having been marked with red dye.

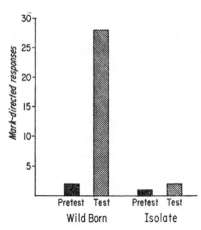

Figure 15. Number of times any marked portion of the skin was touched during a thirty-minute pretest without the mirror and a thirty-minute test by wild-born and isolate chimpanzees (Gallup et al. 1971)

As added evidence for the notion that the formation of a self-concept may be critically tied to early social experiences (Hill et al. 1970), two of three additional young isolation-reared chimpanzees were given twelve weeks of "remedial" social experience by housing the pair together in the same cage at eighteen months of age which, according to Cooley and Mead, should provide for conditions conducive to the emergence of some kind of personal identity. In accord with the prediction, the two chimps given a three-month opportunity to interact did show some signs of being able to recognize their reflections when tested following ten days of mirror exposure, whereas the chimp that remained in isolation failed to show evidence of self-recognition.

There are, however, at least two other, perhaps more parsimonious interpretations of the data obtained using differentially reared chimpanzees. It might be argued, for example, that the inability of isolate chimps to interpret correctly mirrored information about themselves could be indicative of a learning deficit engendered by early and prolonged maternal and peer deprivation.

On the other hand, Harlow, Schlitz, and Harlow (1968) contend that apparent deficiencies in learning ability evidenced by socially isolated primates may in fact be due to heightened levels of emotionality early in the testing regime. For instance, they report that with sufficient adaptation to the testing situation isolate rhesus monkeys do just as well as their feral counterparts on a variety of tasks. In this regard it is significant that none of the isolate chimpanzees showed enhanced emotionality after the first few days of mirror exposure, which was what would be expected since the only appreciable difference between experimental and ordinary housing conditions was the presence of the mirror.

Alternatively, it could be argued that since the isolate chimps never had the opportunity to become familiar with other chimpanzees, perhaps they failed to "speculate" about the curious behavior of the animal depicted in the mirror, who never initiates a social encounter nor reciprocates. Therefore, they may never entertain any hypotheses concerning the significance of the reflection. Although this second interpretation will account for the data, and cannot be ruled out, we tend to favor the idea that the absence of self-recognition is due to a general lack of identity or self-awareness.

The Cooley-Mead interpretation is a more attractive one because it encompasses much more data. Why, for example, should some psychotic patients begin spending excessive amounts of time watching themselves in mirrors and show a progressive inability to recognize their reflections; because they have lost interest in speculating about the identity of the reflection, or because of the loss of personal identity? Indeed, to the extent that viewing time is indicative of the attractive potential of MIS, isolate rhesus monkeys, isolate chimpanzees, and schizophrenic humans have NOT lost interest in the reflection because in all instances they spend inordinate amounts of time looking at mirrors.

As pointed out by Gallup, McClure, Hill, and Bundy (1971) the Cooley-Mead conceptual scheme can be used to account for a number of other curious findings with chimpanzees. Rogers and Davenport (1969), for example, report that the sexual behavior of chimpanzees reared in complete social isolation is less impaired than that of chimps given human maternal care. If the interpersonal nature of self-concept formation holds, then this finding should come as no surprise since the chimpanzee reared by humans would be expected to show a self-concept based on the reflected appraisals of another species which, in turn, could conceivably distort its own species identity.

As support for this interpretation Hayes and Nissen (1971) describe the case of a home-raised chimpanzee named Viki who, when given the task of sorting photographs into an animal and human pile, placed her own picture in the human stack.

Certainly all of this is highly speculative and the answers must await further experimentation. On the other hand, questions often have to be asked before answers can be obtained. Contentment with the wrong answers, or no answers, would seem to be much more dangerous than the risk entailed in asking a question. Perhaps the reason an attempt to operationalize and come to grips with self-awareness has been so long in coming results from a reluctance to even consider the questions.

To return to the question of self-recognition in chimpanzees, a number of additional studies remain to be done. For example, it might be interesting to devise techniques for accelerating the development of self-recognition. One obvious possibility would be to expose simultaneously two familiar cage-mates to the same mirror. Presumably each chimp would be able to recognize the reflection of its partner, and therefore would have considerably more preliminary information with regard to the identity of the "other" unfamiliar animal in the mirror. It would also be interesting to know what effect various drugs and/or neurological "insults" might have on a chimp who has learned to recognize his reflection (see section on Latent Social Stimulus Properties).

SELF-RECOGNITION IN MAN

It may sound ridiculous, but to date better quantitative evidence of self-recognition exists for chimpanzees than for man. Most attempts to assess self-recognition in humans have taken the form of trying to determine when infants learn to identify themselves in mirrors. Unfortunately the vast majority of these studies, particularly the earlier ones, are based on subjective impressions and lack rigorous control procedures.

While almost all investigators agree that prior to the attainment of self-recognition most children treat the image as another child or "playmate," there is very little agreement as to the average age at which children learn to recognize themselves in mirrors. The lack of consensus is not because too few studies have been attempted, but rather seems to have been due to an inability to devise an unconfounded and objective technique. Preyer (1893), for example, was satisfied that his son could recognize his own reflection at fourteen months because he showed evidence of recognizing his mother's image at about that time, a finding which might reflect on an ability not unlike that of a macaque who has learned to recognize objects other than himself in a mirror. Dixon (1957) was content to infer self-recognition anytime a child was observed to look at both his mirror reflection and a corresponding body part, which occurred between six and twelve months of age in a sample of five subjects. Stone and Church (1968) contend that most children recognize themselves in mirrors at around ten months of age.

Darwin (1877) felt that his own boy recognized himself at nine months because when called by name the child would turn to the mirror and say "ah." However, since children are often held in front of mirrors with parents repeatedly calling out their names this could merely mean that the child has learned to associate a name with the reflection, and not that he has acquired explicit self-awareness. Simply labeling the reflection may be quite different from an accurate awareness as to the source and identity of the image, and therefore cannot be used as conclusive evidence for self-recognition. On the other hand, Gesell and Thompson (1934), on the basis of a study of over 500 children, questioned that any self-recognition occurs in early childhood up to fifty-six weeks of age, and Shirley (1933) was also skeptical of early recognition based on her observations of children between forty and fifty weeks.

The only semi-convincing study with humans is a recent one by Amsterdam (1972), in which the assessment of mirror self-recognition was accomplished by marking children with a spot of rouge placed on the side of the nose, and then a few minutes later noting whether the nose was touched when subjects were exposed to a mirror. Using this technique she reports the emergence of self-recognition at between twenty and twenty-four months of age in about 65 percent of her subjects. Unfortunately the procedure employed by Amsterdam may have provided the child with considerable confounding information about the presence of the marks prior to the test of self-recognition.

Of the various human facial features, the sides of the nose are unique in that they are the most readily available to visual inspection without a mirror, and thus mark-directed responses might not be indicative of self-recognition. Rhesus monkeys, for example, are notorious for the efficient removal of paint and dye which has been applied to various body parts for identification purposes, but as previously noted they fail to respond to mirrored cues concerning otherwise visually inaccessible marks on their eyebrows and ears.

Moreover, since the rouge was applied a few minutes before mirror self-confrontation, while the child was fully awake, there is also the very real possibility that subjects may have been responding to tactual cues associated with the marking procedure and not to the reflection of those spots in the mirror. Finally, apparently no provisions were made in the Amsterdam study to monitor and record the number of mark-directed responses made prior to the test of self-recognition. Thus, while it may be introspectively and intuitively obvious that humans recognize themselves in mirrors, a clear and unequivocal experimental demonstration of this capacity has yet to be recorded.

LATENT SOCIAL STIMULUS PROPERTIES

Although most humans eventually do learn to recognize themselves in mirrors there are reasons to suspect that MIS may never completely lose its original, and perhaps more fundamental, social stimulus qualities (Gallup 1971). As already stated, people with serious mental disorders have been known to revert to an other-directed orientation in the presence of their own reflection and commonly show signs of a progressive inability to recognize themselves in mirrors.

Many people have had the rather startling experience of suddenly seeing themselves in an unexpected mirror surface, and responding as if confronted by a stranger (e.g. Wolff 1943). Similarly, the ingestion of certain chemical agents, such as alcohol and marijuana, has caused some people to report a feeling of strangeness and detachment or unfamiliarity with themselves in mirrors (e.g. Kraus 1949). Also there are anecdotal reports of gradual fragmentation or satiation of self-recognition after prolonged inspection of one's own mirror image, and people often find themselves temporarily unable to identify the reflection.

As previously stated, it is well known that performance is often affected by the presence of other organisms, as in the case of chickens who eat more in the presence of other chickens. In humans, Wicklund and Duval (1971) recently found a striking social facilitation effect on the performance of college students tested alone while facing a mirror, as compared to students without mirror-image stimulation. Mark P. Behar, a graduate student working in my laboratory, has been able to replicate this effect of mirror facilitation in an unpublished study by having college students press a simple hand-operated counter in the presence or absence of their own reflection. The average number of counter presses in a five-minute period was significantly higher when subjects were required to respond in front of a mirror, with a mean of 1,089 responses in the MIS condition as compared to 923 without the mirror. Thus, even for normal, self-recognizing adults a mirror image may still carry psychological significance comparable to the presence of another person.

REFERENCES

ABÉLY, P.
    1930   Le signe du miroir dans les psychoses et plus spécialement dans la démence précoce. *Annales Médico-Psychologiques* 88:28–36.

AMSTERDAM, B.
  1972   Mirror self-image reactions before age two. *Developmental Psychobiology* 5:297–305.

BAENNINGER, R.
  1966   Waning of aggressive motivation in *Betta splendens*. *Psychonomic Science* 4:241–242.

BAENNINGER, L., M. BERGMAN, R. BAENNINGER
  1969   Aggressive motivation in *Betta splendens:* replication and extension. *Psychonomic Science* 16:260–261.

BROWN, W. L., A. A. MC DOWELL, E. M. ROBINSON
  1965   Discrimination learning of mirrored cues by rhesus monkeys. *Journal of Genetic Psychology* 106:123–128.

COOLEY, C. H.
  1912   *Human nature and the social order.* New York: Charles Scribner's Sons.

DARWIN, C. R.
  1877   A biographical sketch of an infant. *Mind* 2:285–294.

DAVENPORT, R. K., C. M. ROGERS
  1970   Intermodal equivalence of stimuli in apes. *Science* 168:279–280.

DELMAS, F. A.
  1929   Le signe du miroir dans la démence précoce. *Annales Médico-Psychologiques* 87:227–233.

DIXON, J. C.
  1957   Development of self-recognition. *Journal of Genetic Psychology* 91:251–256.

FAURE, H.
  1956   L'investissement délirant de l'image de soi. *Évolution Psychiatrique* 3:545–577.

GALLUP, G. G., JR.
  1966   Mirror-image reinforcement in monkeys. *Psychonomic Science* 5:39–40.
  1968   Mirror-image stimulation. *Psychological Bulletin* 70:782–793.
  1970   Chimpanzees: self-recognition. *Science* 167:86–87.
  1971   Minds and mirrors. *New Society* 18(477):975–977.

GALLUP, G. G., JR., S. A. CAPPER
  1970   Preference for mirror-image stimulation in finches (*Passer domesticus domesticus*) and parakeets (*Melopsittacus undulatus*). *Animal Behavior* 18:621–624.

GALLUP, G. G. JR., J. Y. HESS
  1971   Preference for mirror-image stimulation in goldfish (*Carassius auratus*). *Psychonomic Science* 23:63–64.

GALLUP, G. G., JR., M. K. MC CLURE
  1971   Preference for mirror-image stimulation in differentially reared rhesus monkeys. *Journal of Comparative and Physiological Psychology* 75:403–407.

GALLUP, G. G., JR., M. K. MC CLURE, S. D. HILL, R. A. BUNDY
  1971   Capacity for self-recognition in differentially reared chimpanzees. *The Psychological Record* 21:69–74.

GALLUP, G. G., JR., W. A. MONTEVECCHI, E. T. SWANSON
1972   Motivational properties of mirror-image stimulation in the domestic chicken. *The Psychological Record* 22:193–199.

GARDNER, R. A., B. T. GARDNER
1969   Teaching sign language to a chimpanzee. *Science* 165:664–672.

GESELL, A., H. THOMPSON
1934   *Infant behavior: its genesis and growth*. New York: McGraw-Hill.

HARLOW, H. F., M. K. HARLOW
1962   The effect of rearing conditions on behavior. *Bulletin of the Menninger Clinic* 26:213–224.

HARLOW, H. F., K. S. SCHLITZ, M. K. HARLOW
1968   Effects of social isolation on the learning performance of rhesus monkeys. *Proceedings of the Second International Congress in Primatology, Atlanta, Georgia*, volume one. New York and Basel: Karger.

HAYES, K. J., C. H. NISSEN
1971   "Higher mental functions in a home-raised chimpanzee," in *Behavior of nonhuman primates*, volume three. Edited by A. M. Schrier and F. Stollnitz. New York: Academic Press.

HILL, S. D., R. A. BUNDY, G. G. GALLUP, JR., M. K. MC CLURE
1970   Responsiveness of young nursery-reared chimpanzees to mirrors. *Proceedings of the Louisiana Academy of Sciences* 33:77–82.

KRAUS, G.
1949   Over de psychopathologie en de psychologie van de waarneming van het eigen spiegelbeeld. *Nederlandsch Tijdschrift voor Psychologie en haar Grensgebieden* 4:1–37.

LISSMANN, H. W.
1932   Die Umwelt des Kampffisches (*Betta splendens* Regan). *Zeitschrift für Vergleichende Physiologie* 18:62–111.

LOTT, D. F., P. N. BRODY
1966   Support of ovulation in the ring dove by auditory and visual stimuli. *Journal of Comparative and Physiological Psychology* 62:311–313.

MAC LEAN, P. D.
1964   Mirror display in the squirrel monkey. *Science* 146:950–952.

MATTHEWS, L. H.
1939   Visual stimulation and ovulation in pigeons. *Proceedings of the Royal Society of London* 126:557–560.

MEAD, G. H.
1934   *Mind, self and society*. Chicago: University of Chicago Press.

MELVIN, K. B., J. E. ANSON
1970   Image-induced aggressive display: reinforcement in the paradise fish. *The Psychological Record* 20:225–228.

OSTANCOW, P.
1934   Le signe du miroir dans la démence précoce. *Annales Médico-Psychologiques* 92:787–790.

PRATT, C. L., G. P. SACKETT
1967   Selection of social partners as a function of peer contact during rearing. *Science* 155:1133–1135.

PREMACK, D.
1971 "On the assessment of language competence in the chimpanzee," in *Behavior of nonhuman primates,* volume four. Edited by A. M. Schrier and F. Stollnitz. New York: Academic Press.

PREYER, W.
1893 *Mind of the child,* volume two: *Development of the intellect.* New York: Appleton.

RITTER, W. E., S. B. BENSON
1934 "Is the poor bird demented?" Another case of "shadow boxing." *Auk* 51:169–179.

ROGERS, C. M., R. K. DAVENPORT
1969 Effects of restricted rearing on sexual behavior in chimpanzees. *Developmental Psychology* 1:200–204.

RUMBAUGH, D. M.
1970 "Learning skills of anthropoids," in *Primate behavior,* volume one. Edited by L. A. Rosenblum. New York: Academic Press.

SCHMIDT, M.
1878 Beobachtungen am Orang-Utan. *Zoologischen Garten* 19:230–232.

SCHULMAN, A. H., J. N. ANDERSON
1972 "The effects of early rearing conditions upon the preferences for mirror-image stimulation in domestic chicks." Paper presented at the meeting of the Southeastern Psychological Association, Atlanta.

SCHUSTERMAN, R. J., R. GENTRY, J. SCHMOOK
1966 Underwater vocalization by sea lions: social and mirror stimuli. *Science* 154:540–542.

SHENTOUB, S. A., A. SOULAIRAC, E. RUSTIN
1954 Comportement de l'enfant arriéré devant le miroir. *Enfance* 7: 333–340.

SHIRLEY, M. M.
1933 *The first two years,* volume two: *Intellectual development.* Minneapolis: University of Minnesota Press.

SIMPSON, M. J. A.
1968 The display of the Siamese fighting fish, *Betta splendens. Animal Behaviour Monographs* 1:1–73.

SMYTHE, R. H.
1962 *Animal habits: the things animals do.* Springfield, Illinois: Charles C. Thomas.

STONE, L. J., J. CHURCH
1968 *Childhood and adolescence* (second edition). New York: Random House.

SWALLOW, R. W.
1937 Ancient Chinese bronze mirrors. Peking: Henri Vetch.

TERNES, J. W., J. A. JEMAIL, J. E. LABORDE
1972 "Social facilitation of extinction in goldfish." Paper presented at the meeting of the Psychonomic Society, St. Louis.

THOMPSON, T. I.
1963 Visual reinforcement in Siamese fighting fish. *Science* 141:55–57.

1967   Visual reinforcement in fighting cocks. *Journal of the Experimental Analysis of Behavior* 7:45–49.

TINKLEPAUGH, O. L.
1928   An experimental study of representative factors in monkeys. *Journal of Comparative Psychology* 8:197–236.

TOLMAN, C. W.
1965   Feeding behaviour of domestic chicks in the presence of their own mirror images. (Abstract.) *Canadian Psychologist* 6:227.

VAN LAWICK-GOODALL, J.
1972   *In the shadow of man.* Boston: Houghton Mifflin.

VON SENDEN, M.
1960   *Space and sight: the perception of space and shape in the congenitally blind before and after operation.* Glencoe: Free Press.

WICKLUND, R. A., S. DUVAL
1971   Opinion change and performance facilitation as a result of objective self-awareness. *Journal of Experimental Social Psychology* 7:319–342.

WITTREICH, W.
1959   Visual perception and personality. *Scientific American* 200:56–60.

WOLFF, W.
1943   *The expression of personality.* New York: Harper.

YERKES, R. M., A. W. YERKES
1929   *The great apes: a study of anthropoid life.* New Haven: Yale University Press.

Capacities of Nonhuman Primates for Perceptual Integration Across Sensory Modalities

CHARLES M. ROGERS and RICHARD K. DAVENPORT

The transfer of information across sensory modalities takes place in normal humans in a wide variety of situations (Freides 1973). This process occurs in the apparent absence of significant association fiber pathways between the functional sectors of the cerebral cortex relating to vision, audition, and touch (Meyers 1967). However, in man an area of parieto-temporal cortex, the angular gyrus (Broadman's area 39) communicates with all these functional sectors (Geschwind 1965). Man's ability to integrate information from the various sensory modalities has been attributed by some to the relatively advanced development of this area. Furthermore, it has been suggested that the ability to form cross-modal association is a prerequisite to the ability to acquire speech (Geschwind 1965; Lancaster 1968). It has been maintained that the advanced development of the angular gyrus is unique in man. This accounts for the unique development of language in this species and, at the same time, for the supposed absence in non-humans of the ability to integrate sensory information. Negative results from experiments attempting to teach monkeys to transfer learned discriminations from one sensory modality to another (for citations see Davenport and Rogers 1970; Ettlinger 1973) have lent support to this position.

An alternative hypothesis is that the ability to match stimuli cross-modally is dependent on verbal mediation (e.g. Ettlinger 1967). Freides (1973) discussed the relevant human research literature at some length and concluded that cross-modal matching does not appear to

Supported by Grant No. GB-28713X from the National Science Foundation and by Grant RR-00165 from the National Institutes of Health.

depend on verbal mediation. Also, Ettlinger (1973) has revised his previous position on the role of language in cross-modal matching, but he still thinks that it is essential to cross-modal transfer. Conceptually, cross-modal matching, which involves the transfer of information from a model presented to one sensory modality to a simultaneously presented discrimination problem in which two or more objects are presented to a second sensory modality, is of a lower order of difficulty than the transfer task in which, presumably, some abstract representation allows the subject to utilize information gained from the solution of a problem in one sensory modality in the solution of the same or a similar problem presented to another modality.

A demonstration that nonhuman primates can perform tasks that require sensory integration would be generally construed as evidence against the necessity of verbal mediation. While there is now ample evidence that chimpanzees can acquire something very close to language under proper tuition (Premack 1970), there is no evidence that anything approximating it is to be found in naive animals.

A demonstration of nonhuman cross-modal integration might lead the anatomist to look more closely at the organization of the angular gyrus in the successful species; however, the possibility exists that there is some other neurological mechanism (possibly in the frontal cortex; perhaps subcortical). There is also the possibility that some alternative form of mediating response might exist in the absence of a verbal one.

Previous attempts to obtain evidence of cross-modal integration in nonhuman primates may have met with failure because of the procedures used. These negative experiments utilized some form of "transfer of training" design in which the subject is taught a discrimination task in one modality and is then presented with the same task in another modality. A positive result is interpreted to have occurred if the subject then learns the second task more rapidly or with fewer errors than he learned the first. The assumption is that some intersensory generalization has taken place permitting the subject to utilize visual experience, for example, in the solution of a tactile problem.

As Ettlinger (1973) has pointed out, a major difficulty with this procedure is the ambiguity of the test situation for the subject. There is no assurance that the subject is aware that there is any connection between step one and step two, that previous experience provides a clue to later solution. The subject may perceive the transfer test as a new problem, unrelated to the previous one. It should be noted that there is another possible source of difficulty in this procedure, a temporal factor. The subject would have to remember a set of clues from the time of termination of the initial discrimination training into the subsequent discrimination.

Our initial approaches to the problem of cross-modal integration in apes were from a different direction. It seemed to us that the subject would be most likely to make generalizations of this sort when all the stimuli were present simultaneously to both modalities and remained available throughout the problem until the choice was made. For this reason we adopted a matching-to-sample procedure. A single object, the sample, was presented to vision alone, and two objects, one identical to the visual object, one different from it, were presented for selection by touch alone (Davenport and Rogers 1970). The subject's task was then to compare the objects and choose the one that felt like the sample looked while he was looking at the sample. Using this procedure, we trained two chimpanzees and one orangutan to the point where they were capable of approximately 75 percent correct performance when tested on a series of forty objects which they had never seen before and which they saw only once during the assessment. Consistent performance at this level is significantly better than chance.

These results have been criticized on the basis that the subjects could attain this level of performance, not by matching across sensory modalities, but by responding on the basis of some other strategy: for example, by responding according to some classification system such as "if the sample is wider than the midpoint of the range of the widths select the wider choice object; and conversely" (Ettlinger 1973). In the first place, any strategy based on characteristics of this sort would require that the animal feel both discriminanda before making a selection. This did not occur; observations of the subjects during critical testing indicate that, in most instances, when (by chance) the subject first encountered the correct match, he selected it without touching the other object. Second, subjects had no opportunity to sample the range of the widths of unique-test objects, which they saw only once, at the time they were required to respond to them. Furthermore, a solution of this sort would appear to require an extraordinarily accurate memory and the ability to make virtually instantaneous comparisons between this remembered standard (drawn from a variety of complex objects of varying dimensions) and the complex discriminanda present during the given choice. Many of the objects did not lend themselves to comparisons to a given standard: how wide is a J-shaped bent wire? Finally, additial testing using randomly assembled unique

objects was conducted on these subjects in further experimental procedures to be described below and they continued to perform at high
levels.

Because previous experimental failures employed monkeys, the
questions arise whether we have utilized an easier task, developed a
better training technique, or demonstrated a phyletic difference between Hominoidea and other Anthropoidea. Ettlinger (1973) has
made the interesting suggestion that the various assessments of cross-
modal ability might facilitate the classification of different mammalian species according to cortical organization and/or cognitive
level. We are currently extending our initial research by training monkeys using procedures that were successful with our apes. It should be
noted here that prolonged training was necessary before our apes
achieved a high level of proficiency in cross-modal matching-to-sample.
A major factor in the training procedure seems to have been the
problem of instructing the subjects on what they were expected to
do in the test situation (related to test ambiguity mentioned above).
For example, a significant portion of the training was in intra-modal
matching, a preliminary step to cross-modal matching. Once the
basic operations, such as the matching strategy, were grasped, the ape
subjects proceeded rapidly toward criterion levels in the cross-modal
training phases.

The ability of apes to perform in the transfer situation, where naive
macaques have failed, should be explored. Ettlinger (1967, 1973) has
proposed that matching and transfer are in fact different processes
tapping cognitive abilities at different levels. He believes that some degree of linguistic capability is needed in order to transfer cross-modally but is not necessary for cross-modal matching. To evaluate
this hypothesis it will be necessary to attempt to teach apes to transfer
cross-modally and to do the same with monkeys that have mastered
cross-modal matching. We shall return to this problem shortly.

It occurred to us (and the question has been raised occasionally
by others) that in an animal like man, in which vision seems to be the
major sensory modality, the utilization of haptic cues might be more
difficult or less efficient. Therefore, we thought it wise to assess
the bidirectionality of the cross-modal matching-to-sample phenomenon, and we undertook to train a group of naive chimpanzees
to make a visual discrimination on the basis of a haptic sample. Our
procedures were essentially the same as those employed in the first
experiment except that we streamlined training a bit by eliminating
some of the mistakes we had made in the first experiment. In this ex-

periment (Davenport, Rogers, and Russell 1973) five of six subjects survived the training period and received critical trial testing with unique objects. Four of these five performed during sixty unique trials above 70 percent accuracy. While their performance was not quite as good as that of the animals in our first experiment, it was significantly better than chance.

A variety of factors may have contributed to the differences in performance: (a) there is a slight temporal delay when the second procedure is used — the subjects released the haptic sample prior to making a selection between the visually presented objects (by touching a covering window) — while in the first experiment the sample was present in the visual field during the haptic selection; although they were not prevented from doing so, the subjects never made their selection while holding the sample; (b) different parts (e.g. lower portion) or aspects (shape, texture, etc.) of the sample might have been sampled selectively by a subject in the second experiment, while in the first experiment all the characteristics were sensorially present to vision simultaneously and the subject could then compare a combination of characteristics simultaneously or could "come upon" discriminative characteristics more readily (in the first experiment he had all the characteristics of the sample available but might not need to use all of those of the discriminanda); (c) the subjects in the second experiment were considerably younger (four to five versus seven to eight years) at the time of critical testing; (d) it may be more difficult to generalize from haptic to visual characteristics than the converse because of the cortical organization of the organism; and (e) it may be more difficult for this species to make discriminations by touch than by sight, without any differences in the cross-modal aspects of the task.

Some of these factors could be explored, but most of them are not central to the issue. For example, it would be of interest to determine possible age differences in sensory integration ability. It would be a relatively easy task to compare visual and haptic discrimination abilities in chimpanzees. However, other questions have occupied our attention.

The possibility that temporal factors may contribute to the difficulty of cross-modal transfer has been mentioned. We have, in fact, explored the effects of imposed delays on the performance of the animals trained to match from haptic to visual stimuli (Davenport, Rogers, and Russell 1975). In this procedure the subjects were permitted to sample the haptic object, were denied subsequent access to it, and were forced to wait for a predetermined interval before the visual discriminanda were presented. Initially, the delays were very short; they were very gradually lengthened as the subjects reached criterion performance at each delay. Forty test trials with objects seen only once before were interposed periodically. Without going into a detailed discussion of the results here, it is sufficient to note that all subjects scored significantly above chance at each level tested, with the exception of the performance of one subject at the five-second level. On a unique-object series presented after training at the twenty-second level, two subjects performed well above significant levels, one just below, and one at chance. Thus, some chimpanzees can retain, over short intervals, a representation of the sample that is sufficiently accurate to permit correct solution of a discrimination in another sensory modality. This implies that they are capable of some sort of symbolic process. It also suggests that the major difficulty of the transfer task may rest elsewhere than simply in temporal factors. We must emphasize, however, that just as with the performance of cross-modal matching-to-sample itself, the subjects received prolonged training in delay before their ability was evaluated.

It is worth noting that, according to most human-memory researchers, we have here, in fact, a demonstrating of long-term memory. However, a discussion of memory or of long-term versus short-term memory and the various implications for central processes or mechanisms is not germane to this discussion.

The logical next step would be to assess the ability of these highly trained chimpanzees to perform a cross-modal transfer task. If the real difficulty with the transfer procedure lies in the area of "telling" the animal what he is supposed to do, then these animals should readily master a transfer problem. Conversely, if, in fact, transfer requires linguistic mediation, our subjects should fail to master it. These chimpanzees are currently being tested on such a task and their performance thus far is promising.

Alternatively, it would seem desirable to attempt to directly train naive subjects to perform a cross-modal transfer task without interposing any matching training. Some of the insights and clues from our previous experiments suggest various procedures which might facilitate communicating to the animal what he is expected to do. This is currently under investigation with a group of orangutan subjects, and it, too, looks promising.

There remains another feature of sensory integration to which we have given some very preliminary consideration, namely, the question of what aspects of the stimulus are transferred. Although we have made only a beginning in this area, we shall briefly discuss experiments that might be characterized as dealing with cue reduction. The initial experiment (Davenport and Rogers 1971) was an extension of our first study in which two chimpanzees and one orangutan were trained to solve a haptic discrimination on the basis of a visual sample (Davenport and Rogers 1970). Full-size color photographs were substituted for a series of unique, not previously experienced, actual objects and were presented as visual samples. Black-and-white photographs of another series of unique objects were subsequently presented as samples.

The performance of the subjects was not affected by the substitution of color photographs; there was no evidence in their performance, or in their behavior during testing, that any change in the sample had occurred. When black-and-white photographs were substituted there was a slight decline in performance, but all subjects continued to perform at levels significantly above chance. No learning to perceive photographs was necessary. Most of the slight decline in performance when black-and-white photographs were substituted can be attributed to the performance of one subject, who was still above chance although performing at a slightly lower level throughout the black-and-white series. It should be emphasized that these results indicate that the apes perceived these photographs of objects AT FIRST SIGHT and utilized the cues they provided just as they had utilized those provided by actual objects.

No further alterations of the sample were made using visual-to-haptic procedures. Following critical trial performance, the haptic-to-visual cross-modal group was also tested on a series of altered visual cues. As in the visual-to-haptic experiments, photographs of unique objects were used to present forty critical trials in each condition. As before, color photographs were followed by black-and-white photographs. In this experiment the series was extended to include half-size black-and-white photographs, high-contrast photographs, and line drawings, in that order.

The performance of the haptic-to-visual group continued to be somewhat poorer than that of the visual-to-haptic group. Whereas the latter performed at 85 percent and 77 percent efficiency on color and black-and-white photographs respectively, the haptic-to-visual group performed at 70 percent correct on each. Although there are too many variables operating to make a valid comparison between the groups, it is interesting to speculate that relatively small reductions in the discriminanda cues might have an effect on performance, while comparable changes in the sample have no effect. This difference could be explained on the basis that cue reductions in the sample lead the subject to explore the discriminanda for differences that reflect cue parameters still present in the sample. Reductions in the discriminanda cues may involve just those sample cues to which the subject attended just prior to making his discrimination. Remember that in haptic-to-visual matching, the subjects released the haptic sample before making a visual choice and rarely resampled it.

Performance on the remainder of the altered visual cue series was at about the same level except when high-contrast photographs were presented. Here the performance dropped to about 62 percent. High-contrast photographs looked essentially like silhouettes. The appearance of many objects was markedly altered in these photographs. Furthermore, there is no way of presenting haptic objects to conform with the plane of presentation of the photographs. Finally, many salient characteristics of shape as well as texture were totally eliminated in the high-contrast photographs.

We know of no satisfactory way of systematically reducing cues in order to produce a series of graded difficulty. Most of the alterations used in these experiments had little effect on the apes' performance (with the exception of the high-contrast photographs). But differences in difficulty could be masked by the small number of subjects, the somewhat erratic performance of the haptic-to-visual group, general practice effects which frequently occur when a series of problems is presented, and differences in discrimination difficulty from one series of objects to another. These series were put together more or less randomly from an assortment of objects, although an effort was made to use widely different objects within a series as well as in pairings. An alternative to the cue reduction procedure which we would like to investigate is the use of drawings in which various characteristics of miscellaneous objects are emphasized or de-emphasized.

A significant finding in the photograph experiments is that photographs were recognized by the apes with apparently no difficulty and that no learning was necessary. Even nonprimates can be TRAINED to discriminate between photographs, but this is, we believe, the first unequivocal demonstration that animals can perceive some photographs without prior instruction.

Obviously, these results have direct implications for the notion that primitive peoples must learn to perceive photographs as representations of real things (Segal, Campbell, and Herskovits 1966; Deregowski 1972). Apes performed about as well when photographs were substituted as they had when actual objects were presented. It is true that in photographs presented to human subjects, the representations were markedly reduced in size — this may have been a major factor interfering with perception. However, a 50 percent reduction in size did not materially affect the performance of our chimpanzees.

There are basically two general theoretical positions regarding pictorial perception (Gibson 1971). According to the point projection theory of pictorial information, representation of a picture on the retina is precisely the same as that of the real object or scene, and no learning is required to perceive a picture.The alternate position, the symbol theory of pictorial information, holds that a picture provides a set of symbols which the perceiver must learn to interpret. Our data lend support to the point projection theory because our subjects had no previous experience with pictures of any sort prior to their sudden appearance in the testing program.

This line of research, along with studies of symbolizing, taps some of the higher cognitive abilities of apes. These are abilities once thought to be unique to man. It suggests that many of the questions that behavioral primatologists have articulated have been much too simple.

REFERENCES

DAVENPORT, R. K., C. M. ROGERS
    1970   Intermodal equivalence of stimuli in apes. *Science* 168:279–280.
    1971   Perception of photographs by apes. *Behaviour* 39:318–320.
DAVENPORT, R. K., C. M. ROGERS, I. S. RUSSELL
    1973   Cross-modal perception in apes. *Neuropsychologia* 11(1):21–28.
    1975   Cross-modal perception in apes: altered visual cues and delays. *Neuropsychologia* 13:229–235.
DEREGOWSKI, J. B.
    1972   Pictorial perception and culture. *Scientific American* 227:82–88.
ETTLINGER, G.
    1967   "Analysis of cross-modal effects and their relationship to language," in *Brain mechanisms underlying speech and language*. Edited by C. H. Millikan and F. L. Darley. New York: Grune and Stratton.
    1973   "The transfer of information between sense-modalities: a neuropsychological revue," in *Memory transfer and information*. Edited by H. P. Zippel. New York: Plenum.
FREIDES, D.
    1973   "Human information processing and sensory modality: crossmodal functions, information complexity, memory and deficit." (Privately circulated.)

GESCHWIND, N.

1965   Disconnexion syndromes in animals and man. *Brain* 88:237–294, 585–644.

GIBSON, J. J.

1971   The information available in pictures. *Leonardo* 4:27–35.

LANCASTER, J.

1968   "On the evolution of speech," in *Primates: studies in adaptation and variability*. Edited by P. Jay, 439–457. New York: Holt, Rinehart and Winston.

MEYERS, R. E.

1967   "Cerebral connectionism and brain function," in *Brain mechanisms underlying speech and language*. Edited by C. H. Millikan and F. L. Darley. New York: Grune and Stratton.

PREMACK, D.

1970   A functional analysis of language. *Journal of the Experimental Analysis of Behavior* 14:107–125.

SEGAL, M., D. T. CAMPBELL, M. J. HERSKOVITS

1966   *The influences of culture on visual perception*. Indianapolis: Bobbs-Merrill.

The Learning and Symbolizing Capacities of Apes and Monkeys

DUANE M. RUMBAUGH

Man is, perhaps, more readily distinguished from other primates by what he does and by what he can do than by his morphology. Without question, man's abilities to learn, to symbolize and conceptualize, to define and even to create problems as well as solve them, to invent and otherwise create, to reflect upon the distant past, and to contemplate the future are profoundly advanced by unknown orders of magnitude over the abilities of all other primate forms. Man is distinguished primarily by his intelligence.

The history of measurement in education and psychology is replete with accounts of theory and methods for quantifying man's intelligence. Although there will be continuing controversy about the nature and measurement of human intelligence, there seems little doubt that the concept of intelligence itself is established. The parameters of intelligence, and the relative contributions of genetics and experience in continuous interaction in determining intellectual competence, are now coming to be understood through systematic inquiry. But questions of how genetics sets the range limits for intelligence, and of how experience in relation to age influences expressed intelligence, are likely to remain for generations to come.

Anthropologists have a continuing interest in assessments of the intelligence of early man, for they have recognized the importance of evolving intelligence in the determination of a wide variety of adaptations. Such assessments are extremely problematic, however, for the intelligence of extinct life forms can only be inferred from indices which are not necessarily closely correlated with either potential or functional intelligence. Fossil skulls and other skeletal materials

For Plate, see p. viii, between pp. 368–369

provide for estimates of cranial capacity and brain/body ratios, but, unfortunately, they can tell nothing about possible evolutionary developments in cytoarchitectonics. Similarly, the products of early man — tools, abodes, fossil remains of his prey, art, etc. — are helpful, but by no means definitive in assessing functional intelligence.

The prospect that comparative studies of the learning processes and skills of extant nonhuman primates might shed light upon the relationship between brain development, a hallmark of primate evolution, and intelligence led me to a program of research which has now spanned more than a decade. It is hoped that, in due course, the results of this research program and of those that follow will facilitate the assessment of the intelligence of early man through the determination of lawful relationships between indirect indices of intelligence and the cognitive capacities of early man.

INTELLIGENCE

The problems of defining intelligence are acknowledged. It is also conceded that operational definitions of intelligence leave much to be desired: to assert that "intelligence" is that which is measured by a device labeled an "intelligence test" does not necessarily provide satisfaction as to the dimensions and parameters of intelligence. For testing animal intelligence, then, it is best that attention be given to those skills which are agreed to as fundamental, the *sine qua non* of intelligence as we know it in man. Few, if any, students of intelligence would deny that the ability to TRANSFER learning is a fundamental process.

It is not possible to achieve quantification of such fundamental processes through field research. As important as field research is for learning about many factors of primate adaptation, the expression of intelligence in nonhuman primates that anticipates intelligence as known in *Homo sapiens* requires the controlled methodology of the laboratory.

LABORATORY RESEARCH ON PRIMATE INTELLIGENCE

Brain evolution has been mentioned as one of the hallmarks of primate evolution. In particular, evolution of the neocortex has been emphasized, and the array of extant primates from prosimian to monkeys and apes provides a rich and reasonably systematic set of graded brains and neural systems for studies that might provide us with a better understanding of the evolutionary course of human intelligence.

Research programs reviewed elsewhere (Rumbaugh 1968, 1970, 1974) support the conclusions that (1) complex learning skills are enhanced by brain development, (2) transfer-of-training skills are similarly enhanced, and (3) with specific reference to transfer-of-training skill, and probably complex-learning skills as well, the great apes are superior to the lesser apes, monkeys and prosimians.

The formulations of Harlow (1949) on the nature of the learning-how-to-learn phenomenon, termed "learning set," and the refinement of methods whereby the development of learning sets can be quantitatively charted, gave great impetus to comparative studies designed to assess the comparative capacities of the complex-learning skills of diverse primate species. Research by Harlow and others indicated that learning-set capacity was positively related to brain development and to ontogeny, and inversely related to brain damage and to age, for example. But as the learning-set training procedures developed by Harlow made no allowance for perceptual/motivational/motor factors, all of which are confounded with the species and age variables, questions remained as to the validity of comparisons between the performances (percentage responses correct) of diverse species, age groups, etc.

To answer those questions it was apparent that equitable cross-species testing methods had to be devised. The challenge was great, however, when in addition to known factors of perceptual/motivational/motor differences among species there were probably many other factors totally UNKNOWN. Even to attempt to mitigate learning/performance differences associated with or produced by species differences in perceptual/motivational/motor characteristics is extremely problematic. For example, in assessing food motivation, how long must a gorilla be deprived of food for it to be as hungry as a squirrel monkey that is deprived for twenty hours? What size should problem objects be for species of widely divergent physical proportions? How can one equate the work factor entailed in the execution of choices for species that differ greatly in morphology and size?

The list of such questions is endless, and makes it almost impossible to define procedures for formal testing that will ensure equity or fairness for the species to be compared. In point of fact, there probably is no way in which equity of testing can be achieved through attempts to build specific apparatuses for each species, or otherwise to approximate equity through complex manipulations of operationally-induced motivations, the incentive values of different rewards, etc.

But as a result of the past decade of research, I now believe that equity in testing across species can be achieved through the use of PERFORMANCE criteria that are demonstrated by the subjects of diverse species immediately PRIOR to the administration of the critical tests used for the determination of the comparative assessments. This approach is one, then, which calibrates subjects on a performance criterion prior to test, rather than one which attempts dubious calibration of test apparatuses, deprivation schedules, etc., in the interests of equitable testing in the context of the species variable.

The testing procedure which entails the demonstration of a performance criterion prior to the procurement of those measures for comparative assessment of complex-learning capabilities is termed the "Transfer Index" (TI; see Rumbaugh 1970 for details). Its origin can be traced to a study program addressed to determination of the complex-learning skills of primates conducted at the San Diego Zoo between 1960 and 1966 (Rumbaugh and McCormack 1967). That program included a series of simple-discrimination, learning-set, discrimination-reversal, and oddity tasks for a variety of primate genera that included monkeys, gibbons, and great apes.

Analysis of the data from discrimination-reversal learning tasks revealed interesting differences between ape and macaque subjects on the one hand and squirrel monkeys on the other. The discrimination-reversal training entailed seven, nine, or eleven trials, randomly determined, on problems in which one object was reliably correct (food-rewarded) and the other object reliably incorrect (not food-rewarded) if chosen. Upon completion of those trials, the reward values of the objects were reversed and remained so for the following ten trials on each problem.

Examination of pre-reversal and post-reversal performances revealed that several of the apes and macaques were doing appreciably better on the post-reversal trials than on the pre-reversal trials. This was significant, for squirrel monkeys were without exception profoundly worse on post-reversal trials compared to pre-reversal trials. The possibility was thus suggested that it might be possible to equate diverse primate species on pre-reversal PERFORMANCE criteria so as to permit defensible and equitable tests immediately thereafter.

Pursuing this line of thought, a number of experimental probes were made to determine the feasibility of defining pretest performance criteria in ways that would allow latitude in terms of numbers of trials, yet not do so with the result that such allowance would in and of itself be the determinant of post-criterial test performance. This work led to the operational definition of two criterial levels of task mastery — 67 percent and 84 percent in terms of percentages of correct responses — whereby criterial achievement was defined in terms of numbers of correct choices after various numbers of training trials.

Upon satisfaction of criterial acquisition in two-choice, object-quality discrimination problems, in which initially one object was reliably correct and rewarded and the other object reliably incorrect and not rewarded, test trials (ten per problem) were given on which the reward values were reversed relative to their assignment during initial training.

Extensive tests have shown repeatedly that in general (with the exception of the genus *Hylobates*), numbers of trials to achieve criteria do not correlate appreciably with performance on the reversal test trials. Accordingly, it is maintained that latitude in terms of trials to criteria can be afforded, within set limits, to primate species so as to allow equitably for extant differences among them in their basic discrimination-learning skills.

It is also maintained that under these conditions the many characteristics, both known and unknown, that might confound assessment of their complex-learning skills are uniquely mitigated, for it is only under specified conditions that test trials are given and it is only those test trials in relation to the pretest criterial performance level that determines the conclusions of comparative assessment.

Trials to criteria are limited to between 11 and 60 in number, in addition to the first training trial. The 67 percent criterial schedule requires 6 or 7 correct choices by the 11th trial (6 and 7 correct being required on alternate problems for which it is on the 11th trial tha, the criterion is achieved), 9 correct by the 14th trial, 10 correct by the 16th trial, 12 correct by the 19th trial, or 14 correct choices within the last 21-trial span as training continues to a maximum of 60 trials for a given problem.

The 84 percent criterial schedule requires 9 correct choices by the 11th trial, 14 correct by the 17th trial, 17 or 18 correct on alternate problems for which it is on the 21st trial that the criterion is achieved, or 17 or 18 correct within the last 21-trial span as training continues to a maximum of 60 trials for a given problem (again, 17 and 18 are required on alternate problems for which it is within the most recent 21 trials that the criterion is achieved).

TI is calculated by determining the percentage of responses correct on the reversal trials two-to-ten for a block of ten problems in which the criterion on each problem was achieved under the stated conditions. That percentage is then divided by the operationally defined criteria mastery level used for the pre-reversal acquisitional training — 67 percent and 84 percent correct.

Figure 1 presents data obtained from the genera indicated in a testing program that obtained two TI values per subject: first after 67 percent, then after 84 percent criterial mastery. It is clear that reversal test performance differed across the genera tested, as reflected both in the TI values (left axis) and in the reversal percentages on which the TI values were, in the main, determined.

TI values greater than 1.15, obtained through use of 67 percent pre-reversal criterial schedule, reflect significant POSITIVE transfer, reversal percentage correct being significantly better than the 67 percent pre-reversal performance. Values of this magnitude were obtained in all of the three great ape genera (*Pan*, *Gorilla*, and *Pongo*), but never in any other genera tested. Further, only the great apes' reversal performance increased in correspondence with an advance of the pre-reversal criterial schedule from 67 percent to 84 percent. On the average, their reversal percentages correct increased 18 percent, a gain almost identical to the difference between the 67 percent and 84 percent pre-reversal criterial schedules.

Pre-reversal and reversal performances for the great apes were positively correlated. By contrast, reversal performances of the talapoins (*Miopithecus*) on the average dropped significantly from about 45 percent to 25 percent correct as the pre-reversal criterion was advanced from 67 percent to 84 percent. The TI values for both gibbons (*Hylobates*) and talapoins dropped significantly as the pre-reversal criterion was advanced from 67 percent to 84 percent; the former because the reversal percentages correct remained essentially unchanged, and the latter for the reason already stated.

In summary, then, there was (1) superiority of the great apes, particularly when tested subsequent to 67 percent criterial mastery where certain representatives of them achieved reversal performances that reflected significant positive transfer from pre- to post-reversal trials, (2) for the great apes a high and positive relationship between the pre-reversal criterial training level employed and reversal performance, (3) for the vervets (*Cercopithecus*) a positive relationship, but not as high as for the great apes, between the pre-reversal criterial training level employed and reversal performance, (4) for the gibbons and lemurs (*Lemur*) no alteration in reversal percentage correct asso-

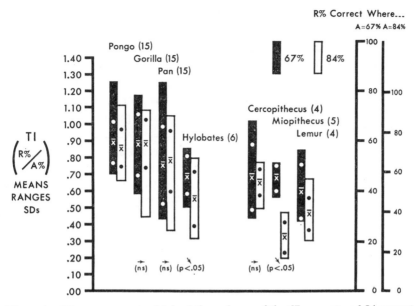

Figure 1.   TI measurements obtained through use of the 67 percent and 84 percent pretest criterial training schedule for great apes, lesser apes, monkeys, and lemurs

ciated with pre-reversal criterial training level, and (5) for the talapoins a very high and negative relationship between pre-reversal criterial training level and reversal performance.

Studies by Conolly (1950) and by Hill (1966) result in the brains of the genera tested being ranked in the following order, from most to least advanced: great ape, gibbon, vervet, talapoin, and lemur. Among the nonhuman primates, then, advanced brain development is associated with facile reversal performance, believed to reflect, in the main, transfer-of-training ability. Less advanced brain development is associated with either less facile transfer (vervets), no alteration in transfer (gibbon and lemur) associated with the amount of learning available for transfer (as determined by pre-reversal criterial training schedules), or with transfer occurring in a way that results in a profound loss in accuracy of performance (talapoin).

As many genera of nonhuman primates remain untested with TI methodology, reasonable caution must be exercised in formulating conclusions now. That observation notwithstanding, it seems to me quite unlikely that the performance levels of the great apes are to be exceeded, even by the cognitively adept macaques (*Macaca*).

Detailed analysis of the great apes' TI data (Rumbaugh and Gill

1973) revealed statistically reliable superiority of gorilla (*Gorilla*) and orangutan (*Pongo*) to chimpanzee (*Pan*) when testing used the 67 percent pre-reversal criterial training schedule. The significance of the difference was not obtained when testing used the 84 percent schedule; however, the rank order from high to low TI values remained: gorilla, orangutan, chimpanzee. Interestingly, this rank order corresponds perfectly with the apes' cranial capacity (Schultz 1965). This relationship is not presented in terms of cause-and-effect, but it is, nonetheless, one that should not be summarily disregarded.

Few would deny that at least in part man's superior intelligence is provided by a brain that is large relative to his body, but probably all would insist that brain size itself is not the *sine qua non* of high-order intellectual expression. To date, TI data on the developing child are not available, but they are being collected; they should be significant to those interested in calibrating the intelligence of man with that of apes.

EMERGENCE OF IDEATIONAL, ABSTRACTIVE LEARNING

In years past, Köhler (1925) and Yerkes and Yerkes (1929) concluded that the great apes possess ideational/abstractive learning capacities not commonly found in monkeys and not reducible to stimulus-response (S-R) learning processes. The reasons for their arguments, however, were based on a variety of observations and impressions, not on the basis of measurements obtained by identical tests administered to apes and monkeys.

Elsewhere (Rumbaugh 1971) an account is provided of a testing paradigm which is believed to be both sensitive to differences in learning processes and equitable for diverse species. The testing paradigm required: first, criterial mastery of two-choice discrimination problems; second, reversal of cue values; and third, the administration of test trials on which there was deletion of either the initially correct or incorrect stimuli with new stimuli substituted in their stead. During criterial training, with the correct stimulus designated A+ and the incorrect stimulus designated B−, on achievement of the criterion (nine correct choices with the span of ten trials) the cue values were reversed so as to make A− and B+. With subjects sophisticated in discrimination-reversal problems, this first A−, B+ trial serves as the cue to reverse choice of objects on subsequent trials if additional rewards are to be obtained, the absence of reward for choice of object "A" being the salient cue or discriminative stimulus.

Now, if the criterion was achieved through the formation of an "approach" HABIT to A+ and an "avoidance" or inhibitory habit to B–, extinction or weakening of the A+ habit and countermanding of the B– avoidance habit would be requisites to facile reversal of choice from object A to object B. On the other hand, if the criterion was achieved through ideational/abstractive learning, the absence of reward for choice of object "A" on the first cue-reversal trial could serve more generally as the occasion (or reason?) for "A" to be avoided and/or for "B" to be approached on the rest of the trials for that problem.

It follows then, the deletion of either A (which became "minus" [–] on the first reversal trial) OR B (which became "plus" [+] on the first reversal trial) should facilitate performance on the ensuing reversal test trials IF achievement of the pre-reversal performance criterion had been achieved through the S-R habit-formation processes. (Deletion of A would obviate extinction of a strong approach tendency interfering with shifting of choice to B, and deletion of B would obviate countermanding of the aversion to B, established through the effects of non-rewarded choices of it during criterial training.) On the other hand, if the pre-reversal performance criterion had been achieved through ideational/abstractive learning, then deletion of A or B would be of little consequence, for sufficient information would remain (the object NOT deleted) for appropriate choice to be determined to obtain reward.

The experimental procedure reflected these considerations. On each of a series of two-choice, object-quality discrimination problems, training continued until the criterion was satisfied. At that time the cue values were reversed (A+ became A–; B– became B+) for the first reversal trial. On the remaining reversal trials there was deletion of either A– or B+ and in their respective steads a new stimulus, C, was substituted and assigned the cue value of the stimulus that had been deleted (if A– deleted, then C was "minus" [–] if B+ deleted, then C was "plus" [+]). A control reversal condition consisted of continuing BOTH A– and B+ throughout all trials post-cue reversal.

Gorillas served as great ape representatives, gibbons served as lesser ape representatives, and the diminutive talapoins served as representatives of monkeys, particularly those with the less-developed brains. Gorillas were viewed as most likely to reflect ideational/abstractive learning (prediction = no difference between reversal test conditions) and talapoins were viewed as most likely to reflect S-R learning processes (prediction = B+, C− and/or A−, C+ reversal test conditions would produce higher performance levels than the control condition of B+, A−). Gibbons, whose brain development is intermediary between gorilla and talapoin, were viewed as "unknown entities" so far as learning process was concerned.

The results of the study are portrayed in Figure 2. The gorillas' performances supported predictions based on ideational/abstractive learning and the talapoins' performances indicated the operation of S-R learning. Interestingly, the gibbons' performances reflected preference of the "C" stimuli, regardless of their assigned cue values. If C was "plus," gibbons were as accurate as the gorillas, but if C was "minus" they were more inaccurate than the talapoins.

The study supported the argument, then, that with brain development there is probably the emergence of new learning processes that can be characterized as ideational/abstractive in properties. With *Homo sapiens'* brain being considerably more developed than the

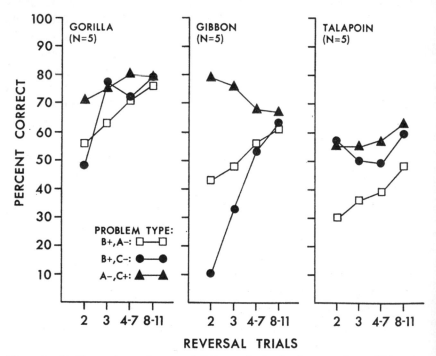

Figure 2. Evidence that primates of different brain development have different learning processes. In relation to the discussion of the text, the control condition is B+, A—, the second reversal condition is B+, C—, and the third reversal condition is A—, C+

ape brain, the neurologic base for high intelligence is apparent.

DID TERRESTRIAL ADAPTATION SELECT FOR INTELLIGENCE?

These and other studies in the comparative learning field are intended to give us a better perspective of human intelligence. In conjunction with considerations of ecological factors, certain guarded inferences might be warranted as to the conditions that selected in a positive way for refinement of the brain and high intellience.

It is the conclusion of this author that there is no reason to question henceforth the superiority of great ape intelligence among the other nonhuman primates. Other studies (see Rumbaugh 1970 for a review) suggest that next in rank-order are the macaques (*Macaca*) and baboons (*Papio*). All other primate genera, gibbons included, are at lower levels of cognitive competence as inferred by performance on tasks that entail facile transfer-of-training abilities, concept-formation, learning-set, and other forms of complex learning.

The majority of *Macaca* genera, all of the *Papio* genera, along with the gorilla and chimpanzee, share a common characteristic — they are all highly adapted to a terrestrial way of life. They do ascend trees, of course, for particular occasions or reasons, but all of them are very much at home on the ground. It is suggested that it has been the evolving of adaptations to terrestrial, as opposed to arboreal, life that has, in the main, selected for refinement of the brain in ways that provide for high intelligence and complex cognitive functions. Exceptions are few, but two of them — notably the orangutan and patas (*Erythrocebus*) — warrant special attention.

The orangutan is enigmatic in that, despite its relatively massive proportions it is primarily an arboreal primate form. Its hands and feet are all highly specialized for grasping and suspension. Orangutans do come to the ground more frequently than was thought even a few years ago (Horr 1972) but they are not well equipped for long, efficient, terrestrial travel. They are, nonetheless, of superior intelligence as assessed by TI methodology, and are, perhaps, even superior to the chimpanzee. Why?

Two possibilities suggest themselves: (1) orangutans are an exception to the thesis that terrestrial adaptation has been the primary force in the evolution of intelligence as we know it in man; or (2) orangutans were selected both for large size and for intelligence during some interval of the distant past when they were either adapted to or were adapting to a terrestrial way of life. Unfortunately, there are no data at present to support the latter possibility, but it should be retained as a hypothesis for future testing should there be abundant discoveries of fossil remains of orangutans in terrestrial environs. Meanwhile, the former alternative is, perhaps, the most defensible.

Regarding the patas monkey, practically nothing is known regarding its skills in the kinds of tasks primarily considered here. Some of my students have tested two specimens with TI methodology; neither did well. It would be unwarranted to conclude from tests of these two animals that the patas either is or is not cognitively advanced. Further discussion is, consequently, unwarranted except to note that IF the patas is not cognitively advanced, perhaps their notorious high-speed running ability has achieved for them the adaptations that other terrestrial primates have achieved through development of cognitive skills.

LANGUAGE: IS IT A UNIQUELY HUMAN ATTRIBUTE?

In another article in this volume, my associates and I describe current research into the possibility that certain nonhuman primates might possess the capacity for linguistic productions, controlled by rules of sentence structure, as we know it in man. It is no accident that in this research, and in the research of others on that topic, apes rather than monkeys were selected as subjects. The research summarized in the first sections of the present paper provides objective basis for that selection.

REFERENCES

CONOLLY, C. J.
  1950   *External morphology of the primate brain.* Springfield, Illinois: Charles C. Thomas.
HARLOW, H. F.
  1949   The formation of learning sets. *Psychological Review* 56:51–65.
HORR, D.
  1972   The Borneo orang-utan. *The Borneo Research Bulletin* 4(2).
HILL, W. C. O.
  1966   *Primates: comparative anatomy and taxonomy*, volume six: *Catarrhini Cercopithecoidea Cercopithecinae.* New York: Wiley.

KÖHLER, W.
1925 *The mentality of apes*. London: Routledge and Kegan Paul.
RUMBAUGH, D. M.
1968 "The learning and sensory capacities of the squirrel monkey in phylogenetic percpective," in *The squirrel monkey*. Edited by L. A. Rosenblum and R. C. Cooper, 255–317. New York: Academic Press.
1970 "Learning skills of anthropoids," in *Primate behavior: developments in field and laboratory research*. Edited by L. A. Rosenblum. New York: Academic Press.
1971 Evidence of qualitative differences in learning processes among primates. *Journal of Comparative and Physiological Psychology* 76(2):250–265.
1974 "Comparative primate learning and its contributions to understanding development, play, intelligence, and language," in *Comparative biology of primates*, 253–281. Edited by B. Chiarelli. New York: Plenum.
RUMBAUGH, D. M., T. V. GILL
1973 The learning skills of great apes. *Journal of Human Evolution* 2:171–179.
RUMBAUGH, D. M., C. MC CORMACK
1967 "The learning skills of primates: a comparative study of apes and monkeys," in *Progress in primatology*. Edited by D. Starck, R. Schneider, and H. J. Kuhn, 289–306. Stuttgart: Gustav Fischer.
SCHULTZ, A. H.
1965 "The cranial capacity and the orbital volume of hominoids according to age and sex," in *Homenaje a Juan Comas* 2:337–357. Mexico City.
YERKES, R. M., A. W. YERKES
1929 *The great apes: a study of anthropoid life*. New Haven: Yale University Press.

Discussion

RUMBAUGH: Our method for assessing the intelligence of nonhuman primates has recently been demonstrated to relate very significantly to the mental age of four-and-one-half-year-old children. Their mental ages were assessed by conventional intelligence testing techniques. They were also administered transfer index testing. The correlation between those two sets of values was +0.76 which is as high can be expected between any two tests of intelligence. At the nonhuman primate level this testing procedure has revealed that in terms of transfer of training abilities, which is absolutely germane to the expression of intelligent behavior, the great apes are without question superior to the lesser apes (represented by the gibbon) and to the Old World monkeys which we tested. We have not tested rhesus macaques but we tested vervets and talapoins. In a test situation in which the great apes manifest significant positive transfer from the pre-training to the test trials, the talapoin, which has a much more primitive, smooth-cortexed brain, reliably manifests significant negative transfer even though in the pre-test performances the great apes and the talapoins do equivalently well. In other words, they learned the material with equal facility. But while the apes transfer to a profound advantage, the talapoins transfer to a profound disadvantage. This work also demonstrates that there are differences in the learning processes of nonhuman primates. These differences in learning process are related to brain development. In an experiment that is relatively complex, we demonstrated that whereas the talapoins learned problems with simple stimulus-response association learning processes the great apes learned abstractively in a way that allowed for much greater adaptiveness on test trials which varied in ways to assess the degrees to which the initial learning was the result of stimulus-response learning instead of abstractive learning. Thus even though there is a continuum of neurological development and increased complexity of the brain in extant primates, there are differences in learning processes with abstractive learning emerging within the great apes quite obviously and profoundly. Thus far cross-modal stimulus equivalence capacity has not been demonstrated in monkeys. This is not to say that they do not possess it, however. That Rogers and Davenport (see Rogers and Davenport, this volume) have demonstrated it quite readily in the great apes, I believe relates to the wisdom of the choice of using apes in language projects rather than monkeys. Harry Harlow commented on the basis of data on Lana's performance (see Rumbaugh et al., this volume) at the end of three months of training that even then she was well beyond what he would expect a rhesus monkey to ever be able to do. And short of hard empirical tests I cannot think of anyone better qualified to offer such an opinion.

LIEBERMAN: One wonders what would have happened to theories of operant reinforcement if chimpanzees had been the initial subjects instead of rats.

RUMBAUGH: Behavioral research portrays that there are many capabilities in nonhuman primates that might not be observed except under the most extreme circumstances. These latent capabilities certainly provide something to be selected for. To the degree that that which is adaptive is contingent upon intelligence we can see where intelligence might have been selected for in a very positive way. Many years ago I demonstrated that though the squirrel monkey mother is normally a passive mother and a quadruped, if you increase the dependency of the infant so that it cannot cling normally, the mother will become very active and care-giving and bipedal in her walk. You would not likely see this in squirrel monkeys in the trees. But that there is this capability in the squirrel monkey suggests that it could have been selected for as infant dependency increased. Intelligence can provide for a great variety of latent adaptive patterns that can see life forms through when the more fixed and rigid behavioral adaptations, as defined by genetics, no longer are sufficient to a changing environment.

Language Skills of Apes and the Evolution of Human Language

Capacities for Language in Great Apes

ROGER S. FOUTS

INTRODUCTION

Any article entitled "Capacities for language in great apes" implies two questions: "What is language?" and "Is language unique to man?" Because language is thought to be unique to man, we must confront the larger question of the nature of man. The question "What is man?" has plagued us throughout historical times; how can a species as wonderful as man not be totally unique in some respect?

One of the earliest definitions of man separated this divine creation from his fellow animals on the basis of man's rational soul. Perhaps it would have been better if the question had remained theological rather than developing into an empirical problem, but later came the trauma that the earth was not the center of the universe. However, the scientists of the day came to the rescue of an ego-shattered human species searching for uniqueness. The rational soul became the ability to reason and this definition lingered for ages. When the definition changed into "the ability to learn from past experience," the species was abruptly confronted with non-uniqueness since extremely simple animals obviously share this same quality. The scientific community again came to the rescue with another well-worn methodology; namely, basing scientific statements on negative evidence or the absence of evidence. In this method, the scientist need only look around and NOT see something. From this he may conclude that the thing not seen in a particular species is totally absent in that species. For example, one of the more recent definitions of man was that he was the only species to use tools. The word was spread to college freshman and man was secure in his divine right to uniqueness. Unfortunately for those who based the uniqueness of man on this criterion, it was soon shown to be inadequate. Several species were observed using tools, even the snubby-beaked Galapagos woodpecker. The next thing some scientists did not see was an animal making a tool. Once again the dichotomy was drawn. Unfortunately for the defenders of our obviously unique species, van Lawick-Goodall (1968), observed chimpanzee behavior that was strikingly similar to tool-making. Because the definition of man as the "tool maker" proved to be unsatisfactory, those who would define the uniqueness were forced to look elsewhere.

Presently, the definition has, for the most part, changed to involve the use of language. Of course "language" has been carefully separated from "communication." It is clear that animals other than man are capable of communication skills, and because some language skills have not been observed in any animal except man, it is compelling to conclude, on the basis of lack of evidence – or negative evidence – that only man is capable of language and that this defines his uniqueness.

Dobzhansky, while maintaining the position that man is unique, fails to define "uniqueness." He stresses the notion of uniqueness so emphatically that one implicitly assumes that he is referring to a difference in kind rather than degree. He points out that all species are unique, but "the human species is the most unique of all. . . . Its most outstanding unique properties are predominantly not in the morphological or physiological but in the psychological realm" (1972 : 418). At no point does he specifically define what he means by the word "psychological," but apparently he refers to the language behavior of man. Quoting Simpson (1964), Dobzhansky comes to the crucial psychological property: "Language is also the most diagnostic single trait of man: all normal men have language; no other now living organisms do" (1972 : 419). Accepting the importance of language as a definition for the uniqueness of man, Dobzhansky cites Hockett's (1959) list of key properties of language. (The six features quoted by Dobzhansky, however, have all been seen to some degree in chimpanzees using American Sign Language [ASL]). But the check list approach to defining language has obvious drawbacks which will be mentioned later. Dobzhansky then quotes from the article by Gardner and Gardner (1969), a report on progress during the first twenty-two months of teaching a chimpanzee (Washoe) to use American Sign Language (ASL) and not a completed study. He connects the Gardners' research with a quote by Bronowski and Bellugi (1970): "the child's ability to analyze out regularities in the language, to segment novel utterances into component parts as they relate to the world, and to understand these parts again in new combinations" (1972 : 421). This, finally, allows him to make his own statement based on the absence of evidence: "The chimpanzee has not mastered this art of analysis and synthesis" (1972 : 421).

The Dobzhansky article is typical of the negative kinds of evidence used to support the notion of the behavioral uniqueness of man as a species. But if negative evidence is all that we can amass to prove man's uniqueness or difference in kind, perhaps we should abandon differences in kind and instead appreciate the remarkable differences in degree in the behavior of different species.

Before proceeding, it should be made clear that it is not known whether or not the Great Apes possess a natural language of their own. There is presently only negative evidence concerning this; but this may be a result of the inability of investigators to "break the code," if a code or language does exist. It is conceivable that chimpanzees may have a language of their own – if we can ever find a universally agreed upon definition of language, and if we are clever enough to make the appropriate observations.

Attempts in the past to define language have generally consisted of a list of the characteristics of language (Hockett 1958; Thorpe 1972). Usually, however, when evidence is presented that a nonhuman species achieves some of these characteristics, the list grows longer in order to exclude the interloper species. If this kind of progression continues we may eventually have a definition of language that isomorphically maps the behavior of human language, in essence a redundant description of the behavior. Such a list would serve to explain nothing, but would exclude every organism that does not meet all of the listed criteria.

One of the more common and prejudicial characteristics of defining language is limiting language to the vocal mode. This is a mistake that is not only wrong, but has served to give some research done on animal communication a rather myopic approach, i.e. focusing on vocalizations at the expense of other modes which might prove more productive in understanding the communication process in a particular species. A scientist studying animal communication should be interested in all possible modes of communication because they are often quite varied. As Marler has said:

In most situations it is not a single signal that passes from one animal to another but a whole complex of them, visual, auditory, tactile, and sometimes olfactory. There can be little doubt that the structure of individual signals is very much affected by this incorporation in a whole matrix of other signals (1965).

Another approach to defining language might be called the structural-physiological approach (Chomsky 1967, 1968; Lenneberg 1967, 1971). This approach depends on the supposition that other animals lack a structure in their brain necessary for language. Often, it seems that speech structures are confused with the hypothesized language structure, which again is probably the result of the emphasis on the vocal mode of communication. Based on this emphasis one could take the ridiculous point of view that deaf people using a gestural mode of communication are not *Homo sapiens*.

The Chomskian view is basically that man has an innate structure in his brain that enables him to have language. This structure is unique to man and is hypothesized to be the result of a mutation. Chomsky's view that the structure is innate is reasonable; but the conclusion that it is specific to either man or language is questionable. It is not plausible that something as complicated as language could be the result of a mutation in one species.

Lenneberg, on the other hand, seems to imply a similar hypothetical structure that not only handles language, but also arithmetic and tool-making. But the structural-physiological point of view has one great weakness in implying that a specific behavior can result from one and only one structure and that no other structures in any other species could equally serve a similar function.

Perhaps an analogy is necessary to make these points clearer. Let us suppose that a Cadillac that has been fully equipped with all the extra cost options is analogous to human language and a Volkswagen is analogous to a chimpanzee using ASL. If you were a person using a checklist you could note that the Cadillac had a large V-8 engine of enormous horsepower, air conditioning, power brakes, power windows, etc. Using your checklist you could say that the Volkswagen had only a few of these characteristics and was therefore not really an automobile. If you adhered to the structural-physiological point of view you could note that the Volkswagen does not have an engine in the front, that it is missing four of its cylinders, that the cylinders are not in the V-8 position and most important of all it completely lacks a radiator. It is obviously not an automobile. The structural-physiological approach overlooks the fact that both vehicles have engines that are capable of getting you from point A to point B on a freeway. Of course, there are differences in comfort, speed, and sophistication in addition to the absence of extra cost options, but are these the essential characteristics?

It has been argued that all attempts to make man different in kind rather than degree by relying on negative evidence, the presence or absence of physiological structures, and check lists of characteristics have basic weaknesses. As an alternative there is the notion that man is different in degree, and that a true dichotomy does not exist. Consider for example, Lashley's (1951) statement:

I am coming more and more to the conviction that the rudiments of every human behavioral mechanism will be found far down in the evolutionary scale and also represented even in primitive activities of the nervous system. If there exist, in human cerebral action, processes which seem fundamentally different or inexplicable in terms of our present construct of the elementary physiology of integration, then it is probable that that construct is incomplete or mistaken, even for the levels of behavior to which it is applied.

The differences between man and other species are profound by our present standards, but they are still differences in degree rather than kind.

Presently, there seems to be no universal agreement upon either a definition of language, or that a definition separating language from communication must at all exist. A behavioral definition using essential characteristics of language seems reasonable. But at this time we do not know what the essential characteristics of language might be. There is one characteristic of language behavior in humans and chimpanzees that seems to be essential to not only language acquisition but to the competent integration of other behaviors as well. It might simply be called rule-following behavior. It appears that animals are able to perceive relationships between events in the environment and between events in the environment and themselves. They seem to be able to incorporate these relationships into their own behavior and then behave in accordance with them. The specific behavior is not important; it might be climbing a tree or it might be using language. For example, a chimpanzee is able to climb trees, any tree, completely novel trees or very familiar ones. But the important point is that he climbs the tree in a lawful fashion; i.e. he always goes up head first and undoubtedly he must combine muscle movements in a novel fashion specific to that particular tree. From one point of view this bears a strong resemblance to a person combining the various constituents of language in order to complete a grammatically correct sentence. But this is presently only an idea that is still in its neonatal stage and will obviously require much more refinement. It is basically the idea that animals have an ability for perceiving rules, incorporating them, and then applying them to appropriate situations. Whether or not this ability is learned or innate is not important; it may be the result of the way our nervous systems operate (Hebb et al. 1973) or because of maturation or experience (Schneirla 1966). This being the case, the empirical data concerning language behavior in the chimpanzee and a few other primates will now be presented. Finally, a note of warning should be given. If conclusions are to be based on these data alone, it must be stressed that the data are incomplete; in fact, probably only a minimal amount has been collected. After the data have been presented some theories related to language origin in early man will be discussed.

ATTEMPTS TO TEACH VOCAL LANGUAGE IN APES

Attempts to teach apes to use vocal speech have had rather limited success. One reason is that the chimpanzee vocal tract is different from the human vocal tract. This, of course, does not preclude the possibility of a clever experimenter overcoming this difference and someday establishing two-way vocal communication with an ape, but present evidence makes that look doubtful. Lieberman, Crelin, and Klatt's (1972) comparative research on the vocal apparatus of man and chimpanzee has shown that the vocal apparatus of a chimpanzee is quite different from that of adult humans. Lieberman claims that since nonhuman primates lack a supralaryngeal pharyngeal region similar to that of adult humans, the nonhuman primates are unable to produce the important human vowels /a/, /i/, and /u/. In addition, nonhuman primates lack proper tongue mobility and thus cannot change the shape of the vocal tract as humans can. Given this information any attempt to teach an ape vocal speech ought to be utterly hopeless. But, there has been success; of course it is relative success. Furness (1916) was able to teach a female orangutan the vocal words *papa* and *cup* which the ape used in a correct manner. Furness noted that neither the orangutan nor the chimpanzee appeared to use the lips or tongue to make their natural vocalization, and this was the major obstacle to acquiring speech. Note that the acquired words did overcome the obstacle of the lips.

Hayes and Hayes (1951, 1952) attempted to teach a young female chimpanzee, Viki, to speak by raising her in their home for over six years. They worked from the premise that a chimpanzee's vocal apparatus is capable of producing human vocal sounds. After intensive training, Viki acquired the four words *mama, papa, cup* and *up;* of course, they were recognizable as English words but were pronounced with a heavy chimpanzee accent. Viki's acquisition of the four words has been the most successful attempt to teach a newborn primate to produce human speech sounds.

These studies lead to two possible conclusions: (1) chimpanzees may not possess the mental abilities to acquire language, or (2) the chimpanzee's vocal apparatus may not be suited to the acquisition of human speech sounds and, therefore, a communication mode other than vocal may be more appropriate.

Sarah

The Premacks (D. Premack 1971a, 1971b; and Premack and Premack 1972) studied the acquisition of language skills in a chimpanzee, Sarah, by dividing language into behavioral constituents "considered fundamental by linguists" and giving Sarah training similar to conditional discrimination of some of these constituents. Premack and Premack (1972: 92) stated that:

we have been teaching Sarah to read and write with various shaped and colored pieces of plastic, each representing a word; Sarah has a vocabulary of about 130 terms that she uses with a reliability of between 75 and 80 percent.

By using pieces of plastic that adhered to a magnetized board, Premack claimed that he was able to train Sarah to use and understand the negative article, the interrogative, *wh* questions, the concept of "name of," dimensional classes, prepositions, hierarchically organized sentences, and the conditional. Premack and Premack (1972: 99) state that:

Sarah had managed to learn a code, a simple language that nevertheless included some of the characteristic features of natural language. Each step of the training program was made as simple as possible. The objective was to reduce complex notions to a series of simple and highly learnable steps ... compared with a two-year old child Sarah holds her own in language ability.

Washoe

Gardner and Gardner (1969; 1971) were successful in establishing two-way communication with their chimpanzee, Washoe. Their success might be attributed to the facts that they used a gestural mode of communication (American Sign Language for the Deaf), a chimpanzee as a subject, and the substantial immersion of Washoe in an environment of sign language. By teaching Washoe to use ASL they successfully avoided the problem of anatomical differences, specifically the lack of tongue mobility in the chimpanzee (Lieberman 1968; Lieberman et al. 1972). By using gestures they capitalized on the chimpanzees' natural ability to use gestures to communicate in the wild (van Lawick-Goodall 1968; Kortlandt 1967) and in captivity (Yerkes 1943; Schenkel 1964; and van Hooff 1971).

Washoe was a wild-collected female chimpanzee between eight and fourteen months of age when she arrived in Reno, Nevada, in June, 1966. She lived in a completely self-contained house trailer in the Gardners' large (5000 square feet) backyard. The members of the research team who worked with Washoe during all her waking hours used only ASL to communicate with Washoe and each other. Each served as a conversing companion, a teacher, and an ASL model. Thus, their major function was to immerse Washoe in an environment of ASL by using it during the general activities of the day.

In addition to the usual way human children acquire language, via imitation, Washoe was also taught signs in somewhat structured situations, i.e. intentional attempts to teach her a new sign or improve the form of a sign she was already using. For example, when Washoe would make a gestural response that resembled an ASL sign, suitable rewards were administered so that the gestural response was shaped into a closer approximation of the sign. The Gardners used this shaping technique to introduce new signs during the first year of the project; however, it became apparant that guidance (molding) was a more efficient method. Guidance involved mechanically guiding Washoe's arms and hands into the correct position and movement for a sign in the presence of stimuli representing the sign. Of course, several of her signs were not intentionally taught; she acquired them by imitating her human companions.

Washoe presently has over 160 different signs in her vocabulary. The vocabulary size is interesting but not nearly so interesting as how she combines her signs. By the time Washoe had eight or ten signs she began combining them sequentially. Washoe used her combination of signs in contextually correct situations; e.g. OPEN FLOWER to be let through the garden gate of a flower garden; KEY OPEN PLEASE BLANKET to have a blanket cupboard unlocked; and FOOD OPEN HURRY to a locked refrigerator. Washoe also showed a preference for sign order in her signing which might be interpreted as the rudiments of syntax. For example, she clearly preferred to use the pronoun sign YOU preceding the sequence of a verb and the pronoun sign ME.

Washoe was tested on her vocabulary in double-blind situations that precluded the possibility of someone inadvertently giving her the correct answer. On a preliminary box test of objects representing signs in her vocabulary, Washoe got fifty-three correct out of ninety-nine; this was far above chance level (three correct out of ninety-nine). Also, Washoe's errors fit into meaningful categories such as animals, grooming articles, and food categories. For example, she might err by signing CAT for a picture of a dog.

In addition to double-blind tests, the Gardners also kept a comprehensive diary of Washoe's signing and also sampled her combinations in various contextual situations.

For a more complete explanation of Project Washoe, see Gardner and Gardner (1971).

ASL RESEARCH USING SEVERAL CHIMPANZEES

In October of 1970, Washoe and the author came to the Institute for Primate Studies in Norman, Oklahoma. The Institute for Primate Studies is a chimpanzee colony directed by W. B. Lemmon. The major research at the Institute is concerned with the general social behavior of chimpanzees. The Institute's facilities and ongoing research proved to be not only an excellent new home for Washoe, but also an excellent place for the expansion of ASL teaching to several chimpanzees. At this point some of the completed studies and findings that have taken place at the Institute will be described.

One of the first studies done at the Institute (Fouts 1973) questioned whether chimpanzees other than Washoe would be able to acquire signs; were there individual differences in the chimpanzees' ability to acquire signs; and was there consistent ease or difficulty in acquiring particular signs across chimpanzees?

In this study, two male and two female chimpanzees were each taught ten signs in ASL. Each chimpanzee was given one to three training sessions a day depending on their cooperativeness on a given day. Molding or guidance (Fouts 1972) was used as the method of teaching the signs during the session. The acquisition rate for each sign was compared on the basis of the number of minutes required to reach a criterion of five consecutive unprompted responses.

After all of the chimpanzees had acquired all of the signs, they were tested in a double-blind box test similar to a test described by Gardner and Gardner (1971). A person hidden behind a blind put an object representing a sign in a box. Another person opened the box so that only the chimpanzee could see its contents and then two blind-observers independently recorded the chimpanzees' sign for the object.

All of the chimpanzees acquired all of the signs. There were individual differences between the chimpanzees in their speed of acquiring signs. The mean number of minutes required to acquire a sign for each chimpanzee were: 54.3, 79.7, 136.4, and 159.1. Also, some of the signs were consistently easy or difficult to acquire for all four chimpanzees.

The percentage of correct responses by the chimpanzees in the double-blind box test were: 26.39 percent, 58.33 percent, 59.72 percent, and 90.28 percent. All of the chimpanzees performed above chance level (one out of nine correct).

We have also begun to gather data concerning the use of ASL in intraspecific communication between chimpanzees. Washoe often signs to the other chimpanzees, but unfortunately many of those whom she signs to either do not have any ASL signs or do not have adequate vocabularies. We have recently (Fouts, Mellgren, and Lemmon 1973) begun a study that we hope will not only tap intraspecific ASL communication, but also the posibility of one chimpanzee acquiring signs from another. We have started this study with two young male chimpanzees, Booee and Bruno, with limited vocabularies (thirty-eight signs each). We are presently exploring situations that are conducive to ASL conversation and recording their conversations. After we have gained sufficient knowledge and data concerning this we will introduce Washoe, with her large vocabulary, into this dyad and watch for ASL sign acquisition among the three chimpanzees in addition to recording their intraspecific ASL communication. Presently, in the early stages, we have observed intraspecific ASL communication in such situations as mutual comforting, food eating (and, when they are in a rare mood, food sharing), and general play activities such as tickle games. For example, Booee was once observed to go to Bruno and ask Bruno to TICKLE BOOEE. Bruno at the time was eating some raisins from one of the experimenters' hands and he signed to Booee BOOEE ME FOOD thus refusing Booee's request. The food eating situation has turned out to be somewhat of a one-way ASL communication because neither of the two males seems to want to share food with the other. For example, when one of the two chimpanzees has a desired fruit or drink the other chimpanzee will sign such combinations as GIMME FRUIT or GIMME DRINK. Generally, when the chimpanzee with the desired food sees this request he runs off with his prized posession. In the mutual comforting situation some of the combinations are such things as COME HUG or COME HURRY. Because this experiment is still in the intitial stages a complete data analysis has not yet been done.

In addition to the chimpanzees at the main primate colony there are chimpanzees being reared in human homes in species isolation (isolated from their species) as a part of a study on maternal behavior. The chimpanzees are also used in species isolation as subjects for the study of ASL acquisition and usage.

We (Mellgren, Fouts, and Lemmon 1973) have recently completed a study examining the conceptual ability of one of these chimpanzees, Lucy, in regard to a category of items she is familiar with, in addition to examining the effect of a new sign on a conceptual category. Lucy was presented with twenty-four different fruits and vegetables. Over a period of four days she was asked what the fruits and vegetables were in order to gather baseline data for the responses to these items. The signs she had in her vocabulary that were food-related signs were: FOOD, FRUIT, DRINK, CANDY, and BANANA. She used FOOD, FRUIT, and DRINK in a generic manner, whereas BANANA was specific to bananas. After the four days of baseline data the sign BERRY was taught to her using a cherry as an exemplar. She was presented with the fruits and vegetables for eight more days in order to determine whether the BERRY sign would generalize to the other berry-like items, or whether it would remain highly specific to cherries as the BANANA sign is specific to bananas. The BERRY sign remained specific to the cherries. After day eight she was taught the BERRY sign using a blackberry as an exemplar. She called the blackberry BERRY for two days and then returned to using FRUIT or FOOD to describe it; BERRY was not only specific to cherry but there seemed to be a resistance to using the sign for other items. This might be analogous to the point when a child linguistically develops from calling all four-footed furry animals "dog" to being able to identify individual species.

Perhaps even more interesting were the serendipitous findings concerning her responses to particular items. Her use of ASL appeared to affect the way she conceptualized these items, that is, how she perceived these items. There were four citrus fruits in the twenty-four items and they accounted for 65 percent of the SMELL responses; they were SMELL FRUITS. She was probably referring to the rather pungent odiferous quality of the four citrus fruits (orange, grapefruit, lemon, and lime). She labeled a radish FOOD the first three days. However, on the fourth day she started to take a bite out of it and then spit it out. She then called it a CRY HURT FOOD and then continued to use CRY or HURT or both to describe it for the next eight days. She mainly used DRINK to describe a quarter piece of watermelon; she also labeled it a DRINK FRUIT twice and a CANDY DRINK three times. There was also a clear preference on her part to use the FRUIT sign to describe the fruit items and the FOOD sign to describe the vegetables. It appears that Lucy was able to use various signs in her vocabulary in novel combinations to describe novel stimuli (e.g. CRY HURT FOOD).

Washoe has also shown signing behavior which involved the novel recombination of signs in her vocabulary to describe a referent she did not have a sign for. For example, I often take Washoe for boat rides in a pond surrounding a chimpanzee island at the Institute. The pond is inhabited by two very territorial and nasty swans. Since I do not have a sign for swan I refer to them with the DUCK sign. Washoe does not have the DUCK sign in her vocabulary so she refers to the swans as WATER BIRDS.

Another study (Fouts, Chown, and Goodin 1973) was done using a young male chimpanzee, Ally, on the relationship between his understanding of the English language and his production of ASL. Ally is also being reared in a human home and thus is constantly exposed to vocal English in addition to having an ASL vocabulary of over seventy signs. The study is comparable to second language acquisition in humans. In the pretraining we used strictly vocal English to test his understanding of ten preselected spoken English words. We gave him vocal English commands such as "bring me the spoon" when the particular object was one of several possible choices. When Ally had met a criterion of five consecutive correct choices for each of the ten words, training was begun. In training the list of ten words was divided into two lists of five. One experimenter taught a sign to the stimulus of a vocal word. Later, a second person, who did not know what had been taught or if the sign had been acquired, tested Ally on all five of the items by asking him WHAT THAT in ASL to each of the five objects. It was a blind procedure to control the possibilty of cueing Ally to the correct answer. Ally tranferred all of the signs from the vocal words to the objects. This is similar to the way a second language is acquired. For example, in a Spanish class a teacher is able to tell the students that *sombrero* means the same thing as hat. Then, if the student has made this association, he is able to label the object hat with the Spanish word *sombrero*.

The experiment also has cross-modal implications. For example, in the pretest phase the vocal stimulus was associated with a visual stimulus. During training a gestural response was taught to the vocal stimulus. Then in testing the appropriate gestural response was used to label the visual stimulus.

⌠ Besides the formal studies of the different aspects of ASL usage in chimpanzees there have been several observations of ASL usage that the chimpanzees generated themselves. For example, Gardner and Gardner (1971) noted that Washoe invented her own sign for bib. A similar event happened in Oklahoma. Lucy, who is being reared in a human home, enjoys going for walks. Unfortunately, there is a busy highway nearby, so a leash is necessary for her own safety. Since I do not know the ASL sign for leash I have not referred to it with a sign. Lucy invented a sign for leash which is a hooking action with her extended index finger on her neck. The leash was obviously something important to her, since she enjoyed going out so much. This is probably the reason she invented the sign for it. But it should be noted that she does not care for the leash; she would much prefer to do without it. This behavior also seems to suggest that she is grasping the symbolic relationship between the signs in ASL and their referents. ⌡

The chimpanzees have also changed the grammatical function of a word; i.e. a noun to an adjective. For example, I was about to teach Washoe the sign MONKEY and while I was preparing the data sheet she turned around and began to interact with a particularly obnoxious macaque in a holding cage behind us. They threatened each other in the typical chimpanzee manner and macaque manner. After I had prepared the data sheet I stopped the aggressive interaction and turned her around so that she was facing two siamangs. I asked her what they were in ASL. She did not respond. After I molded her hands into the correct position for the MONKEY sign three times she began to refer to the siamangs with the MONKEY sign. I interspersed questions referring to various objects that she had signs for in her vocabulary. Next, I turned her toward the adjacent cage holding some squirrel monkeys and she transferred the MONKEY sign immediately to them. After she called the squirrel monkeys MONKEY several times I turned her around and asked her what her previous adversary, the macaque, was and she consistently referred to him as a DIRTY MONKEY. Up until this time she had used the DIRTY sign to refer to feces and soiled items, in other words as a noun. She had changed the usage from a noun to an adjective. In essence, it could be said that she had generated an insult. Since that time she has similarly used the dirty sign to refer to me as DIRTY ROGER, once when I signed to her that I could not grant her request to be taken off the chimpanzee island (OUT ME), and another time when she asked me for some fruit (FRUIT ME) and I signed SORRY BUT I NOT HAVE ANY FRUIT.

Lucy has also used the DIRTY sign in a similar manner. Once she referred to a strange cat she had been interacting with aggressively as a DIRTY CAT, and she has also referred to the leash (which she dislikes) as a DIRTY LEASH.

BEYOND CHIMPANZEES

The capacity to acquire a sign and then use it as a referent for an object or action does not appear to be limited to chimpanzees. But, presently, there are only exploratory incipient studies using other species of apes. I did a short exploratory study using one infant orangutan to determine if he could acquire signs. He did acquire signs (e.g. DRINK, FOOD, TICKLE, etc.) and he also combined them into two-sign combinations. Because of the lack of time on the experimenter's part, the study has not been continued. Most certainly it should not be considered a definitive study, but it can be stated that at least one infant orangutan is capable of acquiring signs. This is not a surprising result since Furness (1916) was able to teach an orangutan two vocal words, which is a comparable result to the Hayes and Hayes' (1951) result with a chimpanzee acquiring four spoken words.

A research project concerning the acquisition of ASL in an infant gorilla has been recently started at Stanford University by Francine Patterson. Patterson (personal communication) informed me that the nineteen-month-old female gorillla she is working with presently uses six signs. The gorilla also uses the MORE sign in combination with FOOD, DRINK, and OUT.

Even though these studies are incomplete, it appears that primates other than chimpanzees and man may have the capacity for ASL acquisition and usage.

LANGUAGE BEHAVIOR IN PROTOHOMINIDS

Because language, as most behavioral patterns, does not leave a fossil record, comparisons of modern nonhuman species must be used to estimate the evolutionary history of language. The language acquisition research done on nonhuman primates has been used to support language origin theories in man. At first glance this may seem a rather tenuous comparison since there have been so many millions of years of separate evolution between man and apes. But, just as there are differences between the species, there are also many similarities, and it is possible that the capacities for language in man and apes may be different in degree rather than kind. It is also possible that early man would have at least had a capacity for language comparable to that of the modern chimpanzee.

The question now is what kind of language was most probably used by early man, vocal or gestural? Hewes (1971, 1973) states that language was most probably gestural. A switchover from gestural to vocal may have occurred in the Middle and Upper Paleolithic which may be associated with the accelerated rate of culture growth during that period. Most likely, there were long periods of overlap or coexistence. Hewes goes on to state that:

It is conceivable that the continuing effectiveness of non-vocal communication across language boundaries, sometimes also involving cultural boundaries which, technologically at least, correspond to separations going back to the late Upper Paleolithic — as in the case of gestural communication with the long-isolated aborigines of Tasmania — rests not so much on learned behaviors which happen to approximate cultural universals, but upon a built-in ability in our species to encode its ideas manually whenever vocal habits prove to be ineffective. To Lenneberg's reasonable claim that the human capacity for language acquisition [he is referring of course to VOCAL language acquisition] is innate, in which he is at one with Chomsky, I would add that propositional communication by means of gestures is a capacity not only innate in man, but, in a rudimentary form at least, may go back to the undivided common stock from which modern pongids and hominids have descended. Manual communication may possibly be seen as more directly representative than speech of the deep cognitive structure on which not only language but all the higher intellectual achievements of mankind depend.

Hewes used the evidence of drawing, painting, and sculpture in the Upper Paleolithic as support for evidence of gestures in that these can be viewed as "frozen gestures."

Hewes' works on glottogenesis are most scholarly and thorough. This is true not only of his articles but also of his bibliography on the subject (Hewes 1971). It would be pretentious of me to attempt to add to his logical scholarly works on this subject. Note that he used the chimpanzee language acquisition research to support his hypothesis concerning glottogenesis.

Stokoe (1972) has commented on Hewes' (1971, 1973) work, in addition to correcting many of the misunderstandings concerning the nature of sign languages which served to further strengthen Hewes' arguments.

Stokoe coins the word *gSign* to refer to gestural manifestations with a sign vehicle in a semiotic system. An *sSign* is equivalent to a *gSign* except that it is another communication mode (speech). Stokoe points out that *gSigns* are not merely isomorphically gestural representations of spoken language, but that "the gSigns of a natural sign language relate differently to their denotata and also have different kinds of denotata unrelated to any spoken language" (Stokoe 1972).

Stokoe also notes the assumption that there exists an unbridgeable gap between the *gSign* as an affect display and the *gSign* as a language element. His arguments show that there is most likely a semiotic and evolutionary continuum between them. The denotative richness of *gSigns* is not the only important potential for language development; also important is their similarity to the physical activities of tool-making and using; i.e. the fact that the dominant hand leads while the subordinate hand lags for both tool-using and *gSigns*. Stokoe also points out that the ability to mold a sign into the correct position would ensure accurate cultural transmission of *gSigns* across generations and this might also explain the high degree of similarity between especially iconic *gSigns* across different cultures. In fact, such iconic signs as *work, touch,* and *pound* could conceivably have aboriginal origins. Also, *gSigns* can be used in several circumstances where *sSigns* cannot (e.g. over large distances); but what of the criticism "What did they do after the campfire went out?" The answer is simply that they most probably did what deaf people do in dark rooms – mold the receiver's hands into the proper gestures. Stokoe says:

This is not to say that sign languages have remained relatively unchanged from Paleolithic times — much of the foregoing has emphasized their adaption to full human language capacity — but it may help to account for the occurrence as long noted (e.g., Mallery, 1972 [1881]) of those g-Sign-denotatum connections to be found universally in human cultures. And Hewes' theory goes far to explain why all this should be so.

There is a good case for language origin being gestural in nature; however, this does not preclude the possibility of a simultaneous development of language using both the vocal mode and the gestural mode. The question need not be perceived in either-or terms. Given what we know about protohominids, it is quite easy to conceive of important situations in a protohominid's life that would best be suited to gestural communication, and other situations where the vocal mode would be the most propitious. However, what would appear to be the most important determiner of which mode would be used (if it were possible that both could be used) is the physiological and structural feasibility of a vocal mode (even more so than for a gestural mode). Because, according to Lieberman et al. (1972), the necessity of having a specifically and properly shaped vocal tract for human speech appears to be the prerequisite for human vocal speech, determining physiological feasibility would be important before we could assume any human-like speech production in the protohominids. But gestural communication is not dependent on any delicate peripheral structures. The presence of limbs on a protohominid probably is all the peripheral structure necessary for some form of gestural communication.

Also, it is important to consider what model is a viable one for speculating about protohominid language. If the extant chimpanzee species is used as the model, then vocalization must be reconsidered in a new light. First, chimpanzee vocalizations do carry information about an individual chimpanzee's reaction to the environment, but given our present knowledge about chimpanzee vocalizations they appear to be emotive in nature; it is almost as if the chimpanzee vocalizations are elicited by situational releasers in the environment. On the other hand, the gestures of chimpanzees seem to have more plasticity; in fact, Kortlandt (1967) has suggested that wild chimpanzees may even have local conventions in their gestural communications.

Further, the problem of changing the vocalization from being emotive in nature to being referential is important to consider. In other words, just how much plasticity was there in protohominid vocalization? If protohominids were comparable to extant chimpanzees, then it would seem that gestures may have accounted for most of their communication. However, even if this were not so, the possibility still remains of an active gestural communication mode existing in the protohominids.

The question, however, is a theoretical one and subject to very little empirical support for either the gestural mode or the vocal mode. Perhaps the real answer will never be known with any certainty.

REFERENCES

BRONOWSKI, J., U. BELLUGI
    1970   Language, name and concept. *Science* 1968:669–673.
CHOMSKY, N.
    1967   "The formal nature of language," in *Biological foundations of language*. Edited by Eric Lenneberg, 397–442. New York: John Wiley.

1968   *Language and the mind*. New York: Harcourt, Brace and World.

DOBZHANSKY, T. H.
1972   "On the evolutionary uniqueness of man," in *Evolutionary biology*. Edited by T. H. Dobzhansky, M. K. Hecht, and W. C. Steere, volume six, 415–430. New York: Appleton-Century-Crofts.

FOUTS, R.
1972   The use of guidance in teaching sign language to a chimpanzee (*Pan troglodytes*). *Journal of Comparative and Physiological Psychology* 80:515–522.
1973   Acquisition and testing of gestural signs in four young chimpanzees. *Science* 180:978–980.

FOUTS, R., W. CHOWN, L. GOODIN
1973   "The use of vocal English to teach American Sign Language (ASL) to a chimpanzee: translation from English to ASL." Paper presented at the Southwestern Psychological Association Meeting in Dallas, Texas, April, 1973.

FOUTS, R., R. MELLGREN, W. LEMMON
1973   "American Sign Language in the chimpanzee: chimpanzee-to-chimpanzee communication." Paper presented at the Midwestern Psychological Association Meeting in Chicago, Illinois, May, 1973.

FURNESS, W.
1916   Observations on the mentality of chimpanzees and orangutans. *Proceedings of the American Philosophical Society* 45:281–290.

GARDNER, B. T., R. A. GARDNER
1971   "Two-way communications with an infant chimpanzee," in *Behavior of nonhuman primates*. Edited by A. M. Schrier and F. Stollnitz, volume four, chapter three. New York: Academic Press.

GARDNER, R. A., B. T. GARDNER
1969   Teaching sign language to a chimpanzee. *Science* 165:664–672.

HAYES, K., C. HAYES
1951   The intellectual development of a home-raised chimpanzee. *Proceedings of the American Philosophical Society* 95:105–109.
1952   Imitation in a home-raised chimpanzee. *Journal of Comparative and Physiological Psychology* 45:450–459.

HEBB, D. O., W. E. LAMBERT, G. R. TUCKER
1973   A DMZ in the language war. *Psychology Today* 6(11):55–62.

HEWES, G.
1971   "New light on the gestural origin of language," in *Language origins: a bibliography*, by G. Hewes. Boulder, Colorado: Published by the author.
1973   Primate communication and the gestural origin of language. *Current Anthropology* 14:5–24.

HOCKETT, C. F.
1958   *A course in modern linguistics*. Toronto: Macmillan.
1959   "Animal 'languages' and human language," in *The evolution of man's capacity for culture*. Edited by J. N. Spuhlere, 32–39. Detroit: Wayne University Press.

KORTLANDT, A.
  1967 "Experimentation with chimpanzees in the wild," in *Progress in primatology*. Edited by D. Starck, R. Schneider, and H. J. Kuhn, 208–224. Stuttgart: Gustav Fischer.

LASHLEY, K. S.
  1951 "The problem of serial order in behavior," in *Cerebral mechanisms in behavior*. Edited by L. A. Jeffress, 112–136. New York: John Wiley and Sons.

LENNEBERG, E. H.
  1967 *Biological foundations of language*. New York: John Wiley.
  1971 Of language knowledge, apes, and brains. *Journal of Psycholinguistic Research* 1:1–29.

LIEBERMAN, P.
  1968 Primate vocalizations and human linguistic ability. *Journal of the Acoustical Society of America* 44:1574–1584.

LIEBERMAN, P., E. CRELIN, D. KLATT
  1972 Phonetic ability and related anatomy of the newborn and adult human, Neanderthal man, and the chimpanzee. *American Anthropologist* 74:287–307.

MALLERY, D. G.
  1972 [1881] *Sign language among North American Indians compared with that among other peoples and deaf mutes*. With a Foreword by Th. A. Sebeok. The Hague: Mouton.

MARLER, P.
  1965 "Communication in monkeys and apes," in *Primate behavior: field studies of monkeys and apes*. Edited by I. DeVore, 544–584. New York: Holt, Rinehart and Winston.

MELLGREN, R., R. FOUTS, W. LEMMON
  1973 "American Sign Language in the chimpanzee: semantic and conceptual functions of signs." Paper presented at the Midwestern Psychological Association Meeting in Chicago, Illinois, May, 1973.

PREMACK, A. J., D. PREMACK
  1972 Teaching language to an ape. *Scientific American* 227:92–99.

PREMACK, D.
  1971a Language in chimpanzee? *Science* 172:808–822.
  1971b "On the assessment of language competence in the chimpanzee," in *Behavior of nonhuman primates*. Edited by A. M. Schrier and F. Stollnitz, volume four, chapter four. New York: Academic Press.

SCHNEIRLA, T.
  1966 Behavioral development and comparative psychology. *Quarterly Review of Biology* 41:283–302.

SCHENKEL, R.
  1964 Zur Ontogenese des Verhalten bei Gorilla und Mensch. *Zeitschrift für Morphologie und Anthropologie* 54:233–259.

SIMPSON, G.
  1964 *This view of life*. New York: Harcourt, Brace.

STOKOE, W.
   1972   "Motor signs as the first form of language." Paper presented at the American Anthropological Association Meeting in Toronto, December, 1972.
THORPE, W.
   1972   "The comparison of vocal communication in animals and man," in *Non-verbal communication*. Edited by R. A. Hinde, 27–47. Cambridge: Cambridge University Press.
VAN HOOFF, J. A. R. A. M.
   1971   *Aspects of the social behavior and communication in human and higher non-human primates*. Rotterdam: Broder-Offset.
VAN LAWICK-GOODALL, J.
   1968   The behaviour of free-living chimpanzees in the Gombe Stream Reserve. *Animal Behaviour Monographs* 1(3):161–311.
YERKES, R. M.
   1943   *Chimpanzees*. New Haven: Yale University Press.

The Language Skills of a Young Chimpanzee in a Computer-Controlled Training Situation

DUANE M. RUMBAUGH, E. C. VON GLASERSFELD,
TIMOTHY V. GILL, HAROLD WARNER, PIER PISANI,
JOSEPHINE V. BROWN, and C. L. BELL

Contrary to the belief that only man is capable of productive linguistic communication, evidence is accumulating which suggests that other life forms, notably the chimpanzee (*Pan*), are capable of mastering at least an elementary vocabulary and possibly syntax. The Gardners (1969, 1971), for example, demonstrated that their chimpanzee, Washoe, mastered a large number of hand-produced signs, which she chained, from time to time, with apparent appropriateness to novel situations. Also, Premack (1970, 1971) has reported that his chimpanzee, Sarah, learned to use plastic objects as words and that she attended to their order of presentation in a way that suggested mastery of rules for sentence structure. The use of hand signs by the Gardners and the use of plastic objects as words by Premack reflect cognizance of the fact that the chimpanzee's vocal apparatus lacks the anatomical and neurological features necessary for the production of phonemes used in human speech (Lieberman 1968; Lieberman, Klatt, and Wilson 1969).

Although the works of the Gardners and Premack have served to renew interest in questions concerned with the possibility that language is not a uniquely human skill, they leave unanswered two important questions: (1) Does the chimpanzee, and possibly other anthropoids as well, have the capacity for linguistic "productivity" (Hockett 1960) which characterizes man's communications? (2) If so, what is the scope of the ape's capacity for language? Will it provide for creative expressions, as descriptions or questions, and will it allow for conversation with man or between apes?

This research was supported by NICHD grant HD 06016-01,02 and by NIH grant RR-00165.

The authors have worked cooperatively — pooling their skills in psychology, psycholinguistics, biomedical engineering, computer technology, and electronics — to design and build a computer-controlled language training situation in order to extend objective and efficient inquiry into the language capabilities of young apes. At the time of this writing, work with a young female chimpanzee, Lana, now almost three years old, has been in progress for seven months. As the technical details of the system have been described elsewhere (Rumbaugh et al. 1973), only the main characteristics of the training situation will be described here.

A large plastic chamber serves both as Lana's home and training situation. With the exception of time for daily out-of-doors exercise, she spends twenty-four hours a day in the chamber. In direct proportion to her mastery of the special language, Yerkish, devised for the research, she can exercise control over the events of the day.

YERKISH

The rules governing the formation of sentences in Yerkish are defined by a modified version of English correlational grammar (von Glasersfeld and Pisani 1970). Correlational grammar differs from traditional grammars in that it does not distinguish between syntax and semantics. Its word-classes are based on a semantic or conceptual classification, not on the morphological surface characteristics of words. Its syntax is based on a detailed specification of relational concepts and their applicability to items of the conceptual word-classes rather than on the very generic syntactic functions or connectives of traditional grammars. Thus, instead of the usual word-class "noun," Yerkish has at present fifteen lexigram-classes of items that can function as "subject" in a sentence; instead of the usual word-class "verb," there are ten lexigram-classes of items that designate different activities; and instead of the traditional subject-verb functions, Yerkish has nine "correlators" representing conceptually different "actor-activity" relations.

As a result of this concept-sensitive syntax, word combinations such as "[the] banana eats" or "Lana drinks [a] banana," which according to traditional grammar would be syntactically correct and only semantically deviant, are improper in the correlational syntax of Yerkish.

In the present implementation of the system (operational since December 1972), sentences are limited to a length of seven lexigrams and an end-sign equivalent to a period. A sentence is defined as the string of lexigrams between a start signal (triggered by the subject's grasping and hanging on to the "GO BAR" above the keyboard) and the period sign.

For the past several months, Lana has obtained all of her food and drinks and, also, movies, music, a toy, a blanket, etc., by formulating the appropriate requests. Lana expresses her communications through the serial selection and depression of the appropriate keys, each one designating a word, on keyboards which are mounted on one wall of her chamber. A computer, which is interfaced with the keyboards, determines if her communications adhere to the rules of Yerkish grammar and, if so, automatically dispenses the incentive or event requested. To date, essentially all of Lana's formulations have been requests, but the system provides flexibility even for eventual conversation between Lana and us, in which case we would use a keyboard functionally equivalent to Lana's while the computer served as the reliable intermediary. All that transpires is recorded by a teletype on punched paper tape for computer analysis and, also, on a typed paper record for visual inspection.

Lana now has fifty lexigrams available at any one time. Eventually she will have 125 lexigrams available, though from day to day or even within the course of a day they need not be a constant set of 125 words. We exercise ready control over the words available to Lana by selectively activating or deactivating the keys in accordance with the demands of certain tests conducted and in the interests of controlling the amounts of certain incentives that Lana can receive. For example, her diet is balanced by deactivating keys for those foods which would be undesirable in unlimited amounts — M&M candies, banana, etc.; at times, all she can request is monkey chow, the main staple of her rations.

Each key is made of clear acrylic plastic. Lights mounted behind the keys allow for (1) no back-lighting, which signals Lana that the keys are inactive, (2) low-level back-lighting, which signals Lana that the keys are active and that correct selection and depression of them will be honored by the computer, and (3) high-level back-lighting, which coincides with depression of the key.

Depression of an active key results in the production of a facsimile of the lexigram, embossed on the key's surface, on one of the projectors positioned above the keyboard (Plate 1). Lexigrams used in a given formulation by Lana are produced from left-to-right in the row of projectors regardless of the arrangement of the lexigram-embossed keys on the keyboard. This display allows Lana to refer to the visual readout of her formulations and, more importantly, provides both Lana and us with a channel of communication whereby questions, answers, and eventually the messages of conversation might be exchanged. The lexigram embossed on each key, then, functions as a word. The design of the keyboards allows for ready relocation of the keys so that only the lexigrams, and not positions of the keys on the keyboard, designate the words and their meanings.

All requests must start with PLEASE, which serves to activate one of the computer's subroutines. Sentence beginnings for other than a specific request must be appropriately composed, just as in conversation between people. All formulations must be terminated with a PERIOD, which serves as a signal to the computer to evaluate the formulation, determine its acceptability in accordance with the Yerkish grammar, and to respond appropriately, as with dispensation of an incentive. Depression of the PERIOD key also results in erasure of the expressed formulation (sentence) by the turning off of the projectors' lamps. All correct formulations, as determined by the computer, regardless of their nature, request or otherwise, are followed by the sounding of a tone intended to signal Lana that her expression has been acknowledged.

TRAINING

Within the first week's training, Lana first became skilled at pressing single lexigram-embossed keys for incentives, such as M&M, juice, water, monkey chow, and milk. Next, she readily learned to depress the PLEASE key prior to pressing the key for the desired incentive and to depress the PERIOD key thereafter. Lana was then required to press any one key of a series of keys which constituted a holophrase; depression of any one of the keys activated all of a given holophrase. With "[ ]" serving to embrace the words of a sample holophrase, she was required, for example, to respond PLEASE [MACHINE GIVE M&M] PERIOD. Upon mastery of that example, she was then required to press PLEASE [MACHINE GIVE] M&M/PERIOD, and then PLEASE/MACHINE/GIVE/M&M/ PERIOD. During this training, the keys were arranged in a row in the same order as they were to be pressed. The next step was to scramble the order of the words for a given sentence within a row, after which they were randomly distributed within a matrix of 25 keys. Finally, words of other sentences, built up through the use of breaking apart holophrases, were present AND active, requiring of Lana that she carefully search and select from a number of keys. The reader should be reminded once again that the positions of the keys were randomly changed from day to day to require that Lana search and discriminate among the keys carefully prior to responding.

In this manner Lana learned to ask for juice, water, banana, monkey chow, a ball, a movie, for the window blind to be removed, and, occasionally, for music. Within the first six weeks she worked for all of her food and liquids. She continues to learn new words to add to her present vocabulary of forty-six words (August 1, 1973) and to learn new sentences.

A major concern was that Lana might never attend to the production of the lexigrams on the projectors above her keyboards, a requisite for conversation with her. This concern proved unwarranted, however, for quite on her own she came to attend to and discriminate between them. Her initial attending to them probably reflects the fact that their illumination coincides in time with the depression of selected keys.

Reading

Fortuitous observations first suggested that she "read" the projected lexigrams. For example, from time to time as she climbed on the GO BAR, she accidentally hit and depressed keys. For instance, when she thus had depressed the key for PLEASE and then subsequently addressed herself to work on the keyboard, she apparently noted that PLEASE was already present on the first of the projectors, for she simply ADDED to the word PLEASE the other lexigrams appropriate to her request for food or drink. Coupled with the following observation regarding Lana's innovative use of the PERIOD key, a number of "reading" experiments were suggested to us (Rumbaugh, Gill, and von Glasersfeld 1973).

Lana learned on her own that if she made an error, either in the selection of an intended key or in the order of depressing an otherwise appropriately selected key, there was nothing to be "gained" by continuing the sentence to completion. Under these conditions, she has come to press the PERIOD key, which serves to "erase" the projectors and the error and to advance in time the opportunity to try once again. After we observed this innovative, adaptive response to errors, we considered that if we were to systematically initiate sentences for her through use of our keyboard, she might attempt to complete ONLY those sentence beginnings that were valid (acceptable to the computer's program) in accordance with her experience, and erase other sentence beginnings that were INVALID in the sense that they could not be completed to the system's satisfaction.

Pursuant to the above considerations, experiments were conducted to determine if Lana would differentially respond to our valid and invalid sentence beginnings by completing or erasing them, respectively. These were viewed as "reading" experiments in the literal sense of the word, for in each of the first two studies there were at least two words in addition to the word PLEASE (required as the first word for all sentences of request) which had to be perceived with reference to (1) meaning and (2) sequence.

Experiment 1   Lana was given six different sets of three words which were presented as starts of sentences with which she was thoroughly familiar. One set was valid (could be built upon and completed to obtain an incentive) and five sets were varied and invalid. The valid beginning consisted of PLEASE MACHINE GIVE, to which Lana could add, at her option, JUICE, M&M, PIECE, OF, and BANANA. (The system requires that three words, PIECE OF BANANA, be added to PLEASE MACHINE GIVE for banana to be dispensed.) In addition to the available options listed, there were other word options which, in accordance with the computer's program, cannot be used if the first three words are PLEASE MACHINE GIVE. They were MACHINE and GIVE (both of which were superfluous in light of the valid beginning given to Lana), MOVIE, MAKE, TIM (the technician), LANA, and MUSIC. As the "machine" MAKES, not GIVES, music and movies, these words could not be used with the beginning PLEASE MACHINE GIVE. Similarly, the options of TIM, LANA, and MAKE could in no way be added to the valid beginning provided Lana, for her training up to the time of this experiment provided no model for their use after PLEASE MACHINE GIVE.

Invalid sentence beginnings were generated through random substitution of the following words for either MACHINE or GIVE or for both MACHINE and GIVE: JUICE, M&M, PIECE, OF, BANANA, MOVIE, MAKE, TIM, LANA, and MUSIC. For example, PLEASE PIECE GIVE, PLEASE MACHINE TIM, and PLEASE MOVIE LANA are all invalid sentence beginnings to which Lana's appropriate response should be a rejection and erasure through prompt depression of the PERIOD key, rather than an attempt at sentence-completion destined to fail.

The valid sentence beginning, PLEASE MACHINE GIVE, occurred every fifth trial, the remaining four trials being a randomly determined series of PLEASE "X" GIVE, PLEASE MACHINE "X," PLEASE "X" "X," with "x" representing a randomly selected word from the foregoing list.

Lana was 100 percent correct in sentence completion on the forty-one presentations of PLEASE MACHINE GIVE and 90 percent correct, defined by erasure through prompt depression of the PERIOD key, on the 114 trials on which she encountered an invalid combination as a sentence beginning.

Experiment 2   All conditions remained constant except for the substitution of the word MAKE for GIVE in the valid sentence-beginning trials. To the beginning, PLEASE MACHINE MAKE, could be added WINDOW OPEN (providing a thirty second view of the out-of-doors), MUSIC, or MOVIE (for a thirty second run of a 16-mm motion picture); however, other available options of M&M, BANANA, and JUICE could not be added successfully, for the machine GIVES, not MAKES, them. From the list of random "x"s, PIECE, OF, and BANANA, were deleted and replaced by WINDOW, OPEN, and WATER.

Lana was 86 percent correct in sentence completion on the forty-one presentations of PLEASE MACHINE MAKE and rejected through erasure 96 percent of the 114 invalid sentence beginnings. That she was somewhat less accurate with PLEASE MACHINE MAKE than she was with PLEASE MACHINE GIVE (Experiment 1) probably reflects her relatively greater, more extensive experience with GIVE than MAKE at the time of the study. That probability notwithstanding, her performance in sentence completion remained at a high level.

With twelve active keys, in both Experiments 1 and 2, from which Lana could select one or more keys, the probability of her being correct by chance on any given trial was about 8 percent. An overall performance of 95 percent correct is sufficient evidence to reject chance as the probable determinant of her actual accuracy. Lana was reading.

Experiment 3   In this experiment, ONLY valid beginnings were presented to Lana: (1) PLEASE, (2) PLEASE MACHINE, (3) PLEASE MACHINE GIVE, (4) PLEASE MACHINE GIVE PIECE, (5) PLEASE MACHINE GIVE PIECE OF, (6) PLEASE MACHINE MAKE, (7) PLEASE MACHINE MAKE WINDOW, (8) PLEASE TIM, (9) PLEASE TIM COME, and (10) PLEASE TIM COME INTO. As all of these sentences could be completed successfully, prompt use of the PERIOD key for erasure was never appropriate.

Lana could choose any or all of the word keys just listed, for they were all active, along with BANANA, M&M, MOVIE, OPEN, and ROOM. Her performance in percent correct when there were from one through five lexigrams provided in the sentence beginnings was, respectively, 80, 70, 76, 74, and 100 percent of a total of ten randomized presentations of each of the beginnings.

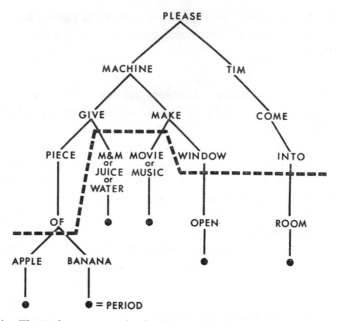

Figure 1.   The various sentence beginnings used in Experiments 3 and 4 are given above the dashed line; all of the keys for these words, except PLEASE, were operative and used by Lana in her attempts to complete the sentences. All of the options below the dashed line were available in Experiment 4; APPLE, JUICE, WATER, MUSIC, TICKLE, and LANA were NOT operative in Experiment 3

Experiment 4   This experiment was identical to Experiment 3 except that the additional options of APPLE, JUICE, WATER, MUSIC, TICKLE, and LANA were added. Figure 1 portrays the possible completions available to Lana as limited by both the specific lexigrams and number of lexigrams included in the sentence beginnings we gave her. Her accuracy scores with sentence-starts from one to five words were 100, 65, 93, 100, and 95 percent, respectively.

The results of these four experiments are taken as evidence that Lana accurately discriminates Yerkish lexigrams (words) presented to her, that she reads their serial order, and accurately discerns whether or not they can be added to in order to obtain various incentives.

Names of Objects

A manifestation of emerging language in the human child is the ability to properly identify various objects by name. Lana's ability to name objects was explored in the following manner.

In July, 1973, the question, ?WHAT NAME OF THIS, was presented systematically to Lana on her projectors. Either M&M candies or slices of banana were shown to her on a plastic tray as this question was posed. Over the course of sixteen days and a total of more than 1,200 training trials she came to respond with 94 percent accuracy within a span of one hundred consecutive trials using either M&M NAME OF THIS or BANANA NAME OF THIS.

We then questioned whether or not she would appropriately name other objects for which she had worked in her language training, i.e. water, juice, a ball, apple, and chow (monkey chow). These five items, along with M&Ms and banana were randomly sequenced in ten lists and presented for a total of seventy trials, ten trials per item. On the first presentation, Lana correctly named ball; however, she failed to name correctly the other four new items. In the first five trials for each of the new items she was 44 percent correct, and in the last five trials for each she was 80 percent correct. (She was 100 percent correct throughout with the presentations of M&Ms and banana.)

On the basis of the fact that she was correct on the FIRST presentation of one of the new items, ball, and improved very rapidly in naming the other objects within the limit of ten trials per item, we concluded that she had learned at least something about the fact that objects in general have names from her earlier training with just M&Ms and banana.

The research was extended by reacquainting her with her blanket and the lexigram for BLANKET, for she had not had access to them for several months. Subsequent to that retraining, Lana was presented with, in turn, blanket and milk and asked, ?WHAT NAME OF THIS. She was correct on both the first and second presentation of each object!

It seems reasonably clear that Lana has learned a considerable amount regarding the mastery of names. We have no evidence at this time that she uses the names symbolically, to represent objects in their absence, but in due course we intend to determine if that is the case.

DISCUSSION

Lana's rapid learning of language-relevant behaviors attests to the value of both the training system and training methods. Further, her achievements give us reason to be optimistic about eventual success in demonstrating that she is capable of linguistic productivity, which hopefully includes conversation with us. At present, however, in the interests of remaining objective rather than fanciful, a very real temptation in this area of research, we stop well short of concluding or even suggesting that Lana has demonstrated productive language capabilities. She has, nonetheless, impressed us with her achievements, and, at times, we believe that the greatest barrier to even more rapid progress on her part is our limited understanding as to how to best convey to her what it is that we are trying to teach. She remains highly motivated and gives us reason to believe that she "enjoys" the challenge of new tasks and disdains the routine.

From time to time, Lana is formulating new sentences which have apparent relevance to recent events. For example, when she completed a lengthy session of answering, ?WHAT NAME OF THIS, for M&Ms, banana, and the five aforementioned items, she shortly typed out the following statement: PLEASE, MACHINE, GIVE PIECE OF THIS. Was it by chance that she did so? Probably so, for she did it just once, in that particular way. On the other hand, it gives us cause to consider that "THIS" possibly came to represent something to her through the course of exhaustive testing, something which she wanted from the MACHINE for further examination. At the very least, it makes us wonder about cognitive processes she may possess which elude full examination.

Language is possibly not a uniquely human characteristic. If it is not, perhaps Lana will be the one to teach us truths which will profoundly alter our views and appreciation of the chimpanzee — and man.

REFERENCES

GARDNER, B. T., R. A. GARDNER
  1969 Teaching sign language to a chimpanzee. *Science* 165:664–672.
  1971 "Two-way communication with an infant chimpanzee," in *Behavior of nonhuman primates*, volume four. Edited by A. M. Schrier and F. Stollnitz. New York: Academic Press.
HOCKETT, CHARLES
  1960 The origin of speech. *Scientific American* 203(3):88–96.
LIEBERMAN, P.
  1968 Primate vocalizations and human linguistic ability. *Journal of the Acoustic Society of America* 4(6):1574–1584.
LIEBERMAN, P., D. H. KLATT, W. H. WILSON
  1969 Vocal tract limitations on the vowel repertoires of rhesus monkey and other nonhuman primates. *Science* 164:1185–1187.
PREMACK, DAVID
  1970 A functional analysis of language. *Journal of the Experimental Analysis of Behavior* 14(1):107–125.

1971 "On the assessment of language competence in the chimpanzee," in *Behavior of nonhuman primates,* volume four. Edited by A. M. Schrier and F. Stollnitz. New York: Academic Press.

RUMBAUGH, DUANE M., TIMOTHY V. GILL, E. C. VON GLASERSFELD
1973 Reading and sentence completion by a chimpanzee *(Pan). Science* 182:731–733.

RUMBAUGH, DUANE M., E. C. VON GLASERSFELD, HAROLD WARNER, PIER PISANI, TIMOTHY V. GILL, JOSEPHINE V. BROWN, C. L. BELL
1973 A computer-controlled language training system for investigating the language skills of young apes. *Behavior Research Methods & Instrumentation* 5(5):382–390.

VON GLASERSFELD, E., P. P. PISANI
1970 The Multistore Parser for hierarchical syntactic structures. *Communications of the Association for Computing Machinery* 13(2): 74–82.

Discussion

[Dr. Rumbaugh and Dr. Fouts summarized their papers and illustrated their research with cine films.]

LIEBERMAN: Linguists have traditionally defined language in terms of its uniqueness to man. This has taken the form of listing characteristics of human languages and then requiring that a system must possess all of the characteristics to be a language. It is a very strange way to approach the problem. This calls to mind Roger Fouts' example of defining a car (see Fouts, this volume). Language is simply a means of communication that transmits new information. The mechanisms that one needs to transmit this new information probably are mechanisms that are innate in the sense that there are various capabilities that you need in order to express this type of behavior. But there is no real evidence that they are unique to human language or for that matter even unique to language in general. One of the things that you need for language is automatized behavior. Sounds are produced automatically in human language but the function of language is not the making of sounds *per se*, it is communication. Chimpanzees make various gestures. And Fouts' chimpazees combine the gestures to transmit new information. Lana pushes keys on a computer (see Rumbaugh et al., this volume). This is also automatic. The important thing is what the animal is doing.

What kinds of functional elements do we recognize in both of these experiments? It is quite clear that the animals are behaving in what we would have to call a linguistic mode. For example, the syntax is doing something. The syntax of language is not there for fun. There are many aspects of syntax that are arbitrary. In some languages the noun will precede the adjective and in some languages it will follow the adjective. It does not make much difference. But other aspects are very functional. One of the attributes of human language is that words do not have unique semantic references. The word BANK can mean the place where you store money or the side of a river. It can be a noun or it can be a verb. We derive the meaning through the sentence. The syntax tells us. In "I will go to the bank and get some money" the meaning of bank is clear. In "Let us bank the road," bank is a verb. Now in both of the chimpanzee studies presented here it is quite clear that they are using language creatively. When Lana produced the sentence, "Please machine give me a piece of this," she extended THIS into a generalized noun phrase, a *wh*-type something. This is a form typical of human language or any language system. Roger, I recall one of your chimpanzees used two references for one word.

FOUTS: Yes, drink and food. For instance the chimpanzee used food as a verb when signing "Food me" though she also referred to FOOD as an object noun.

LIEBERMAN: That is typical of what syntax does. It is functioning there. It is difficult to envision how human language can be separated from animal language except perhaps in matters of speed or message inventory. There are these kinds of differences that might separate human language from the language of an ape. They can be very important behaviorally. You do not need any new mechanisms. For instance compare a digital computer and desk calculator. The same circuit elements are contained in the desk calculator and the digital computer. There are several million more logical connection elements in an IBM 360 than in a small desk calculator. However, the difference between the desk calculator and the large computer is not just that you can do the same sorts of problems faster with the latter. You can also do problems of a kind on the digital computer that you cannot do on the desk calculator. So what makes human language different from the language of other living hominoids? The so-called unique factor in human language is a very simple one. It is that we talk fast.

If I make short pulses you can count them up to a rate of about seven or ten per second. Beyond that they fuse and you hear a continuous tone. Yet human speakers talk at a rate of twenty per second. We really do not transmit twenty sounds per second. The traditional linguistic conception of phonemes or phonetic events as beads on a string is not really valid at the acoustic level. Acoustic cues for consonants like *b* and *t* in the word bat, are squashed onto the vowel. To decode this speech signal we have to go through a very elaborate process. It can be modeled on a computer. The syllable is scrambled in terms of the prospective articulatory gestures producing that acoustic gesture. Then the sound is perceived as composed of the original elements. In order to do this you have to know the size of the speaker. If someone has a vocal tract that is half the length of another person, e.g. comparing a seven-year-old child and an adult, the acoustic signal corresponding with the sound *uh* would be quite different. It would occur in two very different frequency ranges. The acoustic signal that an adult male produces for [ɪ] is identical to the acoustical signal that a small child produces for [ae]. To unscramble this, we normalize on the size of the vocal tract of the speaker that produces it. Thus we use vowels like [i], [u] and [a]. Certain other sounds like [s] also give us acoustic information that allows us to deduce what size vocal tract we are listening to.

We have tested this kind of recognition model on computers. The ability to make these sounds is a very recent acquisition in hominid evolution, probably occurring in the last million years. Hominid forms like La Chapelle, the classic Neanderthal type, who persisted until comparatively recent times could not make these sounds. We reconstructed their vocal tracts. They physically could not make these sounds. Other forms like Steinheim and Skūhl V could produce these sounds. Hence, there were hominids, some of whom were specializing for rapid speech communication, while others probably retained a system that mixed sounds and gestures. This does not mean that the ones who could not talk fast lacked language. It simply means that they were using a very different form of language. These different forms of linguistic behavior are very clearly evidenced by these apes (see Fouts and Rumbaugh et al., this volume).

RUMBAUGH: The language ape projects demonstrate that we have underestimated not only the linguistic capabilities of nonhuman animals but also their intelligence. We are getting far more impressive behavior out of chimpanzees in language training situations than we obtained through the more formal kinds of test procedures that psychologists have used extensively during the last thirty years in discrimination learning. Now we have solid evidence to substantiate a real edge in the learning abilities and transfer of training abilities in the apes. But that edge is really a profound underestimation of what these animals can do when given a very flexible challenging open-ended type of situation such as our language training program.

LIEBERMAN: There is an interesting concomitant to that. Do we in fact know how these animals communicate in the natural environment? Ethologists have tended to follow the Darwinian model a bit too closely.

KORTLANDT: We are still very far from decoding the complete system of communication of chimpanzees in the wild. Primarily what is needed is much more precise observation techniques, for example, video-taping on the spot to analyze and to decode. There are so many movements which they make only rarely. My team members discovered a certain gesture and told me about it. Later I saw that it occurred in zoos where I had worked for several years without recognizing it as a special and highly stereotyped gesture. It had not been noticed by any previous workers who had studied chimps in the wild.

LIEBERMAN: That reminds me of the comment by Daniel Jones, the famous English phonetician, that you do not know the phonetic elements of a language until you know the language.

AUDIENCE: It seems that language learning in apes always starts with questions, nouns, and imperatives. Are there other structures that cannot be interpreted as questions, nouns, and imperatives? If so, is there a special time needed before they can be introduced to such propositions?

RUMBAUGH: We started by having the animal make requests simply in the interest of getting her engaged with the training situation. By beginning with requests, we could require her to work for all of her food and drink, then expand from that point to ever increasing things. Next we introduced a series of questions like, "What name of this?" But we are shooting for nothing short of conversation. Clearly there has to be more than imperatives and questions.

LIEBERMAN: Chimpanzees can use conditional utterances. Premack demonstrated this with plastic markers and Roger Fouts with sign language. A chimpanzee will bargain with you. You might want the chimpanzee to read a book, but the chimpanzee may not want to read the book. So you say, "If chimpanzee will read book, I will tickle chimpanzee." The chimpanzee then reads the book. This is a complicated logical operation. Human infants do not get command of this sort of situation until they are four or five years old. Recall that in these studies we are dealing with juvenile chimpanzees. There is no reason to believe that they are going to proceed much faster than human infants do.

RUMBAUGH: It is important to distinguish whether the thing bargained for with an animal is a result of prolonged training with a given kind of request as Premack did, or they are doing something new on the first trial of the request. In our testing procedures we always try to use trial 1 performance of new questions or new tasks as the measurement of the animal having acquired the concept as opposed to just being conditioned over a period of time to comply with a redundant request.

FOUTS: There is a tendency among researchers to assume that if a chimpanzee has not evidenced a certain behavior that they are incapable of doing so. I fall into this tendency unintentionally because I am often surprised by some of the things that chimpanzees do. For example, I was preparing to teach Washoe the monkey sign. As I was making out the data sheets, she had an aggressive interaction with a macaque in a cage behind us. They threatened and tried to grab each other. I stopped this, turned around, and showed her the siamangs, which are not monkeys. I thought that she would not know the difference. I asked her what they were. There was no response. I gave her three prompts and she began to call them monkey, monkey, monkey. I interjected other things like "What is this?" to my shoe. She would sign shoe. Then I pointed toward the next cage which contained squirrel monkeys. She immediately transferred and they were monkeys too. This went on for a while. Then I turned to the macaque and said, "What is this?" She said, "Dirty monkey, dirty monkey, dirty monkey." Previously she had used the "dirty" sign specifically to refer to feces or to soiled items as a noun. She has since changed it into an adjective and expanded it beyond monkeys. One time she was on the chimpanzee island and I was on the shore. She kept saying, "Out, out me, come out me." I said, "Sorry but you have to stay there" (in sign language). She walked away signing, "Dirty Roger, dirty Roger." She has also done this when she is caged and says, "Give me fruit" or "Give me banana" and I reply, "Sorry, I do not have any." She will turn away and sign, "Dirty Roger, dirty Roger, dirty Roger." These things occurred without any training. And it surprised me. I did not expect it. I do not think that we should rely on negative evidence to establish differences between the chimpanzee and man. We are just beginning these studies. Language acquisition and language skills develop over a lifetime. The estimated maximum lifetime of a chimpanzee is sixty years. It is too early to look at our limits as such.

TUTTLE: I hope that you will make a movie entitled *Dirty Roger*.

LIEBERMAN: In most field studies of primate communication researchers implicitly assume that there is a one-to-one mapping between a particular vocal or gestural sign, and some "emotion." In 1872, Darwin discussed expression of emotions independent of habit and independent of will. He was probably referring to events like the death cry of the rabbit. If a person steps on someone's foot he does not emit the counterpart of a death cry. Instead he gives a very stylized output. The injured person might say "ouch" or simply stare at the offender. There is no direct gestural or vocal expression of the emotions. Further, in human face-to-face communication there is a very elaborate syntax. It depends on the context. But when researchers set out to study nonhuman primates they drop the notion of syntax, i.e. the rules of communication.

For instance, a gorilla might be observed in a number of different situations. Then the researcher asks, "What is the common element in all of these situations? Posing the question that way structures the reply toward a very primitive "emotion." If you did the same thing in studies of human speech, the only conclusion might be that phonation means affective behavior, i.e. two people are coming together. The situation is very complex. Peter Marler's movies of chimpanzees document very complex combinations of gestures and sounds. But the gestures have not yet been analyzed in a very careful way. And the sounds have to date been analyzed in very preliminary ways. A typical ethological paper will have sound spectrographs. Sound spectrographs are nothing in themselves. They are simply analyses performed by a very peculiar instrument that is set to give optimum results for the male human voice under certain very specific conditions. One can publish a sound spectrograph of the cry of a howling monkey, but no analysis has occured.

STRUHSAKER: I do not quite understand your comment that no analysis has been done or that nothing has been achieved by this. Perhaps you would suggest what you would do in a field situation.

LIEBERMAN: It is commonly recognized in studies of human speech that sound spectrographs *per se* tell almost nothing. One cannot read them. The first attempts to use sound spectrographs was to teach the deaf to use them as a means of communication. This failed completely. It is impossible. Experts at reading sound spectrographs have great difficulty telling approximately what is occurring. It is merely an analysis instrument which gives a particular transformation of the signal. In human communications, people use features, e.g. vocal gestures, that can be independently controlled. The basic difference between the sounds *b* and *p* in English relies on the fact that one can independently open the lips and independently move the larynx into position for formation. With *p* one delays the onset of phonation one hundred milliseconds after the release of the lips. In the Spanish *b* the reverse occurs. The speaker starts phonation one hundred milliseconds before release of the lips. These things are universal features of human language. Most apes have the laryngeal and mouth structures to produce these timing relationships. We should study the signals and form hypotheses such as: What kinds of maximal differentiation could these animals make? The techniques are available for acoustical analysis, computer modeling of the vocal abilities, and direct neuroelectric recording.

STRUHSAKER: Does it not depend to a large extent upon the question that you are asking?

LIEBERMAN: Yes.

STRUHSAKER: In addition to being concerned with the social communication, many of these field studies have also been interested in the physical properties of the sounds as they relate to the environment. There have been some extensive studies attempting to relate the adaptive significance of the physical features of sounds to particular habitats. These sonograms allow some measures of the frequency or pitch of the sound which can be related to the physical nature of the habitat. Perhaps you can suggest alternative methods to measure this.

LIEBERMAN: The acoustical information that can be extracted from the environment is very limited. Basically it can be summed up as high frequency propagation falls off very fast as a function of humidity. It is minimal in high humidity or extreme low humidity. It peaks in mid-range. The sound spectrograph typically tends to be used in a way that introduces artifacts. The interpretation does not go beyond the raw acoustic material to the kinds of mechanisms and factors that might be significant to the animal.

STRUHSAKER: Are you familiar with Morton's work with birds? Do you think that his analysis failed to reveal which features of their sounds were significant to them?

LIEBERMAN: Birds are not primates. What is appropriate for the bird in that kind of analysis is not for the primates.

*Capacities for Tool Behavior and
Hominid Evolution*

Primate Tool Behavior

BENJAMIN B. BECK

DEFINITION

Tool behavior refers to tool use and tool manufacture, terms that are widely discussed but inadequately defined. Alcock (1972: 464) defines tool use as "the manipulation of an inanimate object, not internally manufactured, with the effect of improving the animal's efficiency in altering the position or form of some separate object." This would describe a rat pressing a lever for food pellets in a Skinner box, a behavior that few would call tool use. Tool use is defined by van Lawick-Goodall (1970: 195) as "the use of an external object as a functional extension of mouth or beak, hand or claw, in the attainment of an immediate goal." She claims that birds' dropping or throwing stones on eggs to break the shells is tool use, while dropping or throwing eggs on stones is not. The distinction, while intuitively valid, is not derivable from the definition.

A satisfactory definition of tool use must include several qualifications. First, attached parts of the user's own body cannot serve as tools. Karrer (1970) describes as tool use crab-eating macaques (*Macaca fascicularis*) using their tails to secure objects out of arm's reach. If this categorization is valid, then hands, feet, wings, beak, teeth, and the like must also be tools, a premise that few would endorse. It is not necessary, however, to eliminate products of the user's own body as potential tools.

Second, the user must hold or carry the tool *in toto* during or just prior to use and the tool must be free of any fixed connection to the substrate. Chimpanzees (*Pan troglodytes*) are not using tools when they hold tough-skinned fruits and open them by banging them against rocks (van Lawick-Goodall 1968), but they are when they hold the rocks and bang them against the fruits (Rahm 1971). Similarly, chimpanzees are not using tools when they stand on branches and saplings and cause the distal ends to sway toward a conspecific, but they are when they brandish or throw an unattached branch at him (van Lawick-Goodall 1968, 1970). Without this qualification, a monkey traversing a branch to gain access to food must be considered to be using the branch as a tool, a conclusion with which few would agree.

Third, the tool user must establish the critical connection or spatial orientation between tool and incentive that enables the tool to be effective. A wild gibbon (*Hylobates lar*) pulling in a vine (C. Carpenter 1940) or a captive gibbon pulling in a string (Beck 1967) to get attached fruit is not tool use. This restriction excludes, among other behaviors, lever pressing in a Skinner box.

I propose a revision of Alcock's definition: tool use is the manipulation of an unattached environmental object, the tool (not part of the user's body), to alter more efficiently the form or position of a separate object, when the user holds or carries the tool *in toto* during or just prior to use and is responsible for the critical connection between tool and incentive. The grammatical and logical tortuousness of this definition is essential if tool use is to retain integrity as a behavioral category. The logic of previous definitions allowed categorization of almost any behavior as tool use and therefore did not replace intuitive notions.

The present definition excludes as tool use some behaviors that are strikingly similar, in both form and function to those it includes. For example, as noted above, chimpanzees are not using tools when they open fruits by banging them ON rocks, but they are when they bang fruits WITH rocks. Chimpanzees are not using tools when they disperse observers by defecating from the forest canopy, but they are when they achieve the same end by throwing feces. Monkeys are not using tools when their animated displays passively cause branches to fall or rocks to roll toward intruders, but they are using tools if the branches or rocks are held and then thrown or dropped. Further, the definition excludes behaviors that are felt by many to be tool use, e.g. nest building by pongids, which is excluded because the completed nest is not held or carried. If these distinctions are logically but not biologically sound, then tool use may not be justified as a distinct behavioral category.

The present definition is offered without consideration of purposiveness, symbolic mediation, or cognitive understanding of causal relationships. While critical and compelling, such processes are not yet sufficiently subject to operational definition or empirical manipulation to be useful in definition. Further, assessment of the relative contribution of genetic and environmental influences to a tool-using phenotype is not considered germane to the definition of tool use, although it is important in more refined analysis. Likewise, it is irrelevant to definition whether tool use, when learned, is learned by trial and error, observation, or insight.

Given the definition of tool use, the definition of tool manufacture is simply the modification of an object by the user or a conspecific so that it serves more effectively as a tool.

CATALOGUE OF NONHUMAN PRIMATE TOOL BEHAVIOR

The restriction of this catalogue to primates does not imply that tool behavior by other animals is less advanced, less important, or fundamentally different.

Tool behavior by both wild and captive primates is included. Some have argued that because wild primates live under "natural" conditions while captives live under "unnatural" conditions, only tool behavior by the former is relevant. However, it is simplistic and misleading to dichotomize the great variety in primate environments. Differences in the environments of captive and wild primates are often insignificant. Many important field studies of primate behavior have been conducted in towns, agricultural areas, or national parks greatly affected by human enterprise. The success of van Lawick-Goodall in observing tool behavior by wild chimpanzees in Gombe National Park is due largely to habituation of the animals by repeated exposure to humans and to artificial provisioning. In fact, van Lawick-Goodall (1970) notes that the provisioning regime used at her study site has caused a substantial increase in the frequency and efficiency of aimed throwing by the chimpanzees. The native habitat is unquestionably the best setting for understanding the adaptive significance of tool behavior in extant taxa. However, tool behavior by wild primates may be infrequent, and observation is therefore fortuitous and sometimes inferential. The environment of captives can be structured to reinforce tool behavior, thus allowing ready observation and experimental analysis. Experimentation, primarily manipulating environmental factors so as to make probable the observation of tool behavior, has been conducted fruitfully on wild as well as captive primates. Likewise, tool behavior has appeared spontaneously, i.e. without anticipation or intervention by the observer, in captive as well as wild groups. Just as Kummer and Kurt (1965) found a remarkable isomorphism in the social behavior of wild and captive hamadryas baboons (*Papio hamadryas*), there is notable similarity in the tool behavior of wild and captive primates.

I have omitted cases where captives have acquired tool behavior only after repeated demonstrations by humans, e.g. the use and manufacture of stone tools by an orangutan, *Pongo pygmaeus* (Wright 1972), or after patient shaping of the complete response, e.g. the use of a stick to reach food by a gorilla, *Gorilla gorilla* (Yerkes 1927). Such tuition can reveal the organism's capacity for tool use. However, because the capacity may be pleiotropic, resulting from selection for other behavioral complexes, and because extensive training by humans is unlikely in the native habitat, the simple demonstration of a capacity is of limited relevance. I have also omitted cases where captives have used tools totally unlike objects apt to be encountered in the native habitat, e.g. the use of keys and screwdrivers by a chimpanzee (Döhl 1966; Rensch and Döhl 1967). Further, I have omitted reports of tool behavior by primates that have been hand-reared in homes because tuition and distinctively human implements are unavoidable in such settings. In sum, I have included in the following catalogue cases of the use and manufacture of tools by wild and captive nonhuman primates where the observations are directly relevant to the dynamics and evolutionary significance of tool behavior.

TOOL USE

Gorilla (Gorillas)

1.   A wild gorilla, as part of agonistic display, BRANDISHED OR WAVED a pole toward a human (Cordier in Kortlandt and Kooij 1963). Wild gorillas wave twigs to disperse flies (Heck, Matschie in Yerkes and Yerkes 1929).
2.   Captive gorillas CLUB OR HIT unspecified targets with unspecified objects in unspecified context (anonymous in Kortlandt and Kooij 1963).
3.   Wild gorillas, as part of agonistic display, THROW WITHOUT AIMING branches, twigs, leaves, and herbs in the presence of conspecifics and

humans (Geddes, Merfield, Rahm, Rollais in Kortlandt and Kooij 1963; Schaller 1963). Captives, as part of agonistic display, throw without aiming straw, sand, and water in the presence of conspecifics and humans (anonymous in Kortlandt and Kooij 1963; Beck, personal observation).

4.   Captive gorillas, in an agonistic context, THROW WITH AIMING sand, water, and feces toward humans (Beck, personal observation), a carrot at a human (Smith in Kortlandt and Kooij 1963), and, in a play context, an unspecified object at a conspecific (anonymous in Kortlandt and Kooij 1963).

5.   Wild gorillas, as part of agonistic display, DROP OR THROW DOWN branches from trees at humans (Merfield and Miller 1956) and a branch toward an unspecified target (Baumgartel in Kortlandt and Kooij 1963).

6.   Wild gorillas REACH with sticks to get food (Philipps 1950;[1] Pitman 1931). Captive gorillas reach with sticks to get food (Parker 1968) and with a piece of straw to touch urine (Teleki in van Lawick-Goodall 1970).

7.   A captive gorilla used rope to ABSORB from a concavity sweet liquid which was then sucked or licked (Parker 1968).

8.   Wild gorillas DRAPE lobclia leaves and moss on their heads in a play context (Schaller 1963). Captive gorillas drape straw, pieces of wood, and feces on their backs in a context that is not clear (Beck, personal observation) and place straw under their chins in an unspecified context (C. Carpenter 1937). Because the form or position of a separate object apparently was not altered, this may not be tool use as presently defined.

Pan (Chimpanzees)

1.   Wild chimpanzees, as part of agonistic display, BRANDISH OR WAVE sticks, boughs, and saplings at conspecifics, baboons, humans, a leopard model, and their own mirror images (Kortlandt 1965, 1967; van Lawick-Goodall 1968, 1970; Nishida 1970; Reynolds and Reynolds 1965) and an axe at a human (Goodall 1965). Captives, in the same context, brandish or wave sticks at conspecifics, humans, and a leopard model (Köhler 1927; Kortlandt 1965, 1967; Kortlandt and Kooij 1963; Schiller 1957). Wild chimpanzees wave boughs to disperse flies (Sugiyama 1969). Brandishing sticks in a play context is reported

---

[1]   Schaller (1963) reports a personal communication from Philipps that expresses uncertainty about this observation.

for wild chimpanzees (van Lawick-Goodall 1970) and for captives (Köhler 1927; Watty in Kortlandt and Kooij 1963).

2.   Wild chimpanzees, in an agonistic context, CLUB OR HIT conspecifics with sticks and a baboon with a palm frond (Itani and Suzuki 1967;[2] van Lawick-Goodall 1968, 1970). They hit the ground with a stick while pursuing conspecifics (anonymous in Kortlandt 1965; Nishida 1970). Captives, in the same context, club or hit conspecifics with sticks and burlap bags (van Hooff 1973; Köhler 1927; Kollar 1972; Wilson and Wilson 1968), a leopard model with sticks (Kortlandt 1965, 1967), a gorilla with a whip (Steinbacher, Weinert in Kortlandt and Kooij 1963), and a variety of mammals and reptiles with sticks (Kortlandt and Kooij 1963). The behavior has resulted in injury (Wilson and Wilson 1968). A wild chimpanzee clubbed an insect with a stick in a context that is not clear (van Lawick-Goodall 1970). A wild chimpanzee clubbed a conspecific with a tuft of grass during play (van Lawick-Goodall 1970) and captive chimpanzees hit conspecifics with sticks during play (Köhler 1927). A captive clubbed the ground with a stick in a context that is unclear (Wilson and Wilson 1968).

3.   Captive chimpanzees, in an agonistic context, PROD OR JAB conspecifics with sticks (Köhler 1927; Kollar 1972) and humans, dogs, and chickens with sticks and wire in a context that is not clear (Köhler 1927).

4.   Wild chimpanzees, as part of agonistic display, DRAG, HIT, ROLL, OR KICK sticks, stones, and metal drums in the presence of conspecifics (van Lawick-Goodall 1968, 1970). Captives, in the same context, do likewise with wooden boxes and metal drums (Bernstein, personal communication; Köhler 1927). Wild chimpanzees drag sticks in social play (van Lawick-Goodall 1970).

5.   Wild chimpanzees, as part of agonistic display, THROW WITHOUT AIMING sticks, stones, grass, leaves, and a palm nut in the presence of conspecifics (Kortlandt 1962; van Lawick-Goodall 1968, 1970; Nishida 1970; Reynolds and Reynolds 1965;[3] Rollais in Kortlandt and Kooij 1963). Captives, in the same context, throw a variety of materials (often sand, straw, and water) in the presence of conspecifics and humans (Köhler 1927; Kortlandt and Kooij 1963[4]). Wild chim-

[2] Itani and Suzuki note but do not describe use of "a stick for attacking;" I have included their observation here, but the stick may have been used in another way.
[3] Neither Nishida nor Reynolds and Reynolds specify whether throwing was aimed or unaimed; I am assuming it was unaimed.
[4] Kortlandt and Kooij do not specify whether throwing was aimed or unaimed in each of the eighty-seven cases they collected; I am assuming some were unaimed.

panzees throw without aiming a variety of objects in play (van Lawick-Goodall 1968).

6. Wild chimpanzees, in an agonistic context, THROW WITH AIMING sticks, stones of various sizes, banana skins, grass, and other bits of vegetation at conspecifics (Kortlandt 1965, 1967; van Lawick-Goodall 1968, 1970; Watty in Kortlandt and Kooij 1963), stones of various sizes and leaves at baboons (van Lawick-Goodall 1968, 1970; de Leest in Kortlandt and Kooij 1963), stones at a monitor lizard (van Lawick-Goodall 1968), sticks, stones of various sizes, and banana skins at humans (van Lawick-Goodall 1968, 1970; Millot in Kortlandt and Kooij 1963), and branches and saplings at a leopard model (Kortlandt 1965, 1967). Captive chimpanzees, in the same context, throw with aiming sticks, stones of various sizes, sand, and locks at conspecifics (van Hooff 1973; Kortlandt and Kooij 1963; Menzel, Davenport, and Rogers 1970; Wilson and Wilson 1968), sticks, stones, gravel, sand, mud, water, feces, rolls of wire netting, tin cans, and wooden blocks at humans and a variety of other mammals (Köhler 1927; Kortlandt and Kooij 1963; Merfield and Miller 1956; Schiller 1957; Wilson and Wilson 1968), sticks at reptile models (Menzel 1971), and stones at an observation booth (Menzel 1972). Aimed throwing has resulted in injury (van Lawick-Goodall 1970). Wild chimpanzees throw sticks at conspecifics in play (van Lawick-Goodall 1968, 1970) and captives throw stones of various sizes, sticks, and clods of dirt in the same context (Cowper 1971; Köhler 1927; Wilson and Wilson 1968).

7. Wild chimpanzees, as part of agonistic display, DROP OR THROW DOWN branches from trees at humans (van Lawick-Goodall 1970; Owen, Reynolds in Kortlandt and Kooij 1963; Sugiyama 1969) and twigs and bits of vine at a leopard and/or a human (Nishida 1968). Wild chimpanzees drop branches in a context that is not clear (van Lawick-Goodall 1968).

8. Wild chimpanzees INSERT AND PROBE with sticks in subterranean and arboreal ant nests and eat the ants that become attached to the sticks (van Lawick-Goodall 1968, 1970). They probe in termite mounds and dead logs with sticks, twigs, bark, stalks, stems, midveins of leaves, blades of grass, and pieces of vine and eat termites that become attached to the tools (Jones and Sabater Pi 1969; van Lawick-Goodall 1968, 1970; Suzuki 1966, 1969). Van Lawick-Goodall reports that suitable tools were carried some distance to the point of use. Wild chimpanzees also probe in subterranean bee nests with sticks and twigs and eat the honey that adheres to the tools (Izawa

and Itani 1966; Merfield and Miller 1956). They probe with sticks, twigs, and grass in pockets, holes in branches, and holes in tree trunks and smell the end of the tool after it is withdrawn (van Lawick-Goodall 1968, 1970). One inserted leaves and a grass stem into water contained in a hollow and put the wet ends in its mouth (van Lawick-Goodall 1968, 1970). Wild chimpanzees insert twigs into their noses and teeth during autogrooming (van Lawick-Goodall 1970). Wild chimpanzees insert and probe with twigs in termite nests in what appears to be a play context (van Lawick-Goodall 1968, 1970). Captive chimpanzees insert and probe with sticks, twigs, and straw into water tanks and other vessels and lick off the fluid that adheres (Köhler 1927; van Lawick-Goodall 1970). They probe with sticks, twigs, nails, and wooden pegs into holes and crevices in a context(s) that is unclear (van Hooff 1973; Kollar 1972; Menzel, Davenport, and Rogers 1970; Schiller 1957). Captives dip sticks and straws into liquids which they then lick or suck off the tools (Hobhouse 1901; Schiller 1957). They use sticks to groom the dentition of conspecifics (McGrew and Tutin 1973), to scratch themselves (Köhler 1927), and to touch their own genitalia (Menzel, Davenport, and Rogers 1970). One used cotton swabs to groom its own gums, bamboo splinters to probe between the toes of humans, and straw to probe under human fingernails (Merfield and Miller 1956).

Perhaps analogous is captive chimpanzees inserting poles and sticks into long, narrow pipes, tubes, and tunnels in order to procure food placed therein (Birch 1945; Hobhouse 1901; Khroustov in Tobias 1965; Yerkes 1943).

9.   Wild chimpanzees REACH with sticks to touch conspecifics, a dead python, and a banana held by a human (van Lawick-Goodall 1968, 1970). Captives use sticks to touch fire, mice, and lizards (Köhler 1927), a pangolin (Kortlandt and Kooij 1963; van Lawick in van Lawick-Goodall 1970), and food placed near reptile models (Menzel 1971). In these cases, access to the incentive is blocked not by physical obstruction but by fear or reluctance to make direct contact. When access is physically obstructed, captives use sticks and a wide variety of other objects to reach toward and rake in food (Birch 1945; Bourne 1971; Döhl 1966; Guillaume and Meyerson 1930, 1934; Hobhouse 1901; Jacobsen, Wolfe, and Jackson 1935; Jennison 1927; Köhler 1927; Menzel, Davenport, and Rogers 1970; Schiller 1957). In some of these cases, the chimpanzees used short sticks to rake in other sticks of sufficient length to procure the food and retrieved suitable sticks that were not in the same visual field as the food. Captive

chimpanzees extend twigs and straw through cage mesh into processions of ants; when the ants become attached, the tool is withdrawn and the ants are eaten (Köhler 1927). Wild chimpanzees did likewise with grass stems and twigs, although they were not physically obstructed from direct contact with the ant procession (van Lawick-Goodall 1970).

10.   Captive chimpanzees BALANCE AND CLIMB sticks, poles, planks, and a variety of other elongated objects to procure suspended food (Köhler 1927) and in what appears to be a play context (Menzel 1972; Menzel, Davenport, and Rogers 1970).

11.   Captive chimpanzees PROP AND CLIMB branches, poles, ladders, iron bars, and planks to get suspended food (Köhler 1927), to gain accesss to an observation booth and tree tops, and to escape from their enclosure (Menzel 1972). Suitable objects were carried some distance to the point of use and were carried vertically to elevated substrata. In Menzel's group, one chimpanzee propped and held the pole for others to climb.

12.   Captive chimpanzees STACK boxes and metal drums to procure suspended food (Bingham 1929; Köhler 1927; Schiller 1957; Yerkes 1943; Yerkes and Learned 1925; Yerkes and Yerkes 1929) and to procure a balloon (von Buttel Reepen in Bierens de Haan 1931). They make towers containing up to four boxes, some of which are carried some distance to the point of use. Köhler reported that three animals participated in moving a heavy box into position.

13.   Wild chimpanzees POUND OR HAMMER tough-skinned fruits, seeds, and nuts with stones and sticks (Azuma and Toyoshima in Itani and Suzuki 1967; Beatty 1951; Rahm 1971; Savage and Wyman 1843–1844; Struhsaker and Hunkeler 1971). The behavior facilitates access to the edible interior of the fruits and nuts. The stones and sticks appear to be carried some distance to the point of use (Rahm 1971; Struhsaker and Hunkeler 1971). The food objects arc sometimes placed on rocks (Beatty 1951) or in crevices and depressions formed by or in roots (Rahm 1971; Struhsaker and Hunkeler 1971) to provide an anvil. Wild chimpanzees may pound or hammer with sticks on hollow logs or buttresses as part of agonistic display or during high arousal (anonymous in Savage and Wyman 1843–1844; Robillard in Rahm 1971). A wild chimpanzee pounded the ground with a stone in a context that is unclear (van Lawick-Goodall 1970). Captive chimpanzees pound one rock with another in a context that is not clear (Menzel, Davenport, and Rogers 1970).

14.   Wild chimpanzees PRY OR APPLY LEVERAGE with sticks in at-

tempts to separate an arboreal ant nest from a branch (van Lawick-Goodall 1970) and to open boxes containing food (van Lawick-Goodall 1968, 1970). Captive chimpanzees pry with sticks to open feeders (Kollar 1972) and with sticks and iron bars to break cage mesh and to remove the top of a water tank (Köhler 1927). Captives pry with sticks at a cage door (Menzel, Davenport, and Rogers 1970), at a box (Hobhouse 1901), and in cracks and crevices (Schiller 1957).

15.   Wild chimpanzees DIG with sticks to widen the entrance of a subterranean bee nest (van Lawick-Goodall 1970). Captives dig with sticks, pieces of wood, metal rods, and wire in a context that is not clear (van Hooff 1973; Köhler 1927; Kollar 1972) and to procure grass and roots which are eaten (Cowper 1971; Köhler 1927).

16.   Wild chimpanzees use leaves and grass to WIPE blood, feces, urine, ejaculate, sticky food residues and juices, water, and mud from their bodies (anonymous in Merfield and Miller 1956; anonymous in Savage and Wyman 1843–1844; van Lawick-Goodall 1968, 1970). Van Lawick-Goodall and Merfield and Miller's informant saw chimpanzees use leaves to wipe substances from conspecifics. Captives use leaves, straw, twigs, rags, or pieces of paper to wipe off blood, feces, or pus (Köhler 1927). Kortlandt (in Kortlandt and Kooij 1963) notes but does not describe a chimpanzee's use of a stick or fruit as a "toilet aid."

17.   Wild chimpanzees use leaves and grass as sponges to ABSORB water from concavities (van Lawick-Goodall 1968, 1970) and residual fluids and tissue from the skulls of prey animals (Teleki 1973). In some cases the leaves were gathered and carried some distance to the point of use (van Lawick-Goodall 1968, 1970). Captives use straw, rags, bread, and rope to absorb fluids which are then sucked or licked (Cowper 1971; Köhler 1927; Parker 1968). The behavior facilitates collection of the liquid materials for ingestion. Wild chimpanzees use leaves as sponges in play (van Lawick-Goodall 1970).

18.   A wild chimpanzee DRAPED a branch over its back during rain (Izawa and Itani 1966). Captives drape cloth, grass, and leaves on their bodies during rain and cold (Köhler 1927). A wild chimpanzee draped pieces of lichen on its head in a context that is not clear (Reynolds and Reynolds 1965). Captives drape cloth, paper, branches, leaves, fruit skins, stones, and other objects on their bodies in a context(s) that is not clear (Cowper 1971; van Hooff 1973; Köhler 1927; Menzel, Davenport, and Rogers 1970; Yerkes 1943). Draping might not alter the form or position of a separate object and thus may not be tool use as presently defined.

19. Captive chimpanzees BAIT chickens with bread in a context that is unclear (Köhler 1927).

20. Captive chimpanzees use unspecified objects as cups to CONTAIN water scooped from a moat. The water is sometimes drunk or the behavior may appear in a play context (van Hooff 1973).

Pongo (Orangutans)

1. Captive orangutans CLUB OR HIT a snake (Harrisson 1963b), a human (Rabb, personal communication), and unspecified targets (anonymous in Kortlandt and Kooij 1963) with a stick.

2. Captive orangutans THROW WITH AIMING a variety of objects at humans in unspecified contexts (anonymous in Kortlandt and Kooij 1963;[5] Harrisson 1963b; Yerkes and Yerkes 1929) and in play (Harrisson 1963b).

3. Wild orangutans, as part of agonistic display, DROP OR THROW DOWN branches, twigs, and fruits at humans (Attenborough, Hoogerwert, Luitjes, Schultz in Kortlandt and Kooij 1963; Davenport 1967; Harrisson 1963a, 1963b; MacKinnon 1971; Rodman, personal communication; Schaller 1961; Wallace 1869).

4. A captive orangutan INSERTED AND PROBED with sticks in an insect nest (Harrisson 1963b). Perhaps analogous is captive orangutans inserting poles and sticks into narrow pipes, tubes, and tunnels to procure food placed therein (Bourne 1971; Haggerty 1910; Yerkes 1916). Yerkes' subject carried the tool some distance to the point of use.

5. A wild orangutan REACHED with a branch to get an unspecified object, perhaps fruit (Blomberg in Kortlandt and Kooij 1963). Captive orangutans reach toward and rake in food with sticks and cloth (Drescher and Trendelenburg 1927; Haggerty 1910; Parker 1968; Reuvens in Yerkes and Yerkes 1929; Sheak 1922; Yerkes 1916). Reuvens' subject threw a sack over the fruit and used a second sack to retrieve the first and the incentive. A captive orangutan reached with a stick to knock fruit from a human's hand (Rabb, personal communication).

6. Captive orangutans BALANCE AND CLIMB sticks to procure suspended food (Yerkes and Yerkes 1929) and in what appears to be a play context (Rice in Harrisson 1963a).

[5] Kortlandt and Kooij do not specify whether throwing was aimed or unaimed in each of the eleven cases they collected; I am assuming it was aimed.

7.   A captive orangutan STACKED chairs on a table and stood on top in a play context (Rensenbrink 1960).

8.   Captive orangutans POUND OR HAMMER on cage walls and floor with a variety of hard objects in a context(s) that is not clear (Beck, personal observation).

9.   Captive orangutans PRY OR APPLY LEVERAGE with sticks, iron bars, a key, and nails in attempts to break cage mesh and bars or to open boxes containing food (Benchley in Reynolds 1967; Camacho 1907; Darwin 1871; Harrisson 1963a; Hornaday 1922; Vosmaer in Yerkes and Yerkes 1929; Yerkes 1916). Hornaday's subject received cooperative assistance from another orangutan who pulled simultaneously on the lever.

10.   A captive orangutan used rope as a sponge to ABSORB from a concavity sweet liquid which was then sucked or licked (Parker 1968).

11.   Wild orangutans DRAPE boughs over their heads and backs in heavy rain, intense sun, and in the presence of a human (MacKinnon 1971). Captive orangutans drape cloth and straw over their heads and backs at night (Beck, personal observation; Bourne 1971; Harrisson 1963a, 1963b) and before being whipped (Darwin 1871). Wild orangutans drape boughs over their heads and backs in play (MacKinnon 1971) and captives drape cloth, straw, and vegetables over their heads in play (Beck, personal observation; Harrisson 1963a).

12.   A captive orangutan HUNG a length of braided straw over cage bars and swung from it (Hornaday 1922).

Hylobates (Gibbons)

1.   A captive gibbon THREW an unspecified object in an unspecified context. Whether throwing was aimed or unaimed is not specified (anonymous in Kortlandt and Kooij 1963).

2.   Wild gibbons DROP OR THROW DOWN branches on humans (C. Carpenter 1940).

3.   A captive gibbon used pieces of cloth as sponges to ABSORB water from an automatic dispenser. The water was sucked from the cloth or allowed to drip from it to form a puddle from which the gibbon drank. The behavior allowed the animal to avoid drinking directly from the dispenser, from which the water gushed forcibly (Rumbaugh 1970).

4.   A captive gibbon HUNG lengths of rope and hose on cage mesh and bars and swung from them (Rumbaugh 1970).

Cercocebus (Mangabeys)

1.   Captive mangabeys THROW unspecified objects in unspecified contexts. Whether throwing is aimed or unaimed is not specified (anonymous in Kortlandt and Kooij 1963).
2.   Captive mangabeys REACH toward and rake in food with sticks (Guillaume and Meyerson 1934).
3.   Wild mangabeys DIG with sticks to widen the entrance of subterranean insect nests (Jobaert in Kortlandt and Kooij 1963).

Cercopithecus (Guenons)

1.   Wild guenons, in an agonistic context, THROW WITH AIMING sand and gravel at humans (anonymous in Kortlandt and Kooij 1963). A captive threw an unspecified object in an unspecified context. Whether throwing was aimed or unaimed in this case is not specified (in Kortlandt and Kooij 1963).
2.   Wild guenons, in an agonistic context, DROP OR THROW DOWN branches or twigs on humans (anonymous in Kortlandt and Kooij 1963).
3.   A captive guenon BAITED a dog with bread in a context that is not clear (van Lawick-Goodall 1970).
4.   Captive guenons use halves of peanut shells as cups to CONTAIN water (Lombardi, personal communication). The behavior allows the animals to avoid drinking directly from an automatic water dispenser.

Colobus (Colobus Monkeys)

1.   Wild colobus monkeys, in an agonistic context, DROP OR THROW DOWN branches or twigs at humans (anonymous in Kortlandt and Kooij 1963).
2.   Wild colobus monkeys DIG with sticks to widen the entrance of subterranean insect nests (Jobaert in Kortlandt and Kooij 1963).
3.   A wild colobus monkey used leaves as a medicated pad, i.e. WIPED unspecified fluids in an unspecified context (anonymous in Kortlandt and Kooij 1963).

Erythrocebus (Patas Monkeys)

1.   Wild patas monkeys, in an agonistic context, THROW WITH AIMING

rocks and sand at humans (anonymous in Kortlandt and Kooij 1963; De la Brue in Jennison 1927). Captive patas also throw unspecified objects in an unspecified context(s). Whether throwing was aimed or unaimed is not specified in this report (anonymous in Kortlandt and Kooij 1963).

Macaca (Macaques)

1.   Captive macaques THROW unspecified objects in unspecified contexts. Whether throwing is aimed or unaimed is not specified (anonymous in Kortlandt and Kooij 1963).
2.   Wild macaques, in an agonistic context, DROP OR THROW DOWN twigs, branches, and pine cones on humans (anonymous in Kortlandt and Kooij 1963; anonymous in Hall 1963).
3.   Captive macaques REACH toward and rake in food with sticks, cloth, rope, and wire (Hobhouse 1901; Klüver 1937; Verlaine and Gallis in Hooton 1942; Warden, Koch, and Fjeld 1940). Some used short sticks to rake in others of sufficient length to procure the food (Warden, Koch, and Fjeld 1940).
4.   Wild macaques POUND OR HAMMER oysters with stones. The stones are carried some distance to the point of use. The behavior facilitates access to the soft tissue for consumption (A. Carpenter 1887).
5.   Wild macaques WIPE seeds, fruits, and inedible objects with leaves to remove dirt, fungus, and ants (Chiang 1967).

Mandrillus (Drills and Mandrills)

1.   Captive drills and mandrills THROW unspecified objects in unspecified contexts. Whether throwing was aimed or unaimed is not specified (anonymous in Kortlandt and Kooij 1963). Captive mandrills throw sand without aiming in the presence of humans (Beck, personal observation).

Papio (Baboons)

1.   Wild baboons, in an agonistic context, THROW WITH AIMING sand, gravel, stones, and vegetation at humans (anonymous in Kortlandt and Kooij 1963; Rawlinson in Hornaday 1922) and sand and gravel at a crocodile (Owen in Kortlandt and Kooij 1963). Captives, in an agonistic context, throw with aiming rocks, sand, gravel, bananas, and other objects at humans (anonymous in Kortlandt and Kooij 1963;

Bolwig 1961, 1964; Hornaday 1922). A captive threw sticks at a suspended banana to set it moving in an arc that brought it within reach (Bolwig 1961, 1964) and captives threw rods behind or beside food so that they could then be used to rake the food within reach (Beck 1972, 1973a; Bolwig 1964).

2. A captive baboon INSERTED AND PROBED with a blade of grass in a pipe stem and ate the oils extracted therefrom (Marais 1969).

3. Wild baboons REACH with sticks to stir up insects concealed under stones (Roth in Kortlandt and Kooij 1963). Captives use sticks and rods to reach toward and rake in food (Beck 1972, 1973a; Bolwig 1961, 1964; Guillaume and Meyerson 1934; Nellman and Trendelenburg 1926; Protopopov in Klüver 1937). Bolwig's subject used short sticks to procure others of sufficient length to reach the food and retrieved suitable sticks that were not in the same visual field as the food. A female brought a male a suitable rod from a cage that he could not enter (Beck 1973b).

4. A captive baboon BALANCED AND CLIMBED sticks to procure suspended food and in play (Bolwig 1961, 1964).

5. A captive baboon PROPPED AND CLIMBED sticks in play (Bolwig 1961).

6. Wild baboons POUND OR HAMMER tough-skinned fruits with stones (Marais 1969) and a scorpion with a stone (Davison in Kortlandt and Kooij 1963).

7. Captive baboons PRY OR APPLY LEVERAGE with steel rods in the crevice between their cage wall and door (Beck, personal observation) and with a stick to move heavy objects covering food or while digging (Bolwig 1964).

8. Wild baboons DIG with sticks to widen the entrance of subterranean insect nests (Jobaert in Kortlandt and Kooij 1963). A captive baboon dug with sticks in a context that is unclear (Bolwig 1964).

9. A wild baboon WIPED sticky fluid from her face with a stone and another wiped blood from his lip with a corn cob (van Lawick-Goodall, van Lawick, and Parker 1973).

Presbytis (Langurs)

1. A wild langur, in an agonistic context, THREW WITH AIMING an unspecified object at an unspecified target (anonymous in Kortlandt and Kooij 1963).

Alouatta (Howler Monkeys)

1. Wild howler monkeys, in an agonistic context, DROP OR THROW DOWN branches and twigs on humans (anonymous in Kortlandt and Kooij 1963; C. Carpenter 1934; Dampier in C. Carpenter 1934).
2. There are two third-hand observations of wild howler monkeys using leaves to WIPE bleeding wounds (Azara, Buffon in C. Carpenter 1934). The use of small sticks and fruit as "toilet aids" is noted but not described (Chippendale in Kortlandt and Kooij 1963).

Ateles (Spider Monkeys)

1. Wild spider monkeys, in an agonistic context, DROP OR THROW DOWN branches and twigs at humans (anonymous in Kortlandt and Kooij 1963; C. Carpenter 1935).

Cebus (Capuchin Monkeys)

1. Wild capuchin monkeys, in an agonistic context, CLUB OR HIT a rattlesnake with sticks and other objects (Chippendale in Kortlandt and Kooij 1963). Captives, in an agonistic context, club or hit conspecifics and a rhesus monkey with a stick (Cooper and Harlow 1961). Captives club unspecified targets with unspecified objects in unspecified contexts (anonymous in Kortlandt and Kooij 1963).
2. A captive capuchin monkey, in an agonistic context, PRODDED OR JABBED a conspecific with a stick (Cooper and Harlow 1961).
3. Captive capuchin monkeys, in an agonistic context, THROW WITH AIMING sticks and other objects at humans and dogs (Romanes 1882). They throw sticks to dislodge suspended food (Bierens de Haan 1931) and throw sticks, belts, tethered rodents, and other objects behind or beside food so that these could then be used to rake in the food (Cope in Bierens de Haan 1931; Klüver 1933, 1937). Captives also throw unspecified objects at unspecified targets in unspecified contexts. Whether throwing was aimed or unaimed in these cases is not specified (anonymous in Kortlandt and Kooij 1963).
4. Wild capuchin monkeys, in an agonistic context, DROP OR THROW DOWN nuts and debris on coatimundis (Kaufman 1962) and branches or twigs on humans (anonymous in Kortlandt and Kooij 1963).
5. Wild capuchin monkeys INSERT AND PROBE with twigs to pick insects from beneath bark (Thorington in Jay 1968). Perhaps analogous is captive capuchin monkeys inserting sticks into narrow pipes,

tubes, and tunnels to procure food placed therein (Harlow 1951; Klüver 1933, 1937).

6. Captive capuchin monkeys REACH toward and rake in food with sticks, cloth, wire, belts, cords, tethered rodents, and a wide variety of other objects (Bierens de Haan 1931; Cooper and Harlow 1961; Cope in Bierens de Haan 1931; Harlow 1951; Klüver 1933, 1937; Romanes 1882; Warden, Koch, and Fjeld 1940). In some of these cases, the monkeys used short sticks to rake in other sticks of sufficient length to procure the food and retrieved suitable sticks that were not in the same visual field as the food. A captive capuchin monkey used a stick to reach toward and knock down suspended food (Bierens de Haan 1931; Harlow 1951; Klüver 1933, 1937).

7. Captive capuchin monkeys BALANCE AND CLIMB sticks to get suspended food (Bierens de Haan 1931; Harlow 1951).

8. A captive capuchin monkey PROPPED AND CLIMBED a stick to get suspended food (Bierens de Haan 1931).

9. A captive capuchin monkey STACKED boxes and tins to procure suspended food. The monkey made towers containing up to three elements, some of which were carried some distance to the point of use (Bierens de Haan 1931).

10. Wild capuchin monkeys POUND OR HAMMER oysters with stones (anonymous in Jennison 1927). Captives pound or hammer nuts, insects, eggs, and sugar cubes with rocks, blocks of wood, and other hard objects. The behavior facilitates access to the edible interior of the nuts, insects, and eggs (Bierens de Haan 1931; Klüver 1933; Kooij and van Zon 1964; Nolte 1958; Romanes 1882; Tobias 1965; Vevers and Weiner 1963).

11. Captive capuchin monkeys WIPE their bodies with odorous objects or substances (Hill 1960; Nolte 1958). This behavior might not alter the form or position of a separate object and thus may not be tool use as presently defined. Wild capuchin monkeys' use of sticks or fruit as "toilet aids" is noted but not described (Chippendale in Kortlandt and Kooij 1963). Captives wrap sticky bananas in leaves before picking them up (Katz and Katz 1936).[6]

12. A captive capuchin BAITED ducks with bread and killed them when they came within reach (Boulenger 1937).

---

[6] Katz and Katz studied three green monkeys and three capuchin monkeys and do not specify which or how many performed this behavior; I am assuming it was the capuchin(s).

Pithecia (Sakis)

1. Wild sakis, in an agonistic context, DROP OR THROW DOWN branches or twigs on humans (anonymous in Kortlandt and Kooij 1963).

Saimiri (Squirrel Monkeys)

1. Wild squirrel monkeys, in an agonistic context, DROP OR THROW DOWN branches or twigs on humans (anonymous in Kortlandt and Kooij 1963).
2. A wild squirrel monkey REACHED with a stick to sweep a piece of fruit across the ground to dislodge ants from it (Chippendale in Kortlandt and Kooij 1963).

TOOL MANUFACTURE

Gorilla (Gorillas)

1. Wild gorillas DETACH potential tools from the substrate. They break off branches and twigs, pull up grass, and pull off leaves prior to throwing them without aiming (Schaller 1963).

Pan (Chimpanzees)

1. Wild chimpanzees DETACH potential tools from the substrate. They break off branches, saplings, or boughs prior to brandishing them, throwing them (with and without aiming), and using them to knock a banana from a human's hand (Kortlandt 1965, 1967; van Lawick-Goodall 1968, 1970; Reynolds and Reynolds 1965). They break off sticks and twigs and pick grass stems prior to inserting and probing with them in ant and termite nests (Jones and Sabater Pi 1969; van Lawick-Goodall 1968, 1970; Suzuki 1966). They pick grass and leaves prior to wiping or using them as sponges to absorb water (van Lawick-Goodall 1968, 1970). Captives break branches from trees and pieces from a fixed footscraper prior to reaching with them for food (Köhler 1927) and a captive broke off a branch prior to propping and climbing it (Menzel 1972).

2.   Captive chimpanzees SUBTRACT elements from unattached objects to make them (more) suitable as tools. They strip and discard leaves from sticks, twigs, and the midvein of a palm leaf, pull and discard strips from blades of grass, and pull and discard fibers from pieces of bark prior to inserting and probing with them in ant and termite nests. They also remove parts of these tools that become bent or broken during use (Jones and Sabater Pi 1969; van Lawick-Goodall 1968, 1970; Suzuki 1966). They strip and discard leaves from sticks prior to using them as levers to pry open food boxes (van Lawick-Goodall 1968, 1970). Captives strip and discard leaves from branches prior to using them to reach food (Köhler 1927) and remove and discard leaves from a twig prior to inserting and probing with it in a conspecific's mouth during dental allogrooming (McGrew and Tutin 1973). They break off crosspieces and split rectangular and circular pieces of wood to produce objects slender enough to be inserted in a tube to acquire food (Khroustov in Tobias 1965) and remove wood slats from a crate and use them to reach food (Köhler 1927). They remove a stopper from a hollow stick so that it can be joined (*vide infra*) with another to be used for reaching food (Köhler 1927). They remove sand and stones from boxes so that the boxes can be positioned beneath suspended food (Köhler 1927).

3.   Captive chimpanzees ADD OR COMBINE unattached objects to make them suitable as tools. They join two and three sticks to make a tool long enough to reach food (Köhler 1927; Schiller 1957).

4.   Wild chimpanzees RESHAPE unattached objects to make them (more) suitable as tools. They bite splinters from the ends of sticks to form chisel-edged shafts to pry open food boxes (van Lawick-Goodall 1970). They crumple and masticate leaves and grass to increase their absorbency for collecting water from concavities (Goodall 1964; van Lawick-Goodall 1968, 1970). Captives remove splinters from sticks to sharpen them for jabbing (Köhler 1927) and taper sticks so that they can be inserted into others and used to reach food (Köhler 1927). They bend small clumps of straw and unroll coils of wire to make reaching tools of sufficient firmness and length respectively (Köhler 1927).

Pongo (Orangutans)

1.   Wild orangutans DETACH potential tools from the substrate. They break off branches prior to dropping or throwing them down (Daven-

port 1967; Harrisson 1963a, 1963b; MacKinnon 1971; Schaller 1961; Wallace 1869).

2. A captive orangutan COMBINED AND RESHAPED unattached objects to make them suitable as a tool. He braided pieces of straw to make a "rope" which he hung over cage bars and from which he swung (Hornaday 1922).

Hylobates (Gibbons)

1. Wild gibbons DETACH potential tools from the substrate. They break off branches prior to dropping or throwing them down (C. Carpenter 1940).

Macaca (Macaques)

1. Captive macaques DETACH potential tools from the substrate. They break off branches prior to reaching with them for food (Verlaine and Gallis in Spence 1937).

Alouatta (Howler Monkeys)

1. Wild howler monkeys DETACH potential tools from the substrate. They break off branches prior to dropping or throwing them down (C. Carpenter 1934).

2. There are two third-hand reports that wild howler monkeys RESHAPE unattached objects to make them (more) suitable as tools. They masticate leaves prior to wiping bleeding wounds (Azara, Buffon in C. Carpenter 1934).

Ateles (Spider Monkeys)

1. Wild spider monkeys DETACH potential tools from the substrate. They break off branches prior to dropping or throwing them down (C. Carpenter 1935).

Cebus (Capuchin Monkeys)

1. A captive capuchin monkey DETACHED potential tools from the substrate. He broke off a fern frond, lengths of stick, and pieces of

newspaper prior to reaching with them for food (Klüver 1933, 1937).
2. Wild capuchin monkeys SUBTRACT elements from unattached objects to make them (more) suitable as tools. They peel and discard bark from twigs prior to inserting and probing with them beneath bark for insects (Thorington in Jay 1968).
3. A captive capuchin monkey RESHAPED unattached objects to make them (more) suitable as tools. He rolled pieces of newspaper to make reaching tools of sufficient length and firmness (Klüver 1933).

The modes of tool behavior (throwing, reaching, stacking, etc.) used to organize this catalogue are arbitrary, reflecting only the little commonality that could be found in the diverse reports consulted. Few authors provide the precise descriptions of motor patterns essential for more fundamental behavioral categorization. For example, brandishing and clubbing are listed as separate modes, but they may only be minor variants of the same motor pattern.

That reports of tool behavior on the part of some genera greatly outnumber those by others may represent genuine phyletic differences in the capacity for or frequency of tool behavior, or may simply reflect differences in the frequency and conditions of observation. For example, there are more reports of tool use by baboons than by mangabeys. Baboons may in fact be more capable of using tools and may use them more frequently. On the other hand, baboons have been studied more intensively and under conditions where tool use is more likely to be seen. While phyletic differences undoubtedly exist, the possibility of sampling error precludes their estimation from the catalogue alone.

FUNCTIONS OF TOOL USE

Hall (1963), Kortlandt and Kooij (1963), and van Lawick-Goodall (1970) have dichotomized tool use as agonistic and nonagonistic, probably reflecting the sterile argument over whether man's first tools were weapons. Examination of the catalogue reveals that most primate taxa that use tools in agonistic contexts do so in nonagonistic contexts as well. Chimpanzees hit leopard models, conspecifics, hard-shelled nuts, and suspended fruits with sticks. Any behavioral capacity is apt to be utilized in every context in which it is advantageous.

I prefer to substitute function for context as a basis for superordinate categorization of tool use. Most nonhuman primate tool use falls into one of three functional categories: extending the reach of the user, increasing the mechanical force that the user can exert, or augmenting the user's display.

Extension of reach is advantageous when an animal cannot move near enough to an incentive to reach it directly. Wild primates, who can move with little restriction, rarely confront such a situation, but captives frequently face an incentive out of reach beyond cage bars or a moat. At times, an animal may not be physically restricted from moving close enough to an incentive to reach it directly but may be ambivalent because the incentive is associated with fear-producing or unpleasant stimuli. An infant sibling cradled in the arm of an aggressively protective mother, food placed near reptile models, and ant-covered fruit are examples of such situations. Access to an incentive may also be prevented if the incentive resides in a concavity whose size or configuration precludes direct reaching. Insects in subterranean nests and food in long narrow tubes are examples of such a situation. The modes of tool use used by nonhuman primates to extend their reach are inserting and probing, reaching, balancing and climbing, propping and climbing, and stacking, five of the twenty-one different modes of tool use appearing in the catalogue.

Nonhuman primates increase the mechanical force that they can bring to bear on their environment by increasing mass (using a stone rather than a hand to hammer fruit), decreasing elasticity (again hammering with a stone or a hard stick rather than a hand), concentrating force on a small point (jabbing with a stick or piece of wire), increasing speed or acceleration (clubbing a leopard model with the end of a long stick rather than a hand), and utilizing leverage (prying with a stick). The modes of tool use used by nonhuman primates to increase mechanical force are clubbing or hitting, prodding or jabbing, aimed throwing, pounding or hammering, prying or applying leverage, and digging, six of the twenty-one different modes of tool use appearing in the catalogue.

Nonhuman primates frequently utilize inanimate environmental features in their displays toward conspecifics, predators, and human intruders. Some passively dislodge dead branches or stones which fall or roll toward the intruder. Others slap or stamp on the ground, tree trunks, or branches, or they sway saplings or branches violently. None of these behaviors are tool use as presently defined. However, nonhuman primates detach, hold, and then drop or throw down objects, throw objects without aiming, brandish or wave objects, and drag, hit, kick, or roll objects to augment their displays. These comprise an additional four of the twenty-one modes appearing in the catalogue.

In all, tool use functioning to extend reach, increase mechanical force, and augment display accounts for fifteen of the twenty-one modes (more than 70 percent) listed in the catalogue. Further, the percentage of observation of these modes is even higher; tool use in several of the remaining six modes has been seen very rarely. While many nonhuman primates apply a variety of tools to a variety of objects in a variety of ways, they do so in the service of remarkably few functions.

ONTOGENY OF TOOL BEHAVIOR

Although the sensory, motor, and cognitive capacities utilized for tool behavior are genetically influenced, there are several lines of evidence which indicate that nonhuman primate tool patterns are learned. For example, the opportunity to explore and manipulate environmental objects increases the probability that those objects will be used as tools. Also, the frequency of tool use is contingent, in part, on resulting reinforcement. Further, increasingly skilled tool use results from continued opportunity for rewarded practice.

The learning process most commonly underlying tool behavior is trial-and-error learning. Trial-and-error learning differs from operant conditioning only in that the latter is under the design and control of human investigators. Both rest on an identical fundamental tenet: there will be an increase in the frequency of a response that is followed by positive reinforcement. Among primates, there are two main sources of response variation from which fortuitous reinforcement produces tool use: object manipulation during environmental exploration motivated only by curiosity (Butler 1965) and object manipulation during agonistic display (*vide supra*). By chance, an individual is apt to use an object as a tool during display or exploration and, if the response is fortuitously rewarded, he will perform that response more frequently. Further, inefficient motor elements of the response will become less frequent because they do not produce reinforcement, and efficient elements will be linked in a skillful response sequence. In their reviews, Alcock (1972), Hall (1963), and van Lawick-Goodall (1970) emphasize the role of trial-and-error learning in nonhuman tool use. Beck (1972, 1973a) has demonstrated experimentally that baboons' use of tools to get food is learned by trial and error. Many still assume that tool behavior, at least in primates, is based on an advanced learning process. On the contrary, most primate tool behavior is acquired by trial and error, a learning process ubiquitous among vertebrates.

Trial-and-error learning of tool behavior is based on the compound probability that a suitable response is performed and that it is performed under circumstances where it will be reinforced. Because the probability of both is undoubtedly low for wild primates, the rarity of their tool behavior is understandable. Tool behavior by captives is more common because critical resources are provided, making exploratory object manipulation more probable. Finally, the greatest variety and frequency of tool behavior is produced by training, where responses are channeled and are followed by immediate reinforcement. The learning process involved in each setting is identical. The difference is in the probability of the occurrence and reinforcement of unusual responses.

Several characteristics of individuals acquiring tool behavior by trial and error can be predicted. If the response originated from exploratory manipulation, those animals that explore most are most likely to learn the behavior. Of a group of six hamadryas baboons (*Papio hamadryas*) and another group of eight Guinea baboons (*Papio papio*), the animal who learned to use a tool had been the most frequent manipulator of the tool (Beck 1972, 1973a). Because sexually immature primates are more likely than adults to engage in exploratory manipulation (Menzel 1966), young animals are more likely than adults to learn tool use in this way. When the problem setting is limited so that only one animal at a time can engage in relevant exploratory manipulation, dominance, and the determinants thereof, will be operative. In each of Beck's experiments, the most dominant subadult animal became the tool user. When tool use originates from agonistic display, those individuals who engage in object manipulation most frequently in this context, e.g. adults, are likely to become tool users. In general, any factor that tends to be associated with increased object manipulation will also be operative in determining those individuals who will learn to use tools by trial and error.

Another learning process involved in the acquisition of tool behavior is observation learning. Following Hall and Goswell (1964) and Spence (1937), there are three types of observation learning. The first, known as social facilitation, consists simply of increased readiness to perform a response upon observation of a conspecific performing the same response. The response is typically well established in the behavioral repertoire of both observer and demonstrator so that, in a sense, learning is not occurring at all. An example is the contagious spread of alarm calls or contact calls in a baboon group. There is no documented case of social facilitation operating in nonhuman primate tool behavior.

The second type of observation learning is stimulus enhancement, in which the consequences of a demonstrator's behavior in a specific situation influence the orientation of an observer's behavior in the same or a similar situation. Van Lawick-Goodall (1968, 1970) notes that infant chimpanzees watch attentively as their mothers use stems and stalks to secure food from subterranean termite nests. Subsequently, the infants manipulate stems and stalks more frequently but not necessarily more skillfully. Beck (1973a) has noted that captive Guinea baboons, after extensive opportunity to observe a dominant group member use a tool to get food, touch the tool more frequently than they did before. In primates, stimulus enhancement supports increased manipulation of any stimuli associated with positive reinforcement. A primate observing an object being used as a tool is more likely to manipulate that object and is thus more likely to learn to use it as a tool by trial and error.

A third type of observation learning is imitative copying, in which a naive observer effectively reproduces the motor elements, in sequence and with coordination, of a demonstrator's behavior. Proof of imitative copying must be based on detailed comparison of response topography and has not yet been provided for the acquisition of tool behavior by nonhuman primates. Van Lawick-Goodall (1968, 1970), Menzel (1972), and Beck (1973a) felt that some imitative copying was occurring among their subjects but could not offer definitive proof.

Thus, of the three types of observation learning, only stimulus enhancement has been proven to operate in the acquisition of tool behavior by nonhuman primates. Observers manipulate relevant stimuli more and they may copy elements of a demonstrator's behavior. However, they must still learn the behavior individually by trial and error; observation learning merely accelerates the course of individual acquisition. This suggests re-examination of the common speculation that observation learning is important in the acquisition of tool behavior by nonhuman primates. It should be noted that merely synchronous appearance of a novel behavior pattern among members of a primate group is not evidence for observation learning; each individual may be learning the behavior by trial and error as a result of changes in the opportunity for manipulation or changes in the reinforcement contingencies offered by the environment.

When observation learning is involved in the acquisition of tool behavior by nonhuman primates, several predictions can be made about the animals that will learn in this way. Because primate observation learning is undoubtedly visual, any factor that promotes proximity and visual access to a demonstrator will also promote observation learning. The dissemination of potato and wheat washing in the Koshima troop of Japanese macaques (*Macaca fuscata*) revealed that maternal and sibling relationships are such factors. Adults seldom in the vicinity of the demonstrator did not acquire the behavior. Menzel (1972) and Kawai (1965) found that personal affinity to a skilled demonstrator supports observation learning. Because subordinates frequently watch dominants, the direction of observation learning, all else being equal, will be downward as opposed to upward in the dominance hierarchy. The paucity of information acquired by baboons after repeated opportunity to watch a skilled tool user (Beck 1973a) compared with the considerable transfer of information among chimpanzees (van Lawick-Goodall 1968, 1970; Menzel 1972) indicates that pongids may have a greater capacity for observation learning of tool use than do cercopithecines.

The third learning process involved in the acquisition of tool behavior is insight. Köhler (1927), who reported insightful solution of tool problems by chimpanzees, felt that insight had two attributes. One, which was descriptive, was that the complete solution to complex problems occurred too suddenly to be adequately explained by trial and error. The second, which was unobservable, was that solution resulted from the animal's perception and understanding of critical relationships rather than from mechanistic stimulus-response associations.

Spence (1938) showed that sudden solution can occur in trial-and-error learning, but he used simple two-choice discriminations with which his subjects had prior experience. His analysis may not apply to more complex, novel problems. Birch (1945) argued that when only the empirically verifiable attributes of insight are examined, clear evidence remains that insight is a qualitatively unique learning process. Beck (1967) reported insightful solution by gibbons of problems that did not involve tool use. He defined insight as the sudden appearance of a complete solution immediately following a period of non-problem-directed responding, which in turn follows a period(s) of incorrect attempts. Thus it is not sudden solution alone but sudden solution after a period free of problem-directed responding that is the criterion. The definition is operational and verifiable and makes no reference to unobservable mentalistic events. Van Lawick-Goodall (1970) felt that she observed a least one case of insightful learning of tool use and Yerkes (1943) reports at least one case. Some solutions to some tool problems by Köhler's chimpanzees appear to have been insightful, but many were by trial and error (Chance 1960). Beck (1973b) reports the occurrence of insight in cooperative tool use by captive hamadryas baboons. A male knew how to use a tool to get food but was too large to enter an adjacent cage where the tool was placed. A smaller female learned insightfully to retrieve and bring the tool to the male. That these are the only convincing examples indicates that insight, operationally defined, is rarely involved in the acquisition of tool behavior by nonhuman primates. However, only on the first few performances can behavior acquired by insight be distinguished from that acquired by trial and error. The reinforcement attained by insightful acquisition of tool behavior probably occurs more frequently response, which thus quickly loses its insightful character. Therefore, insightful acquisition of tool behavior probably occurs more frequently than it is observed.

The operational definition of insight as a unique learning process without reference to specialized psychological events does not imply that such events are nonexistent or unimportant. I believe, although I cannot yet demonstrate, that monkeys and apes are capable of forming concepts and of understanding complex relationships. Primates, I am quite sure, lead rich ideational existences. However, conceptualization and comprehension of relationships should not be equated with or limited to information acquired by insight. I feel that both occur during even trial-and-error and observation learning. The work of Davenport and Rogers (1970, 1971), using operant techniques, and of Gallup (1970) indicates that at least pongids are capable of forming sophisticated concepts. Conclusive demonstration of the inferred psychological events awaits techniques that will make them subject to operational definition and empirical manipulation. Meanwhile, I suggest that the impatient sceptic find an opportunity to watch an untrained monkey or ape solve a novel, complex problem.

TOOLS AND HUMAN EVOLUTION

Several points emerge which may aid in understanding human evolution. First, the definition of tool use is arbitrary. A logically consistent definition excludes some behaviors that are very similar to those that are included, and excludes behaviors that many feel to be tool use. Until the tool behavior of even extant forms can be adequately defined, speculation about the tool behavior of extinct forms should be tempered.

Most nonhuman primate tool behavior is acquired by trial and error, a learning process ubiquitous among vertebrates. It is therefore unnecessary and probably erroneous to postulate that tool use among basal hominids involved a more advanced or more specialized type of learning.

Extant apes and monkeys have the sensory, motor, and cognitive capacities to learn to use and manufacture tools without training. Thus, complex, learned tool behavior may have been present before the hominid grade was attained. Consideration of chimpanzee tool behavior led Lancaster (1968) to postulate tool behavior among Pliocene hominoids. Even baboons, commonly used as a model of an even more primitive grade than that represented by chimpanzees, can and do use tools. In fact, Boese (personal communication) and Ransom and Ransom (1971) observed a baboon behavior that may represent a unique mode of nonhuman tool use: socially stressed males pick up and hold infants to inhibit attack by other males or to gain proximity to adult females. The variety of baboon tool use, including cooperative tool use, indicates that tool use in the hominid lineage may predate even the Pliocene.

Chimpanzees, quite proficient tool users, show declining numbers and shrinking distribution, while monkeys, which use tools infrequently, remain well established in the same range. Thus tool use does not necessarily confer significant competitive advantage. Alcock (1972) suggests that tool use acts not to eliminate competitors but rather to allow invasion of a vacant niche which is unavailable to competitors. The notion that the tool behavior of one hominid species was operative in the extinction of closely related, competing forms may not be valid.

It is unlikely that any object used as a tool by an extant wild primate would be preserved naturally so as to be recognized as a tool several million years from now. Likewise, the first tools used and manufactured by hominid ancestors are not apt to be recovered. Tool behavior undoubtedly predates even the oldest recognizable artifacts.

These points indicate that the critical importance attributed to tool behavior in the differentiation and radiation of hominids should be re-examined. I believe that language behavior was far more important in shaping hominid evolution. Language allowed rapid, widespread transfer of information between and within generations and thus allowed one individual to profit, without hazard, from the experience of countless others. Language allowed the assumption and recognition of context-specific roles which are advantageous in small, complex societies. Language also allowed planned, cooperative subsistence patterns.

Tool behavior was of limited importance in human evolution until man, unlike any extant nonhuman primate, began to power his tools with energy other than that derived from his own metabolic processes and from gravity. This development, which is really the origin of technology, is the only aspect of tool behavior that stands as a distinctive milestone in the hominid career.

REFERENCES

ALCOCK, J.
  1972 The evolution of the use of tools by feeding animals. *Evolution* 26:464–473.

BEATTY, H.
  1951 A note on the behavior of the chimpanzee. *Journal of Mammalogy* 32:118.

BECK, B.
  1967 A study of problem solving by gibbons. *Behaviour* 28:95–109.
  1972 Tool use in captive hamadryas baboons. *Primates* 13:277–295.
  1973a Observation learning of tool use by captive Guinea baboons (*Papio papio*). *American Journal of Physical Anthropology* 38:579–582.
  1973b Cooperative tool use by captive hamadryas baboons. *Science* 182:594–597.

BIERENS DE HAAN, J.
  1931 Werkzeuggebrauch und Werkzeugerstellung bei einem niederen Affen (*Cebus hypoleucus* Humb.). *Zeitschrift für Vergleichende Physiologie* 13:639–695.

BINGHAM, H.
  1929 *Chimpanzee translocation by means of boxes.* Comparative Psychology Monographs 5(3).

BIRCH, H.
  1945 The relation of previous experience to insightful problem solving. *Journal of Comparative Psychology* 38:367–383.

BOLWIG, N.
  1961 An intelligent tool-using baboon. *South African Journal of Science* 57:147–152.
  1964 Observations on the mental and manipulative abilities of a captive baboon (*Papio doguera*). *Behaviour* 22:24–40.

BOULENGER, E.
1937   *Apes and monkeys.* New York: McBride.
BOURNE, G.
1971   *The ape people.* New York: New American Library.
BUTLER, R.
1965   "Investigative behavior," in *Behavior of nonhuman primates,* volume two. Edited by A. Schrier, H. Harlow, and F. Stollnitz, 463–490. New York: Academic Press.
CAMACHO, L.
1907   Do animals reason? *Scientific American* 96:515.
CARPENTER, A.
1887   Monkeys opening oysters. *Nature* 36:53.
CARPENTER, C.
1934   *A field study of the behavior and social relations of howling monkeys.* Comparative Psychology Monographs 10(2).
1935   Behavior of red spider monkeys in Panama. *Journal of Mammalogy* 16:171–180.
1937   An observational study of two captive gorillas. *Human Biology* 9:175–196.
1940   *A field study in Siam of the behavior and social relations of the gibbon.* Comparative Psychology Monographs 16(5).
CHANCE, M.
1960   Köhler's chimpanzees — how did they perform? *Man* 59:130–135.
CHIANG, M.
1967   Use of tools by wild macaque monkeys in Singapore. *Nature* 214:1258–1259.
COOPER, L., H. HARLOW
1961   Note on a cebus monkey's use of a stick as a weapon. *Psychological Reports* 8:418.
COWPER, A.
1971   Observations on chimpanzees in Chester Zoo. *Revue du Comportement Animal* 5:39–44.
DARWIN, C.
1871   *The descent of man, and selection in relation to sex.* London: Murray.
DAVENPORT, R.
1967   The orang-utan in Sabah. *Folia Primatologica* 5:247–263.
DAVENPORT, R., C. ROGERS
1970   Intermodal equivalence of stimuli in apes. *Science* 168:279–281.
1971   Perception of photographs by apes. *Behaviour* 39:318–320.
DÖHL, J.
1966   Manipulierfähigkeit und "einsichtiges" Verhalten eines Schimpansen bei komplizierten Handlungsketten. *Zeitschrift für Tierpsychologie* 23:77–113.
DRESCHER, K., W. TRENDELENBURG
1927   Weiterer Beitrag zur Intelligenzprüfung an Affen (einschliesslich Anthropoiden). *Zeitschrift für Vergleichende Physiologie* 5:613–642.

GALLUP, G.
 1970   Chimpanzees: self-recognition. *Science* 167:86–87.
GOODALL, J.
 1964   Tool-using and aimed throwing in a community of free-living chimpanzees. *Nature* 201:1264–1266.
 1965   "Chimpanzees of the Gombe Stream Reserve," in *Primate behavior*. Edited by I. DeVore, 425-473. Chicago: Holt, Rinehart and Winston.
GUILLAUME, R., I. MEYERSON
 1930   Recherches sur l'usage de l'instrument chez les singes. *Journal de Psychologie* 27:177–236.
 1934   Recherches sur l'usage de l'instrument chez les singes III. *Journal de Psychologie* 31:497–554.
HAGGERTY, M.
 1910   Preliminary experiments on anthropoid apes. *Psychological Bulletin* 7:49.
HALL, K.
 1963   Tool-using performances as indicators of behavioral adaptability. *Current Anthropology* 4:479–494.
HALL, K., M. GOSWELL
 1964   Aspects of social learning in captive patas monkeys. *Primates* 5: 59–70.
HARLOW, H.
 1951   "Primate learning," in *Comparative psychology*. Edited by C. Stone, 183–238. New York: Prentice-Hall.
HARRISSON, B.
 1963a *Orang-utan*. Garden City, New York: Doubleday.
 1963b Education to wild living of young orang-utans at Bako National Park, Sarawak. *Sarawak Museum Journal* 11:221–258.
HILL, W.
 1960   *Primates*, volume four. Edinburgh: Edinburgh University Press.
HOBHOUSE, L.
 1901   *Mind in evolution*. New York: Macmillan.
HOOTON, E.
 1942   *Man's poor relations*. Garden City, New York: Doubleday, Doran.
HORNADAY, W.
 1922   *The minds and manners of wild animals*. New York: Scribner's.
ITANI, J., A. SUZUKI
 1967   The social unit of chimpanzees. *Primates* 8:355–381.
IZAWA, K., J. ITANI
 1966   Chimpanzees in Kasakati Basin, Tanzania. *Kyoto University African Studies* 1.
JACOBSEN, C., J. WOLFE, T. JACKSON
 1935   An experimental analysis of the functions of the frontal association areas in primates. *Journal of Nervous and Mental Disease* 82:1–14.
JAY, P.
 1968   "Primate field studies and human evolution," in *Primates*. Edited by P. Jay, 487–519. Chicago: Holt, Rinehart and Winston.

JENNISON, G.
1927   *Natural history: animals.* New York: Macmillan.
JONES, C., J. SABATER PI
1969   Sticks used by chimpanzees in Río Muni, West Africa. *Nature* 223:100–101.
KARRER, R.
1970   The use of the tail by an Old World monkey. *Primates* 11:171–175.
KATZ, D., R. KATZ
1936   Some problems concerning the feeding behaviour of monkeys. *Proceedings of the Zoological Society of London,* 579–582.
KAUFMANN, J.
1962   Ecology and social behavior of the coati, *Nasua narica,* on Barro Colorado Island, Panama. *University of California Publications in Zoology* 60:95–222.
KAWAI, M.
1965   Newly-acquired pre-cultural behavior of the natural troop of Japanese monkeys on Koshima Islet. *Primates* 6:1–30.
KLÜVER, H.
1933   *Behavior mechanisms in monkeys.* Chicago: University of Chicago Press.
1937   Re-examination of implement-using after an interval of three years. *Acta Psychologica* 2:347–397.
KÖHLER, W.
1927   *The mentality of apes* (second edition). London: Routledge and Kegan Paul.
KOLLAR, E.
1972   Object relations and the origin of tools. *Archives of General Psychiatry* 26:23–27.
KOOIJ, M., J. VAN ZON
1964   Gooiende Seriema's. *Artis* 9:197–201.
KORTLANDT, A.
1962   Chimpanzees in the wild. *Scientific American* 206:128–138.
1965   How do chimpanzees use weapons when fighting leopards? *American Philosophical Society Year Book,* 327–332.
1967   "Experimentation with chimpanzees in the wild," in *Neue Ergebnisse der Primatologie.* Edited by D. Starck, R. Schneider, and H.-J. Kuhn, 208–224. Stuttgart: Gustav Fischer.
KORTLANDT, A., M. KOOIJ
1963   Protohominid behavior in primates (preliminary communication). *Symposia of the Zoological Society of London* 10:61–68.
KUMMER, H., F. KURT
1965   "A comparison of social behavior in captive and wild hamadryas baboons," in *The baboon in medical research.* Edited by H. Vagtborg, 65–80. Austin: University of Texas Press.
LANCASTER, J.
1968   On the evolution of tool-using behavior. *American Anthropologist* 70:56–66.

MAC KINNON, J.
1971 The orang-utan in Sabah today. *Oryx* 11:141–191.

MARAIS, E.
1969 *The soul of the ape.* New York: Atheneum.

MC GREW, W., C. TUTIN
1973 Chimpanzee tool use in dental grooming. *Nature* 241:477–478.

MENZEL, E.
1966 Responsiveness to objects in free-ranging Japanese monkeys. *Behaviour* 26:130–150.
1971 Communication about the environment in a group of young chimpanzees. *Folia Primatologica* 15:220–232.
1972 Spontaneous invention of ladders in a group of young chimpanzees. *Folia Primatologica* 17:87–106.

MENZEL, E., R. DAVENPORT, C. ROGERS
1970 The development of tool using in wild-born and restriction-reared chimpanzees. *Folia Primatologica* 12:273–283.

MERFIELD, F., H. MILLER
1956 *Gorilla hunter.* New York: Farrar, Straus.

NELLMAN, H., W. TRENDELENBURG
1926 Ein Beitrag zur Intelligenzprüfung niederer Affen. *Zeitschrift für Vergleichende Physiologie* 4:142–200.

NISHIDA, T.
1968 The social group of wild chimpanzees in the Mahali Mountains. *Primates* 9:167–224.
1970 Social behavior and relationship among wild chimpanzees of the Mahali Mountains. *Primates* 11:47–87.

NOLTE, A.
1958 Beobachtungen über Instinktverhalten von Kapuzineraffen (*Cebus apella* L.) in der Gefangenschaft. *Behaviour* 12:183–207.

PARKER, C.
1968 The use of tools by apes. *Zoonooz* 41:10–13.

PHILIPPS, T.
1950 Man's relation to the apes. *Man: Journal of the Royal Anthropological Institute* 272:168.

PITMAN, C.
1931 *A game warden among his charges.* London: Nisbet.

RAHM, U.
1971 L'emploi d'outils par les chimpanzés de l'ouest de la Côte-d'Ivoire. *La Terre et la Vie* 25:506–509.

RANSOM, T., B. RANSOM
1971 Adult male-infant relationships among baboons (*Papio anubis*). *Folia Primatologica* 16:179–195.

RENSCH, B., J. DÖHL
1967 Spontanes Öffnen verschiedener Kistenverschlüsse durch einen Schimpansen. *Zeitschrift für Tierpsychologie* 24:476–489.

RENSENBRINK, H.
1960 Sarina en de stoelen. *Artis* 5:206–210.

REYNOLDS, V.
1967 *The apes.* Evanston: Harper and Row.

REYNOLDS, V., F. REYNOLDS
   1965   "Chimpanzees of the Budongo Forest," in *Primate behavior*. Edited by I. DeVore, 368–424. Chicago: Holt, Rinehart and Winston.

ROMANES, G.
   1882   *Animal intelligence*. London: Kegan Paul, Trench.

RUMBAUGH, D.
   1970   "Learning skills of anthropoids," in *Primate behavior*, volume one. Edited by L. Rosenblum, 1–70. New York: Academic Press.

SAVAGE, T., J. WYMAN
   1843–1844   Observations on the external characters and habits of the *Troglodytes niger* Geoff. and on its organization. *Boston Journal of Natural History* 4:362–386.

SCHALLER, G.
   1961   The orang-utan in Sarawak. *Zoologica* 46:73–82.
   1963   *The mountain gorilla*. Chicago: University of Chicago Press.

SCHILLER, P.
   1957   "Innate motor action as a basis of learning," in *Instinctive behavior*. Edited by C. Schiller, 264–287. New York: International Universities Press.

SHEAK, W.
   1922   Disposition and intelligence of the orang-utan. *Journal of Mammalogy* 3:47–51.

SPENCE, K.
   1937   Experimental studies of learning and the higher mental processes in infra-human primates. *Psychological Bulletin* 34:806–850.
   1938   Gradual versus sudden solution of discrimination problems by chimpanzees. *Journal of Comparative Psychology* 25:213–224.

STRUHSAKER, T., P. HUNKELER
   1971   Evidence of tool-using by chimpanzees in the Ivory Coast. *Folia Primatologica* 15:212–219.

SUGIYAMA, Y.
   1969   Social behavior of chimpanzees in the Budongo Forest, Uganda. *Primates* 10:197–225.

SUZUKI, A.
   1966   On the insect-eating habits among wild chimpanzees in the savanna woodland of west Tanzania. *Primates* 7:481–487.
   1969   An ecological study of chimpanzees in a savanna woodland. *Primates* 10:103–148.

TELEKI, G.
   1973   The omnivorous chimpanzee. *Scientific American* 228:32–42.

TOBIAS, P.
   1965   *Australopithecus, Homo habilis*, tool-using and tool-making. *South African Archaeological Bulletin* 20:167–192.

VAN HOOFF, J.
   1973   "The Arnhem Zoo chimpanzee consortium: an attempt to create an ecologically and socially acceptable habitat," in *International zoo yearbook*, volume thirteen. Edited by N. Duplaix-Hall, 195–203. London: Zoological Society of London.

VAN LAWICK-GOODALL, J.
  1968   The behaviour of free-living chimpanzees in the Gombe Stream
         Reserve. *Animal Behaviour Monographs* 1(3):161–311.
  1970   "Tool-using in primates and other vertebrates," in *Advances in the
         study of behavior,* volume three. Edited by D. Lehrman, R. Hinde,
         and E. Shaw, 195–249. New York: Academic Press.
VAN LAWICK-GOODALL, J., H. VAN LAWICK, C. PARKER
  1973   Tool-use in free-living baboons in the Gombe National Park, Tan-
         zania. *Nature* 241:212–213.
VEVERS, G., J. WEINER
  1963   Use of a tool by a captive capuchin monkey (*Cebus apella*). *Sym-
         posia of the Zoological Society of London* 10:115–118.
WALLACE, A.
  1869   *The Malay Archipelago.* London: Macmillan.
WARDEN, C., A. KOCH, H. FJELD
  1940   Instrumentation in cebus and rhesus monkeys. *Journal of Genetic
         Psychology* 56:297–310.
WILSON, W., C. WILSON
  1968   *Aggressive interactions of captive chimpanzees living in a semi-
         free-ranging environment* (Publication ARL-TR-68-9). Holloman
         Air Force Base, New Mexico: 6571st Aeromedical Research
         Laboratory, Aerospace Medical Division, United States Air Force
         Systems Command.
WRIGHT, R.
  1972   Imitative learning of a flaked stone technology — the case of an
         orangutan. *Mankind* 8:296–306.
YERKES, R.
  1916   *The mental life of monkeys and apes: a study of ideational be-
         havior.* Behavior Monographs 3.
  1927   *The mind of a gorilla.* Genetic Psychology Monographs 2.
  1943   *Chimpanzees: a laboratory colony.* New Haven: Yale University
         Press.
YERKES, R., B. LEARNED
  1925   *Chimpanzee intelligence and its vocal expressions.* Baltimore: Wil-
         liams and Wilkins.
YERKES, R., A. YERKES
  1929   *The great apes.* New Haven: Yale University Press.

Discussion

[Dr. Beck summarized his paper.]

BECK: I would like to direct some comments to my paleoanthropologist colleagues. This is largely generated by some of the discussion that occurred in a previous session (see *Paleoanthropology: morphology and paleoecology*). If as I have shown (see Beck, this volume) the definition of tool use among extant primates is so difficult and so arbitrary, we must be very cautious about glib statements concerning the tool use, tool manufacture, and culture (which may be equated with tool use) of extinct primates. We have been much too free in our use of these terms when dealing with extinct primates. Secondly, an overwhelming proportion of the tool behavior of nonhuman primates is acquired by simple accidental trial-and-error learning. Thus we need not postulate sensory, motor, and cognitive capacities equivalent to those observed in extant man in order to discuss tool behavior in the hominid lineage. My experimental studies demonstrated that baboons can use tools quite facilely when their environment makes tool use possible and reinforcing. In fact, one experiment showed that baboons are capable of cooperative tool use with division of labor. This has not been reported even for chimpanzees. So even the cercopithecine monkeys are capable of tremendous variety and sophistication in tool behavior. We should bear this in mind in viewing the potential for tool behavior by representatives in the hominid fossil record. Futhermore, tools that are used by wild extant primates today would not be recognizable as tools a few days after use. We should not think of tool use in the hominid career as beginning with manufactured stone tools in the fossil record. Extensive and sophisticated tool use and perhaps even a dependency on tools probably far predates the earliest manufactured stone tools. This also should be borne in mind when one makes statements like that of Tobias (see Tobias in *Primate functional morphology and evolution*) that a very important factor in the divergence of *Homo* was their dependency on tools. Indeed we find manufactured stone tools only with hominids but this does not mean that their antecedents were not using tools considerably and in ways critical for their own natural history. In sum, I suspect that tool use goes far back in the hominid lineage and certainly predates the discovery of the earliest manufactured stone tools which I think is now dated at somewhere around 2.6 million years B.P. I would also speculate that when we find evidence for tools "manufactured to a set and regular pattern," i.e. actual tool cultures, this strongly argues for the existence of some sort of linguistic communication. My research on baboons and survey of the literature on chimpanzees evidences that the amount of information gathered by an individual simply observing a skilled tool user is very minimal. Chimpanzees probably gain more than baboons, but it is still minimal. Thus, it is unrealistic to postulate that we should suddenly find regular tool traditions springing up in the hominid lineage that are based on one animal observing others through successive generations. We should think more in terms of one animal "telling" others how to do it.

LIEBERMAN: If you were to write a formal grammar of the retouching of a biface you would obtain a context sensitive phrase structure grammar. But if you wished to produce the formal grammar of a tool of Levalloisian technique you would probably need a transformational grammar.

RUMBAUGH: In order for tool use to occur it is important to have materials available that lend themselves to competent tool use. It is quite clear that primates in captivity are much more inclined to tool use and evidence more flexible tool usage than primates in the field primarily because at least in some contexts there is a wide variety of fine durable materials available to them. So the animals interact with them and discover through trial-and-error the various attributes of the materials and various reinforcements that can be obtained through their employment.

BECK: That is why I say that the capacity for tool use is really only seen when the environment makes it both possible and reinforcing, i.e. there is a pay-off and there are the materials to work with. Many wild primates probably have the capacity for tool use but simply do not utilize the capacity.

KORTLANDT: There are definite regional traditions of tool use in the wild. Several observers in the western part of the Ivory Coast have reported that chimpanzees use sticks and hammer open fruits on the exposed roots of trees. This has not been observed in any other area.

STRUHSAKER: During three years of study in western Uganda, we detected no evidence that chimpanzees use sticks or stones to open hard fruits. Perhaps with more observations something like this will be found. However, neither of the two species of fruit that they were opening with sticks and stones in the Ivory Coast occur in Uganda. Possibly the fruits necessary for this kind of operation simply are not available.

Biographical Notes

BENJAMIN B. BECK (1939–) is Research Curator and Curator of Primates at the Chicago Zoological Park, Brookfield, Illinois, and Research Associate and Lecturer at the University of Chicago, where he received his Ph.D. in 1967. He is primarily interested in primate cognition and has studied primate sensory processes, locomotion, and social behavior. He has conducted field studies of mammalian and avian behavior and ecology.

CHARLES BELL (1936–) is an electronics technician at Yerkes Regional Primate Research Center at Emory University in Atlanta, Georgia. He received his education at the Southern Technical Institute and at the Georgia Institute of Technology. His major research interests lie in the application of electronics to behavior and biomedics.

GILBERT K. BOESE (1937–) was born in Chicago. He received his B.A. from Carthage College, Carthage, Illinois in 1959, an M.S. from Northern Illinois University in 1965, and a Ph.D. in Pathobiology from The Johns Hopkins University in 1972. He was Assistant Professor of Biology at Elmhurst College until 1970 and is presently an Associate Director of the Chicago Zoological Park, Brookfield, Illinois. His special interests are primate social behavior and ecology.

JOSEPHINE V. BROWN (1933–) was born in Rotterdam, Holland, and received her education at Emory University, Atlanta, Georgia. She is a member of Phi Beta Kappa and the Society of Sigma Xi. Her major research interests are in the areas of perceptual and cognitive development of newborn infants, and mother-infant interaction. She is an Associate Professor of Psychology at Georgia State University.

RICHARD K. DAVENPORT (1930–   ) is currently Professor of Psychology at the Georgia Institute of Technology and Psychobiologist at the Yerkes Regional Primate Research Center of Emory University, Atlanta, Georgia. He was educated at the University of North Carolina and the University of Kentucky. He joined the Yerkes Center in 1957 and began studying the behavioral effects of early restriction in chimpanzees. He has done fieldwork with orangutans in Sabah, Malaysia. He is now primarily interested in perception in apes, monkeys, and in human children with severe reading problems.

WOLFGANG P. J. DITTUS (1943–   ) is a post-doctoral fellow with the Smithsonian Institution, Washington, D.C. He received his B.Sc. and M.Sc. from McGill University, Canada, and his Ph.D. in Zoology from the University of Maryland in 1974. He has published on the development of singing behavior in the cardinal bird, and he is presently preparing publications dealing with primate behavior and socioecology based on his three and one-half years of field research on the toque monkey of Sri Lanka.

NORRIS M. DURHAM has been on the faculties of the Pennsylvania State University and Wayne State University. Presently he is an Assistant Professor in the College of Human Biology at the University of Wisconsin-Green Bay. His doctorate is in physical anthropology from the Pennsylvania State University where he studied under Doctors C. R. Carpenter and Paul T. Baker. He has carried out research at Yerkes Regional Primate Research Center, and in Peru, French Guinea, and Surinam.

ROGER S. FOUTS (1943–   ) is an Assistant Professor of Psychology at the University of Oklahoma. He was a Research Associate at the Institute for Primate Studies and the Department of Psychology at the University of Oklahoma from 1970–1973. He received a Ph.D. in Psychology at the University of Nevada at Reno. His major research concerns the acquisition and usage of American Sign Language by non-human primates.

GORDON G. GALLUP, JR. (1941–   ) is Professor of Psychology at Tulane University. He received his Ph.D. from Washington State University in 1968. His research interests include cognitive capacities in primates, learning, ethology, comparative psychology, and behavior genetics. Currently his work concerns tonic immobility ("animal hypnosis") and its relation to various kinds of human psychopathology.

TIMOTHY V. GILL (1947–   ) is a Behavioral Technician at Yerkes Regional Primate Research Center at Emory University. He received his education at Emory University and Georgia State University. His major areas of interest are developmental, comparative, and psycho-linguistics.

KENNETH E. GLANDER (1940–   ) is Assistant Professor of Anthropology at Duke University. He received his B.A. from the University of Texas at Austin in 1969, an M.A. from the University of Chicago in 1971, and a Ph.D. in Anthropology from the University of Chicago in 1975. His special interests include primate ecology, resource distribution and utilization, anatomical correlates of dietary specialization, and primate adaptive strategies.

ROBERT S. O. HARDING (1931–   ) was born in New York City. He received his B.A. from Harvard in 1952, and M.A. from the University of California, Berkeley, in 1970, and a Ph. D. from the same institution in 1973. He is currently an Assistant Professor of Anthropology and Assistant Curator of Physical Anthropology at the University Museum at the University of Pennsylvania. His research interests include primate ecology and the evolution of behavior.

CLAUDE MARCEL HLADIK (1936–   ) was born in Paris. He began field observations on the primates of Ceylon in 1959 and 1960, when he was a student at the University of Paris. His researches were focused on the diet of primate species in the wild, in correlation with their anatomical and physiological characteristics as well as their behavioral patterns. The ecological aspect of this research was conducted in the field in association with the botanical researches of his wife, ANNETTE HLADIK. This long-term study has been partly published in a series of papers concerning a total of 38 primate species observed in the wild. In the past he has been associated with research programs of the Smithsonian Institution, in Central America (Barro Colorado; 1967–1968) and in Asia (Sri Lanka; 1969–1970). He is now Research Fellow of the C.N.R.S. (National Center of Scientific Research, France) and is based at the Museum of Natural History (Brunoy, France). He is currently conducting field studies on the lemurs of Madagascar (1970–1974) and on the apes of Gabon (1966–1971, 1972–1975).

DOROTHY J. KLEIN (1939–   ) received a B.A. in Anthropology from from the University of California at Berkeley in 1964.

LEWIS L. KLEIN (1938–   ) studied anthropology at the University of California, Berkeley, where he received an M.A. (1961) and a Ph.D. (1972). He has taught in the Anthropology Department of the University of California, Berkeley, and in the Anthropology and Zoology Departments at the University of Illinois.

JAMES LOY (1943–   ) is presently an Assistant Professor of Anthropology at the University of Rhode Island. His formal training began at the University of Tennesee (B.S., 1965) and was continued at Northwestern University (M.A., 1966; Ph.D., 1969). He has studied the behavior of both free-ranging and captive macaques and patas monkeys on the island colonies of the Caribbean Primate Research Center (Puerto Rico). Prior to moving to Rhode Island, he held the position of Scientist-in-Charge of the La Parguera (Puerto Rico) primate colony.

L. D. MECH studied biology at Cornell University and received his Ph.D. at Purdue in 1962. His dissertation dealt with the ecology of wolves and moose on Isle Royale in Michigan. He has taught at McAllister College in St. Paul, Minnesota. Since 1968 he has been studying the spatial organization of wolf packs in northeastern Minnesota. He is currently a research biologist with the United States Fish and Wildlife Service.

JOHN F. OATES (1944–   ) was born in N. Wales. He studied Zoology at University College London, receiving his B.Sc. in 1966. He subsequently undertook research on the ecology of rodents and prosimian primates in East Nigeria, working at the University of Nigeria, Nsukka. That project was suspended at the outbreak of the Nigerian civil war. He returned to Africa in 1970 under the auspices of the New York Zoological Society to undertake a field study of the black-and-white colobus monkey. On the basis of this study he was awarded a Ph.D. from the University of London in 1974.

ROGER PETERS received a B.A. at the University of Chicago in 1965, taught mathematics at New College in Sarasota, Florida, and received a Ph.D. in Psychology at the University of Michigan in 1974. His dissertation dealt with olfactory communication and spatial behavior in the wolves of northeastern Minnesota. He is currently a lecturer in the

Department of Psychology at the University of Michigan and is working on a book on the role of hunting in human evolution.

PIER PAOLO PISANI (1937–) was born in Rome, Italy. He was educated at Tech College, Vercelli, Italy, and with the IBM Training Course, IBM Italia, Milan, Italy. His major areas of interest lie in nonnumerical computer programming and various problems in cybernetics. He is a Research Associate at the University of Georgia, Athens, Georgia.

CHARLES M. ROGERS (1923–) received his B.A. from Lafayette College in 1948 and a Ph.D. in Experimental Psychology from Yale in 1954. He has been an Associate Professor at Auburn University since 1973. He spent several years as a Psychobiologist at the Yerkes Regional Primate Research Center of Emory University and a year as Visiting Associate Professor at the University of Guelph. His major interests lie in the general areas of animal behavior and comparative psychobiology.

DUANE M. RUMBAUGH (1929–) is Chairman and Professor of Psychology at Georgia State University, Atlanta, Georgia. He received his education at the University of Dubuque, Dubuque, Iowa; Kent State University; and the University of Colorado, Boulder, Colorado. He is an APA fellow (div. 1 and 7); AAAS fellow; Sigma Xi; Fellow of the San Diego Zoological Society; American Men and Women of Science; AAAS Chautauqua Course Lecturer for College Teachers; and has been an invited lecturer to twenty different universities. His major research interests are in comparative behavioral primatology and developmental psychology.

GRAHAM S. SAAYMAN (1939–) is Senior Lecturer in Psychology at the University of Capetown. He received his B.A. Honours from the University of Natal in 1961, an M.A. from McMaster University in Canada in 1963 and a Ph.D. from the University of London in 1967. He was a Research Fellow at the Mammal Research Institute of the University of Pretoria between 1968 and 1969, during which time he studied the influence of hormonal and ecological factors on the social behavior of baboons in the northern Transvaal and in the Kruger National Park. He then spent four years studying captive and free-swimming dolphins as Animal Behaviorist at the Port Elizabeth Museum and Oceanarium. He took up his present post in April 1974.

THOMAS THANE STRUHSAKER (1938–   ) was born in Lansing, Michigan. He received his B.S. in the biological sciences from Michigan State University in 1960 and his Ph.D. in zoology from the University of California, Berkeley, in 1965. Since 1962 he has been conducting field studies on primates particularly in Uganda, Kenya, and Cameroun, but also has zoological field experience in Senegal, the Ivory Coast, Equatorial Guinea, Tanzania, Zaire, Madagascar, Mexico, Trinidad, Panama, Argentina, Columbia, India, Japan, and Canada. In 1966 he joined the Institute for Research of Animal Behavior (a unit of the New York Zoological Society and Rockefeller University) and in 1972 transferred to the successor organization of this institute, The Center for Field Biology and Conservation of the New York Zoological Society.

AKIRA SUZUKI (1939–   ) was born in Japan. He studied animal ecology at the Tokyo University of Education and physical anthropology at Kyoto University, and is now at the Primate Research Institute, Kyoto University. He studied the ecology of snow-living Japanese monkeys since 1962 and of the savanna-living and forest-living chimpanzees in East Africa since 1964.

RUSSELL HOWARD TUTTLE (1939–   ) is Associate Professor of Anthropology and Evolutionary Biology at the University of Chicago and Visiting Research Scientist at Yerkes Regional Primate Research Center of Emory University. He received a B.Sc. degree (Anatomy, 1961) and an M.A. (Anthropology, 1962) from the Ohio State University and a Ph.D. (Anthropology, 1965) from the University of California, Berkeley. He has conducted field studies on nonhuman primates and associated fauna in Rhodesia, Ceylon, Kenya, and Tanzania. His principal research on the functional morphology and evolutionary biology of primates has been conducted at primate research centers, museums, and anthropological institutes in the United States, Japan, Switzerland, and Italy. He is the editor of *The functional and evolutionary biology of primates* (1972) and author of more than thirty scientific papers.

ERNST VON GLASERSFELD (1917–   ) was born in Munich, Germany, and is now Assistant Professor of Psychology, University of Georgia, Athens, Georgia. He received his education at Zuoz College, Switzerland, Zurich University, Switzerland and the University of Vienna. He is a consultant for Information System Architectonic, Bethesda, Maryland. His major research interest is language analysis and artificial intelligence.

HAL WARNER (1917–   ) is Assistant Professor and Chief of the Bio-medical Engineering Lab at Yerkes Regional Primate Research Center of Emory University. He received his education at the Drexel Institute of Technology, the University of Pennsylvania, and Temple University. He is a member of the Research Society of America (Sigma Xi) and General Electric's Elfun Society (a society for engineering managers and high-level scientific contributors). His major interest is in bio-medical engineering.

Index of Names

Abély, P., 332
Alcock, J., 413–414, 436, 440
Aldrich-Blake, F. P. G., 82, 184, 205
Alexander, B. K., 158, 159, 166, 195
Altmann, J., 250, 295
Altmann, S. A., 38, 54, 77, 166, 190, 191–193, 205, 250, 252, 295
Amsterdam, B., 321, 336
Anderson, J. N., 317
Andradi, L., 125
Anson, J. E., 312
Anthoney, T. R., 213
Archer, A. L., 246, 251
Ardrey, R., 153, 256
Asanov, S. S., 191, 193
Atz, J. W., 279

Baenninger, L., 313
Baenninger, R., 313
Baggaley, D., 259
Baker, Paul T., 87
Baldwin, J. D., 156, 168
Banage, W. B., 259
Barnicot, N. A., 120
Barreda, M. Víctor, 87
Bartlett, D., 248
Bartlett, J., 248
Bazan, Q., 88
Beattie, J., 170, 171
Beatty, H., 421
Beck, Benjamin B., 11, 40, 235–236, 241, 302–304, 413–441, 449–450
Beg, Mirza Azhar, 158

Behar, Mark P., 337
Bell, C. L., 391–400
Bellugi, U., 372
Benson, S. B., 310
Bergman, M., 313
Bernstein, I., 120, 125, 154, 155, 162, 169, 418
Bert, T., 206, 218, 223
Bertrand, M., 158, 328
Bierens de Hann, J., 421, 428
Birch, H., 420, 438
Bingham, H., 421
Blankenship, L., 246
Boelkins, R. C., 146, 147
Boese, Gilbert K., 205–228, 231–233, 240–241, 440
Boese, Wilma B., 205
Bolwig, N., 183, 427
Bossert, W. H., 111
Boulenger, E., 430
Bourne, G., 420, 423–424
Bowers, J. M., 158, 159, 166, 196
Bradbury, J., 37
Brody, P. N., 310
Bronowski, J., 372
Brooks, A. C., 251
Brosset, A., 3
Brown, Josephine V., 391–400
Brown, W. L., 329
Buechner, H. K., 125
Bundy, R. A., 334
Burt, W. H., 110
Butler, R., 435
Bygott, David, 261

Caldwell, D. K., 181
Caldwell, M. C., 181
Camacho, L., 424
Campbell, B. G., 289, 292
Campbell, D. T., 350
Capper, S. A., 315–316
Carpenter, A., 426
Carpenter, C. R., 38, 54, 61, 68, 76, 87, 95, 144, 155, 166, 168, 169, 414, 417, 424, 426, 428, 432
Carroll, R., 37
Castell, R., 168
Chalmers, N. R., 40, 169
Chance, M. R. A., 166, 439
Charles-Dominique, P., 15, 16, 31
Chiang, M., 426
Chivers, D. J., 30, 31, 54, 76
Chomsky, N., 374, 385
Chown, W., 382
Church, J., 335
Clark, J. D., 283
Clutton-Brock, Tim, 103, 117–119
Colinonsky, Celestino, 87
Conaway, C. H., 153, 167, 188, 193
Condit, I. J., 77
Conolly, C. J., 359
Cooley, C. H., 331, 332–334
Cooper, L., 428
Corner, E. J. H., 77
Coult, A. D., 171
Count, E. W., 153, 163, 170
Cowan, I. M., 290
Cowper, A., 419, 422
Crelin, E., 376
Crisler, L., 281, 284, 290
Crook, J. H., 30, 37, 166, 195, 205

Dandelot, P., 103
Dart, R. A., 247, 251–252, 254, 289, 292–293
Darwin, Charles, 335, 407, 424
Dathe, H., 130
Davenport, Richard K., 329, 334, 343–351, 368, 419–423, 432, 439
David, G. F. X., 191
Deevey, E. S., 133
DeKeyser, P. L., 223
Delmas, F. A., 332
Denham, W. W., 37
Deraniyagala, P. E. P., 139
Deregpwski, J. B., 350
DeSilva, G., 125
DeVore, I. K., 30, 157, 166, 168, 182–183, 190, 205–206, 219, 224, 252,

282, 287, 292, 295
Dittus, Wolfgang P. J., 125–149, 231–242
Dixon, J. S., 294, 311, 335
Dobzhansky, T. H., 372–373
Dölh, J., 416, 420
Drescher, K., 423
DuMond, F. V., 156, 168
Dunbar, R. I. M., 184, 206, 213, 218, 223
DuPuy, A., 223
Durham, Norris M., 87–101
Duval, S., 337

Eaton, G., 187, 193
Eckstein, P., 182, 186, 189
Eisenberg, J. F., 3, 4, 21–22, 24–25, 30, 37, 120, 125, 127, 148, 168, 196, 232
Estes, R., 281, 286, 291
Ettel, P. C., 275
Ettlinger, G., 343–346

Farook, S. M. S., 125
Faure, H., 322
Feeney, P. P., 54, 55
Ferguson, S. N. U., 131
Fisera, Dolores, 205
Fjeld, H., 426, 429
Fooden, J., 162
Ford, C. D., 171, 172, 173
Fouts, Roger S., 371–387, 403–404, 406
Fox, R., 166; *The imperial animal* (with Tiger), 153
Fraenkel, G. S., 55
Freides, D., 343
Frisch, J. E., 195
Furness, W., 384
Furuya, Y., 120

Gaillard, D. R., 223
Gallup, Gordon G., Jr., 309–337, 439
Gardner, B. T., 329, 372, 377–379, 383, 391
Gardner, R. A., 329, 372, 377–379, 383, 391
Gartlan, J. S., 30, 37, 154, 166, 169
Gautier, J. P., 31
Gautier-Hion, A., 31, 195
Gentry, R., 310
Geschwind, N., 343
Gessell, A., 336
Gibson, J. J., 351
Gilbert, C., 183, 188–191
Gill, Timothy V., 359, 391–400

Gillman, J., 183, 188, 189, 190–191
Glander, Kenneth E., 37–55, 235–236, 238–240, 455
Goddard, J., 281, 286, 291
Goldfoot, D. A., 187
Goodall, J., 26, 28, 169, 273, 302, 304, 305, 417. *See also* Van Lawick-Goodall, J.
Goodin, L., 382
Goss-Custard, J. D., 184
Goswell, M., 437
Gould, R. A., 283
Graham, C. E., 189
Guillaume, R., 420, 425, 427
Green, Steven, 103
Groves, C. P., 103
Guggisberg, C. A. W., 287

Habenstein, R. W., 171
Haber, G., 291
Haggerty, M., 423
Hagnauer, Werner, 37
Hailman, J. P., 155
Hairston, N. G., 54
Hall, K. R. L., 30, 82, 155, 157, 163, 166, 168, 169, 182–183, 205–206, 219, 224, 426, 433, 436–437
Hamburg, D. A., 195
Hamilton, Alan, 103
Hanby, J. P., 186, 188
Harding, Robert S. O., 245–256, 302
Harlow, Harry F., 195, 320, 333, 355, 368, 428–429
Harlow, M. K., 320, 333
Harrison, B., 423–424, 432
Hartman, C. G., 193
Hausfater, G., 165, 168
Hayashi, K., 277
Hayes, C., 376, 384
Hayes, K. J., 334, 376, 384
Hebb, D. O., 376
Herbert J., 182, 186–187, 193
Heinrich, B., 168
Hendrickx, A. G., 188–190
Henry, G. M., 139
Herskovits, M. J., 350
Hess, J. Y., 314–315
Hewes, G., 385
Hewett-Emmett, D., 120
Hill, S. D., 333–334
Hill, W. C. O., 125, 205, 213, 359, 429
Hladik, A., 76, 77, 80, 120, 147
Hladik, C. M., 3–32, 38, 49, 54, 55, 76, 77, 80, 120, 147

Hobhouse, B., 420, 422, 426
Hockett, C. F., 372–373, 391
Hodgen, G. D., 189
Hoff, Charles J., 87
Holden, Mrs. Wy, 125
Holdridge, L. R., 38
Holmes, R. T., 114
Hooton, E., 426
Hornaday, W., 424, 426–427, 432
Horr, D., 363
Hunkeler, P., 421

Imanishi, K., 158, 163, 182, 195, 259
Isaac, G., 255
Itani, Junichiro, 144, 147, 259, 273, 418, 420–422
Izawa, K., 419, 422

Jackson, T., 420
Jacobsen, C., 420
Janzen, D., 37, 38, 46
Jay, P., 10, 11, 120, 168, 193, 195, 429, 433
Jemail, J. A., 314
Jennison, G., 420, 426, 429
Johansson, E. D. B., 189
Jolly, A., 19, 166, 167, 275
Jones, C., 419, 430–431
Jones, M. L., 130

Kano, T., 272
Kaplan, S., 280, 297
Karrer, R., 413
Katende, A. B., 103
Katz, D., 429
Katz, R., 429
Kaufmann, J. H., 156, 159, 188, 193, 194, 428
Kawai, Masao, 157, 158, 159, 163, 259, 438
Kawamura, S., 158, 159
Keverne, E. B., 193
Kesall, J. P., 285, 290
Kingdon, J., 247, 259, 275
Klatt, D., 376, 391
Kleiman, D., 125
Klein, Dorothy J., 59–84, 231, 235
Klein, Lewis L., 59–84, 95, 99, 231, 235, 236–239
Klingel, H., 181
Klopfer, P. H., 155
Klüver, H., 426–429, 433
Knobil, E., 189

Koch, A., 426, 429
Koford, C. B., 144, 145, 146, 147, 160, 188, 190
Köhler, W., 360, 417–418, 419–423, 431, 438–439
Kollar, E., 418, 420, 422
Kondo, Shiro, 259
Kooij, M., 416–420, 422–430
Kortlandt, Adriaan, 301–304, 378, 387, 406, 416–420, 422–430, 451
Koyama, N., 159
Krantz, G., 296
Kraus, G., 337
Kriewaldt, F. H., 188, 190
Kuehn, R. E., 22, 168
Kuhme, H., 281, 286–287, 295
Kuhn, H. J., 103
Kummer, H., 165, 166, 205–206, 209, 211, 215, 219–220, 224, 226–227, 231, 236, 416
Kurt, F., 232, 416

Laborde, J. E., 314
Lancaster, J. B., 182, 190, 192–195, 343, 440
Lashley, K. S., 375
Laughlin, W. S., 283, 288
Learned, B., 421
Lee, R. B., 29, 190, 192, 194, 254, 288
Lemmon, W. B., 379–381
Lenneberg, E. H., 374, 385
Lieberman, P., 368, 376, 378, 387, 391, 403–409, 450
Lindburg, D. G., 159, 191
Linnaeus, Carolus, 125
Lissmann, H. W., 310
Little, E. L., Jr., 46
Lockhard, R. B., 279
Lorenz, K., 153
Lott, D. F., 310
Lowther, G. R., 181, 196–197, 265, 295–296
Loy, James, 153–174, 186–187, 190, 194
Loy, Kent M., 153, 156, 157, 160, 161

MacLean, P. D., 311, 312
McClure, H. E., 40
McClure, M. K., 312, 317–320, 332, 334
McCormack, C., 356
MacDonald, G. J., 190
McDowell, A. A., 329
McGrew, W., 431
McKay, G. M., 4, 127
MacKinnon, J., 423–424, 432

MacRoberts, M. H., 158, 161
Mallery, D. G., 386
Malmi, W., 247–248
Manley, G., 5
Manske, David, 205
Marais, E. N., 195, 251, 427
Marler, Peter, 103, 120, 373, 408
Marsden, H. M., 164
Martin, R. D., 18
Matthews, L. H., 310
Mead, G. H., 331, 333–334
Mech, L. David, 279–298
Mellgren, R., 380–381
Melvin, K. B., 312
Menzel, E., 419–422, 431, 436–437, 438
Merfield, F., 417, 419–420, 422
Meyers, R. E., 343
Meyerson, I., 420, 425, 427
Michael, R. P., 182, 186, 189, 193
Miller, H., 417, 419–420, 422
Missakian, E. Z., 146, 147, 159, 161
Mizuhara, H., 147
Montevecchi, W. A., 312–314
Morgan, Elaine, 242
Morris, D., 256
Moynihan, M. H., 3, 25
Muckenhirn, N. A., 22, 120, 125
Murdock, G. P., 171, 172
Murie, A., 284, 290, 294

Napier, J. R., 103, 147
Napier, P. H., 103, 147
Nathan, M. F., 206, 213, 218, 223
Neill, D. D., 189
Nellman, H., 427
Neville, M. K., 147
Nishida, T., 197, 261, 273, 417–419
Nishimura, A., 144
Nissen, C. H., 334
Nolte, A., 429
Nomura, T., 191, 195

Oates, John F., 103–121, 233, 242
Opler, C., 37
Opler, Paul, 37
Opler, T., 37
Oppenheimer, J. R., 24, 79, 80
Ostancow, P., 332

Parker, C., 417, 422–424, 427
Patterson, Francine, 384
Pearson, H. A., 45
Peters, Roger, 279–298, 301, 303–305
Petter, J. J., 3, 14, 19, 20

Philipps, T., 417
Phillips, W. W. A., 127
Phoenix, C. H., 186
Pilbeam, D., 174
Pimlott, D. H., 285
Pisani, Pier, 391–400
Pitelka, F. A., 110, 114
Pitman, C., 417
Poirier, F. E., 120, 169
Pratt, C. L., 320
Premack, A. J., 377
Premack, D., 329, 344, 377, 391, 406
Preyer, W., 335
Pribram, K. H., 328

Quick, H. F., 134

Rahm, U., 29, 103, 414, 417, 421
Ramaswami, L. S., 191
Ransom, B. S., 185, 211, 219, 440
Read, C., 292
Rensenbrink, H., 424
Rensch, B., 416
Reynolds, F., 29, 169, 197, 260, 273, 417, 422, 424, 430
Reynolds, V., 29, 169, 197, 273, 417, 419, 422, 430
Richard A., 19, 38, 68
Richards, C., 240
Ripley, S., 8, 10, 11, 125
Ritter, W. E., 310
Roberts, P., 167
Robertson, L. T., 186, 188, 191
Robinette, W. L., 246, 251
Robinson, E. M., 329
Rogers, Charles M., 329, 334, 343–351, 368, 419–423, 439
Romanes, G., 428–429
Rowell, T. E., 154, 163, 168, 169, 170, 182–186, 188–189, 191–192, 196, 205, 246, 252
Rudran, R., 5, 6, 22, 120
Rukuba, M. L. S. B., 103
Rumbaugh, Duane M., 235, 304, 329, 353–364, 367–368, 391–392, 395, 403, 405–406, 424, 450, 457
Russell, I. S., 347
Rustin, E., 322
Rutter, R. J., 285

Saayman, Graham S., 168, 181–198, 205, 252
Sabater, Pi, J., 419, 430–431
Sackett, G. P., 320

Sade, D. S., 146, 153, 155, 156, 158, 159, 160, 161, 163, 164, 165, 170, 193, 195
Sarich, V. M., 120
Savage, T., 421
Schaller, G. B., 29, 30, 169, 181, 196, 265, 272, 276, 282, 286, 287, 291–292, 294–296, 417, 423, 430, 432
Schenkel, R., 378
Schiller, P., 417, 420–422, 431
Schiltz, S., 333
Schjelderup-Ebbe, T., 155
Schmidt, M., 310
Schmidt-Nielsen, K., 54
Schmook, J., 310
Schneirla, T., 376
Schulman, A. H., 317
Schultz, A. H., 360, 423
Schusterman, R. J., 310
Sclater, W. L., 251
Scott, B., 37
Scott, Norman, 37
Scow, Kate, 205
Segal, M. D., 350
Sheak, W., 423
Shentoub, S. A., 322
Shirley, E. K., 54
Shirley, M. M., 336
Siddiqi, M. Rafiq, 158
Simonds, P. E., 158, 162
Simons, E. L., 275
Simpson, G., 372
Simpson, M. J. A., 310
Slobodkin, L. B., 54
Smith, C. C., 18
Smith, F. E., 54
Smythe, R. H., 310
Soderlund, Richard, 205
Sorenson, M. W., 167
Soulairac, A., 322
Southwick, C. H., 127, 147, 158
Spence, K., 432, 437–438
Stabenfeldt, G. H., 189
Stokoe, W., 385–386
Stoltz, L. P., 185, 190, 192, 252
Stone, L. J., 335
Struhsaker, Thomas T., 26, 82, 103–121, 169, 188, 233–234, 236, 241–242, 408–409, 421, 451
Strum, S., 248
Sugiyama, Y., 10, 158, 162, 304, 417, 419
Sussman, R .W., 19, 20
Sutcliffe, A. J., 293

Suzuki, Akira, 259–277, 418–419, 421, 430
Suzuki, Takako, 259
Swallow, R. W., 309
Swanson, E. T., 312–314

Tayler, 181, 184, 196–197
Teleki, G., 26, 247, 252–253, 255, 283, 288, 292, 296, 302–305, 417, 422
Ternes, J. W., 314
Thompson, T. I., 312, 336
Thorington, R. W., Jr., 78, 433
Thorpe, W., 373
Tiger, L., 153, 166, 170, 173; *The imperial animal,* 153
Tinklepaugh, O. L., 329
Tobias, P., 197, 420, 429, 431; *Antecedents of man and after,* 450
Tolman, C. W., 311
Trendelburg, W., 423, 427
Tutin, C., 431
Tuttle, Russell, 3, 11, 37, 40, 231, 241–242, 407

Vandenbergh, J. G., 146, 182, 193–194
Van Hooff, J. A. R. A. M., 378, 418–419, 420, 422–423
Van Lawick, H., 265, 427
Van Lawick-Goodall, J., 40 ,188, 197, 252–253, 261, 265, 266, 283, 288, 292, 330, 372, 378, 413–415, 417–422, 425, 427, 430–431, 433, 436–439; *My friends the wild chimpanzees,* 301. *See also* Goodall J.
Van Zon, J., 429
Vargas, Cezar, 87
Vehrencamp, S., 37
Verheyen, W. N., 103
Vessey, S., 146
Vevers, G., 429
Vogel, Christian, 120, 242, 304

Von Ebers, Margaret, 205
Von Glaserfeld, E. C., 391–400
Von Senden, M., 322

Wass, S., 125
Wadsworth, F. H., 46
Wagner, H. O., 68
Wallace, A., 423, 432
Warden, C., 426, 429
Warner, Harold, 391–400
Waser, P., 277
Washburn, S. L., 182, 190, 193, 195, 205, 252, 282, 287, 292, 295
Weiner, J., 429
Welegalla, J., 186
Whittaker, R. H., 54
Wicklund, R. A., 337
Wilson, A. P., 146, 147
Wilson, C., 418–419
Wilson, E. O., 111
Wilson, W. H., 391, 418–419
Wittreich, W., 322
Wolfe, J., 420
Wolff, W., 337
Woodburn, J., 27, 254–255
Wright, R., 416
Wyman, J., 421
Wynne-Edwards, V. C., 30

Yakimov, V. P., 304–305
Yerkes, A. W., 310, 360, 416, 421, 423–424, 439
Yerkes, R. M., 310, 360, 378, 416, 420, 421–424
Yoshiba, K., 120, 146, 168, 190
Young, S., 281

Zuckerman, S., 181–182, 186, 189, 195–196
Zumpe, D., 189

Index of Subjects

Acacia, 275
Adina, 5
Aepyceros melampus, 246–247, 249
Africa, 3, 26, 28, 31, 103, 119, 171–172, 192, 205, 207, 242, 247, 251–252, 260–261, 266–275. *See also* Names of individual countries
Alces alces, 280, 284–285, 290
Alouatta, 21–22, 31, 37–55, 59, 70, 75–78, 87, 168, 237–240, 408; tool-manufacturing behavior of, 432; tool-using behavior of, 428
Alouatta palliata, 31, 37–55, 76, 237–240, 408; diet of, 21–22, 237, 239; dominance in, 168; drinking behavior of, 49, 55; effects on habitat by, 50–52; feeding posture of, 48–50; feeding rates of, 49; group size of, 53; habitat of, 37–55; movements of, 45; resource utilization by, 37–55; selectivity of food species by, 53–55; social structure of, 22, 237; utilization of primary resources by, 52–53
Alouatta seniculus, 59, 70; feeding habits and diet of, 76–78; site population density of, 75; subgroups of, 76
American Sign Language, 372, 377–384
Anacardiaceae, 42, 46
Anectine, 41
Anestrus, 182
Annonaceae, 42
Antelope. *See Rhynchotragus kirki*
Anthropoid apes, social life and ecology of, 26–30

Anthropoidea, 346
Anuradhapura, 126–128, 130–132, 137–138, 148–149
Aotus, 25, 87, 98
Aotus trivirgatus, 89, 91–92; diet of, 25; feeding groups of, 98; social structure of, 25
Apocynaceae, 42, 88
Aquila verreauxi, 247
Araliaceae, 42
Arctocebus, 3, 31
Astrocaryum standleyanum, 24
Ateles, 59–84, 87, 89–97, 99–101, 168, 231, 235, 237–239; tool-manufacturing behavior of, 432–433; tool-using behavior of, 428
Ateles belzebuth, 59–84, 231, 235–239; diet and feeding behavior of, 67–71, 239; dominance hierarchy of, 73–74, 168; feeding competitors of, 70; isolates from subgroup of, 61–62; relationship of diet to subgroups of, 71–75; site population density of, 75; social organization of, 73, 236–237; subgroup associations of, 63–67, 231; subgroup composition of, 62–63, 72–73; subgroup size of, 60–61, 83; subgroup spacing of, 60
Ateles geoffroyi, 24, 31, 80; diet of, 22; social organization of, 22
Ateles paniscus, 89–97, 100; food trees utilized by, 94; group size of, 93–94; living area of, 93; subgroups of, 94–95

Australian Aborigines, 283
Australopithecus, 252; hunting coopera-
   tion by, 289, 296; hunting strategy
   by, 293; social organization and dom-
   inance in, 173–174
Australopithecus africanus, 174
Axis axis, 4
Aztecs, 172

Baboons (savannah). *See Papio cyno-
   cephalus*
Balanites, 275
Barbary apes. *See Macaca sylvana*
Bignoniaceae, 42
Bixaceae, 42
Black-and-white Colobus monkey. *See
   Colobus guereza occidentalis*
Blackfoot Indians, 171
Black spider monkey. *See Ateles pa-
   niscus*
Blue duiker. *See Cephalophus monticola*
Blue monkey, 253, 261, 266–267
Bombacaceae, 42, 88
Bonnet macaque. *See Macaca radiata*
Boraginaceae, 42
Bottlenose dolphins. *See Tursiops adun-
   cus*
Brachiaria, 272
Brosimum, 69, 74
Bubo nipalensis blighi, 139
Buffalo. *See Syncerus caffer*
Burma, 125
Burseraceae, 42
Bushbuck, 302
Bushpig, 302

Caesalpinaceae, 42, 270, 272
Callithricidae, 25. *See also Saquinus
   geoffroyi*
Callophylum, 70
Canada, 171–172
Canis aureus, 138
Canis lupus, 196, 279–281, 293–295;
   cognitive mapping by, 293; persist-
   ence in hunting of, 280–281; hunting
   cooperation of, 284–286; hunting
   strategy of, 289–291; zone of "owner-
   ship" of, 285
Canthium, 171
Cape hare. *See Lepus capensis*
Cappardaceae, 43
Capucin monkeys. *See Cebus apella;
   Cebus capucinus*

Carassius auratus, 314, 318
Caribou. *See Rangifer tarandus*
Carucaceae, 43, 88
Catarrhini, 182, 185, 191
Cebidae, 84
Cebus, 13, 31, 59, 75, 79–83, 87, 91,
   96, 99–101, 238; tool-manufacturing
   behavior of, 433; tool-using behavior
   of, 428–430
Cebus albifrons, 89, 91, 99
Cebus apella, 59, 70, 70–83, 238; diet of,
   80–82; group pattern and size, 79–80;
   site population density of, 75; social
   organization of, 80–81
Cebus capucinus, 22–24, 31, 80; diet of,
   24; grooming in, 24; social structure
   of, 24
Celebes monkeys. *See Cymopithecus
   niger*
Celtis durandii, 113, 115–116, 234, 267–
   268, 270
Cephalophus monticola, 262–263, 265,
   267
Cercocebus albigena: census in Uganda
   of, 106; dominance hierarchy in, 169;
   tool-using behavior of, 425
Cercocebus atys, 169
Cercopithecus, 31, 103, 106, 116, 125,
   165, 168–169, 186–188, 191, 288,
   358–359, 367, 438; tool-using behavior of, 425, 449
Cercopithecus aethiops, 116, 119, 186–
   188, 252, 288, 367; copulation after
   birth among, 191; dominance hier-
   archy in, 169; pregnancy and sexual
   receptivity of, 188; sexual activity of,
   186–188; transfer index tests on, 358–
   359
Cercopithecus ascanius, 106
Cercopithecus lhoesti, 106
Cercopithecus mitis, 106
Cervus elaphus, 290
Cervus unicolor, 127–128
Ceylon, 3–16, 18–21, 24–25, 121, 125–
   149, 231, 234, 242
Chaffinches, 310
Cheirogaleus medius, 16
Chickens, domestic. *See Gallus gallus*
Chimpanzees. *See Pan troglodytes trog-
   lodytes; Pan troglodytes schweinfurthi*
Chrysophyllum, 70, 74
Cochin, 172–173
Cochlospermaceae, 43
Colobus, 3, 31, 103–121, 233–234, 241–

242, 261, 265–267, 283; tool-using behavior of, 425
Colobus badius rufomitratus, 119
Colobus badius temminckii, 119
Colobus badius tephrosceles, 103–121, 234, 241–242, 252, 265; activity time allotment of, 112–113; census of, 106–107; daily ranging patterns of, 111–112, 117; diet of, 113–119, 234; dominance hierarchy of, 108–109, 117; grooming among, 108; group size and composition of, 107, 234; home range of, 104–105, 110–111, 116–118; infant relations among, 108; intergroup relations of, 110, 117; inter-individual spacing of, 107, 117; mating systems of, 109; trees utilized by, 105–106
Colobus guereza occidentalis, 103–121, 241–242, 261, 265, 267; activity time allotment of, 112–113; census of, 106–107; daily ranging patterns of, 111–112, 116; diet of, 113–119, 234; dominance hierarchy of, 108–109; grooming among, 108; group size and composition of, 107, 116, 118, 234; home range of, 105, 110–111; infant relations among, 108; intergroup relations of, 110, 118; inter-individual spacing of, 107, 119; mating systems of, 109, 116; trees utilized by, 105–106
Colobus polykomos, 120
Colombia, 59–75
Combretum, 268, 275
Costa Rica, 38–55
Coula edulis, 29
Crab-eating macaques. *See Macaca fascicularis*
Crocuta crocuta, 196, 289
Cynometra, 265–268, 270
Cynopithecus niger, 162

Dall sheep. *See Ovis dalli*
Deer. *See Odocoileus virginianus*
Delphinid species, 181–182, 196
Desplatzia lutea, 265
Dog, hunting, African. *See Lycaon pictus*
Dominance, 73–74, 153–174, 303–305; age and, 164; basic and dependent rank and, 157; behavior related to, 156; concept and measurement of, 154–156; in fossil hominids, 173–174;

functions of, 165–167; in hominids, 170–174; in *Macaca,* 153–156, 158–166, 174; maternal rank and, 162–164; mating frequency and, 158, 166; in New World monkeys, 167–168; in Old World monkeys, 168–169; in Prosimians, 167; rank acquisition and, 162–164; reduction of aggression and, 166; reproductive state and, 164; social organization and, 166–167
Drypetes sepiaria, 8–11, 13

Eira barbara, 89
Elaeocarpaceae, 43
Elephas maximus, 127
Elk. *See Cervus elaphus*
Erythrocebus patas, 235–236, 313, 363–364, 425–426; dominance hierarchy in, 165; range of, 236; self-awareness and aggression in, 313–314; tool-using behavior of, 425–426; transfer index methodology on, 363–364
Estrous and menstrual cycles, 182–189, 191–197
Ethiopia, 205
Euoticus elegantulus, 32
Euphorbiaceae, 88
Euterpe, 70, 75, 80

Fabaceae, 43, 46
Felis chaus, 139
Felis pardalis, 89
Felis viverrina, 139
Felis wiedi, 89
Felis yagouaroundi, 89
Ficus, 8–10, 30, 74, 76–86, 94–95, 97, 265, 270
Flacourtiaceae, 43

Gaboon, 26–30
Galago crassicaudatus, 167
Galapagos woodpeckers, 372
Galictis, 89
Galidia, 20
Gallus gallus, 310–313, 317, 337
Gambia, 232
Garcinia, 272, 275
Gazella spp., 246–248, 251–252, 281–282, 286, 289
Gazella thomsoni, 246–248, 251–261
Gazelles. *See Gazella thomsoni*
Gibbon. *See Hylobates lar*
Gigantopithecus, 275

Giraffa camelopardis, 287
Goldfish. *See Carassius auratus*
Gorilla. *See Pan gorilla gorilla; Gorilla gorilla beringei*
Gorilla gorilla beringei, 275–277, 355, 358–363, 408; dominance heirarchy in, 169; ideational/abstractive learning tests on, 361–362; nomadiac range of, 272; tool-manufacturing behavior of, 430; tool-using behavior of, 416–417; transfer index tests and results on, 358–360; use of American Sign Language by, 384
Guinea baboon. *See Papio papio*
Guinea fool. *See Numida mitrata*

Hadza, 255–256
Haliaectus leucogaster, 139
Haliastur indus indus, 139
Hamadryas baboons. *See Papio hamadryas*
Hapalemur griseus, 20
Hedge sparrows, 310
Heisteria, 69
Hippocrataceae, 43
Hominids, 170–174, 196–197, 247, 252, 254–256, 259, 275–277, 279, 283–284, 295–298, 304, 348, 371–376, 403–405. *See also Australopithecus; Homo;* ability of to learn and symbolize, 353–354; adaptability of, 3; big game hunting by, 292–293; cognitive mapping by, 295–297; cooperation in hunting by, 288–289, 296–298; dominance-subordination system of, 170–173; evolution of theories for, 196, 405; fossil, 173–174, 353–354, 449–450; hunting behavior of, 247, 252, 255–256, 259, 275–277, 279, 283, 304; intelligence of, 353–355, 360; language ability of, 364, 372–376, 384–387, 391, 400, 403–404, 407–408; manufacturing of stone tools by, 450; hierarchy in, 170–173; self-awareness in, 311, 328, 330, 334–337; social behavior and organization of, 153, 197; hierarchy in, 170, 173; tool-using behavior of, 440–441, 449–450; transfer of information by, 343–344. *See also Homo*
Hominoidea, 346
Homo, 296, 354, 362, 373, 405, 450. *See also* Hominids
Homo neanderthalensis, 405

Homo sapiens, 296, 354, 362, 374
Howler monkey. *See Alouatta pallaita; Alouatta seniculus*
Humpback dolphins (*Sousa*), 197
Hyeans. *See Crocuta crocuta*
Hyeronima, 70
Hylobates lar, 30, 301, 328, 361–363, 367; dominance hierarchy in, 169; ideational/abstractive learning tests on, 361–362; observational learning in, 438–439; tool-manufacturing behavior of, 432; tool-using behavior of, 414, 424; transfer index measurement on, 356–359
Hylobatidae, 30

Ichthyophaga ichthyaetus pulmeiceps, 139
Impala. *See Aepyceros melampus*
India, 10, 103, 120, 125, 147, 168, 172–173, 191, 242
Indian langur, 190–192
Indri, 3, 29, 31
Inga, 89, 94, 97
Iriartea, 70, 75, 80
Ivory Coast, 451

Japanese macaque. *See Macaca fuscata*

Karos–Pilopata, 90–92
Kasi, 127
Kenya, 168, 205, 245–247
Ketupa zeylonensis zeylonensis, 139
Khaya anthotheca, 267
!Kung Bushmen, 197, 254–255, 272, 283
Kwakiutl, 171–172

Lagothrix, 87, 91–92, 99–101
Lagothrix lagothrica, 89, 91–92, 100; body size of, 95; dirt of, 95–98; distribution of, 95; dominance hierarchy of, 96–98; grooming of, 97–98; group size of, 96–97
Language, 371–387, 391–400, 403–409; attempts to teach apes, 376–384; 382–400; definition of, 373–375; evolution of, in Hominidea, 376, 384–387, 405; Yerkish, 392–400
Lauraceae, 43, 88
Leaf monkeys. *See Presbytis senex; P. Entellus*
Leguminoseae, 88
Lemur, 16, 19–20, 167, 358–359
Lemur catta, 16, 19, 167

Lemur fulvus, 20
Lepilemur, 3, 16–19, 31
Lepilemur leucopus, 16–18
Lepus capensis, 247–248, 252
Lion. *See Panthera leo*
Loris, 3–4, 18–19, 31, 127
Loris tardigradus, 4, 14–16, 127, 354
Lupuna, 94–95, 97
Lutra, 89
Lycaon pictus, 279, 281–282, 293–295; cognitive mapping by, 294; hunting cooperation of, 286; hunting strategy of, 291; persistence in hunting of, 281–282

Macaca, 4, 11–14, 31, 82, 125–149, 186–195, 231, 238, 312, 317–321, 328–329, 333–336, 346, 367–368, 383, 407, 413, 438; dominance hierarchy in, 153–156, 158–166, 174; learning task tests and TI on, 356, 359; tool-manufacturing behavior of, 432; tool-using behavior of, 426
Macaca arctoides, 328
Macaca assamensis, 125
Macaca fascicularis, 162, 190, 328, 413
Macaca fuscata, 144–147, 158–159, 161–162, 166, 186, 191–193, 195, 438; birth season of, 192–193, 195; copulatory activity of, 186, 191; dominance hierarchy in, 158–159; observation learning by, 438; rank in, 159
Macaca mulatta, 127, 144–147, 149, 166, 189–195, 367–368; aggressive behavior of, 155, 160; aggressive encounters of, 160; birth season of, 192–195; dominance in, 159–162; group size in, 161; infant mortality in, 191; masturbation by, 194; mating behavior of, 186, 190; migration among, 191–192; mirror preference of, 317–321; mother-sib ranking in, 160–161; self-awareness in, 312, 317–321, 328, 333–334, 336
Macaca nemestrina, 162, 187, 312
Macaca radiata, 125, 162, 189
Macaca sinica, 4, 11–14, 31, 125–149, 231; age classes in, 138, 149; biomass of, per unit area, 143–144, 147, 149; death rate in infants of, 135–136; diet of, 13; dominance hierarchy in, 141; fertility of, 130–132, 145; life tables of, 133–138; longevity of, 130; migration of, 139–141, 145–146; mortality

of, 136–139, 141, 146–149; movement of, 13; net reproductive rate (Ro) of, 142, 149; sex ratio at birth of, 132–133; social organization of, 13; survival curve of, 136; weights of, 143–144
Macaca sylvana, 161–162
Macaque. *See Macaca sinica*
Macromiscoides aculeatus, 29
Madagascar, 3, 16–22, 26
Maesopsis, 267–268, 270
Malaya, 30
Malpighiaceae, 43
Mandrillus, 426
Mangabey. *See Cercocebus albigena*
Masai, 171
Meliaceae, 43
Mellaceae, 88
Melopsittacus undulatus, 315–318
Melursus ursinus, 128
Mexico, 172
Microcebus, 18–19
Microcebus murinus, 16
Mimosaceae, 43, 46
Mimosa pudica, 11
Miopithecus talapoin, 195, 358–359, 361–362, 367
Mirror Image Stimulation (MIS), 309–337; hominid self-recognition and, 335–337; preference for mirrors and, 314–321; primate self-recognition and, 321–335; social stimulus properties of, 311
Moose. *See Alces alces*
Moraceae, 43, 46
Morus, 270
Mountain gorilla. *See Gorilla gorilla beringei*
Myriathus arboreus, 265
Myrtaceae, 43, 88

Naja n. naja, 139
Nandi, 171
Nigeria, 172
Night monkey. *See Aotus trivirgatus*
Numida mitrata, 248
Nyctaginaceae, 43

Odocoileus virginianus, 281, 284–285, 289–290
Oecophylla longinoda, 29
Olacaceae, 43
Omnivore, 32
One-button quail. *See Turnix sylvatica*

Orangutan. *See Pongo*
Orthoptera, 27
Ovis dalli, 290

Palmetto, 89, 94–95, 97
Paltothyreus tarsatus, 29
Panama, 21–26, 28
Panda oleosa, 29
Pan gorilla gorilla, 29–30, 31
Panthera, 4, 89, 128, 196, 279, 282, 286
  –287, 289, 291–292, 294–295
Panthera leo, 196, 279, 289; cognitive
  mapping by, 294–295; hunting cooperation of, 286–287; hunting persistence of, 282; hunting strategy of, 291–
  292
Panthera onca, 89
Panthera pardus, 128
Pan troglodytes schweinfurthi, 188, 197
Pan troglodytes troglodytes, 26–30, 174,
  259–277, 279, 292, 295–296, 348–
  351, 363, 368, 372–384, 413–415,
  417–423; carrying behavior of, 264–
  265, 420; census in Uganda of, 106;
  cooperation in hunting by, 288; cooperative working of, 265; cross-modal
  integration of, 344–346, 348–349;
  diet of, 26–27, 252, 254, 269–272;
  dominance hierarchy in, 169, 303,
  305; food sharing of, 264, 276; grooming of, 420; home range of, 274, 276;
  land utilization by, 272; language
  ability of, 344, 376, 387, 391–400,
  403–408; meat-eating and hunting
  behavior of, 247, 252–255, 259–267,
  301–305; movement patterns and behavior of, 272–275; persistence in
  hunting of, 283; seasonal food adaptation of, 268–272; self-awareness and
  MIS in, 322–335; social structure of,
  27–29, 255, 272–273, 275–276; termite
  "fishing" behavior of, 28, 266, 419–
  420, 431; tool-manufacturing behavior of, 430–431; tool-using behavior
  of, 259, 265–266, 372, 413–415, 417–
  423, 437–438, 440, 450–451; transfer
  index tests and results on, 358–360;
  use of American Sign Language by,
  372, 377–384, 391
Papilionoideae, 43, 272
Papio, 82, 157, 165, 174, 183–186, 188–
  193, 196, 205–228, 231–232, 237, 245
  –256, 277, 279, 282–283, 287–288,
  292, 295, 301–305, 363, 416, 419, 439;

communicative gestures of, 206; tool-
  using behavior of, 426–427, 433, 436–
  437, 440, 449–450
Papio anubis, 185, 205; diet of, 247, 254;
  dominance ranking in, 250; herding
  behavior of, 211; home range of, 245;
  "instinctive" protein need of, 252, 254;
  meat-eating and hunting behavior of,
  245–256; sexual behavior of, 220–
  221; troop size of, 245
Papio cynocephalus, 168, 174, 188–192,
  205, 279, 287–288, 292, 295, 301–305;
  dominance hierarchy in, 165, 168,
  185, 303; estrous cycle of, 183–186;
  mating systems of, 183–186, 190;
  meat-eating behavior of, 277, 302–
  304; migration of, 192; persistence in
  hunting of, 282–283; pregnancy and
  sexual receptivity in, 188–189; range
  of, 277; sexual behavior in, 219–222;
  social organization of, 157
Papio hamadryas, 191, 205–206, 215,
  219–222, 231–232, 237, 416, 439;
  birth season of, 193; copulatory behavior of, 220; herding behavior of,
  211; male-female bonds of, 206;
  social unit of, 205, 219, 227–228;
  tool-using behavior of, 416, 436
Papio papio, 205–228, 232; copulatory
  behavior of, 219–222; grooming interactions of, 206, 209–212, 217, 226;
  group movement of, 223–225; "harems" of male, 223; herding behavior
  in, 211–218, 227–228; "nearest neighbor" tests on, 208–209; "prancing"
  display of, 213–214; sexual behavior
  of, 206, 219–222; social development
  of, 222–224, 227–228; spatial relationships of, 206–209; subgroups of,
  206, 209, 223–228; tail wrap in, 227;
  tool-using behavior of, 436
Papio ursinus, 183–195, 188–192, 205;
  infant mortality in, 190; mating systems in, 184–185, 190; pregnancy and
  sexual receptivity in, 188–189; sexual
  preference in, 185, 220
Paradise fish, 312
Parakeets, domestic. *See Melopsittacus*
  undulatus
Parinari, 272, 275
Passer domesticus domesticus, 315–317
Patas monkey. *See Erythrocebus patas*
Perodicticus, 3
Perodicticus potto, 32

Peru, 87–101
Pigeon, 310
Pigtail macaque. *See Macaca nemestrina*
Piliocolobus, 103
Pinnipeds, 195–196
Piperaceae, 43
Pipile cumanensis, 70
Pithecia, 430
Platyrrhini, 21–26
Polonnaruwa, Ceylon, 126–135, 137–138, 142, 144–149
Polygonaceae, 43
Polyrhachis militaris, 29
Pongidae, 84
Pongo, 363–364, 376; cross-modal transfer tasks by, 348–349; tool-manufacturing behavior of, 432; tool-using behavior of, 416, 423–424; transfer index tests and results on, 358–360; vocal language of, 384
Pongo pygmaeus, 416
Pouteria, 70
Presbytis, 3–11, 13, 19–22, 31, 120–121, 127, 138–139, 147–148, 168–169, 188, 234, 242; tool-using behavior of, 427–428
Presbytis cristatus, 120
Presbytis entellus, 4, 8–11, 13, 19, 22, 40–ii, 120–121, 127, 138, 148, 234; copulation in, 188; diet of, 8, 242; dominance hierarchy in, 168; home ranges of, 8; social structure of, 10
Presbytis johnii, 120, 168–169
Prestbytis senex, 4, 5–8, 11, 19–20, 22, 40–i, 120–121, 127, 138, 147–148, 234, 242
Procavia habessenica, 247
Procolobus, 103
Propithecus verreauxi, 16, 19
Prosimian. *See Galago crassicaudatus; Lemur catta; Loris tardigradus; Tupaia longipes*
Protium, 69
Pseudolmedia, 69
Pseudospondias, 267, 270
Python molurus pimbura, 139

Ramapithecus, 173–174
Ramphastos tucanus, 70
Randium dumetorum, 13
Randomized Individual Observation (RIO), 40–41
Rangifer tarandus, 281, 284, 290–291
Raphicaerus campestris, 247, 251

Rat. *See Rattus norvegicus*
Rattus norvegicus, 297, 368, 413
Red colobus monkey. *See Colobus badius tephrosceles*
Red spider monkey. *See Ateles geoffroyi*
Redtailed monkey, 253, 266
Rheedia, 69
Rhesus monkey. *See Macaca mulatta*
Rhodesia, 252
Rhynchotragus kirki, 247–249, 251–252
Ring dove, 310
Rock hyrax. *See Procavia habessenica*
Rosaceae, 43
Rubiaceae, 43, 88
Rufus-naped tamarin. *See Saguinus geoffroyi*
Rutaceae, 44

Saber-toothed tiger. *See Smilodon*
Saguinus geoffroyi, 25, 31
Saimiri, 59, 70, 74–75, 78–80, 83, 87, 89, 91, 98–99, 167–168, 312, 355–356, 368, 383, 430
Saimiri sciureus, 59, 70, 74–75, 78–80, 83, 89, 91, 311–312, 355–356, 368, 383; diet of, 78–79; dominance hierarchy in, 167–168; site population density of, 75; subgroups of, 78, 98–99; tool-using behavior of, 430
Sapindaceae, 44
Sapotaceae, 44, 46, 88
Scheelea zonensis, 24
Schleichera oleosa, 13
"Secondary compounds" (trees), 45–46, 54
Semnopithecus, 127
Senegal, 207, 223
Sernylan (phencyclidine hydrochloride), 325
Siamang. *See Symphalangus syndatylus*
Siamese fighting fish, 312–314
Sifaka. *See Propithecus verreauxi*
Simarouba, 44, 69
Smilodon spp., 289
Spider monkey. *See Ateles belzebuth*
Spilornis cheela spilogaster, 139
Spitzaetus cirrhatus ceylonensis, 139
Steinbok. *See Raphicerus campestris*
Sterculiaceae, 44, 88
Strychnos, 13, 272, 275
Strychnos potatorum, 13
Stumptail macaque. *See Macaca arctoides*
Sus scrofa, 128

Symphalangus syndactylus, 30, 383, 407

Syncerus caffer, 287, 289

Takasakiyama, 146–147, 192
Talapoin monkey. *See Miopithecus talapoin*
Tamiasciurus, 18
Tanzania, 117, 252, 254–255, 260, 266–274
Tapirus terrestris, 89
Tarchonanthus camphoratus, 246
Tarenna, 272
Tasmanian Aborigines, 385
Tayassu tapacu, 89
Tiliaceae, 44
Tinta, 94, 97
Tool behavior: catalogue of nonhuman, 415–433; definition of, 413–415; evolution of hominid, 440–441, 449–451; observation learning of, 437–439; ontogeny of, 435–439; trial-and-error learning of, 435–436, 439, 449–450
Tool manufacture: catalogue of nonhuman primate, 430–433; definition of, 415
Tool use: agonistic contexts of, 434; definition of, 413–415, 440, 449; evolution of hominid, 440–441, 450; functions of, 433–435; mechanical force increase of, 434–435
Tragelaphus scuptus, 267
Tragulus meminna, 4
Transfer Index (TI), 356–360, 363–364
Transvaal, 192
Trecullia africanus, 265
Tree shrew. *See Tupaia longipes*
Trees, 42–55, 69–81; effects of monkeys on, 50–52; fruits of, 46–48, 51, 69–71; leaf production of, 47; list of, 42–44,

50; in Peru, 88–89; "secondary compounds" of, 45–46, 54
Tupaia, 167
Tupaia longipes, 167
Tursiops aduncus, 196
Turnix sylvatica, 247, 249

Uapaca, 272, 275
Uganda, 103–121, 168, 233–234, 252, 260, 451
Uragoga, 272

Verreaux's eagle *See Aquila verreauxi*
Vervet monkey. *See Cercopithecus aethiops*
Vipera russelli pilchella, 139
Virola, 69
Vitex, 272, 275

Walsura piscidia, 8–9
Washoe, 372, 382–384, 391, 407; use of American Sign Language by, 372
Weaver finch. *See Passer domesticus domesticus*
White-headed piping guan. *See Pipile cumanensis*
White-throated capuchin. *See Cebus capucinus*
White-throated toucan. *See Ramphastos tucanus*
Wolf. *See Canis lupus*
Woolly monkey. *See Lagothrix lagothrica*

Yarina, 89
Yellow baboon, 190–191
Yerkish language, 392–400
Yoruba, 172

Zati, 125
Zebra, 181